THE MOST
TRUSTED NAME
IN **TRAVEL**

UTAH

By Mary Brown Malouf

FROMMER'S STAR RATINGS SYSTEM

Every hotel, restaurant, and attraction listed in this guide has been ranked for quality and value. Here's what the stars mean:

★ Recommended
★★ Highly Recommended
★★★ A must! Don't miss!

AN IMPORTANT NOTE

The world is a dynamic place. Hotels change ownership, restaurants hike their prices, museums alter their opening hours, and buses and trains change their routings. And all of this can occur in the several months after our authors have visited, inspected, and written about these hotels, restaurants, museums, and transportation services. Though we have made valiant efforts to keep all our information fresh and up-to-date, some few changes can inevitably occur in the periods before a revised edition of this guidebook is published. So please bear with us if a tiny number of the details in this book have changed. Please also note that we have no responsibility or liability for any inaccuracy or errors or omissions, or for inconvenience, loss, damage, or expenses suffered by anyone as a result of assertions in this guide.

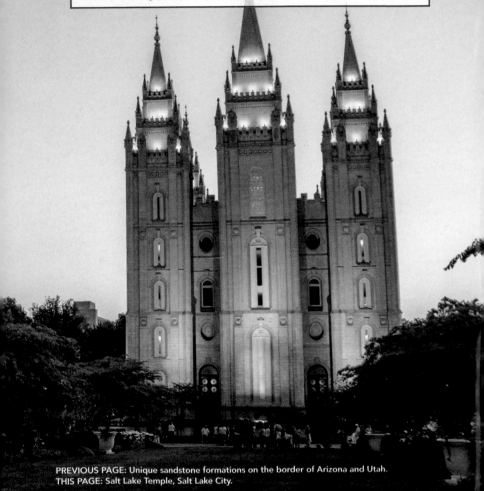

PREVIOUS PAGE: Unique sandstone formations on the border of Arizona and Utah.
THIS PAGE: Salt Lake Temple, Salt Lake City.

CONTENTS

Slot canyon in Grand Staircase-Escalante National Park

A LOOK AT UTAH

I n Utah, you can come face-to-face with ancient giant dinosaurs, observe some of the last of the Old West's bison, and then dine in restaurants run by James Beard Award–winning chefs. Utah's culture runs the gamut from Mesozoic to modern, but Utah must be seen to be believed. From the Mirror Lakes in the High Uintas with its deep forests to the incredible rock formations in the southern National Parks, the landscape in Utah comprises some of the country's most beautiful scenery. Natural Utah is best seen on a driving and hiking trip, so you can take in the magnificent vistas on roadside turnouts (do stop) as well as the tiny desert flora and oddities like the cryptobiotic soil, which allows many things to grow in the desert rock. Utah's landscape is a living lesson in biology and geology, lending to an understanding of the planet's formation. But it's also a reminder of the peace and tranquility to be found in the natural world, the unique sense of wonder that nature inspires, and an inspiration to help preserve these natural wonders.

Utahns call it the "license plate" arch, and Delicate Arch in Arches National Park has indeed become the iconic symbol of Utah. If you can, schedule your hike to coincide with sunset for a truly unforgettable experience. See p. 312.

This incredible feat of architecture, designed and constructed by the early Mormon pioneers, the Tabernacle is the home of the famous Tabernacle Choir. Go on a tour so you can hear the famous pin drop. See p. 62.

Joseph Smith, founder of the Church of Jesus Christ of Latter-day Saints, famously had 40 wives, beginning the Mormon polygamous practice, which was ended in 1890. The statue is by Mahonri Young, a grandson of Brigham Young. See p. 70.

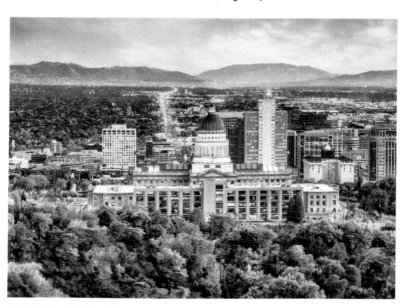

Salt Lake City skyline by night.

Mormon marriages may be "sealed" in the temple, and the beautiful building is a favorite site for wedding portraits.

The Beehive House was a residence of Brigham Young, the second president of the Church of Jesus Christ of Latter-day Saints and the leader who brought the Mormons to Utah. According to the Book of Mormon, "deseret" means "honeybee" and represents the state motto of industry. See p. 64.

Bridal Veil Falls is the end destination for one of the most beautiful hikes in Provo Canyon; the trail is comfortable for all skill levels. See p. 159.

Ensign Peak is a small mountain peak at the north end of the Salt Lake Valley, with amazing city views. Two days after arriving in the Salt Lake Valley, Brigham Young and other leaders climbed the mountain and from there they laid out in their minds the future city of Salt Lake. See p. 49.

Eccles Stadium is the home of the University of Utah Utes, part of the Pac-12 Conference. The annual game between the "U" and the "Y" (nickname for Brigham Young University) has been jokingly dubbed "The Holy War" and is one of the biggest football events of the year. See p. 64.

25th Street, downtown Ogden. Legend has it that the streets under Ogden are threaded with tunnels once used by bootleggers and other outlaws. See p. 84.

A drive to Antelope Island is the best way to see the Great Salt Lake and understand its strange beauty. It's home to herds of pronghorn and deer, hundreds of migratory birds, and a big herd of bison. See p. 82.

For many, the Utah Arts Festival marks the beginning of the summer festival season.

THE HIGH MOUNTAINS

The Mirror Lake Highway in the High Uintas in the north of state is bejeweled with pristine alpine lakes, like lovely Butterfly Lake.

Dappled light through the forests of northern Utah creates a magical atmosphere. Especially in summer, this part of the state provides a cool haven. But in the fall, the yellow aspens and red maples make the area a color explosion.

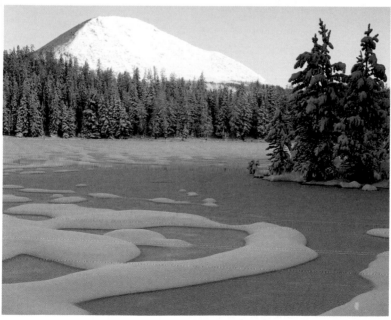

Sunrise in the Uinta Mountains.

Eons ago, Utah was under the water of prehistoric Lake Bonneville and a prime habitat for dinosaurs. Dinosaur National Park is one of the best places to view dinosaur fossils and to understand the value and the process of their excavation. See p. 175.

Mount Timpanagos and Silver Lake. See p. 120.

Sunday Market, Park City. See p. 126.

Family picnic at Sundance Ski Resort. See p. 151.

Utah snow is exceptionally powdery due to unique climatic conditions. All the resorts offer lessons and slopes appropriate for every age, making skiing a great family activity.

Snowbird Resort and its neighbor, Alta, offer some of the most challenging ski slopes in the West. See p. 123.

Many Utah kids are pretty much raised on skis, learning to navigate the slopes through school programs and resort lessons. It becomes a lifelong sport.

The famous Egyptian Theater on Park City's Main Street hosts live performances of all kinds and is the famous epicenter of the Sundance Film Festival, though now films are also screened in many other venues. See p. 143.

Solitude Ski Resort, up Big Cottonwood Canyon, is one of the quieter resorts and popular with Salt Lakers because it's only half an hour from city to slopes. See p. 120.

RED ROCKS

Of all Utah's national parks, Capitol Reef is the least famous, but it is no less spectacular than its siblings, with red and golden sandstone, canyons, and striking rock formations. See p. 321.

Canyonlands National Park is the largest of the state's parks and covers so many varied land-scapes that it's hard to see it all. See p. 315.

The Narrows is one of Zion National Park's most popular features. Hiking along the trails involves walking in the water some of the time and the whole trail threads its way between sheer red sandstone walls. See p. 227.

One of dozens of natural arches in Canyonlands, many consider Moab Angel Arch to be the most beautiful. It's a long, winding trail to the arch, but worth it. Not far, Molar Rock pokes up looking somewhat like a giant's extracted tooth. See p. 315.

Bryce Canyon's hoodoos, the thousands of rock formations jutting from the floor of a red rock canyon, define this national park. See p. 237.

If Goblin Valley looks familiar, it's because you've seen it in multiple movies, including Galaxy Quest, where it stands in for a sci-fi landscape. See p. 326.

To best appreciate Bryce Canyon, hike the Navajo Loop Trail from the rim of Bryce Canyon through towering Douglas pines down to the hoodoos. This is deservedly the most popular trail in the park. See p. 242.

Picture-perfect Kodachrome Basin lives up to its name. See p. 253.

Although most people consider skiing the primary winter recreation in Utah, the southern red rock country in the wintertime takes on a whole otherworldly look, with snowcaps on the formations and a shower of white powder on the colorful formations.

Winter in Zion National Park is one of Utah's best-kept secrets. Obviously, there are fewer people, but temperatures can be surprisingly mild, and snow at the higher elevations means you can add cross-country skiing to the options of activities. Wildlife viewing can be excellent at this time of year. See p. 217.

Moab is a popular base for exploring some of Utah's best sights, but the attraction is not the town itself, it's the magnificent trails and vistas so close at hand. See p. 292.

THE BEST OF UTAH

Welcome to the mystery of unique Utah, the first (and so far, the only) state to be awarded three stars by Michelin. Yep, the whole state was recognized, as opposed to a single establishment—who knew that could even happen? One of the most contradictory states in America, the landscape and cultures of Utah run the gamut from one extreme to the other: The unfathomably beautiful landscape, from red desert rocks to mountain forests, is populated by cultures just as disparate. Salt Lake City is the heart of the conservative Church of Jesus Christ of Latter-day Saints, one of a handful of religions founded in America. But the city is also home to the seventh highest LGBTQ population in the country. Utah's landscape accounts for both the strong environmentalist movement in the state and the interests of extraction industries; the same mineral-rich land is coveted by companies who want to harvest the bounty and those who want to preserve it as is. Utah is home to some of the world's best and busiest ski resorts, yet they are just a half-hour away from empty desert. The 175-mile-long Wasatch Front, from Ogden through Salt Lake and down to Provo, is home to 85% of Utah's population—much of the rest of the state is an incredible landscape ready for you to explore.

CITIES **Salt Lake City** is the largest city in the state, home to Temple Square and the Utah State Capitol. To the north, **Ogden** is worth a visit for its historic mountain-man downtown core and proximity to three ski resorts in Ogden Valley. **Provo,** to the south, is home to Brigham Young University and the gateway to Provo Canyon and Sundance Resort.

COUNTRYSIDE The **Wasatch Mountains** provide both a stunning backdrop to the urbanized Wasatch Front and a year-round playground, featuring more than a dozen ski resorts (Alta and Deer Valley among them) and hundreds of miles of hiking and mountain-biking trails. **Mount Timpanogos** is the second-highest mountain

Grand Staircase-Escalante
National Monument
Orginal Boundary

in the range and home to Timpanogos Peak National Monument. **Southern Utah** is a desert wonderland, and home to five national parks.

EATING & DRINKING Utah's food scene has exploded in recent years. There are still plenty of traditional American eateries, but the innovative, locally sourced fare has become nationally renowned. Besides local trout and game, the state is now internationally recognized as a center for fine chocolate and cheese. Utah's liquor laws are famously complicated but you can certainly get a drink in Utah now and the state is home to dozens of craft breweries and distilleries, most of which offer tours and tastings.

NATIONAL PARKS There is not be a better place in the United States to appreciate "America's best idea." Utah has five national parks: **Arches, Canyonlands, Capitol Reef, Bryce Canyon,** and **Zion.** In addition, it has seven national monuments: Bears Ears, **Grand Staircase-Escalante, Natural Bridges, Rainbow Bridge, Cedar Breaks, Hovenweep, Timpanogos Cave,** and **Dinosaur.** It also has a Navajo Nation national park—**Monument Valley.**

THE best UTAH EXPERIENCES

o **Exploring Bryce Canyon National Park:** Bryce is among Utah's most scenic parks. It is also one of its most accessible. Several trails lead down into the canyon—more like walks than hikes, so just about everyone can get to know this beautiful jewel up close. Part of the Rim Trail is even wheelchair accessible. The colorful rock formations are panoramically impressive when viewed from the rim but become fanciful works of art as you walk among them. See chapter 11.

o **Enjoying Capitol Reef National Park:** This tranquil park combines history—from prehistoric to pioneer—with scenery. And it's not too demanding, either: This is the park to visit with parents or grandparents. Wander through the frontier orchards of Fruita, hike the Capitol Gorge Trail, stroll up the Grand Wash, or sit under the stars roasting marshmallows over a campfire. See chapter 12.

o **Houseboating on Lake Powell:** Kick back and relax while floating on the deep blue waters of manmade Lake Powell, with towering red rocks all around and an azure sky above. Feeling warm? Slip over the side for a dip in the cool water. Want a little exercise? Anchor yourself, and hike to the surrounding natural beauties, such as the Rainbow Bridge. See p. 285.

THE best VIEWS

o **The Narrows, Zion National Park:** The sheer, 1,000-foot-high walls enclose you in a 20-foot-wide world of hanging gardens, waterfalls, and sculpted sandstone arches, with the Virgin River running beneath your boots—literally. The Narrows are so narrow that you can't walk beside the river. Instead, you have to wade right in it—but the surreal landscape makes it worth getting your feet wet. See p. 227.

- **Boulder Mountain Viewpoints (btw. Escalante and Torrey):** The panoramas from the road along the crest of Boulder Mountain are extraordinary—don't skip a single viewpoint along the drive. You can see Capitol Reef, miles to the east, and the valleys and lakes nestled in between. See p. 265.
- **The Queen's Garden, Bryce Canyon National Park:** Carved in stone by Mother Nature, these thousands of colorfully striped spires present a magnificent display when viewed from the rim. From the trail below, they dazzle as the early-morning sun throws them into stark relief. See p. 245.
- **Monument Valley Buttes at Sunset:** Impressive at any time, these stark sentinels of the desert take on a particularly dignified aura when the setting sun casts its deep colors over them, etching their profiles against a darkening sky. Although the park generally closes before sunset, you can arrange a sunset tour upon request—it's well worth the cost. See p. 336.

THE best FAMILY-VACATION EXPERIENCES

- **Camping at Cherry Hill Camping Resort (Ogden):** This fun-filled campground offers something for everybody: a water park with slides, pools, and a pirate ship, plus miniature golf, batting cages, and aeroball (kind of like basketball). It's like camping in a theme park. See p. 99.
- **Taking a Ride on the Heber Valley Historic Railroad:** Take a trip back in time on the "Heber Creeper," so called because of the way this historic steam train inches up the canyon from Provo. A ride on this once-proud passenger and freight line lets you experience travel the way it was in your grandparents' day. See p. 144.
- **Exploring Northeast Utah's Dinosaurland:** This is the real *Jurassic Park*—no special effects needed. First stop: Utah Field House of Natural History State Park in Vernal. Examine an actual dinosaur dig and stroll through the Dinosaur Garden to admire the 18 life-size dinosaurs and other prehistoric creatures. Next, head to Dinosaur National Monument to see and touch—yes, touch—real fossilized dinosaur bones. See chapter 8.
- **Discovering Zion National Park:** The Junior Ranger Program, available at most national parks, is extensive here, with morning and afternoon activities for kids all summer. They'll have so much fun they won't notice they're learning about what makes this natural wonder so special. See p. 223.

THE best HIKING TRAILS

- **Indian Trail (Ogden):** Easily accessible from downtown Ogden, this 4.3-mile trail takes you into a thick forest of spruce and fir, and onto a mountainside that offers spectacular views of Ogden Canyon, including a beautiful waterfall. See p. 94.

o **Hidden Piñon Trail, Snow Canyon State Park (St. George):** This fairly easy self-guided nature trail has breathtaking panoramic views. Wander among lava rocks, into canyons, and over rocky flatland, along a trail lined with Mormon tea, cliffrose, prickly pear cactus, banana yucca, and other wild desert plants. See p. 195.

o **Lower Emerald Pools Trail, Zion National Park:** If green is your color, you'll love this trail—algae make three pools glow a deep, rich shade of emerald. The first part of the trail, navigable by wheelchairs with assistance, leads through a forest to the Lower Emerald Pool, with its lovely waterfall and hanging garden. The small pool just above it is so still and calm that the reflection in the water of the towering cliffs above looks like a photograph. See p. 227.

o **Navajo Loop/Queen's Garden Trail, Bryce Canyon National Park:** This not-too-difficult trail lets you truly experience magical Bryce Canyon. Start at Sunset Point and get the hardest part out of the way first. You'll pass Thor's Hammer, ponder the towering skyscrapers of Wall Street, and visit with majestic Queen Victoria herself—one of the park's most fanciful formations. See p. 245.

o **Lower Calf Creek Falls, Grand Staircase-Escalante National Monument:** Plan to spend most of the day here. The riverside hike with cliffs soaring on either side (look for Anasazi grain caches tucked in the rocks) ends in a 126-foot-high waterfall and refreshing swimming hole. Bring a picnic and enjoy the perfect desert oasis. See p. 258.

o **Angels Landing, Zion National Park:** *Be warned:* This is one of the most perilous trails in Utah, but the view from the top of this steep, strenuous trail from its forested beginning to its ultimate crag is unparalleled—you actually look down on raptors soaring below. See p. 227.

THE best MOUNTAIN BIKING

o **Park City:** Some 350 miles of prime trails radiate out into the sage- and evergreen-laden open space surrounding Utah's best-known ski town. See p. 134.

o **Brian Head Resort:** At 11,307 feet, there may not be a lot of oxygen, but the air is pure and clear, and the biking is great—especially when you can ride a chairlift up and bike down. Trails are everywhere, each with more magnificent scenery than the last. See p. 209.

o **Dave's Hollow Trail:** Just outside the entrance to Bryce Canyon National Park, this trail heads off into the national forest. The double track takes you through sun-dappled glades surrounded by tall ponderosa pines and spruce trees, all the way to fishing and camping at Tropic Reservoir. See p. 244.

o **Moab Slickrock Bike Trail:** A rite of passage for serious mountain bikers, this challenging yet rewarding trail takes 4 to 5 hours to complete. You'll enjoy breathtaking views of the Colorado River far below, the La Sal Mountains towering above, and the red sandstone formations of Arches National Park in the distance. See p. 300.

THE best FISHING & WATERSPORTS

o **Strawberry Reservoir:** The number-one trout fishery in Utah for both cutthroat and rainbow, this gem of a lake is set magnificently among tall pines. You're really out in the woods here: The nearest town of any size is 30 miles away. So pick your spot and cast a line for dinner—you can't beat fresh-caught trout cooked over an open fire. See p. 150.

o **Jordanelle Reservoir, Jordanelle State Park:** Not far from Park City, the wide area at the dam of this boomerang-shaped reservoir is perfect for speedboats, water-skiers, and personal watercraft. The southeast end is designated for low-speed boating. Wherever you go, you'll have the beautiful Wasatch Mountains on all sides. See p. 146.

o **The Green River through Dinosaur National Monument:** The best way to see this spectacularly desolate country is from the river, the way explorer John Wesley Powell did in 1869. Crave excitement? Run the foaming rapids. But if peace and quiet is your thing, float mindlessly in the placid waters and leave your troubles behind. See p. 177.

o **Lake Flaming Gorge:** Smaller and more intimate than Lake Powell—and located in a gloriously colorful setting—Lake Flaming Gorge is one of Utah's real hidden treasures. You can skim the water on skis or relax topside on a houseboat. As for the fishing, if you feel like the big ones always get away, this is the place for you—they're *all* big here. See p. 181.

o **Lake Powell:** This sprawling reservoir has what seems like zillions of finger canyons reaching off the main watercourse of the Colorado River. You could spend weeks—maybe even months—water-skiing, swimming, fishing, exploring the myriad side canyons, and loafing about in the sun. See p. 285.

o **The Colorado River near Moab:** Tackle the placid stretches on your own in a canoe or kayak, or sign up with one of the outfitters and shoot the rapids. Whatever your style, a trip down the spectacular, scenic Colorado River is an adventure you won't forget. See p. 301.

THE best WILDLIFE-WATCHING

o **Rock Cliff, Jordanelle State Park:** More than 160 species of birds, both resident and migratory, are found here. The park is an especially good place to spot eagles and other raptors that nest locally. Boardwalks and trails traverse the riparian wetlands, giving you a chance to observe wetlands life while reducing your ecological footprint. See p. 147.

o **Flaming Gorge National Recreation Area:** Take to the water to vie for a glimpse of the majestic bighorn sheep. In spring and early summer the imposing beasts are sometimes seen on Kingfisher Island and near Hideout Canyon, on the north side of the reservoir. Keep your eyes peeled for the lovely osprey and rare peregrine falcon, occasionally spotted near their nests on the high rocky spires above the lake. See p. 182.

o **Coral Pink Sand Dunes State Park (near Kanab):** If you climb the dunes early in the morning, you're sure to see the footprints of jackrabbits, kangaroo rats, and the occasional mule deer or coyote. But the park is also a habitat for scorpions and fascinating but poisonous (and sometimes bioluminescent) arachnids that often prey on each other. Humans aren't their natural targets, but it's best to keep your distance. See p. 212.

o **Escalante Petrified Forest State Park (Escalante):** Willows and cottonwoods line the banks of the reservoir, one of the few wetlands birding sites in southern Utah. The park is home to a wide variety of ducks, plus coots, herons, and swallows. You might also see eagles, ospreys, American kestrels, and other raptors. Cottontail and blacktail jackrabbits, squirrels, and beavers inhabit the area as well. See p. 260.

o **Antelope Island in the Great Salt Lake:** Famous for its migratory bird population—millions of birds congregate on its shores—Antelope Island is also home to one of largest and oldest herds of bison, who roam the prairies, crags, and shores of this unique ecosystem. Other inhabitants include mule deer, jackrabbits, pronghorn, bobcats, and coyotes. The bison population is controlled by the annual bison roundup—one of the most authentic western experiences in the country and open to the public. See p. 82.

THE best DOWNHILL SKIING

o **Snowbasin (Ogden Valley):** Families love Snowbasin because there's something for everyone here, no matter what your ability. The resort is particularly popular with intermediate skiers, who love the long, easy, well-groomed cruising runs. Experts can expect challenges, including an abundance of untracked powder and Utah's third-highest vertical drop. See p. 107.

o **Beaver Mountain (The Northern Wasatch Front):** Visiting this small, family-oriented ski area is like going home—it's just plain comfortable. There's no glitz, no fancy anything, just lots of personal attention, plenty of snow, and great terrain with beautifully maintained trails. See p. 108.

o **Alta (Little Cottonwood Canyon):** All serious skiers must make a pilgrimage to Alta. It offers the best skiing in the state—and some of the lightest powder in the world—especially for advanced skiers willing to hike a bit for perfect conditions. If you're not up to black-diamond level yet, don't worry: Beginners and intermediates will find plenty of cruising ground, too. See p. 122.

o **Park City and Deer Valley:** These resorts offer not only excellent powder skiing on a variety of terrains, but also the best shopping, nightlife, lodging, and dining in all of Utah's ski areas—and for that matter, in all of Utah. Park City is the party town; Deer Valley is its grown-up, sophisticated sibling. And they're less then 5 minutes apart by road, so you can take advantage of both. See p. 126 and p. 129.

THE best PLACES TO DISCOVER AMERICAN INDIAN CULTURE

o **The Great Gallery in Horseshoe Canyon, Canyonlands National Park:** In a remote, hard-to-reach section of Canyonlands National Park is the Great Gallery, an 80-foot-long panel of rock art dating back several thousand years. It's one of the biggest and best prehistoric murals you'll find anywhere. See p. 321.

o **Monument Valley Navajo Tribal Park:** You've seen Monument Valley Navajo Tribal Park immortalized in movies, on TV, and in advertisements. While the Old West may be gone, many Navajos still call this area home. A Navajo guide can give you the Navajo perspective on this majestic land and take you to areas not otherwise open to visitors. See p. 334.

o **Hovenweep National Monument:** This deserted valley contains some of the most striking and isolated archaeological sites in the Four Corners: the remains of curious sandstone towers built more than 700 years ago. These mysterious structures keep archaeologists guessing. See p. 340.

o **Mesa Verde National Park (Colorado):** The largest archaeological preserve in the country is also home to the most impressive cliff dwellings in the Southwest. The sites run the gamut from simple pit houses to extensive cliff dwellings, all fascinating to explore. See p. 342.

o **Bears Ears National Monument:** The controversial treasure trove of Anasazi artifacts and ruins is wide open to exploration, but please recognize that these are sacred lands to the Navajos and act accordingly. See p. 333.

THE best LUXURY HOTELS

o **The Grand America Hotel** (Salt Lake City; www.grandamerica.com; ✆ 800/621-4505): Built for the 2002 Olympics, the Grand America occupies an entire city block in downtown Salt Lake City and offers top-notch service, amenities, and decor. The marriage of superb design and deluxe furnishings has resulted in exquisitely comfortable guest rooms and suites. See p. 56.

o **Hotel Monaco** (Salt Lake City; www.monaco-saltlakecity.com; ✆ 800/294-9710): This hotel mixes traditional and contemporary styling in rooms that brim with an eclectic array of patterns, textures, and colors. The pet-friendly Monaco lets you bring your animal companion along, and even provides a loaner goldfish on request. See p. 56.

o **Montage Deer Valley** (Park City; www.montagedeervalley.com; ✆ 435/604-1300): Opened in 2010, the Montage Deer Valley (the first outside Southern California) looms above the resort, with luxury (and rates) similarly at the pinnacle of the resort. See p. 137.

o **Stein Eriksen Lodge** (Deer Valley; www.steinlodge.com; ✆ 800/453-1302): Grandly elegant, yet warm and welcoming, with cozy niches in the dignified lobby and lavishly comfortable suites. Attendants in the whirlpool, sauna, and fitness room are on hand to pamper and attend to your every need, but they're so unobtrusive that you'll feel right at home—contentedly, luxuriously at home. See p. 138.

○ **Amangiri** (near Lake Powell; www.amanresorts.com; © **877/695-8999**): A secluded, minimalist desert compound, Amangiri offers design, comfort, service, and opulence that are nothing short of superlative. Rooms are ultra-chic, with two outdoor sitting areas each (the suite even has a private pool), and transcendent views. See p. 291.

THE best BED & BREAKFASTS

○ **Inn on the Hill** (Salt Lake City; www.innonthehillslc.com; © **801/328-1466**): Two blocks from both the Utah State Capitol and Temple Square, this stately mansion atop Capitol Hill is one of Salt Lake City's greatest B&Bs, thanks in no small part to its tremendous city and mountain views. Look for original details—such as wavy and stained-glass windows and steam heat. See p. 57.

○ **Atomic Chalet** (near Ogden; www.atomicchalet.com; © **801/745-0538**): Growing up in the shadow of a nuclear power plant near San Diego gave Wes Welch the inspiration for the name of his (and his wife, Keri's) inn, but his experience as a professional volleyball player in the European Alps inspired its style and service. See p. 98.

○ **Blue Boar Inn** (Midway; www.theblueboarinn.com; © **888/654-1400**): Named for a watering hole in Robin Hood lore, the Blue Boar Inn is tucked into an upscale neighborhood in historic Midway, under the beautiful mountain vista of Wasatch Mountain State Park. This is a special property, with a dozen attractive and plush guest rooms named for poets and authors. See p. 151.

○ **Hines Mansion Luxury Bed & Breakfast** (Provo; www.hinesmansion.com; © **800/428-5636**): A Victorian mansion ripe with vintage charm, this is a wonderful place to celebrate a wedding anniversary or romantic occasion, with complimentary sparkling cider and two-person whirlpool tubs in every room. See p. 162.

○ **Green Gate Village Historic Bed & Breakfast** (St. George; www.greengatevillage.com; © **800/350-6999**): One of the most delightful lodgings in St. George, this B&B inn is actually 10 separate buildings—all restored pioneer homes from the late 1800s, sitting in their own flower-filled little "village" across the street from Town Square. See p. 198.

○ **Stone Canyon Inn** (near Bryce Canyon National Park; www.stonecanyoninn.com; © **866/489-4680**): Quiet seclusion, loads of charm, and absolutely splendid views are only three of the reasons why this inn is so highly recommended—it is also very upscale and the place to come to be pampered. Each of the six guest rooms is unique, with queen- or king-size beds, handsome wood furnishings, and a classic Western look. The luxurious cottages each have two bedrooms and two bathrooms, a gas fireplace, full kitchen, and a private deck with a hot tub. See p. 250.

o **Sunflower Hill Luxury Inn** (Moab; www.sunflowerhill.com; ℂ **800/662-2786**): Loaded with country charm, this delightful B&B makes you feel like you're at Grandma's, where family relics surround you and handmade quilts keep you warm at night. What's more, this may be the quietest lodging in Moab, and the grassy, shady grounds are especially inviting on a hot day. See p. 304.

THE best LODGES

o **Zion Lodge** (Zion National Park; www.zionlodge.com; ℂ **435/772-7700**): The original lodge, built in 1924, burned in 1966, but the replacement, built in 100 days, captures the period rusticity and charm in the heart of Zion National Park. The cabins are especially charming. See p. 230.

o **Red Canyon Lodge** (Flaming Gorge National Recreation Area; www.redcanyonlodge.com; ℂ **435/889-3759**): Not really a lodge at all, this group of delightful 1930s cabins was remodeled in the 1990s. Your choice of TV- and telephone-free accommodations ranges from rustic to luxurious and the forest setting, complete with a private lake, is spectacular. See p. 185.

o **The Lodge at Bryce Canyon** (Bryce Canyon National Park; www.brycecanyonforever.com; ℂ **877/386-4383**): This handsome sandstone and ponderosa-pine lodge is the perfect place to stay while visiting the national park. The suites are outfitted with white wicker furniture, ceiling fans, and sitting rooms. But go for one of the cabins—the high ceilings give the impression of spaciousness, and the gas-burning stone fireplaces and log beams make them positively cozy. See p. 248.

THE best RESTAURANTS

o **Log Haven** (Salt Lake City; log-haven.com; ℂ **801/272-8255**): The epitome of Utah dining, this much-awarded restaurant offers fine dining, Utah-style—a combination of rusticity and sophistication. Set in an antique log cabin nestled in forested Millcreek Canyon, Chef David Jones' menu features bison and elk as well as beef and chicken, and a special low-cal/ high-impact menu offers hearty but healthy fare. See p. 60.

o **HSL** (Salt Lake City; hslrestaurant.com; ℂ **801/539-9999**): Chef Briar Handly's first restaurant, Handle, in Park City, drew accolades from the minute it opened. Its sister restaurant, HSL in SLC, is equally known for inventive, constantly evolving chef-driven cuisine. The General Tso's cauliflower is a local favorite and the place is famous for its fried chicken. See p. 59.

o **Glitretind Restaurant** (Park City; www.steinlodge.com; ℂ **435/649-3700**): Located in the elegant Stein Eriksen Lodge, this equally stylish restaurant may be the best dining experience in the entire state. The Glitretind serves

UNIQUELY utahn FARE

They say you can't know a place until you've eaten its food. This is a high and low list of foods peculiar to Utah. Try as many as you can. Or dare.

Pastrami burger: Just like it sounds—a burger topped with a pile of pastrami—this is Utah's signature burger. It's available many places, but the classic is served at **Crown Burgers.** Multiple locations, but near downtown Salt Lake, head to 377 E. 200 South. http://crown-burgers.com. ℂ 801/532-1155.

Fry sauce: Fry sauce—basically a pink mix of mayo and ketchup—is such a popular condiment in Utah that they made a collectible 2002 Olympics pin depicting it. A must for your fries.

Beehive cheese: This prizewinning cheddar, made in Uintah County, north of Salt Lake City, is cow's milk cheese aged and rubbed with various flavorings—Hatch chilies or lavender and espresso or Redmond salt and honey. You can buy it online (www.beehivecheese.com), at their retail creamery (2440 E 6600 S, Suite 8, Uintah; ℂ **801/476-0900**) or at **Caputo's Gourmet Market & Deli** (314 W Broadway, SLC; www.caputos.com; ℂ 801/531-8669), which sells many Utah cheeses and other foods.

Raspberry milkshake: Raspberries from the Bear Lake area on the border of Utah and Idaho are locally famous. Because of the beautiful location, development is encroaching on farmland, but Bear Lake raspberries are still a byword in Utah and raspberry milkshakes are the locals' favorite way to eat them. Many burger joints and ice cream shops sell a version of it, but you can try one of the originals at LeBeau's Drive-In, 69 N. Bear Lake Blvd, Garden City (ℂ **435/946-8821**).

Artisanal chocolate: Utah has become the unlikely center of artisanal chocolate in the U.S. Companies like Amano Artisan Chocolate, Solstice Chocolate, Millcreek Cacao Roasters, and Ritual Chocolate have won international awards competing with the finest European chocolate. Find a great selection at Caputo's (see above).

Utah scones: Forget the jam and clotted cream—your Utah scone won't need it. Unlike a traditional scone, the Utah model is a piece of fried dough, like the Latin sopapilla or Navajo fry bread. They're traditionally served with honey butter, but local 24-hour eatery **Sconecutter** (2040 State St., SLC; ℂ **801/485-9981**) makes sandwiches with them.

Redmonod Salt: It surprises many that Utah's local salt has nothing to do with the Great Salt Lake. It's actually mined from a deposit left by an ancient inland sea. Unrefined and full of natural minerals, this pinkish salt has a round, almost slightly sweet flavor that makes other salts taste flat. It's a great souvenir or gift to take home. Find it at **Harmons Grocery** (www.harmons grocery.com), with 18 locations.

innovative meals that change with the seasons but always incorporate local game. Plus, it all comes with views of the spectacular Wasatch Mountains. See p. 141.

o **Communal** (Provo; www.communal.com; © **801/373-8000**): A farm-to-table restaurant relying on local growers serves seasonal American food in a cool but comfy family-style setting. See p. 164.

o **Painted Pony** (St. George; www.painted-pony.com; © **435/634-1700**): The Painted Pony is the best restaurant between Las Vegas and Salt Lake City—though its vibe is more California than Utah. The creative menu includes twists on familiar dishes such as seared ahi with wasabi aioli. See p. 201.

o **Hell's Backbone Grill & Farm** (Boulder; http://hellsbackbonegrill.com; © **435/335-7464**): Nationally recognized by the "New York Times," "O, The Oprah Magazine," and the "Wall Street Journal," Hell's Backbone Grill is a story as much as it is a restaurant. Situated in a remote and gorgeous part of the state near Capitol Reef, the chef/owners manage a 6-acre farm as well as flocks of chickens and goats to provide their customers with literally farm-fresh food. See p. 264.

THE best OF THE PERFORMING ARTS

o **Mormon Tabernacle Choir (Salt Lake City):** Hear the glorious sounds of this world-renowned choir in its home on Temple Square. When not on tour, the choir rehearses Thursday evenings and performs Sunday mornings. Both events are open to the public, free of charge. See p. 62.

o **Utah Symphony (Salt Lake City, Park City):** Starting with the pioneers, Utah has a long history of excellent music. The Utah Symphony is at home in Abravanel Hall (marked by the huge Dale Chihuly sculpture in the lobby) but tours worldwide and provides the soundtrack to films in the Sundance Summer series. See p. 79.

o **Utah Shakespeare Festival (Cedar City):** This nationally respected venue for Shakespeare's plays and other theatrical works makes an Elizabethan-worthy event out of theater every summer in Cedar City. The pre-play "Greenshow," a series of seminars on costume, set design, and acting, expand and enrich the experience. See p. 206.

THE best SCENIC DRIVES

Sometimes a drive-by is the best way to look at landscape. It's an overview, not the intimate experience of a hike, but can make the most of your time and energy, and is universally attainable. Here are some of the prettiest.

o **Flaming Gorge-Uintas National Scenic Byway:** This was the state's first national forest scenic byway, known as "Wildlife Through the Ages." It runs between Vernal and Manila on US Highway 191 and Utah Highway

44 and climbs through foothills to the 1-billion-year-old exposed geological core of the Uinta Mountains near Flaming Gorge National Recreation Area. There's high desert, forest, and a huge variety of wildlife. See p. 171.

o **Potash Scenic Byway:** This 44-mile byway northeast out of Moab takes you along the spectacular Colorado River Gorge to the ghost town of Cisco, a former railroad town that died when the interstates bypassed it. Stop along the way for Fisher Towers' majestic red rock spires set against the snowy La Sal Mountains. See p. 311.

o **Mirror Lake Scenic Byway:** One of the highest roads in Utah, this 56-mile stretch of State Road 150 begins in Kamas, Utah, and climbs into the Uinta Mountains before dropping down to the Wyoming border. Glassy lakes, waterfalls, deep forests, and long vistas make this drive especially nice in summer. *Tip:* Stop at the **Samak** (Kamas spelled backwards, get it?) **Smoke House & Country Store** (http://samaksmokehouse.com) for a snack.

o **Hell's Backbone Scenic Drive:** A Civilian Conservation Corps engineering projects that linked Boulder, the last frontier town in the state that still relied on mules to deliver the mail, with Escalante, made famous by its tortuous Hole-In-The-Rock Expedition. One of the most difficult roads built, the route makes its way along a winding spine of rock. On one side, look down to Calf Creek, on the other, look as far as Capitol Reef. See p. 264.

o **Moki Dugway:** A dirt and gravel road, Utah Route 261 just north of Mexican Hat, Utah is a steep (10% grade), staggering switchback road carved into the face of the cliff called Cedar Mesa. The State of Utah recommends that only vehicles less than 28 feet in length and 10,000 pounds in weight attempt to negotiate this road. Constructed in 1958, it's a breathtaking ride. Subject to closures due to weather. For the intrepid only, with four-wheel drive.

o **Burr Trail:** Another wild 4WD trail, this road starts out paved, but that doesn't last long—most of the way is dirt and gravel. Take it slow to be safe and to allow time to take in views of the Henry Mountains, the colorfully contorted Waterpocket Fold, red Circle Cliffs, and Long Canyon. Not passable in wet weather. See p. 272.

UTAH IN DEPTH

Utah is one of the most beautiful and most misunderstood places in the United States. Because of the state's ever-changing liquor laws and its strong association with the Church of Jesus Christ of Latter-day Saints (LDS; the Mormons), many expect Utah to be a strange and, well, slightly dull place. But visitors usually come away with a more nuanced notion of the Beehive State, one that includes breathtaking scenery, friendly locals, well-managed cities, and a unique history. To appreciate Utah, you need to meet its modern-day culture as well as understand the state's strange history and the pervasive influence of the Church of Jesus Christ of Latter-day Saints.

UTAH TODAY

Some people think Utah is stuck in the 1950s—quaintly or annoyingly so, depending on your perspective. This time warp is due in large part to the strong LDS church influence and the corollary Mormon emphasis on old-fashioned family values, which make Utah a notably family-oriented state. Mormons go to church on Sundays and Mondays are traditionally designated as "family home evenings."

So, don't expect to find a lot of wild nightlife here—Utah is famously sober. Attitudes toward alcohol in Utah are considerably more conservative than what you'll find in neighboring states and rules are correspondingly complex. The abolishment of the law requiring imbibers to be members of an establishment's "club," signaled a brief softening of the state's attitudes towards liquor, but subsequently rules have tightened again. The confusing "Zion Curtain" requires that drinks be mixed out of sight of customers ostensibly so children can't see, though the law has been somewhat modified so that restaurants can choose a "Zion Moat" instead—a 10-foot buffer zone from bars where children are banned. In 2017, Utah lowered its blood-alcohol content for driving under the influence from 0.08% to 0.05%, the first state in the country to adopt the tougher limit. And then there are confusing rules about which establishments children are allowed to enter. For clarification, visit **http://utah.com/state-liquor-laws.** For those of us who enjoy a glass of wine or beer or a mixed drink with lunch or dinner need to choose our restaurants carefully. Nevertheless, the bar scene is booming in Salt Lake City. Craft or artisanal cocktails are particularly popular and many of them use locally made spirits, bitters, mixers, and beer.

As the state's demographic shifts, and more outsiders move to Utah, further changes are taking place. Escapees from California's smog, crime, crowds, and taxes have brought their mountain bikes and West Coast philosophy to southern Utah's national park country, while others have been lured to the Wasatch Front, particularly between Salt Lake City and Provo, near the ski hills and burgeoning high-tech industry. These newcomers have brought demands for more services, better restaurants, upscale shops, and a greater range of activities—though they're also accused, by some Utahns, of bringing with them the very problems they sought to escape.

The wilderness versus development debate is the top hot topic in Utah. Utahns are engaged in an ongoing battle between business interests, who see federal lands as prime targets for development or resource extraction, and environmentalists, who are intent on preserving one of the last true wildernesses of the American West. The wilderness-preservation side sees the business people as greedy land-grabbers who care nothing for the future and regard lands only as a commodity to be exploited. Ranchers, loggers, and miners see the environmentalists as selfish, well-off newcomers who don't care that other people need to earn a living and want the government to designate vast wilderness areas as their personal playgrounds.

As Utah looks toward the future, the state is trying to tackle these problems as well as huge population growth along the Wasatch Front and its increasing air pollution. During the 2000s, the Olympics helped catalyze growth: Utah grew an incredible 24%—more than double the national average—thanks largely to a high birth rate but also to an influx of newcomers from California and elsewhere. The Beehive State remains the youngest state in the U.S. (the median age is about 27 years old) and is poised for even more growth in the years ahead. The current challenge for the state is to balance all of this growth (and the problems that accompany it) with the quality of life that accounts for at least some of the growth.

LOOKING BACK: UTAH HISTORY

THE FIRST PEOPLES   The first known inhabitants of Utah were the Desert Gatherers, who, from around 9000 B.C., wandered about the Great Basin and Colorado Plateau searching for food and following the herds. Being nomadic, they left little evidence of their time here. The Ancestral Puebloan (also called Anasazi) culture arose in the Four Corners region at about the time of Christ. By A.D. 1200, their villages were scattered throughout present-day Utah. For some reason—possibly drought—by 1300 the villages had been abandoned, leaving the ruins seen standing today at Hovenweep National Monument and other sites. The descendants of these early people—Shoshone, Ute, Goshute, and Paiute—were among the Native Americans inhabiting the area when the first Europeans arrived.

Another prehistoric group, the Fremont peoples, settled in central Utah and established small villages of pit houses. They arrived about A.D. 1200, but had disappeared by the time the first Europeans reached Utah. Evidence of Utah's indigenous population can be seen all over the state.

Spanish explorer Juan Maria Antonio Rivera and his European expedition arrived at the Colorado River near present-day Moab in 1765. Eleven years later, two Spanish Franciscan friars, Atanasio Domínguez and Silvestre Vélez de Escalante, searching for overland route to missions in California, reached Utah Lake and mapped it, hoping to return to establish a Spanish colony. Spain did not pursue the idea, however, and the next Europeans to explore the area were fur traders in the early 1800s. Then, in July 1847, Brigham Young led the first Mormons (a nickname for members of the Church of Jesus Christ of Latter-day Saints) into the Salt Lake Valley, and the flood of Mormon immigrants began. These were the people who established Utah as we know it today.

MEET THE MORMONS   The Church of Jesus Christ of Latter-day Saints was born in the 1820s when Joseph Smith had a revelation: After much prayer asking which Christian church he should join, Smith was told by God and Jesus that he would be the one to restore the church that Christ established when he walked the earth. An angel named Moroni then gave Smith some ancient inscribed gold tablets that, under divine inspiration and with the aid of seeing stones, he was able to translate into the Book of Mormon. In 1830, Smith and his followers published the Book of Mormon and founded the Church of Jesus Christ of Latter-day Saints (LDS) in upstate New York. Smith's revelations and the fervor with which his followers believed and tried to spread the word bred hostility among their more skeptical neighbors; the early Mormons were soon forced to leave New York.

Smith and his followers settled in Ohio and Missouri in the early 1830s. A few years of prosperity were followed by more strife, and the growing Mormon community was once again forced to flee. They established their church headquarters at Nauvoo, Illinois, reclaiming a swampy area along the Mississippi river. Within a few years, Nauvoo was the second-largest city in Illinois. Also during these years, the practice of polygamy began slowly and quietly among church leaders. Both their nonconformism and their success bred fear and anger in their opponents, who considered Smith and his followers a political, economic and religious threat. In 1844, a mob stormed the jail in Carthage, Illinois, where Joseph Smith and his brother Hyrum were being held on treason charges, and murdered them.

Brigham Young, a confidant of Smith, became the second leader of the church, displaying a genius for organization in the evacuation of Nauvoo and the subsequent migration westward in search of a new Zion. In 1846, the Mormons headed west from Illinois, establishing winter quarters on the far side of the Missouri River, near present-day Omaha, Nebraska.

FOUNDING ZION   In the spring of 1847, Brigham Young started out with the first group of emigrants—two children, three women, and 143 men. When the first group reached the mouth of Emigration Canyon and looked out upon the empty Salt Lake Valley, Young reportedly said, "This is the right place." Within hours of their arrival, the pioneers had begun building an irrigation system and establishing fields for growing food. In the next few days, Young chose the site of the temple and laid out the new city in a grid system beginning at the southeast corner of Temple Square.

That first year almost ended the settlement before it had properly begun. The sod roofs leaked; provisions ran low, forcing the pioneers to eat whatever they could find, including the sego lily bulb (now the state flower); a late frost damaged the wheat and vegetables; and drought damaged more crops. Then a plague of crickets descended on what was left. After two weeks of devastation, the crickets were effectively eliminated by the California gulls (now Utah's state bird) that came from the Great Salt Lake to devour the insects by the thousands, and enough of the crops were saved to feed the pioneers. A monument in Temple Square commemorates their deliverance from famine. It seems strange to hear gull cries in the middle of a city in the desert, but the birds still populate the Great Salt Lake.

By the end of 1848, almost 3,000 Mormons had arrived in the Salt Lake Valley. It was now a part of the United States, ceded to the Union by Mexico. In 1849, the Mormons petitioned to have their territory declared the State of Deseret, a name that comes from the Book of Mormon and means "honeybee" (hence all the beehive symbolism—Utah is not actually a big honey producer, a fact which confuses some visitors.) Denied statehood, the territory of Utah—named after the Ute tribe—was created in 1850, with Brigham Young as territorial governor. Although it was no longer officially run by the church, the territory was assured of its continued influence: The vast majority of voters were Mormons who elected church leaders to positions of authority in the civic domain as well.

In these years, non-Mormons—or "Gentiles," as the Mormons call them—began traveling through the valley, many on their way to or from the gold fields of California. Salt Lake City was an ideal spot for resting and resupplying before setting out again. The Mormons often bought horses, livestock, and supplies, reselling what they didn't need to other travelers. The travelers who passed through to rest and trade took with them a collection of sometimes-confused ideas about the Mormons, including their fascinating practice of polygamy. The journals of these travelers gave the nation its first real knowledge—however incomplete—of Mormon faith and customs.

THE UTAH WAR In 1857, a new governor was sent from Washington to supplant Young. Fearing that he would be rejected, President Buchanan sent federal troops to escort him. The Mormons harassed the troops by driving off their livestock and attacking their supply trains, forcing them to winter in western Wyoming. Although the Mormons were prepared to fight to keep the army out, neither Brigham Young nor President Buchanan wanted bloodshed. As the new governor entered Salt Lake City, Mormon families packed their belongings and awaited the order to move.

An estimated 30,000 Mormons left their homes in Salt Lake City and the northern settlements, moving south over a period of two months, leaving the capital virtually deserted by mid-May. The exodus drew national and international attention and placed the U.S. government in quite an unfavorable light—the government had persecuted innocent people, steamrolling over the fundamental right to religious freedom. An uneasy peace was finally established, the Mormons returned to their homes, and the two groups lived side by side until the outbreak of the Civil War, when the army was called back east.

BECOMING THE BEEHIVE STATE After the close of the Civil War, attention was again directed toward the enforcement of anti-polygamy laws, and many Mormons were imprisoned. Finally, in 1890, the church leaders issued a statement: Based on a revelation from God, the church was no longer teaching plural marriage and no person would be permitted to enter into it. With this major bar to statehood removed, Utah became the 45th state on January 4, 1896.

The Depression hit Utah hard; the unemployment rate reached 35% and per capita income was cut in half. Not until World War II was industry brought back to life. Several military bases established during the war became permanent installations, and missile plants were built along the Wasatch Front. After the war, steel companies reopened, the mining industry boomed, and high-tech businesses moved in. By the mid-1960s, the economy base had shifted from agricultural to industrial.

Dams were built—including the controversial Glen Canyon Dam, which created Lake Powell, and Flaming Gorge Dam, which created Lake Flaming Gorge—to further the cause of industry and to ensure water and energy supplies. They also provided recreational opportunities for a modern society with an increasing amount of discretionary income and free time. Ski resorts began opening in the Wasatch Mountains. In the early 1980s, after outsiders started showing interest in Utah as a recreational playground, Salt Lake City International Airport and the city's cultural center, the Salt Palace complex, expanded.

As the mining industries began winding down, tourism and service industries grew; today, they account for more of the state's economy than any other industry. In the 1990s, the state lobbied hard to be named the host of the 2002 Winter Olympics, and then built numerous venues and roads to assure that the games would be a success. The Mormons, who spent their first decades fleeing from outsiders, are now welcoming them with open arms, and they're coming in droves.

A LOOK AT MODERN MORMONISM—OR, YES, YOU CAN GET A DRINK IN UTAH

Utah is a Mormon state. Not officially, of course—strict state and federal laws are meant to keep church doctrine out of government—and not as much as in the past, when practically all Utahns (and definitely all the decision-makers) were LDS church members. But because about 55% of the state's population belong to the Church of Jesus Christ of Latter-day Saints, and most of them take their religion very seriously, the state legislature is dominated by Mormons and it's hardly surprising that the teachings and values of the church have a strong influence in the voting booth and echo throughout the halls of government.

Although conflict is inevitable as government and community leaders try to adapt to Utah's growing cultural diversity, this discord means little to most visitors, who come to Utah to experience its scenery, recreation, and history. What you'll discover is that Utah is much like the rest of the United States, although generally not as hip as California nor as multicultural as New York or New Mexico.

What Mormons Believe

Mormons are Christians, believing in Jesus Christ as the son of God and the Bible as the word of God, as do all the many offshoots of Christianity. But a significant difference is the role played by the **Book of Mormon,** which they believe to be God's word as revealed to and translated by church founder Joseph Smith.

This book tells of two tribes of people who left Israel in biblical times and made their way to the Western Hemisphere. Mormons believe that these people were the ancestors of today's Native Americans. The Book of Mormon teaches that after his resurrection, Christ spent about 40 days among these people, preaching, healing, and establishing his church. The Mormons believe that Joseph Smith was commanded to restore the church as organized by Christ during his ministry on earth.

The first four principles of the faith are belief in Jesus Christ, repentance, baptism by immersion, and the laying on of hands to receive "the Gift of the Holy Ghost" (in which a priest places his hands on a church member for the transference of spirituality). Another important tenet of the church is respect for the supreme authority of church leaders and the belief in the revelations from God to these leaders.

The family unit is of paramount importance to Mormons, and they believe that marriage lasts literally forever, transcending death. They believe that sex outside of marriage and homosexuality are sins—yet, in another contradiction, Salt Lake City has a large gay population and elected a gay mayor. The church encourages the family to work, play, and study together, and young adults—most men and some women—generally spend 1 or 2 years as missionaries. Mormons also believe in the baptism and redemption of those already dead—hence their strong interest in genealogy. (The popular website **Ancestry.com** grew out of the Mormons' meticulous family recordkeeping.)

It's practically impossible to discuss the church without discussing polygamy, which caused so much antagonism toward church members in the 19th century. Polygamy came about as a "revelation" to church founder Joseph Smith in the 1840s; it was practiced by a relatively small percentage of church members, and was outlawed by church officials in 1890. Today, polygamy is prohibited both by church doctrine and state law, although it does continue among an estimated 30,000 rebels, who have left the church to practice their own brand of fundamentalist Mormonism.

These polygamists have brought unwanted media attention to Utah in recent years. The kidnapping of 14-year-old Elizabeth Smart in 2002 and a separate failed kidnapping attempt in 2003 in Salt Lake City both occurred in connection with polygamy. Smart was eventually found unharmed, and police arrested a man described as a self proclaimed prophet and polygamist who had been thrown out of the Church of Jesus Christ of Latter-day Saints for "activity promoting bizarre teachings and lifestyle far afield from the principles and doctrines of the church."

Warren Jeffs, then leader of the Fundamentalist Church of Jesus Christ of Latter-day Saints (based just across the Utah border in Colorado City, Arizona) and self-proclaimed prophet, was placed on the FBI's Ten Most Wanted List when he went on the lam to avoid prosecution for arranging illegal marriages between his adult male followers and underage girls, sexual conduct with minors, and incest. His 2006 arrest near Las Vegas and subsequent trials in Utah and Texas made national headlines. In 2011, he was convicted of sexually assaulting underage girls and sentenced to life in prison.

What Mormonism Means for Visitors to Utah

The strong religious influence on the state has brought about some strange laws regarding alcoholic beverages, although it's definitely not true that you can't get a drink here. Cigarettes and other tobacco products are also readily available, but smoking is prohibited by state law in all restaurants—legislation that is common across much of the United States. Although cola drinks contain caffeine, the church doesn't specifically prohibit their consumption. Some Mormons drink Coke or Pepsi; others refrain. You'll generally have no trouble at all purchasing whatever type of soft drink you want, with or without caffeine. Coffee, however, may not routinely be served in the morning; especially in small-town B&Bs, you may have to ask.

Although the Mormons of Utah can be pretty tough on themselves regarding the above-mentioned "sins," most Utahns are fairly tolerant of others' beliefs and lifestyles. But be sure to use public transportation, taxis, uber, or Lyft if you're planning on imbibing—Utahns are strict about public intoxication. And be forewarned: Mormons are practically missionaries by definition, and will, with only the slightest encouragement, want to enthusiastically help you see the wisdom of their ways.

Because the church emphasizes the importance of family, you'll see lots of kids in Utah; the state is noted for having the highest fertility rate in the nation, year after year. This also makes Utah a very kid-friendly state, with plenty of family-oriented activities and attractions. Overall, prices for kids and families are reasonable. And because many Mormon families observe Monday evening as a time to spend together, sports facilities, amusement parks, and similar venues often offer family discounts on Mondays; if you're traveling with your family, watch for them.

About 55% of Utah's population are LDS church members, but church membership varies greatly from community to community, so the number of Mormons you'll encounter will vary considerably. Although it's the world headquarters of the church, Salt Lake City is just under half Mormon, while some of the smaller towns approach 100%. Of the major cities, Provo has the strongest church influence. And although St. George was historically a major stronghold for church members, recent migration from other parts of the United States (mainly Southern California) is gradually diluting that influence. You'll probably find the least church influence in Ogden, Park City, and Moab, which, in recent years, have attracted large numbers of outsiders.

EATING & DRINKING

Utah has traditionally been a very meat-and-potatoes destination, but in recent years, there has been a boom in culinary creativity centered in Salt Lake City and the state's ski resorts. The liquor laws are constantly being tweaked by the Legislature, so there are still some quirks: Some establishments require you to purchase food in order to get a drink and can sell only beer and other low-alcohol-content drinks. There is a flourishing microbrewery culture here, a smattering of wineries, and new distilleries opening all the time. As of this printing, there are more than 14 craft distilleries in Utah.

In this book, restaurants categorized as expensive typically charge $15 to $40 for a dinner main course, moderate means $10 to $20 for a dinner main course, and inexpensive indicates most main courses are under $10 for dinner.

WHEN TO GO

Deciding when to visit Utah depends on what you want to do and which places you want to see. Those traveling without children will likely want to avoid visiting during school vacations. Ski resorts are most popular during the Christmas and New Year's holidays (and the room rates accordingly shoot into the stratosphere), and national parks are inundated with visitors in July and August. The best time to visit the parks and almost everything else in southern Utah is spring or fall; summer is too hot, particularly in St. George.

Weather

Utah has four seasons, but because of the wide range of elevation—from 2,200 to 13,528 feet—conditions vary considerably across the state. Generally, as in other desert states, summer days are hot but nights are cool. Winters are cold and snowy, except in southwest Utah's "Dixie" (which includes St. George), where it seldom gets very cold and snow is rare. Mountain temperatures are always pleasantly cool and can be quite cold at night, even in summer.

Average Monthly High/Low Temperatures (°F/°C) & Precipitation (in./cm)

		JAN	FEB	MAR	APR	MAY	JUNE	JULY	AUG	SEPT	OCT	NOV	DEC
MOAB	Temp. (°F)	37/17	42/22	53/30	65/40	75/48	87/57	92/64	89/61	82/54	68/42	49/27	39/20
	Temp. (°C)	2/–8	5/–5	11/–1	18/4	23/8	30/13	33/17	31/16	27/12	20/5	9/–2	3/–6
	Precip. (in.)	0.8	0.7	0.7	0.6	0.6	0.4	0.4	1.2	0.7	0.8	0.7	0.5
	Precip. (cm)	2	1.8	1.8	1.5	1.5	1	1	3	1.8	2	1.8	1.3
ELEV. 4,000'													
PARK CITY	Temp. (°F)	33/12	38/17	43/22	55/30	63/36	74/44	82/50	80/50	71/41	60/31	43/21	33/13
	Temp. (°C)	0/–10	3/–8	6/–5	12/0	17/2	23/6	27/10	26/10	21/4	15/0	6/–6	0/–10
	Precip. (in.)	2.8	1.6	2.1	1.2	1.6	1.1	1.9	1.6	1.8	1.5	1.7	2.7
	Precip. (cm)	7.1	4.1	5.3	3	4.1	2.8	4.8	4.1	4.6	3.8	4.3	6.9
ELEV. 7,000'													
ST. GEORGE	Temp. (°F)	53/24	59/29	67/35	76/42	85/49	96/57	101/65	99/63	93/53	80/41	65/30	54/24
	Temp. (°C)	11/–4	15/–1	19/1	24/5	29/9	35/13	38/18	37/17	33/11	26/5	18/–1	12/–4
	Precip. (in.)	1.4	1.6	1.6	0.9	0.6	0.3	0.8	1.1	0.8	1	0.9	1.2
	Precip. (cm)	3.7	4.2	4.2	2.2	1.6	0.8	2.1	2.7	2	2.6	2.3	3
ELEV. 2,880'													
SALT LAKE CITY	Temp. (°F)	37/20	43/24	52/31	62/38	72/46	83/54	92/62	90/61	80/51	66/40	50/30	39/22
	Temp. (°C)	2/–6	6/–4	11/0	16/3	22/7	28/12	33/16	32/16	26/10	18/4	10/–1	3/–5
	Precip. (in.)	1.3	1.2	1.8	2	1.8	0.9	0.7	0.8	1.1	1.3	1.3	1.3
	Precip. (cm)	3.3	3	4.6	5.1	4.6	2.3	1.8	2	2.8	3.3	3.3	3.3
ELEV. 4,330'													

Holidays

Banks, government offices, post offices, and many stores, restaurants, and museums are closed on the following legal national holidays: January 1 (New Year's Day), the third Monday in January (Martin Luther King, Jr., Day), the third Monday in February (Presidents' Day), the last Monday in May (Memorial Day), July 4 (Independence Day), the first Monday in September (Labor Day), the second Monday in October (Columbus Day), November 11 (Veterans' Day/Armistice Day), the fourth Thursday in November (Thanksgiving Day), and December 25 (Christmas). The Tuesday after the first Monday in November is Election Day, a federal government holiday in presidential-election years (held every 4 years, and next in 2020). Pioneer Day is an official state holiday celebrated July 24 to commemorate the arrival of Brigham Young and the Mormon pioneers in 1847; many businesses and attractions are closed and a big parade marches downtown Salt Lake City.

Utah Calendar of Events

JANUARY

Sundance Film Festival, Park City and other locations. Sponsored by Robert Redford and originally connected to his Sundance Resort, this festival honors the best Independent films with screenings and seminars. But frankly, many people just come to see the celebrities on Main Street, not the movies. Visit www.sundance.org for schedules and information on obtaining tickets. Late January.

FEBRUARY

Freestyle World Cup Ski Races, Deer Valley. This event is made up of sanctioned World Cup races and demonstrations. The location: the Champion and White Owl ski runs on Deer Valley's 2002 Olympic runs. Call © **435/649-1000.** Early February.

Bryce Canyon Winter Festival, Bryce. This winter celebration, with snowshoe tours and other activities, takes place amid the colorful rock formations of the Bryce Canyon

National Park area. Call ☎ **435/834-5341.** Mid-February.

MARCH

Hostlers Model Railroad Festival, Ogden. Fans of model trains gather at historic Union Station, where trains of all shapes and sizes are on display; model-train collectors can locate those hard-to-find items. Call ☎ **801/394-4952,** or visit www.hostlers.info. Early March.

St. George Art Festival, St. George. This outdoor fine-arts festival draws artists and visitors from all over the American West. Call ☎ **435/627-4500,** or visit www.sgartfestival. com. Mid-March.

APRIL

Easter Rendezvous, Ogden. A gathering of mountain men at Fort Buenaventura, with black-powder shooting contests and other early-19th-century activities. Call ☎ **801/399-8099.** Early to mid-April.

April Action Car Show, Moab. A grand display of vintage hot rods, classic cars, and more, plus a Saturday night cruise down Main Street and fun contests. Call ☎ **800/635-6622,** or visit http://moabcar show.org. Late April.

MAY

Golden Spike Reenactment, Golden Spike National Historic Site, Promontory. This reenactment commemorates the moment in 1869 when rail lines from the East and West coasts were joined, linking the nation. A must for historic-railroad buffs. Call ☎ **435/471-2209,** or check out www.nps. gov/gosp. May 10.

Great Salt Lake Bird Festival, Farmington. Birders from across the country flock to this festival, which takes place at the Davis County Fair Park, midway between Salt Lake City and Ogden. Call ☎ **801/451-3286,** or visit www.greatsaltlakebirdfest.com for more information. Mid-May.

JUNE

Harmons Best Dam Bike Ride, Logan. More than 1,500 participants pedal miles along Cache Valley's back roads. The money raised goes to help in the battle against multiple sclerosis. Call ☎ **801/424-0113.** Mid-June.

Utah Shakespeare Festival, Cedar City. This professional theater festival produces several plays by William Shakespeare, plus a few contemporary offerings. Call ☎ **800/752-9849,** or check out www.bard. org. Late June through August.

Downtown Farmers Market, Salt Lake City. This Saturday market (8am–2pm) is held in Pioneer Park, the site of the first Mormon encampment. Only locally grown and made food allowed for sale. There is also a group of curated art and crafts vendors as well as buskers, performers, and crowds of people. In winter, the market moves indoors to the Rio Grande railway station. Visit www. slcfarmersmarket.org. June through October.

JULY

Deer Valley Music Festival, Deer Valley. This festival is the summer home of the Utah Symphony, which performs outdoors with a schedule of notable guest musicians. Order a box lunch from Deer Valley's famous kitchen, bring a low lawn chair or sit on the grass. Call ☎ **801/533-6683,** or visit www. deervalleymusicfestival.org for more information. July to August.

AUGUST

Railroaders' Festival, Golden Spike National Historic Site. Reenactments of the Golden Spike ceremony, which united the nation by rail, plus a spike-driving contest, railroad handcar races, and a buffalo-chip-throwing contest. Call ☎ **435/471-2209,** or visit www.nps.gov/gosp. Early or mid-August.

SEPTEMBER

Greek Festival, Salt Lake City. Greeks are a big part of Utah culture; the music, dance, and food of Greece are featured, plus tours of the historic Holy Trinity Greek Orthodox Church. Call ☎ **801/328-9681,** or visit www. saltlakegreekfestival.com. Early September.

Moab Music Festival, Moab. Live classical, jazz, bluegrass, and other types of music are presented in a beautiful red-rock amphitheater and other locations. For more information, check out www.moabmusicfest. org, or call ☎ **435/259-7003.** Early to mid-September.

Utah State Fair, Salt Lake City. This fair has live entertainment, a horse show, rodeo, livestock judging, arts and crafts exhibits, and typical state-fair fun. Visit www.utah-statefair.com, or call ☎ **801/538-8400.** Mid-September.

Oktoberfest, Snowbird. This is a traditional celebration, with German music, food, and, of course, beer. Call ☎ **801/933-2110,** or visit www.snowbird.com. Mid-September to mid-October.

OCTOBER

Huntsman World Senior Games, St. George. This is an extremely popular Olympics-style competition for seniors, with a variety of athletic events. Call ☎ **800/562-1268,** or check out www.seniorgames.net. Mid-October.

Bison Roundup, Antelope Island State Park. Stop by the park and watch the annual bison roundup. Take binoculars and get a close-up view of the bison as they receive their annual

medical exams. Call ☎ **801/773-2941,** or visit https://stateparks.utah.gov. Late October to early November.

NOVEMBER

Ogden Christmas Parade and Christmas Village, Ogden. A parade begins the Christmas season, and the municipal park is transformed into a Christmas village, with thousands of lights, music, and animated decorations. Call ☎ **801/629-8253,** or visit www.ogdencity.com/452/Christmas-Village. Late November through December.

Temple Square Christmas Lights, Salt Lake City. A huge, spectacular display of Christmas lights adorns Temple Square. Call ☎ **801/240-4872.** From the Friday after Thanksgiving to January 1.

DECEMBER

New Year's Eve, Salt Lake City. The city traditionally throws a big, public New Year's Eve party, with food, entertainment, and activities for the whole family. No champagne, however. For up-to-date details, go to www.downtownslc.org/events.

LAY OF THE LAND

You can easily split Utah into three distinct regions: the Colorado Plateau, in the southern half of the state, where all those fantastic rock formations are; Rocky Mountain Utah, with rugged peaks, stately pines, deep blue lakes, and most of the state's residents; and the Great Basin Desert, the big, middle-of-nowhere to which you've always wanted to send that cousin you never really liked.

Truth be told, though, certain sections of Utah do just have a whole lot of nothing. Then again, large expanses of "nothing" may be the rarest landscapes of all. This book is organized by destination, based on where you probably will want to go.

Eighty percent of Utah's population lives in the Rocky Mountain region of the **Wasatch Front,** the 175-mile-long north-central section of the state from Logan to Provo. **Salt Lake City** is Utah's most populous city, as well as its most cosmopolitan. It's also the international headquarters of the Church of Jesus Christ of Latter-day Saints; the church's world headquarters, Temple Square, is Utah's most-visited attraction. Keep in mind that Salt Lake City is still a relatively small city and not as sophisticated or glitzy as New York or Los Angeles (maybe that's what makes it so likable). As any real-estate agent

RESOURCES FOR greener TRAVEL

In addition to the resources for Utah listed above, the following websites provide valuable wide-ranging information on sustainable travel. For a list of even more sustainable resources, as well as tips and explanations on how to travel greener, visit www.frommers.com/planning.

o **Responsible Travel** (www.responsibletravel.com) is a great source of sustainable travel ideas; the site is run by a spokesperson for ethical tourism in the travel industry. **Sustainable Travel International** (https://sustainabletravel.org) promotes ethical tourism practices, and manages an extensive directory of sustainable properties and tour operators around the world.

o In the U.K., **Tourism Concern** (www.tourismconcern.org.uk) works to reduce social and environmental problems connected to tourism. The **Association of Independent Tour Operators** (**AITO**; www.aito.com) is a group of specialist operators leading the field in making vacations sustainable.

o In Canada, the website **Green Living** (www.greenlivingonline.com) offers extensive content on how to travel sustainably, including a travel and transport section and profiles of the best green

will tell you, one advantage Salt Lake City has over all other Western cities its size is its location; within an hour's drive is some of the best downhill skiing in the United States. Here also is that anomaly of nature, the vast **Great Salt Lake,** eight times saltier than any of the world's oceans.

This brings you to the rest of the Wasatch Front. In this book, the section that's roughly north of Salt Lake is designated the **Northern Wasatch Front.** Here you'll find historic **Ogden; Logan,** Utah's northernmost town of any size; the national historic site where the Central Pacific and Union Pacific railroads met in 1869; and several ski resorts. The mountains that offer skiing in winter also provide numerous opportunities for hiking, horseback riding and biking in summer.

The areas east and south of Salt Lake City are designated in this book as the **Southern Wasatch Front.** This region contains beautiful **Big** and **Little Cottonwood Canyons,** which have some of the state's best skiing, as well as great hiking and biking in the summer; **Park City,** Utah's premier ski-resort town—and a delightful destination year-round—with a historic Main Street dominated by intriguing shops and restaurants; some fun spots just outside of Park City, including a historic railroad, Strawberry Reservoir (a real gem of a lake), and several nice state parks; Robert Redford's Sundance Institute; and **Provo,** a small, conservative city that's home to Brigham Young University.

The western side of Utah, beginning west of Salt Lake City, is dominated by the vast, salty nothingness of the Great Basin Desert, which includes the pristinely white Bonneville Salt Flats, a terrain so flat that you can actually see shops and services in Toronto, Vancouver, and Calgary.

- In Australia, the national body that sets guidelines and standards for ecotourism is **Ecotourism Australia** (www.ecotourism.org.au). The **Green Directory** (www.thegreendirectory.com.au), **Green Pages** (www.thegreen pages.com.au), and **Eco Directory** (www.ecodirectory.com.au) offer sustainable travel tips and directories of green businesses.

- **Carbonfund** (www.carbonfund.org), **TerraPass** (www.terrapass.org), and the **Cool Climate Network** (http://coolclimate.berkeley.edu) provide info on "carbon offsetting," or offsetting the greenhouse gas emitted during flights.

- The **"Green" Hotels Association** (www.greenhotels.com) recommends green-rated member hotels around the world that fulfill the company's stringent environmental requirements. **Environmentally Friendly Hotels** (www.environmentallyfriendly hotels.com) offers additional green accommodation ratings.

- **Sustain Lane** (www.sustainlane.com) lists sustainable eating and drinking choices around the U.S.; also visit **www.eatwellguide.org** for tips on eating sustainably in the U.S. and Canada.

the curvature of the earth. The Flats are also famous for the land-speed records set on them.

Northeastern Utah is home to two terrific recreational areas that creep into the adjoining states: **Flaming Gorge National Recreation Area,** which wanders into Wyoming, and nearby **Dinosaur National Monument,** which extends into Colorado. Both are what one might call "Undiscovered Utah," because they're really off the beaten path and not what most people imagine when they think of the state—consider this part of Utah well worth a visit.

The **Colorado Plateau,** which extends along the state's entire southern border and halfway up the east side, is where all five of Utah's national parks are located, and for good reason. Ancient geologic forces, erosion, oxidation and other natural processes have carved spectacular rock sculptures—delicate and intricate, bold and stately—and painted them in a riot of color. This is quite likely why you've come to Utah in the first place, and these chapters will help you spend your time wisely and enjoyably. Check out chapter 10 on **Zion National Park** for hints on avoiding the crowds at the state's most popular national park; and see if you agree that **Bryce Canyon National Park** (chapter 11), with its marvelous stone sculptures (called hoodoos), is the West's best. Chapter 12 explains why **Capitol Reef National Park** is one of Utah's hidden treasures, and chapter 14, **"From Moab to Arches & Canyonlands National Parks,"** directs you to some of the best ways to explore eastern Utah's beautiful red-rock country.

But the Colorado Plateau is more than national parks. This area offers historic Mormon sites; live theater, dance, and music; as well as skiing and the state's best golf. If you're heading in from Las Vegas, St. George is the first Utah town you'll see.

Utah's best destination for watersports—maybe the best in the West—is **Lake Powell and Glen Canyon National Recreation Area.** A boating vacation here is the stuff that stressed-out big-city dreams are made of.

Finally, the **Four Corners Area** is in Utah's very southeast corner. Spectacular American Indian sites, such as **Hovenweep National Monument,** make a visit here truly worth the drive through the West's vast, empty spaces.

RESPONSIBLE TOURISM

The perpetual debate continues throughout Utah: natural gas drilling and mineral extraction versus recreation and conservation. The Bush administration opened up parcels of federal land near Canyonlands National Park for bidding to natural gas exploration in 2008; the move was condemned and quickly reversed after the Obama administration took over. Likewise, Escalante has been the center of the development-vs.-ecological-preservation debate in Utah since President Bill Clinton made it a national monument in 2000. Locals decried the move, saying it would wreck the economy, and the increased tourism didn't stop President Donald Trump from shrinking the size of both Grand Staircase-Escalante and Bears Ears National Monument, recently created by President Barack Obama. All these areas are still political points of contention, but whatever their official status, they are spectacular places worth visiting.

The **Wasatch Mountain Club** (www.wasatchmountainclub.org; © **801/463-9842**), can offer a number of resources to eco-minded visitors to the Beehive State, with activities geared toward the eco-conscious outdoor lover. Many hotels and resorts in Utah have begun green initiatives, ranging from cutting down on laundry to installing solar panels, in recent years. Be sure to ask hotels about their green policies and initiatives to get a good grasp before you book a room. As for getting around in a green fashion, public transportation is great on the Wasatch Front, but nonexistent in the more remote corners of Utah.

The best way to experience sustainability is by connecting with Utah's wild soul on a trek along the state's myriad hiking trails or a campout in one of its many campgrounds. To lessen your impact, go off the grid on an overnight backpacking trip. **Leave No Trace** (www.lnt.org) is an educational nonprofit that expands on the backpacker's credo to leave any campsite in the same condition—or better off—as when one found it. Backpacking is a refreshing counterpoint to modern life that will give perspective on the issues of sustainability and personal energy dependence.

TOURS

Despite the fact that escorted tours require big deposits and predetermine hotels, restaurants, and itineraries, many people derive security and peace of mind from the structure they offer. Escorted tours—whether navigated by bus, motor coach, train, or boat—let travelers sit back and enjoy the trip without having to drive or worry about details, with a price tag that often includes everything from airfare to hotels, meals, tours, admission costs, and local transportation. They take you to the maximum number of sights in the minimum amount of time with the least amount of hassle. These tours are particularly convenient for people with limited mobility, and they can be a great way to make new friends.

On the downside, you'll have little opportunity for serendipitous interactions with locals. The tours can be jam-packed with activities, leaving little room for individual sightseeing, whim, or adventure—plus they often focus on the heavily touristed sites, so you may miss out the lesser-known gems.

Adventure & Wellness Trips

Utah is an ideal destination for an adventure- or wellness-oriented trip. The national parks are perfect for both, and the spas at Utah's numerous ski resorts and in and around St. George have deservedly earned a national reputation for excellence. See chapter 4, "The Active Vacation Planner," and individual destination chapters for more information.

Guided Tours

City Sights Bus Tours, 3359 S. Main St., Ste. 804 (www.saltlakecitytours. org; © **801/534-1001**), offers several tours of Salt Lake City and the surrounding area. **Tauck Tours** (www.tauck.com; © **800/788-7885**) offering tours throughout the state.

Many companies offer specialized tours for outdoor enthusiasts. See chapter 4, "The Active Vacation Planner," for more information.

Volunteer & Working Trips

Home to several thousand cats, dogs, and other animals at any given time, **Best Friends Animal Sanctuary,** 5001 Angel Canyon Rd., in Kanab (www. bestfriends.org; © **435/644-2001**), offers numerous opportunities for visitors to volunteer for a few hours or an entire vacation, set in the beautiful Southern Utah red rock country (see box, p 213).

Volunteer trail crews offer another great opportunity for visitors to lend a hand while visiting Utah. Many state and national parks and other recreation areas have programs for volunteer trail crews; contact a specific park or area for additional information.

The **International Volunteer Programs Association** (www.volunteer international.org) has a list of questions to help you determine the intentions and the nature of a volunteer program. For general info on volunteer travel, visit **www.volunteerabroad.org** and **www.idealist.org.**

SUGGESTED UTAH ITINERARIES

3

E ventually, you'll have to face it: There is so much to see in Utah that you won't be able to fit it all into one trip. Lifelong Utahns are *still* discovering secret canyons and historical sites. It's easy to be overwhelmed by all the splendid national parks, ski resorts, and wilderness areas; the temples, tabernacles, and historic sites of the Church of Jesus Christ of Latter-day Saints; the genuine Old West destinations, from mining towns and steam trains to saloons and shootout locales; and the traces left by the ancient people who first lived here.

In this chapter we've created several itineraries that will help you plan the most efficient routes to Utah's must-see destinations, from a jam-packed 1-week tour of the Utah's greatest hits to a 2-week leisurely exploration of our stunning national parks.

The following itineraries are all driving tours. If you plan to visit Salt Lake City only or head to a major resort to ski for a week, you can get by without a car, but most of the top destinations here— including all of the national parks—require a bit of a drive. Utah is a vast state, with its sights and attractions spread out, so you'll end up doing some driving to get from one to another. One consolation is that traffic congestion is practically nonexistent, even in cities. Services along rural highways are often limited, though, so motorists need to keep an eye on fuel levels during long-distance hauls. That hand-painted roadside sign that says NO GAS NEXT 50 MILES may be more accurate than you think. And cell phone serve can be iffy.

Suggested Utah Itineraries

Utah in One Week

Utah in Two Weeks

Utah for Families

Utah's National Parks

UTAH IN 1 WEEK

If you only have a week, this itinerary gives you a good overview of the state's highlights. This trip starts and ends in Salt Lake City, taking in historic sites, Mormon culture, and some beautiful red-rock scenery along the way.

Days 1 & 2: Salt Lake City ★

Temple Square, the world headquarters of the Church of Jesus Christ of Latter-day Saints (LDS), is the heart of the city and in some ways, the state. Four days after the Saints entered Salt Lake Valley and Brigham Young apocryphally declared "this is the place," Young chose the site for the temple. The sprawling square houses lovely gardens and statuary, and visitor centers with exhibits on the church's history and beliefs. If possible, attend a performance of the renowned Mormon Tabernacle Choir. Stop in (briefly) at the **Beehive House,** built in 1854 as church leader Brigham Young's family home, and the **Church History Museum.**

When you've had enough of Mormon lore, go to the other end of downtown and visit Salt Lake's **City Library.** It houses a unique collection of zines but you're not there for the reading material. You're here for the architecture, the outdoor fountains, and the view. The roof is landscaped with native plants—and honeybee hives, tended by the library's resident beekeeper.

Up on the east benches, the stunning **Natural History Museum of Utah** tells the state's history through science, starting with geology and moving chronologically through paleontology and native cultures. Its crown jewel is the fantastic collection of dinosaur and other fossils displayed in unique and fascinating ways. (You can "walk over" a dinosaur dig.) The views of the city from the museum are spectacular.

Day 3: Park City ★★

Park City, the famed ski town with its roots in mining, is a beautiful 30-minute drive from Salt Lake. In winter, you can test your skills at one of the nearby ski resorts and in summer, you can check out the **Utah Olympic Park,** built for the 2002 Olympics. It's open year-round for tours and other winter and summer activities. Try tubing down the Nordic Jump or experiencing the speed of an Olympic bobsled ride. Go downtown and spend a few minutes in the **Park City Museum**—home to the old territorial jail in its basement (it's worth a look)—and pick up a copy of the *Park City Main Street Historic Walking Tour* brochure, which leads you to 45 buildings and historic sites that have survived the decades. See p. 126.

Day 4: Price

Make time for a stop in Price on your way south. The town began as a railroad and coal-mining center but is now best known for its dinosaurs.

Stop at the **CEU Prehistoric Museum,** operated by the College of Eastern Utah, to see h*u*ge skeletons of an allosaurus, a Utahraptor, and a strange duck-billed dinosaur known as the prosaurolophus. If time and enthusiasm permit, drive about 35 miles out of town to the **Cleveland-Lloyd Dinosaur Quarry** to see excavations and the bones of more than 70 dinosaurs. See p. 327.

Days 5 & 6: Arches National Park ★★ & Moab

One of Utah's easiest-to-see national parks, **Arches National Park** (p. 308) is famous for its mind-boggling sandstone rock formations. (Example: the arch on the Utah license plate.) Take your time on both the scenic drive and hiking trails to take in the otherworldly desertscape of natural stone arches, towers, and other unlikely sandstone formations. Make the adjacent town of Moab your headquarters, and take a break to cool off at the nearby **Scott M. Matheson Wetlands Preserve** (p. 296), a lush oasis along the river that attracts more than 200 species of birds, plus river otters, beavers, and muskrats. See chapter 14.

Day 7: Back to Salt Lake City

It's a long drive back to Salt Lake City, but you might want to stop in **Provo** (p. 155) to explore some of its fine museums, especially the excellent **Museum of Art** on the campus of Brigham Young University, or the equally renowned **Springville Museum of Art** in nearby Springville. (Note: Take an ice cream break at Rockwell Ice Cream in Provo.)

UTAH IN 2 WEEKS

Even 2 weeks is not enough time to see all that Utah has to offer, but you will be able to see a bit more of everything. This tour assumes you're flying in and out of Salt Lake City and renting a car. If, on the other hand, you don't need to return to the state capital, you'll have extra time to explore the national parks. The "Utah in 1 Week" itinerary provides the base for your trip.

Days 1 & 2: Salt Lake City ★

Start your adventure in Salt Lake City by following the first 2 days in the "Utah in 1 Week" itinerary and be sure to dine in one of the City's great restaurants and pop into a bar. Salt Lake's dining scene has exploded in recent years. *Salt Lake* magazine and *City Weekly* both have good dining guides.

Day 3: Park City ★★

It's on to Park City, an Old West mining town. Follow the recommendations on day 3 of "Utah in 1 Week."

Day 4: Heber Valley Historic Railroad ★★

A short, pretty drive from Park City, the 100-year-old excursion train in Heber City is your ticket to Utah's past. Rides ranging from 1½ to 3 hours are offered on both steam and vintage diesel trains. See p. 144.

Day 5: Price

On your way south, spend day 5 as described on day 4 of "Utah in 1 Week."

Days 6–8: Arches National Park ★★ & Moab

Look to days 5 and 6 in "Utah in 1 Week" for suggestions on exploring the best of Arches National Park and Moab. Spend a day in Canyonlands National Park's Island in the Sky District—usually less crowded than other parts of the park.

Days 9 & 10: Capitol Reef National Park ★★★

This well-kept secret offers brilliantly colored, unexpectedly shaped rock formations, along with a variety of historic sites and a pioneer orchard. The Fremont River feeds a lush oasis in this otherwise barren land; in fact, 19th-century pioneers found the soil so fertile that they established the town of **Fruita,** named for the orchards they planted. You can explore the buildings and even pick fruit in season. Hikers should look for the rock wall where pioneers "signed in," and explore canyons that were a favorite hideout of famed outlaw Butch Cassidy. See chapter 12.

Days 11–13: Bryce Canyon National Park ★★★

The drive down Utah 12 to Bryce Canyon is one of the most scenic routes in Utah. You'll see thousands of intricately shaped hoodoos, those mysterious rock formations Stop at the aptly named **Inspiration Point.** Then hit the colorful **Queen's Garden Trail,** named for a formation that resembles Britain's Queen Victoria, or take a leisurely stroll along the **Rim Trail** for some spectacular views. See chapter 11.

Day 14: Back to Salt Lake City

It's a long drive back to Salt Lake City, but plan a stop in **Provo** (p. 155) to explore the excellent **Museum of Art** on the campus of Brigham Young University.

UTAH FOR FAMILIES

Utah is super family-friendly. Utah's designation of having highest birth rate in the country means there is always consideration for kids. Admission fees for children are usually low, and many tourist attractions offer family packages that are priced considerably lower than the per-person rate. There are lots of family-centric events, and most destinations throughout this book have special activities for kids. This 12-day itinerary, which begins and ends in Salt Lake City, offers plenty for the kids while also providing lots to interest the parents.

Days 1–3: Salt Lake City

It would be easy to spend a week or more here. Start with a stroll through **Temple Square,** taking in the remarkable Tabernacle. Pop into the **Beehive House,** built in 1854 as church leader Brigham Young's family home. Nosh one of the famous rolls next door at **Lion House.** Other family-friendly stops include **Clark Planetarium,** with star shows, light shows, and big-screen movies; **Utah's Hogle Zoo,** home to 1,100 animals; and the kid-oriented **Discovery Gateway,** which houses 140 exhibits, including a kid-size grocery store and an outdoor "flight for life" exhibit. Consider a day-trip to nearby **Ogden** (take the Frontrunner train) for the **Lagoon** amusement park and the terrific family attractions—like skydiving—at the **Salomon Center.** Or opt for a trek to **Antelope Island** in the Great Salt Lake. Its unique eco-system makes it a major flyway for birds, while bison, pronghorn, and coyotes are commonly seen and the trails over rocks and grass to the island's highest points are fun for kids. Fortify yourself with a bison burger at **Island Buffalo Grill** on Bridger Bay.

Day 4: Heber Valley Historic Railroad ★★

This 100-year-old excursion train in Heber City provides a genuine and soot-filled look into the past. Rides ranging from 1½ to 3 hours are offered on both steam and vintage diesel trains. Most kids, including the kids at heart, prefer the steam trains. Less soot. See p. 144.

Days 5–7: Bryce Canyon National Park ★★★

This picturesque park is a long drive down I-15 and then along some back roads, but it's well worth the trip. Bryce contains thousands of intricately shaped hoodoos—those sci-fi rock formations that would look at home on Mars—colored in a palette of red, orange, and brown. Kids will especially like hiking the **Queen's Garden Trail,** where they can spot a variety of whimsically named formations, such as **Thor's Hammer.** See chapter 11.

Days 8 & 9: Capitol Reef National Park ★★★

Heading back north, take the incredibly scenic Utah 12 to Capitol Reef, a secret gem of a national park full of brightly colored and oddly shaped rock formations, along with a handful of historic sites. Be sure to visit the 1896 **Fruita Schoolhouse,** authentically furnished with wood and wrought-iron desks, a wood-burning stove, and textbooks. Nearby, the **orchards** planted by the Mormon settlers (and tended by park workers) continue to thrive. Go ahead and pick some fruit—the rangers have all the supplies. See chapter 12.

Day 10: Price

One word: dinosaurs. They're the reason you want to stop in Price. The **CEU Prehistoric Museum** exhibits huge skeletons of an allosaurus, a Utah raptor, and a duck-billed prosaurolophus. For the true dinophile, drive about 35 miles out of town to the famous **Cleveland-Lloyd Dinosaur Quarry,** where you'll find the relics of more than 70 dinosaurs. See p. 327.

Days 11 & 12: Back to Salt Lake City

Return to Salt Lake City and catch up on attractions you missed the first time, such as **This Is the Place Heritage Park.** The park is home to slightly kitschy but interesting **Old Deseret Village,** a pioneer village comprising original and reproduction buildings that, in summer, becomes a mid-1800s living-history museum, complete with costumed villagers and a variety of activities, including wagon rides. Another good choice is **Liberty Park,** with trails, a small lake with ducks and paddleboat rentals, a playground, a children's garden, a kiddie amusement park, a museum, and the excellent Tracy Aviary. See chapter 5.

UTAH'S NATIONAL PARKS

All those iconic buttes and mesas you remember from Western movies and thought were in Arizona or Wyoming? They're actually in Utah. The state has 5 major National Parks, 2 National Monuments, and 2 National Recreation Areas. In addition, the Navajo Nation is home to wondrous Monument Valley Park, along the Arizona state line. Visit these sites in a somewhat circuitous loop for what is probably the best national park tour in the American West. This trip begins and ends in St. George; air travelers will probably fly to Las Vegas and rent a car there. The tour can be done in 2 weeks, but is much more satisfying done in 3 weeks as described here. With extra time you can easily add the North Rim of the Grand Canyon (see *Frommer's Arizona and the Grand Canyon,* Frommer Media).

Day 1: St. George

Stock up on supplies in town before heading to the parks, but also make some time for—yes, more dinosaurs. The **St. George Dinosaur Discovery Site at Johnson Farm** showcases some 2,000 fossilized dinosaur tracks. The **Jacob Hamblin Home,** built in 1862, provides a peek into a pioneer home, typical of those found throughout the West, except for its two identical bedrooms—one for each of Hamblin's wives. The exquisite 1876 **St. George Tabernacle,** has a pine interior finished by pioneers to look like exotic hardwoods, and even marble. See p. 190.

Days 2–4: Zion National Park ★★

Famous for its mammoth natural stone sculptures and unbelievably narrow slot canyon, Zion is the crown jewel of Utah's Mighty Five. Hop on the shuttle bus that runs the length of the **Zion Canyon Scenic Drive,** getting off to take in the trails. Take the easy **Riverside Walk,** which follows the Virgin River down a narrow canyon through hanging gardens. Especially pleasant on hot days, the **Lower Emerald Pools Trail** traverses a forest of oak, maple, fir, and cottonwood trees, leading to a waterfall, a hanging garden, and a shimmering pool. See chapter 10.

Days 5 & 6: Glen Canyon National Recreation Area ★★★

This national recreation area is best known for **Lake Powell** and its 1,960 miles of shoreline. This is a boating destination, so you'll want to either **rent a boat** to go exploring, fishing, or swimming, or take a guided boat trip. Whichever you do, be sure to save time for **Rainbow Bridge National Monument,** which is in the recreation area and easily accessible by boat. Believed to be the largest natural bridge in the world, this "rainbow turned to stone" is held sacred by the Navajo. See p. 281.

Days 7 & 8: Monument Valley Navajo Tribal Park

To many of us, Monument Valley *is* the Old West we've seen in movies and on TV. Part of the vast Navajo Nation, the park has a 17-mile self-guided **loop road** that lets you hit most of the major scenic attractions, or you can get a more personalized tour with a **Navajo guide.** Either way, you'll see classic Western scenery made famous in movies such as the 1939 classic "Stagecoach," which stars a young John Wayne. Be sure to see the movie exhibits at **Goulding's Trading Post Museum.** See p. 334.

Days 9–12: Arches ★★ & Canyonlands National Parks ★★

Beloved for its captivatingly beautiful red-and-orange rock formations, this area holds two national parks that flank the lively town of Moab. **Canyonlands National Park** (p. 315) is a hikers' park. Stop at the **Grand View Point Overlook,** in the **Island in the Sky District,** and hike the **Grand View Trail,** which is especially scenic in late afternoon. **Arches National Park** (p. 308) is easier to explore than Canyonlands. Take the scenic drive and walk a few trails—on the **Devils Garden Trail** you can see 15 to 20 arches, including picturesque **Landscape Arch.**

Days 13 & 14: Capitol Reef National Park ★★★

This well-kept secret offers brilliantly colored rock formations with a bit of history. The Fremont River created a lush oasis in this otherwise barren land where 19th-century pioneers settled the town of **Fruita,** named for the orchards they planted. Today you can explore the town and even pick fruit in season. Hikers can examine **Pioneer Register,** a rock wall where traveling pioneers "signed in," and explore canyons where famed outlaw Butch Cassidy is said to have hidden out between robberies. See chapter 12.

Days 15–18: Scenic Utah 12 & Bryce Canyon National Park ★★★

From Capitol Reef, go south on Utah 12 over Boulder Mountain and through **Grand Staircase–Escalante National Monument** (p. 254); stop for a meal at renowned Hell's Backbone Grill and take the short but spectacular hike to Calf Creek Falls before heading to **Bryce Canyon National Park.** Spend the night in the park or nearby so you can be on the rim of Bryce Amphitheater at sunrise—the best time to see the colorful and whimsical rock formations known as hoodoos. Top trails here include the colorful **Queen's Garden Trail,** named for a formation that resembles Britain's Queen Victoria. See chapter 11.

Days 19 & 20: Cedar Breaks National Monument ★

This small, high-altitude park has a 5-mile road that offers access to Cedar Breaks' scenic overlooks and trailheads. Hike **Spectra Point Trail** along the rim for changing views of the red and pink rock formations. Enjoy the fields of wildflowers, especially colorful in late July and August, and ponder the fascinating 1,500-year-old bristlecone pines. See p. 203.

Day 21: Back to St. George

Back in St. George, catch the historic Mormon sights you missed earlier, or possibly take in a few rounds of **golf** at one of St. George's eight splendid greens. One of Utah's most scenic parks, **Snow Canyon State Park** offers an abundance of opportunities for photography and hiking, and a respite from the heat in summer. See p. 195.

THE ACTIVE VACATION PLANNER

4

Two thirds of Utah is public land—and that means it belongs to you. Together, Utah's national parks, monuments, recreational areas, national forests, state parks, and millions of acres of land managed by the Bureau of Land Management create an enormous outdoor playground where you can cast for trout or herd cattle, go rock climbing or four-wheeling, sail or ski.

This chapter provides a primer for those folks who are new to planning active vacations or who haven't been to the Utah before; up-to-date information on visiting Utah's public lands; and descriptions of activities you can enjoy in Utah, including the best places to pursue your interests, and the information you need to get started. You'll find more details in the appropriate regional chapters.

PREPARING FOR YOUR ACTIVE VACATION

What to Pack & What to Rent

Planning for a trip into the great outdoors may conjure images of vacationers loaded down with golf clubs, skis, cameras, tents, canoes, and bikes. It's a hassle to travel with too large a load, so plan ahead what activities you really think you're going to try and leave the what-if stuff at home.

How you pack is important for safety and fuel economy. If a car or light truck is your mode of transportation, try to keep the heaviest items between the axles and as close to the floor of your vehicle as possible. If you have a bike rack on the rear bumper, make sure the bike tires are far from the exhaust pipe; one local bike shop owner once mentioned that he does a good business replacing exhaust-cooked mountain-bike tires. Those with roof racks will want to measure the total height of their packed vehicles before leaving home. Underground parking garages often have less than 7 feet of clearance.

One alternative to carrying all that stuff is renting it. Camping equipment, ski equipment, mountain bikes, boats, and water toys are all readily available for rent in places where these activities are popular. You'll find many rental sources listed throughout this book.

When you visit to Utah, be prepared for a land of extremes—one that often has an unforgiving climate and terrain. Those planning to hike or bike should take more drinking water than they think they'll need—experts recommend at least 1 gallon of water per person per day on the trail—as well as high-SPF sun block, hats and other protective clothing, and sunglasses with ultraviolet protection. Summer visitors should carry rain gear for the typical afternoon thunderstorms, plus jackets or sweaters for cool evenings. Winter visitors will need not only warm parkas, gloves, and hats, but also lighter clothing—the bright sun at midday, even in the mountains, can make it feel like June.

Staying Healthy & Safe in the Outdoors

The wide-open spaces and rugged landscape that make Utah such a beautiful place to explore can also be hazardous to your health, especially if you're not accustomed to the extremes here; see "Health" and "Safety," in "Fast Facts: Utah," in chapter 16, for details on dealing with desert climes and high altitudes. The isolation of many of the areas that you'll seek out means there may be no one around to help out in an emergency. So, like any good Boy or Girl Scout, be prepared. Carry a basic first-aid kit that includes a pair of tweezers— very handy for removing tiny cactus spines from tender flesh. Most important of all, check with park offices, park rangers, and other local outdoor specialists about current conditions before heading out.

Outdoor Etiquette

Many outdoor areas in Utah are quite isolated; although you're probably not the first human being to set foot here, you may feel as if you are. Not too long ago, the rule of thumb was to "leave only footprints"; these days, we try not even to do that. Pack out all trash, stay on established trails, be careful not to pollute water, and, in general, do your best to have as little impact on the environment as possible. The best among us go even further, carrying a small trash bag to pick up what others have left behind.

ADVENTURE TRAVEL

Opportunities for adventure travel are plentiful in Utah—as are some terrific outfitters to help you plan and execute your trip. You can take part in a cattle drive, thrill to the excitement of white-water rafting on the Green or Colorado rivers, scale a sheer rock wall in Zion National Park, or head out into some of the most spectacular scenery in the country in a four-wheel-drive vehicle. The variety of tours available seems almost endless, but tour operators can help you find the one for you. In many cases, you can work with an operator to plan your own customized trip—all it takes is money.

IN THE maze

Located on the west side of Canyonlands National Park, the **Maze** is one of the most spectacular places in the Lower 48. It's also one of the most remote and unforgiving places anywhere, making it a good idea to have one of the state's many excellent guide services showing you the way. **Escape Adventures** (www.escapeadventures.com; ℭ **800/596-2953** or 801/824-3934) and **Utah Outventures** (www.utahoutventures.com; ℭ **801/824-3934**) are two options. *Be forewarned:* The Maze, along with Angels Landing (see p. 227), made "Outside" magazine's list of most dangerous hikes in America.

Several companies offer guided hiking/mountain-biking trips into the Maze, one of the riskiest hikes in Utah. It's wise to go with a guide who can lead the way—and also cook up three meals a day on this multi-day adventure. You can ride and bike, then catch a plane back to Moab.

Camp the first night on the brink of the Maze with a view of gnarled sandstone in reds, oranges, tans, and whites, then start hiking through the Maze—its labyrinthine nickname is well earned.

Below are some of the most respected national companies operating in Utah. Most specialize in small groups and have trips geared to various levels of ability and physical condition. They also offer trips in a range of price categories, from basic to luxurious, and of varying length. Numerous local outfitters, guides, and adventure travel companies are discussed throughout this book. For a complete list of outfitters in Utah, as well as a lot of other useful information and Web links, contact the **Utah Office of Tourism** (www.utah.com; ℭ **800/200-1160** or 801/538-1030).

○ **AdventureBus** (www.adventurebus.com; ℭ **888/737-5263** or 909/633-7225) offers trips on customized buses with an emphasis on outdoor adventures, including multisport and mountain biking tours in the Arches, Zion, and Bryce Canyon national parks areas, as well as Hovenweep National Monument.

○ **Austin-Lehman Adventures** (www.austinlehman.com; ℭ **800/575-1540** or 406/655-4591) offers guided multiday mountain biking, hiking, and combination tours in the Zion, Bryce Canyon, and Canyonlands national parks areas.

○ **Backroads** (www.backroads.com; ℭ **800/462-2848** or 510/527-1555) offers a variety of guided multiday road biking, mountain biking, and hiking tours in the areas surrounding southern Utah's national parks.

○ **Bicycle Adventures** (www.bicycleadventures.com; ℭ **800/443-6060** or 425/250-5540) offers guided multiday hiking and biking excursions in the Zion and Bryce Canyon national parks areas.

○ **Escape Adventures** (www.escapeadventures.com; ℭ **800/596-2953**) offers guided multiday hiking, mountain biking, road cycling, and multisport trips in the Canyonlands, Arches, Bryce Canyon, Zion, and Capitol Reef national parks areas.

4

THE ACTIVE VACATION PLANNER | Adventure Travel

- **The World Outdoors** (www.theworldoutdoors.com; ℭ **800/488-8483** or 303/413-0946) offers a variety of trips, including multisport adventures that include hiking, mountain biking, and kayaking to the Canyonlands area, plus hiking/biking trips in the vicinities of Bryce Canyon, Zion, and the north rim of the Grand Canyon.

UTAH'S NATIONAL PARKS

For many people, the best part of a Utah vacation is exploring the state's five national parks (www.nps.gov). Unfortunately, these beautiful national treasures have become so popular that they're being overrun by visitors at a time when the federal government is cutting budgets, making it difficult for the parks to cope with their own success.

The parks are busiest during summer, when most children are out of school, so try to visit at almost any other time. Fall is usually best. Spring is okay, but it can be windy and there may be snow at higher elevations. Winter can be delightful if you don't mind the snow and cold. If you have to travel in summer, be patient. Allow extra time for traffic jams and lines, and try to hike some of the longer and lesser-used trails (ask a ranger for recommendations).

OUTDOOR ACTIVITIES A TO Z

Utah offers a surprisingly wide range of outdoor activities, from desert hiking and four-wheeling to fishing and, of course, skiing. Among the many online outdoor-recreation information sources are the very informative and user-friendly **Public Lands Information Center** website, www.publiclands.org, and **Visit Utah,** www.visitutah.com. For information about fishing, hunting, and wildlife Utah's **Department of Natural Resources** (https://wildlife.utah.gov) is your go-to; detailed maps are available at their offices in Salt Lake City.

You'll have no trouble finding detailed topographic maps—essential for wilderness trips—plus whatever equipment and supplies you need— this is truly a do-it-yourself kind of state. Plus, every single ranger encountered in researching this book was happy to help visitors plan their backcountry trips. In addition, many sporting-goods shops are staffed by area residents that are familiar with both their region and local activities. In almost all cases, if you ask, there will be someone willing and able to help you make the most of your trip.

BOATING For a state that's largely desert, Utah certainly has a lot of lakes and reservoirs, from huge Lake Powell in the south to Lake Flaming Gorge in the north. Both of these lakes are national recreation areas and have complete marinas with boat rentals. Don't forget the state parks, such as Jordanelle, which is near Park City, and **Quail Creek**—with the state's warmest water— near St. George. A favorite is the picturesque but chilly Strawberry Reservoir, southeast of Park City in the Uinta National Forest. For information on boating in state parks, contact **Utah State Parks** (www.stateparks.utah.gov; ℭ **800/322-3770** or 801/538-7378).

passes = PAID ADMISSION ON MOST FEDERAL LANDS

Those who enjoy vacationing at national parks, national forests, and other federal lands have opportunities to save quite a bit of money by using the federal government's annual passes. The America the Beautiful—National Parks and Federal Recreational Lands Pass costs $80 and is good for 1 year from the date of purchase for the general public. It provides free admission for the pass holder and those in his or her vehicle to recreation sites that charge vehicle entrance fees on lands administered by the National Park Service, U.S. Forest Service, U.S. Fish and Wildlife Service, Bureau of Land Management, and Bureau of Reclamation. At areas that charge per-person fees, the passes are good for the pass holder plus three additional adults. Children 15 and under are admitted free.

The Senior Pass is available for U.S. citizens and permanent residents 62 and older for a lifetime fee of $80 (or an annual fee of $20), while the Access Pass, provides free entry for U.S. citizens and permanent residents with disabilities. The Senior and Access passes also provide 50% discounts on some fees, such as camping.

The Senior and Access passes must be obtained in person at national parks, U.S. Forest Service offices, and other federal recreation sites, but the general-public version can be purchased in person, by phone (© 888/275-8747, ext. 1), or online at http://store.usgs.gov/pass, a website that also provides complete information about the passes.

CAMPING   Utah is the perfect place to camp; in fact, at some destinations, such as Canyonlands National Park, it's practically mandatory. Just about every community of any size has at least one commercial campground, and campsites are available at all the national parks and national recreation areas (though they're often crowded in summer) and most state parks. Those who can stand being without hot showers can often find free or very reasonable campsites just outside the national parks, in national forests, and on Bureau of Land Management lands. Other good bets are Utah's state parks, especially Kodachrome, just outside Bryce Canyon National Park; Coral Pink Sand Dunes, just west of Kanab; and Snow Canyon, near St. George.

A growing number of state and federal campgrounds allow visitors to reserve sites, although often only in the busy summer months. Throughout Utah are more than 100 national forest campgrounds and numerous state parks that will also reserve sites. To check on campground reservation possibilities for federal properties, contact Recreation.gov, which combined the old ReserveUSA and National Park Reservation Service into one portal, **Recreation.gov** (© **800/444-6777**), or use the link from the individual park's website. For reservations for campgrounds in state parks, contact **Utah State Parks** (www.stateparks.utah.gov; © **800/322-3770**).

CATTLE DRIVES   Opportunities abound for you to play cowboy on cattle drives that last from a single day to a week or longer. You can actually take part in the riding and roping, though the conditions are generally much more comfortable than what real cowboys once experienced on cattle drives. Each cattle drive is different, so you'll want to ask very specific questions about food, sleeping arrangements, and other conditions before plunking down your cash. It's also a good idea to book your trip as early as possible. A good company is **Rockin' R Ranch** (www.rockinrranch.com; © **801/733-9538**), located north of Bryce Canyon National Park; it's got a business office at 10274 S. Eastdell Dr. in Sandy, Utah.

FISHING Utah has more than 1,000 lakes, plus countless streams and rivers, with species that include rainbow, cutthroat, Mackinaw, and brown trout, plus striped bass, crappie, bluegill, walleye, and whitefish. **Lake Flaming Gorge** and **Lake Powell** are both great fishing lakes, but **Strawberry Reservoir** is Utah's premier trout fishery. Fly-fishing is especially popular in the Park City area and in the streams of the **Wasatch-Cache National Forest** above Ogden. Contact the **Utah Division of Wildlife Resources** (www.wildlife.utah.gov; © **801/538-4700**) for the weekly statewide fishing report.

Fishing licenses are available from state wildlife offices, sporting-goods stores, and the Division of Wildlife Resources website (www.wildlife.utah.gov). Keep in mind that several fishing locations, such as Lake Powell and Lake Flaming Gorge, cross state lines, and you'll need licenses from both states.

FOUR-WHEELING The Moab area, and Canyonlands National Park in particular, are probably the best-known four-wheeling destinations in Utah, but there are also plenty of old mining and logging roads throughout the national forests and on Bureau of Land Management (BLM) land. Those with dune buggies like to head for **Coral Pink Sand Dunes State Park,** west of Kanab. For information on four-wheeling, contact Utah State Parks, the U.S. Forest Service, and the BLM (p. 295).

GOLF Utah's golf courses are known for their beautiful scenery and variety of challenging terrains. They range from mountain courses set among the beautiful forests of the Wasatch to desert courses with scenic views of red-rock country. The warm climate of St. George, in Utah's southwest corner, makes this area a perfect location for year-round golf, and St. George has become the premier destination for visiting golfers—the area's Sunbrook Golf Course is probably Utah's best public course. In northern Utah, the course at the Homestead Resort near Park City is well worth the trip. A free directory of the state's 80-plus courses is available from the Utah Office of Tourism, or check out the **Utah Golf Association** at www.uga.org.

HIKING Hiking is the best—and sometimes only—way to see many of Utah's most beautiful and exciting areas. This is especially true in Utah's five national parks, where most people stick to the paved roads. Flaming Gorge National Recreation Area and the **Wasatch Mountains** around Ogden and Logan are also laced with trails the trails on BLM land around Moab and in rugged Grand Staircase–Escalante National Monument, east of Bryce

LIFE ON THE open road: RV AND TENT VACATIONS

One of the best ways to explore Utah, especially in the warm months, is in an RV—a motor home, truck camper, camper trailer—or a tent. If you own an RV, have the mechanical systems checked out before you go as there are some very steep grades in Utah. After that's done, pack up and go. If you don't have an RV or a tent, you can rent one.

Why Camp?   Many of the best places in Utah, such as **Goblin Valley State Park** and **Canyonlands National Park,** have no lodging. If you don't house yourself, you'll end up sleeping 30 or 40 miles away and missing the spectacular sunrises and sunsets, seeing a lot of wildlife, and that rare feeling of satisfaction that comes from living the experience rather than merely visiting it.

You will be roughing it—no mint on your pillow—but there is no better way to appreciate the outdoors than to be in it, especially when the outdoors is as spectacular as this.

Renting an RV   Renting a tent, a pop-up tent trailer, or a small pickup-truck camper is very affordable, but renting a motor home will probably end up costing as much as driving a compact car, staying in moderately priced motels, and eating in family-style restaurants. That's because motor homes go only a third (or less) as far on a gallon of gas as compact cars, and they're expensive to rent—generally between $1,000 and $1,500 per week in midsummer, when rates are highest.

If you're flying into the area and renting an RV upon arrival, choose your starting point carefully. Because most of Utah's national parks are closer to Las Vegas than Salt Lake City, you could save by starting and ending your trip in Vegas. The country's largest RV rental company, with outlets in Las Vegas and Salt Lake City, is **Cruise America** (www. cruiseamerica.com; *C* **800/671-8042**). You'll see their vehicles everywhere in Utah. RV rentals are also available from El Monte RV (www.elmonte.com; *C* **888/337-2214**). Information on additional rental agencies, as well as tips on renting, can be obtained online from the **Recreation Vehicle Rental Association** (www.rvra.org).

Choosing a Campground   Camping in national parks, federal lands, state parks, and more is discussed in the relevant sections of this book. For a brochure on the campgrounds in Utah's state parks, contact Utah State Parks (p. 172). Members of the **American Automobile Association** (AAA) can request the club's free "Southwestern CampBook," which includes campgrounds and RV parks in Utah, Arizona, Colorado, and New Mexico. Major bookstores carry several massive campground directories, including "Trailer Life Directory" (www.trailerlife directory.com) and "Woodall's North American Campground Directory" and other Woodall's titles (www.woodalls. com), though you won't want to own these unless you're committed to frequent camping.

Canyon. Some of Utah's state parks are as breathtaking as the federal parks and many have good trails, including Kodachrome, near Bryce Canyon National Park; Jordanelle, near Park City; Dead Horse Point, just outside the Island in the Sky District of Canyonlands National Park; and **Escalante,** in the town of Escalante.

Weather in Utah can run to extremes—from brutal summer heat around St. George to the likelihood of ice and snow on high mountain trails from fall through spring. Because of loose rock and gravel on trails in the southern part of the state, wear good hiking boots with aggressive soles and firm ankle support.

HORSEBACK RIDING   It's fun to see the Old West the way the pioneers did—from the back of a horse. Although you won't find many dude ranches in Utah, you can find plenty of stables and outfitters who lead rides lasting from an hour to several days. Try a ride at Bryce and Zion national parks—it's hard to beat the scenery—although you'll likely be surrounded by lots of other riders and hikers. If you'd like a bit more solitude, head north to the mountains around Logan in the Wasatch Front or to Flaming Gorge National Recreation Area.

HOUSEBOATING   Among the best ways to experience either Lake Powell or Flaming Gorge Lake is from the water itself. Marinas at each lake rent houseboats, although you'll find the best selection at Lake Powell. Houseboats provide all the comforts of home—toilets, showers, sleeping quarters, and full kitchens—but in tight quarters. Some of the larger ones have facilities for up to 12 people. You don't have to be an accomplished boater to drive one: Houseboats are easy to maneuver, and can't go very fast. No boating license is required, but you'll need to reserve your houseboat in advance, especially in summer, and send in a sizable deposit.

MOUNTAIN BIKING   Although there are a few areas where road biking is popular (especially in Zion National Park), Utah really belongs to mountain bikers. Just be sure you have plenty of gears—grades can be steep. Moab claims to be Utah's mountain biking capital, but there's no dearth of opportunities in other parts of the state, either. Be aware that mountain bikes must remain on designated motor-vehicle roads in most national parks, but are welcome almost everywhere in areas administered by the U.S. Forest Service and the BLM. In addition to the exciting and often challenging Slickrock trails of Moab, you'll find excellent trail systems just outside of Zion and Bryce Canyon national parks. The warm-weather biking at **Brian Head Resort,** near St. George, is another great option.

RIVER RAFTING, KAYAKING & CANOEING   The Green and Colorado rivers are among the top destinations in the United States for serious white-water as well as flat-water rafting; they're also popular with kayakers and canoeists. A favorite river trip, with plenty of white water, is down the **Green River** through **Dinosaur National Monument.** Trips on the Green also start in the town of Green River, north of Moab. The Colorado River sees more boaters than the Green, and has a greater range of conditions, from flat, glassy waters to rapids so rough they can't be run at all. Most Colorado River trips start in Moab. Several companies rent rafts, canoes, or kayaks, and give you some instruction. They'll also help you decide which stretches of river are

THE ACTIVE VACATION PLANNER | Outdoor Activities A to Z

suitable for your abilities and thrill-seeking level, and can arrange for a pickup at the takeout point. See chapter 14 for details on contacting these outfitters. A worthwhile and lesser-known river trip runs along the **San Juan River** in Bluff. This relaxing excursion will take you to relatively unknown archaeological sites and striking rock formations. See chapter 15.

Note: Water is always an issue in the West; reports on statewide river flows and reservoir information are available from the **Colorado Basin River Forecast Center** (www.cbrfc.noaa.gov; © 801/539-1311 for recorded information).

ROCK CLIMBING This dizzying sport is growing so much in Utah that several popular areas have imposed moratoriums on bolting, and allow climbers to use existing bolt holes only. Among the more dramatic rock-climbing spots is **Zion National Park,** where climbing is as much a spectator sport as a participatory activity. You'll also find some inviting walls in **Snow Canyon State Park** near St. George, in **Logan Canyon, Ogden Canyon,** and throughout the Wasatch Mountains in the Salt Lake City area.

SKIING & OTHER WINTER SPORTS Utahns like to brag that their state has "the greatest snow on earth"—and one winter trip just might convince you they're right. Utah's ski resorts are characterized by absolutely splendid powder, runs as scary or mellow as you'd like, and a next-door-neighbor friendliness many of us thought was extinct. With a few notable exceptions—particularly Park City, Deer Valley, and Snowbird—you won't find the posh atmosphere and high-end amenities that dominate many of the ski resorts next door in Colorado, but you won't find the high prices, either. What you will discover are top-notch ski areas that are surprisingly easy to reach—half are within an hour's drive of Salt Lake City Airport. And they're relatively uncrowded, too: Utah generally receives fewer skiers than Colorado, so you'll see fewer lift lines and plenty of wide-open spaces.

Cross-country skiers can break trails to their hearts' content in Utah's national forests, or explore one of the developed cross-country areas. Particularly good are the mountains above **Ogden** and the old logging and mining roads southeast of Moab. Several downhill resorts, including **Brian Head, Sundance,** and **Solitude,** offer groomed cross-country trails, and some of the hiking trails at **Bryce Canyon National Park** are open to cross-country skiers in winter. Snowmobilers can generally use the same national forest roads as cross-country skiers, and both head to **Cedar Breaks** National Monument in winter, when those are the only ways to get into the park.

Growing in popularity is **snowshoeing,** which is not only easy, but cheap **Bryce Canyon National Park** is one of the best parks for this sport.

Call © 888/999-4019 for the daily avalanche and mountain weather report from the **U.S. Forest Service** (www.wrh.noaa.gov/slc); © 866/511-8824 for statewide road conditions (http://commuterlink.utah.gov); and © 801/524-5133 for weather information. Contact **Ski Utah** (www.skiutah.com; © 800/754-8824 or 801/534-1779) for statewide ski resort information.

4

THE ACTIVE VACATION PLANNER

Outdoor Activities A to Z

WILDLIFE-VIEWING & BIRDING The great expanses of undeveloped land in Utah make it an ideal habitat for wildlife, and, in most cases, it isn't even necessary to hike very far into the backcountry to spot creatures. There's plenty for you to see—water birds at many lakes and reservoirs, elk and antelope in the Wasatch Mountains, lizards and snakes in the red-rock country of the south, and deer and small mammals practically everywhere. All of the national parks and many state parks have excellent wildlife-viewing possibilities: **Coral Pink Sand Dunes** near Kanab is known for its luminescent scorpions, and **Escalante State Park** is the best wetlands bird habitat in southern Utah. Hikers on **Boulder Mountain,** near Escalante, are likely to see deer, elk, and wild turkeys, and birders will enjoy the wide variety of songbirds found here.

The mountains above **Ogden** and **Logan** and the forests around **Brighton** and **Snow Basin** are especially good places to spot elk, deer, and even moose. The relatively remote **Flaming Gorge National Recreation Area** is one of the best areas in the state to find wildlife, so don't be surprised if a pronghorn (improperly called antelopes) joins you at your campsite. Birders have a good chance of seeing ospreys, peregrine falcons, swifts, and swallows along the cliffs; and hikers on the **Little Hole National Recreation Trail,** just below Flaming Gorge Dam, should watch for a variety of birds, including bald eagles in winter. Antelope Island State Park in the Great Salt Lake is another good destination for bird-watchers.

SALT LAKE CITY

Take the short hike up to Ensign's Peak and see Salt Lake Valley from Brigham Young's point of view: a big placid expanse between the Wasatch Mountains on the east and the Oquirrh Range and Great Salt Lake on the west. The city and its suburbs are at an elevation of 4,226 feet. Utah's capital and major population center is small as far as American cities go, with a population of just over 193,000. (The entire metropolitan area, stretching from Ogden to Provo, is about 1.2 million.) But travelers come from around the world to visit Temple Square, world headquarters of the Church of Jesus Christ of Latter-day Saints (LDS), and to hear the inspired voices of the unequaled Mormon Tabernacle Choir. The city is also a base for a growing community of outdoor enthusiasts and home to vibrant dining, arts, and music scenes. An outdoor summer concert (there are many) in Salt Lake is a sublime marriage of landscape and art.

5

THINGS TO DO   The required attraction is **Temple Square,** heart of he worldwide LDS church—one of the few homegrown religions in the United States. Admire the outside of the many-spired temple with its mysterious symbols. You can't go in, but you can enter the **Tabernacle** and be sure to do so. Salt Lake is also home to several excellent **museums,** the **University of Utah** campus, and plenty of shopping and sightseeing.

ACTIVE PURSUITS   Salt Lake City's location is enviable for outdoors enthusiasts: To the east are the **Wasatch Mountains,** with skiing, biking, and hiking; to the west are the **Great Salt Lake** and **Antelope Island State Park.** The nearest ski and snowboard resorts are in Big and Little Cottonwood Canyons, within an hour's drive of downtown: **Alta, Snowbird, Solitude, and Brighton.**

RESTAURANTS & DINING   Salt Lake City has a good dining scene that's only getting better. Creative **New American** cuisine is prominent, as are American standbys like steaks and hamburgers. **Downtown** is a prime dining district, as is the **Cottonwood Heights** area to the southeast.

NIGHTLIFE & ENTERTAINMENT The highly acclaimed **Utah Symphony & Opera** and **Ballet West** are among the country's best. **Downtown** bustles with all sorts of nightlife, from all-ages music venues to brew pubs and cocktail bars. There are also bar strips on **South State Street** and **Sugar House.**

ORIENTATION

Arriving

BY PLANE Direct flights connect Salt Lake City to almost 95 cities in the United States and Canada (Delta Air Lines even offers nonstop service between Salt Lake City and Paris, London, and Amsterdam). **Salt Lake City International Airport** (© 800/595-2442 or 801/575-2400; www.slcairport. com) is located just north of I-80 at exit 115, on the west side of the city.

The airport is a main hub for **Delta Air Lines.** Other airlines flying in and out of Salt Lake City include **American Airlines, Continental Airlines, Frontier Airlines, JetBlue Airways, Southwest Airlines, United Airlines,** and **Alaska Airlines.** See chapter 16 for the websites for these airlines.

BY CAR Salt Lake City is 303 miles north of St. George, 238 miles northwest of Moab, 45 miles north of Provo, and 35 miles south of Ogden. You can reach it from the east or west via I-80 and from the north or south via I-15.

BY TRAIN Amtrak's **California Zephyr** stops in Salt Lake City on its route from Emeryville, California, to Chicago. The station is at 340 S. 600 West (© 800/872-7245; www.amtrak.com).

Visitor Information

Visit Salt Lake, your main source for information about Salt Lake, is headquartered downtown in the **Salt Palace Convention Center,** 90 S. West Temple (© 800/541-4955 or 801/534-4900; www.visitsaltlake.com). It's open daily from 9am to 7pm (closed major holidays), and is right next door is a city institution, **Utah Museum of Contemporary Art** (p 71).

Additional information centers, open 24 hours, can be found in the baggage areas in Salt Lake City International Airport Terminals I and II. A **state information center** is located downtown at Council Hall, 300 N. State St. (© 801-538-1398); it's open Monday through Friday from 9am to 5pm, and Saturday and Sunday from 10am to 5pm.

5

Orientation

SALT LAKE CITY

Glide-By Art Collection

The Salt Lake City International Airport has a growing collection of art that travelers can peruse while cruising the airport's moving sidewalks. It's a multimedia assemblage of art that the airport has been accruing since 1977. See something you like? Call © 801/575-2096 for additional details on the artists and artworks represented on the airport walls.

Salt Lake City Neighborhoods

City Layout

Salt Lake City is laid out in a simple grid system, decreed by Brigham Young and centered on Temple Square. The roads surrounding the Square are North Temple, South Temple, West Temple, and Main Street, with the center of town at the southeast corner (the intersection of Main and South Temple), which is the site of the Brigham Young Monument. The numbers in the road names increase from here by 100s in the four cardinal directions, with West Temple taking the place of 100 West, 100 North called North Temple, and 100 East known as State Street.

Addresses may seem confusing at first, but are really quite clear once you get accustomed to them. For instance, 1292 S. 400 West lies almost 13 blocks south of Temple Square and 4 blocks west, and 243 N. 600 East is about 2 blocks north and 6 blocks east. Note that Lyft, Uber, and GPS direction systems are sometimes confused by these addresses.

A variety of detailed city maps can be purchased at most bookstores. The "Salt Lake Visitors Guide," available free at the visitor center, includes maps showing the approximate location of many restaurants, motels, and attractions.

The Neighborhoods in Brief

Downtown This is most likely where you'll spend the bulk of your time. The downtown area, centered on Temple Square, is a business district, an entertainment and dining destination, and the administrative center for the LDS Church. Church offices, the Family History Library, the Church History Museum, and other church buildings surround the Square. Within a few blocks south, west, and east are hotels, restaurants, stores, and two major shopping centers. Within a couple of blocks are the Salt Palace Convention Center, the George S. and Dolores Dore Eccles Theatre (opened in 2016 as the new premier venue in Salt Lake City), the Maurice Abravanel Concert Hall, and the Capitol Theatre. The City Creek development opened in 2012, bringing upwards of 1,000 new residents downtown and an open-air mall with a retractable roof.

Capitol Hill The Capitol Hill district lies north of the Square and encompasses the 40 acres around the Utah State Capitol Building and Council Hall. Some lovely old homes are located in the blocks surrounding the Capitol.

Marmalade District The quaint houses and narrow streets a few blocks west of the Capitol are known as the Marmalade District. The streets in this small area were named for the nut and fruit trees brought in by early settlers, and the houses represent a variety of the city's early architectural styles.

Sugar House Southeast of downtown, Sugar House was named for a never-completed sugar mill and is one of the valley's longest-standing neighborhoods. Today, it's populated by the young and hip and features a quirky collection of stores, galleries, and eateries, though gentrification is filling the area with more national chains.

Avenues District The Avenues District lies east of the Capitol and north of South Temple. Most of the larger homes here date from the silver boom in Little Cottonwood Canyon, and were built by successful miners and merchants. Today, the charming old houses command a high price.

Getting Around

BY CAR This is an easy city to explore by car, in large part because of the wide streets, in another Brigham Young–design edict. (Young said the streets should be wide enough for a wagon team to turn around without "resorting to profanity.") National car-rental companies here include **Advantage** (www.advantage.com; ✆ 800/777-5500 or 801/322-6090), **Alamo** (www.alamo.com; ✆ 800/462-5266 or 801/575-2211), **Avis** (ww.avis.com; ✆ 800/331-1212 or 801/575-2847), **Budget** (www.budget.com; ✆ 800/527-0700 or 801/575-2500), **Dollar** (www.dollar.com; ✆ 800/800-5252 or 801/575-2580), **Enterprise** (www.enterprise.com; ✆ 800/261-7331 or 801/715-1617), **Hertz** (www.hertz.com; ✆ 800/654-3131 or 801/575-2683), and **National** (www.nationalcar.com; ✆ 800/227-7368 or 801/575-2277). All of these companies either have offices at the airport or will deliver a car to the airport for you. You can contact the main **ground transportation desk** at the airport at ✆ **801/575-2477.**

Many **public parking lots** are situated in the downtown area, costing from $3 to $15 per day. Some lots are free with validation from participating merchants or restaurants. Always ask.

Street parking downtown is metered—that's what those blue robot-looking things are. Key in the number of your parking space, swipe your credit card, key in how much time you need, and go. If you're going to be in Salt Lake for a few days, it's worthwhile to download the **free parking app** on your smartphone. Parking is free on weekends.

BY PUBLIC TRANSPORTATION The **Utah Transit Authority** (www. rideuta.com; ✆ **888/743-3882** or 801/743-3882) provides bus and train service throughout the city, with a "free fare zone" in the downtown area. You can ride free within this zone, getting on and off as many times as you'd like. The fee for traveling in the other zones is $2.50 per person, $1.25 for seniors and those with disabilities, or $6.25 for a day pass. Children 5 and under can ride free with a fare-paying adult. Some buses are wheelchair accessible, and all have bicycle carriers. **TRAX,** a light-rail system also operated by the Utah Transit Authority, with the same contact information and same rates as the Utah Transit Authority's bus service (albeit free in the downtown area), runs 19 miles from Draper Town Center (in the smaller southern city of Draper) north to Salt Lake Central Station in downtown Salt Lake City, with another line running northeast from the city of West Jordan to the University of Utah. The **TRAX Green Line** can take you from the airport into town and around town. The trains are wheelchair accessible and bicycles are permitted. The FrontRunner train connects Ogden to Salt Lake City and Provo; one-way base fares are $2.50 ($1.25 for seniors and travelers with disabilities) with 60¢ for each additional stop (30¢ for seniors and travelers with disabilities). Route schedules and maps for both the buses and light rail are available at malls, libraries, and visitor centers.

BY TAXI For a taxi, contact the **City Cab** (✆ **801/363-5550**), **Yellow Cab** (✆ **801/521-2100**), or Ute Cab (✆ **801/359-7788**), all available 24 hours a day. Of course, the usual Uber and Lyft services are also available and for a fun tour of downtown, try a **BikeTaxi** (www.slcbiketaxi.com). Join the **GREENbike** program (greenbikeslc.org) and see the city on your own two wheels. A network of bike stations is located within a few blocks of one another. As a bike-sharing member, you can unlock any of the specially designed bikes at any station and ride it to any other bike station.

[FastFACTS] SALT LAKE CITY

Emergencies Dial ✆ **911** for police, fire, or ambulance.

Hospitals **LDS Hospital**, 8th Avenue and C Street (https://intermountain healthcare.org/locations/ lds-hospital; ✆ **801/408-1100**), **University of Utah Hospital**, 50 N. Medical Drive (https://healthcare. utah.edu/locations/hospital; ✆ **801/581-2121**); and **Salt** Lake Regional Medical Center, 1050 E. South Temple (www.saltlakeregional. com; ✆ **801/350-4111**), all have 24-hour emergency rooms.

Newspapers & Magazines The two major daily newspapers are the "Salt Lake Tribune" (www.sltrib.com) and the LDS–owned "Deseret Morning News" (www.deseretnews.com). "Salt Lake" magazine (www.saltlakemagazine.com) is a hip, slick publication with a section on current events and a great dining directory. The "Salt Lake City Weekly" (www.cityweekly.net) is the local alternative paper. Other free publications, "SLUG" (Salt Lake Underground) and "Catalyst," offer alternative views of the city.

Police For emergencies, call ℭ **911**. For non emergencies call ℭ **801/799-3000.**

Post Office The main post office is at 1760 W. 2100 South; the branch closest to downtown is at 230 W. 200 South (www.usps.com for hours and locations of other post offices; ℭ **800/275-8777** or 801/532-5501).

Road & Traffic Conditions For statewide road and traffic conditions, visit www.utahcommuterlink.com, or call ℭ **866/511-8824** or 511.

Taxes Sales tax in Salt Lake City is 6.85%; restaurant tax totals 7.85%; lodging taxes total about 12.6% within the city limits, about 11% to 13% in Salt Lake County outside the municipal boundaries.

Weather Call ℭ **801/575-7669** for weather reports.

WHERE TO STAY

Finding comfortable, conveniently located accommodations in Salt Lake City, usually at relatively reasonable rates, is no trouble at all. The building boom of new rooms for the 2002 Olympics supplied lots of lodging, but Salt Lake is booming again and new hotels are still opening.

Among the more affordable major chains and franchises (usually charging about $50–$100 for two people) with locations in Salt Lake City are **Econo Lodge,** 715 W. North Temple (www.choicehotels.com; ℭ **877/233-2666** or 801/363-0062), and **Quality Inn Downtown,** 616 S. 200 West (www.choicehotels.com; ℭ **801/534-0808**).

Frankly, for sightseeing in Salt Lake City or the mountains, airport lodging is inconvenient, but if you must, there's **Comfort Suites Airport** (www.choicehotels.com; ℭ **877/424-6423** or 801/715-8688), **Hampton Inn Downtown** (www.hamptoninn3.hilton.com; ℭ **800/426-7866** or 801/741-1110), and **Radisson Hotel Salt Lake City Airport** (www.radisson.com; ℭ **800/333-3333** or 801/364-5800).

A bit more expensive (generally in the $200–$300 range), the **Salt Lake City Marriott City Center,** 220 S. State St. (ℭ **866/961-8700** or 801/961-8700; www.marriott.com), and the **Hilton Salt Lake City Center,** 255 S. West Temple (ℭ **800/445-8667** or 801/328-2000; www.hilton.com), are among the best full-service chain options downtown.

If you're basing yourself in metro Salt Lake to ski, you may want to consider the **Residence Inn Salt Lake City Cottonwood,** 6425 S. 3000 East (at I-215) (ℭ **888/236-2427** or 801/453-0430; www.marriott.com), which has excellent access to the resorts in Big and Little Cottonwood Canyons. Winter rates start at $179 (including a hearty buffet breakfast) for studios with queen beds and pullouts and full kitchens.

You can often find the lowest hotel rates available online through the **Salt Lake Convention and Visitors Bureau** website, www.visitsaltlake.com.

Where to Stay & Eat in Downtown Salt Lake City

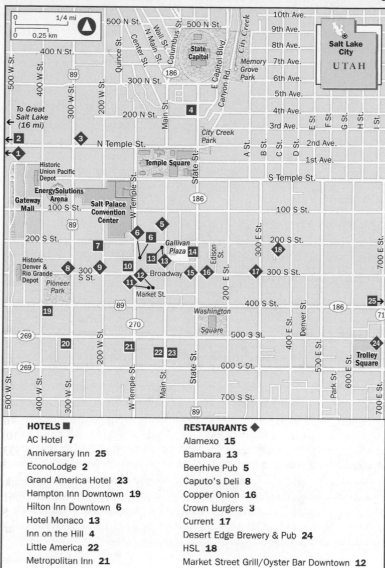

HOTELS ■
AC Hotel **7**
Anniversary Inn **25**
EconoLodge **2**
Grand America Hotel **23**
Hampton Inn Downtown **19**
Hilton Inn Downtown **6**
Hotel Monaco **13**
Inn on the Hill **4**
Little America **22**
Metropolitan Inn **21**
Quality Inn **20**
Salt Lake City
   Marriott City Center **14**
Peery Hotel **10**

RESTAURANTS ◆
Alamexo **15**
Bambara **13**
Beerhive Pub **5**
Caputo's Deli **8**
Copper Onion **16**
Crown Burgers **3**
Current **17**
Desert Edge Brewery & Pub **24**
HSL **18**
Market Street Grill/Oyster Bar Downtown **12**
New Yorker **11**
Red Iguana **1**
Settebello **9**
Spencer's Steaks & Chops **6**

Very Expensive

The Grand America Hotel ★★★ Built for the Olympics, this opulent downtown hotel is the place to stay for those who want the utmost in service and accommodations, and are willing to pay for it. Occupying an entire city block in downtown Salt Lake City, the Grand America is reminiscent of majestic European hotels, with ornate Italian chandeliers and plenty of hand-tooled marble and granite. The exquisitely designed rooms include 880-square-foot deluxe executive suites and beautifully appointed "premiere" rooms with patios and balconies overlooking the pool and garden areas. The concierge floor has a lounge. All rooms are equipped with large-screen TVs, three telephones, and the finest quality furnishings.

555 S. Main St. www.grandamerica.com. ℂ **800/621-4505** or 801/258-6000. 775 units, including 396 suites. $229–$429 double; $339–$5,000 suite. **Amenities:** 2 restaurants; concierge; executive level; fitness center; indoor Jacuzzi; 1 indoor and 1 outdoor heated pool; free Wi-Fi.

Expensive

AC Hotel Salt Lake City Downtown ★★ The newer concept from Marriott, the AC offers sleek, minimalist European design and a cool lounge. The downtown location is convenient for business and tourist purposes and the continental breakfast, included in some rates, features local foods.

225 W. 200 South. www.achotels.marriott.com. ℂ **385/722-9600.** 164 units. $179–$209 double. Some rates include continental breakfast. Pet-friendly ($75 one-time fee). **Amenities:** Bar; fitness center; free Wi-Fi.

The Anniversary Inn–Fifth South ★ A favorite with local couples, the Anniversary Inn makes a fun romantic getaway in the fantasy-style of the '70s, with themed rooms like the Jungle Safari (which features an elephant-trunk shower), and the treehouse-themed Swiss Family Robinson. The most popular is the luxurious Romeo and Juliet Suite, complete with marble, columns, and a sweeping circular staircase. Built on the site of an early-20th-century brewery in a quiet, shady nook east of downtown, the inn has fun details in every room, as well as fireplaces, two-person jetted tubs, and surround-sound systems. Cheesecake and sparkling cider are waiting in your room at check-in; continental breakfast is delivered in the morning. You might also check out the 14-room Anniversary Inn in the historic Kahn Mansion, 678 E. South Temple, which shares a website, a phone, and a similar sensibility with its larger sister property.

460 S. 1000 East. www.anniversaryinn.com/fifth-south. ℂ **800/324-4152** or 801/363-4900. 36 themed suites. $139–$299 double. Lower weekday rates. Rates include continental breakfast. **Amenities:** Free Wi-Fi.

Hotel Monaco ★★ Effortlessly combining a generous dose of class with just a dash of quirk, Salt Lake City's boutique Hotel Monaco occupies the 14-story former Continental Bank Building, built in 1924 and home of the world's first drive-through teller. The colorful lobby mixes classic and contemporary, as do the flamboyant rooms, which captivate with an eclectic array of patterns and colors. Many rooms have spectacular city views. There's complimentary wine at 5pm nightly. Pets are allowed; the hotel will even provide a goldfish for your room if you'd like. The Monaco is also home to an excellent destination restaurant, Bambara (p 58).

15 W. 200 South. www.monaco-saltlakecity.com. © **800/805-1801** or 801/595-0000. 225 units, including 20 suites. $151–$209 double; $219–$391 suite. Lower weekend rates often available. Valet parking $24. Pets accepted (free). **Amenities:** Restaurant (Bambara; see review, p. 58); lounge; concierge; exercise room; room service; free Wi-Fi.

Inn on the Hill ★★

Two blocks from both the Utah State Capitol and Temple Square, this stately 11,000-square-foot mansion atop Capitol Hill—built by a local luminary in 1906—has been a B&B since the 1990s and is a city gem. Most rooms are on the first and third floors, with one king-size or queen-size bed, a large television, and a private bathroom with jetted tub. You'll find plenty of original architectural details, such as wavy and stained-glass windows and steam heat, and you'll enjoy tremendous city and mountain views.

225 N. State St. www.innonthehillslc.com. © **801/328-1466.** 13 units, including 1 carriage house. $165–$210 double; $220 carriage house. Rates include breakfast. **Amenities:** Movie library; free Wi-Fi.

Little America Hotel ★

While now overshadowed by its sister property, the Grand America, the Little America is still among Salt Lake City's finest hotels, and it's probably the locals' favorite—just check out the crowd at breakfast. Choose from standard courtside units to extra-large deluxe tower suites in the 17-story high-rise—all are gracefully yet comfortably appointed in French Provincial style. The locally popular coffee shop opens at 6am; there's also a steakhouse and lounge on-site. The hotel has a second-floor sun deck with an indoor/outdoor pool plus an additional beautifully landscaped outdoor pool.

500 S. Main St. www.saltlake.littleamerica.com. © **800/453-9450** or 801/596-5700. 850 units, including 4 suites. $120 and up double; $189–$400 suite. **Amenities:** 2 restaurants; lounge; concierge; health club; Jacuzzi; 2 pools (outdoor heated, indoor/outdoor heated); room service; sauna, free Wi-Fi.

Peery Hotel ★★

A top choice for those who appreciate the ambience of a vintage property, the Peery is the only truly historic hotel in downtown Salt Lake City. Completed in 1910, it has been fully renovated and restored to its former European-style elegance, offering comfortable, tastefully decorated accommodations. The lobby is delightful, with old-style pigeonholes for letters and a grand staircase to the upper floors. Each unique, handsomely appointed room contains period furnishings and pedestal sinks with antique brass fixtures in the bathroom. And it keeps getting better, with a new replica of the original sign on the roof, an awning that doubles as a deck, and upgrades of the rooms and the exterior. Some units have fridges, and a few suites have jetted tubs. The entire hotel is nonsmoking.

110 W. 300 South (Broadway). www.peeryhotel.com. ℰ **800/331-0073** or 801/521-4300. 73 units, including 10 suites. $169–$199 double. Rates include continental breakfast. Parking $12/day. **Amenities:** Restaurant, concierge; exercise room; free Wi-Fi.

Moderate

Metropolitan Inn ★   This one-time chain motel is now a first-rate independent, clad in colorful stucco and equipped with stylish guest rooms. Art Deco reproductions and prints of "Wizard of Oz" characters hang above the beds (the Wicked Witch of the West excluded). Rooms have either one king-size bed or two queen-size, and the suite has a microwave, fridge, and two couches. The dinky outdoor pool is summer-only, and a computer is available in the lobby for guests traveling without their own.

524 S. West Temple. www.metropolitaninn.com. ℰ **801/531-7100.** 60 units, including 1 suite. $85–$136 double. Rates include continental breakfast. Pet-friendly ($25/3 nights) **Amenities:** Outdoor heated seasonal pool, free Wi-Fi.

Camping

Salt Lake KOA/VIP   This huge, well-maintained campground is the closest camping and RV facility to downtown Salt Lake City. Facilities include an outdoor pool (open May 1–Sept 15), a hot tub (open year round), a playground, a basketball court, Wi-Fi, coin-op laundry machines, several bathhouses, a convenience store with RV supplies, propane, an RV/car wash, well-maintained grassy areas for tents, and large shade trees. It offers 14 instant phone hookups, 200 sites with 50-amp power, and a jogging/pet-walk/bicycle trail behind the campground.

1400 W. North Temple. https://koa.com/campgrounds/salt-lake-city. ℰ **800/562-9510** or **801/328-0224.** 208 sites (18 tent sites, 190 hookups for RVs), 2 cabins. Campsites $37 tents and $55–$65 RVs; camping cabins $75–$126. Advance reservations recommended May–Sept. Pets accepted (free). **Amenities:** Jacuzzi; outdoor pool; free Wi-Fi.

WHERE TO EAT

Salt Lake City restaurants are more casual than those in most major American cities. The service is generally excellent and very friendly.

Expensive

Bambara ★★ NEW AMERICAN   A favorite lunch destination for the downtown business crowd, Bambara's slick dining room is the ideal pre- or post-theater dinner spot—right across the street from Capitol Theater. It's also a great place for people-watching, with windows on the busy (for Salt Lake City, that is) intersection of Main and 200 South. The menu brings a host of influences to the table, from Japanese to Italian to French, intermingling them without any one tradition overwhelming the others. The dinner menu changes regularly but always includes a delectable Utah corn bisque, a nice selection of beef and seafood, and a vegetarian dish. Breakfast is fairly traditional, and lunch brings sandwiches, steaks, and a scrumptious burger topped with local cheddar cheese and horseradish aioli. The popular two-course "Powers" lunch is named after the chef. The menu changes but it's always good. Service is understated and excellent. Full liquor service is available.

In the Hotel Monaco, 202 S. Main St. www.bambara-slc.com. ℭ **801/363-5454.** Reservations recommended. Breakfast $9–$15, lunch $9–$25, dinner $20–$46. Mon–Fri 7–10am and 11:30am–2:30pm; Sat–Sun 8am–2pm; dinner daily 5:30–10pm.

The Copper Onion ★★★ NEW AMERICAN Featuring one of Salt Lake's most creative menus, the Copper Onion serves an eclectic array of dishes in a classic but casual atmosphere. Dinners include pasta dishes, meat loaf, and heirloom chicken, with a nice array of seasonal side dishes like sautéed spinach with cashews and raisins or cauliflower with anchovy cream and capers. Lunch and brunch strike a similar note, ranging from house-made pasta dishes to huevos rancheros. There is a full bar that mixes specialty cocktails like cucumber gimlets and brandy Alexanders.

111 E. Broadway. www.thecopperonion.com. ℭ **801/355-3282.** Reservations recommended. Main courses $8–$18 lunch and brunch, $13–$33 dinner. Mon–Thurs 11:30am–3pm and 5–10pm; Fri 11:30am–3pm and 5–11pm; Sat 10:30am–3pm and 5–11pm; Sun 10:30am–3pm and 5–10pm.

Current Fish & Oyster ★★★ SEAFOOD & MORE The soaring ceiling, reclaimed exterior, mezzanine, and open kitchen elicit a "wow" response from first-timers before they've eaten a bite. The menu highlights seafood from different regions of America—San Francisco, Monterrey, South Carolina, New Orleans, Chicago, New York City—and why not? Utah is landlocked but absolutely fresh seafood is just a flight away. Current also places a high priority on sustainable seafood, so rest easy about that. Preparations tend to be classic: whole branding, caramelized salmon, shrimp and grits, crab cakes, and oysters on the half shell. There are lots of non-fish entrees too and the wine list is excellent. Sunday suppers are prix-fixe ($50), with three courses and no substitutions.

279 E. 300 South. www.currentfishandoyster.com. ℭ **801/326-3474.** Main courses $9–$23 lunch and $22–$38 dinner. Mon–Fri 11am–4pm; daily 4–10pm.

HSL ★★★ CONTEMPORARY AMERICAN Much-lauded chef Briar Handly (a James Beard semi-finalist) opened his first restaurant, Handle, in Park City, but it wasn't long before he expanded the concept and opened another place in Salt Lake. Handly is one of the most innovative chefs in town but that doesn't mean his food is pretentious or expensive. Offerings run the gamut from inventive grain dishes and vegetables to a beefcheek burger to some of the best fried chicken we've had. But it's the oddities such as hearth-roasted cabbage and General Tso's cauliflower that you need to try. This is a place to be adventurous, trust the chef, and explore the constantly changing menu. A great bartender and craft cocktail list, a pleasingly eclectic interior, and friendly service round out the experience. Oh, and the brunch is killer.

418 E. 200 South. hslrestaurant.com. ℂ **801/539-9999.** Main courses $12–$17 lunch and brunch and $16–$32 dinner. Thurs–Fri 11am–2:30pm, Sat–Sun brunch 10am–2:30pm. Sun–Thurs 5–9pm, Fri–Sat 5–10pm.

Log Haven ★★ NEW AMERICAN   Located in a historic log mansion (1920) 4 miles up Millcreek Canyon in the Wasatch National Forest (about 20 min. from downtown), Log Haven has garnered a reputation as Salt Lake City's most romantic restaurant. The seasonally changing menu is creative and diverse, with sushi, game, and more traditional fare—steak and potatoes—to be expected. On a recent visit, the menu included a grilled bison bavette steak with caramelized cauliflower and house-cured pancetta; tomato pappardelle pasta with olives, kale, fava beans, and ricotta; and "alpine nachos," featuring Yukon gold potato chips, raclette cheese, and forest mushrooms. Log Haven's antique charm, nestled in the forest setting with waterfalls and flower gardens in the warm weather and snow-covered evergreens in the winter, blends wilderness and civilization. Its rustic elements combine with elegant sensibilities to maintain a sense of history while pushing the culinary envelope—not an easy task. Service is impeccable, and full liquor service is available.

6451 E. Millcreek Canyon Rd. www.log-haven.com. ℂ **801/272-8255.** Reservations recommended. Main courses $27–$45. Daily 5:30–9pm.

Spencer's for Steaks and Chops ★★ STEAK/CHOPS   This sophisticated steakhouse is the perfect spot to celebrate a special occasion, or to just sit back and enjoy a truly excellent steak. The handsome dining room is reminiscent of a library in a British lord's country home, with dark wood, tapestry-like wall coverings, vintage photos, and intimate and comfortable booths. Beef is king here—aged, well-marbled USDA prime beef that is simply and perfectly prepared. The New York strip and the super-tender filet mignon come heartily recommended. Other dinner selections served a la carte include bison ribeye, peppercorn-seared ahi, double-cut lamb chops, and free-range chicken. Don't miss the delectable loaded hash browns topped with applewood bacon, sharp white cheddar, chives, and sour cream. The lunch menu includes the same steaks, as well as burgers, chicken sandwiches, and entree salads. Spencer's also has an extensive list of wines and single-malt Scotches.

Located in Hilton Salt Lake City Center, 255 S. West Temple. ℂ **801/238-4748.** www. spencersforsteaksandchops.com. Reservations recommended. Lunch items $11–$32, dinner main courses $22–$69. Daily 11:30am–11pm.

Inexpensive

Garlic burgers are a Utah staple and the most famous are at the low-key, to put it nicely, watering hole known as the **Cotton Bottom Inn** where to eat your burger with a beer and old tunes on the jukebox; it's at 2820 E. 6200

South (www.cottonbottominn.com; ☏ **801/273-9830**). The pizzas at **Sette-bello,** 260 S. 200 West (www.settebello.net; ☏ **801/322-3556**) are strictly Neapolitan-style. **Beerhive Pub,** 128 S. Main St. (☏ **801/364-4268**), features American pub fare, a good selection of beer, and a narrow trough of frost at the bar to keep your pint cold to the last swig. For quick, cheap, and family-friendly eats, head to **Tonyburgers,** with several locations in the metro area, including one close to downtown at 613 E. 400 South (www.tonyburgers.com; ☏ **801/419-0531**). And if you must try the (in)famous Salt Lake pastrami burger—that's right, a pile of sliced pastrami on top of a hamburger—better go to **Crownburger** (www.crown-burgers.com), with four Salt Lake loca-tions, including one at 377 E. 200 South (☏ **801/532-1155**), and one on the east side at 3190 S. Highland Dr. (☏ **801/467-6633**).

Caputo's ★ DELICATESSEN   A stalwart lunch stop, Caputo's is located in an upscale market on the west side of downtown. On one side, it's a gour-met Mediterranean shop, with its own cheese caves and the city's best selec-tion of chocolate. On the other side, you can order at the counter, take a seat in the semi-industrial interior or on the patio, and wait for your number to be called. The sandwiches and salads are terrific, made with fresh and flavorful ingredients, with an emphasis on Italian standbys. New Orleans–style muf-fulettas, meatball subs, and roasted peppers on focaccia are among the mouth-watering selections. Salads, pasta dishes, and daily specials are available. There's also a great selection of ready-to-heat meals and charcuterie. Caputo's has four locations throughout the valley, each with slightly different offerings.

The main store is at 314 W. 300 South. www.caputos.com. ☏ **801/531-8669.** Sand-wiches and salads $5–$9. Mon–Sat 9am–7pm; Sun 10am–5pm.

Red Iguana ★ MEXICAN   Another local favorite, owned and operated by the Cardenas family, Red Iguana is one of the few Mexican joints anywhere that specializes in mole—the spicy sauce named for a Nahuatl (Aztec) word meaning concoction. Just as the colorful dining room nearly overwhelms the eyes, the amarillo mole served over chicken nearly overwhelms the taste buds with its fiery combination of aji amarillo and guajillo peppers, vegetables, and spices. Other enticing variations of mole include verde, negro, red pipian with peanuts and pumpkinseeds, and several more. The menu doesn't begin and end with mole, however: A full slate of Mexican standards, seafood, and egg dishes is available, as are beer, wine, and margaritas. Whatever time of day you go, there's sure to be a line. There's a second location at 866 W. South Temple (☏ **801/214-6050**), and a takeout version, Taste of Red Iguana, at the City Creek Food Court, 28 S. State St. (☏ **801/214-6350**).

736 W. North Temple. www.rediguana.com. ☏ **801/322-1489.** Most dishes $7–$17. Mon–Thurs 11am–10pm; Fri 11am–11pm; Sat 10am–11pm; Sun 10am–9pm. From downtown, follow North Temple west under the I-15 overpass; the restaurant is on your right.

EXPLORING TEMPLE SQUARE

This is literally sacred ground for members of the Church of Jesus Christ of Latter-day Saints (LDS), also known as Mormons. (See chapter 2, "Utah in Depth," to learn about the history of the church and modern Mormonism.) The 10-acre **Temple Square ★★★** is enclosed by 15-foot walls, with a gate in the center of each. In addition to the church buildings, the square houses lovely gardens and statuary, and the North and South visitor centers, which have exhibits on the church's history and beliefs, interactive videos, and films. Also in the North Center is an 11-foot-tall replica of the awe-inspiring sculpture *Christus,* a statue of Christ by the Danish artist Bertel Thorvaldsen.

The majestic **Temple** is used only for the LDS church's most sacred ceremonies and is not open to the public. Work began on the six-spired granite structure in 1853, and it took 40 years to complete.

The oval **Tabernacle** seats about 3,500 people and has one of the West's largest unsupported domed roofs. The Tabernacle has fantastic acoustics— even if you don't have time for a performance, stop in and listen to the famous pin drop, an amazing demonstration that happens during every guided tour.

On Thursday evenings at 7:30pm, you can listen to the **Mormon Tabernacle Choir ★★★** rehearse (except when they're on tour; call © **801/240-4150,** or visit www.mormontabernaclechoir.org for the current schedule). During the summer months and in December, rehearsals move from the Tabernacle to the Conference Center to accommodate larger audiences. On Sunday mornings you can attend their broadcast from 9:30 to 10am (you must be seated by 9:15am). The choir, composed entirely of volunteers, was formed shortly after the first pioneers arrived; many husband-and-wife members and families participate, sometimes over several generations. The Tabernacle organ has been rebuilt a number of times, and has grown from the original 2,000 pipes and two manuals to 11,623 pipes and five manuals. The organ is said to have an instantly recognizable signature sound. Half-hour organ recitals take place year-round, Monday through Saturday at noon, Sunday at 2pm. At peak times, an additional 2pm recital is often scheduled Monday through Saturday. Admission to these performances is free.

The Gothic-style **Assembly Hall** was constructed in 1880 from leftover granite from the Temple and has lovely soaring white spires and stained-glass windows. Free concerts are offered here most weekends; inquire at a visitor center for schedules. Two monuments stand in front of the Assembly Hall: One depicts a pioneer family arriving with a handcart filled with their belongings, and the second commemorates the salvaging of the first crops from a plague of Mormon crickets (California gulls swooped down and ate the insects).

Guided tours of the square, lasting approximately 45 minutes and available in 30 languages, leave every hour from 8am to 9pm. They begin at the flagpole west of the Salt Lake Temple; personnel in the visitor center can direct you. Tour guides provide a general history of the church (touching upon the church's doctrine) and take you around the square, briefly explaining what you are seeing. The Tabernacle tour includes a fascinating demonstration of the incredible acoustics: the group is ushered to the last row of seats while someone stands at the podium and drops three pins—the sound is as clear as a bell.

The square is bounded by Main Street on the east and North, South, and West Temple streets. The LDS Church controversially purchased the stretch of Main Street on the square's east side, closed it to traffic, and transformed it into a lovely park with trees, flowers, walking paths, and benches; a large reflecting pool dominates the area, displaying a mirror image of the Temple.

Across North Temple Street from the Square is the mammoth **Conference Center of the Church of Jesus Christ of Latter-day Saints** (© **801/240-0075**). This huge complex has a main auditorium for worship services, meetings, and cultural events, seating 21,000 people. During the bi-annual LDS Conference, the building is packed and so is downtown.

When the church leaders realized there would be 4 acres of roof over the conference center, they decided to do something special with it. So the designers created a wild landscape reminiscent of a Utah mountain on top of the roof. Among the flora are bristlecone pines, aspens, Serbian spruces, 21 native meadow grasses, and 300 varieties of Utah wildflowers. An immense fountain flows in four directions and eventually into the Conference Center spire, from which it cascades 67 feet down the south face of the building. The roof is a serene oasis in the middle of a busy modern city—people sit or stroll and enjoy the views of the city set against the Wasatch Mountains. But you have to have a guide.

The Conference Center is usually open Monday through Saturday from 9am to 9pm (the roof closes at 8:30pm); free, guided tours of the complex are offered except during special events.

Visitor centers are also open daily from 9am to 9pm; tours are given between 9:15am and 8:15pm. Hours are reduced on Christmas. Call © **800/363-6027** or 801/531-1000 for more information, or browse **www. visittemplesquare.com**. The TRAX train stops right out front, at the Temple Square station. Allow 1 to 3 hours to tour the square.

MORE TO SEE & DO IN & AROUND SALT LAKE CITY

Church History Museum This collection of church art and artifacts, started in 1869, includes Utah's earliest Mormon log home, rare 1849 Mormon gold coins, and a scale model of Salt Lake City in 1870. The history of the LDS Church is related in the exhibits that describe each of the church presidents, from Joseph Smith to present; activities include multimedia programs, films, and puppet shows. There's also a museum shop. Allow 1 hour. 45 N. West Temple. www.history.lds.org. © **801/240-3310** or 240-4615. Free admission. Mon–Fri 9am–9pm; Sat and most holidays 10am–5pm. TRAX: Temple Square.

Family History Library ★★ This incredible facility contains what is probably the world's largest collection of genealogical records under one roof. (It shares its database and resources with Ancestry.com.) You can easily spend hours here immersed in discovering the whos, whats, wheres, and whys of your family history. The growing collection comprises a substantial number of records from around the United States, fairly comprehensive data from the British Isles, and vital record information from 110 other countries. Most of the records, which date from about 1550 to 1930, are from governments, various churches and other organizations, and individuals.

The Mormons believe that families are united for eternity through marriage and other sacred ordinances given in the temples. These ordinances, such as baptism ceremonies, can be done on behalf of ancestors—hence the interest in tracing all deceased family members.

When you enter the library, help is available to assist with your research. There are forms you can fill out with any and all data you already know (so come prepared with copies of whatever you have), and you will be directed from there. An orientation is given to newcomers and includes a handout and a map of the library. Volunteers are stationed around the library to help with anything you need.

Some of the records are in books, and many have been converted to microfilm, microfiche, and computer files. The volunteers will show you how to use any unfamiliar machines. One of the easiest ways to begin a search is to start with the place where your ancestors lived, because records are organized first by the geographical origin.

35 N. West Temple. www.familysearch.org. © **801/240-6966** or 801/240-2584. Free admission. Mon 8am–5pm; Tues–Fri 8am–9pm; Sat 9am–5pm. Closed major holidays and July 24. TRAX: Temple Square.

University of Utah Members of the Church of Jesus Christ of Latter-day Saints opened the University of Deseret in 1850, just 2½ years after they arrived in the Salt Lake Valley. It closed 2 years later, due to lack of funds and the greater need for primary education, but reopened in 1867 as a business academy. The name changed in 1892, and the growing school moved to its present location in 1900. The university now sprawls over 1,500 acres on the east side of the city (from the center of town, take Utah 186 east to the campus).

The University is also home to the Utah Museum of Fine Arts, Red Butte Garden and Arboretum, and the Natural History Museum of Utah.

201 Presidents Circle. www.utah.edu. © **801/581-7200.** TRAX: University Line.

Historic Buildings & Monuments

Beehive House ★ This house was built in 1854 as Brigham Young's family home. Young also kept an office here and entertained church and government leaders on the premises. Young, a lover of New England architecture, utilized much of that style in his house, including a widow's walk for surveying the surrounding desert. Today, visitors can get a glimpse of the lifestyle of

What to See & Do in Downtown Salt Lake City

Beehive House **8**
Brigham Young Monument **10**
Capitol Building, Capitol Hill **2**
Church History Museum **5**
City Creek Center **11**
City Library **18**
Clark Planetarium **14**
Conference Center of
  the Church of Jesus Christ
  of Latter-day Saints **4**
Council Hall **3**

Discovery Gateway **13**
Family History Library **6**
Gallivan Plaza **17**
Governor's Mansion **16**
Joseph Smith Memorial Building **9**
The Leonardo **19**
Liberty Park **20**
Pioneer Memorial Museum **1**
Salt Palace Convention Center **15**
Temple Square **7**
Utah Museum of Contemporary Art (UMOCA) **12**

this famous Mormon leader by taking a guided half-hour tour of the house. It has been decorated with period furniture (many pieces original to the home) to resemble its appearance when Young lived here, as described in a journal kept by his daughter Clarissa. Young's bedroom is to the left of the entrance hall. The Long Hall, where formal entertaining took place, is on the second floor; it was also used as a dormitory to house visitors. Young's children gathered in the sewing room, where they helped with chores, bathed by the stove, and studied Mormon principles. Only one of Young's 27 wives lived in the Beehive House at a time; the rest, with some of the children, lived next door in the **Lion House** (now a banquet facility and restaurant open Mon–Sat from 11am–8pm) or in other houses. Built of stuccoed adobe in 1855 through 1856, the Lion House was named for the stone lion guarding its entrance.

Before you leave, you'll see the **Eagle Gate,** a 76-foot gateway that marked the entrance to the Brigham Young homestead, located at the corner of State Street and South Temple. It's been altered several times over the years, and the original wooden eagle has been replaced by a 4,000-pound metal version with a 20-foot wingspan.

67 E. South Temple. www.lds.org/placestovisit. © **801/240-2681.** Free admission. Daily 9am–8:30pm (last tour at 8pm). TRAX: Temple Square; walk a half-block east.

5 **Brigham Young Monument** This marker, near the southeast corner of Temple Square, was placed here to honor Young, the other pioneers who accompanied him here in 1847, and the countless Native Americans and fur trappers who preceded them.

At Main and South Temple sts.

Capitol Building ★ Built between 1912 and 1916 of unpolished Utah granite and Georgia marble—and restored and earthquake-proofed from 2004 to 2008—the Utah State Capitol, considered one of the finest examples of Renaissance Revival style in the West, rests on a hill in a beautifully landscaped 40-acre park. The state symbol, the beehive (representing industry and cooperation), is a recurring motif both inside and out. Those who don't want to take the free tour can explore on their own.

The **Rotunda,** which stretches upward 165 feet, is decorated with murals painted during the WPA years (the four largest depict important scenes in the state's early history) and houses several busts of prominent historical figures,

---

The Connect Pass

The Salt Lake Convention and Visitors Bureau sells the **Connect Pass,** which covers admission at 13 local attractions. A 1-day pass costs $36 for adults, $32 for seniors 65 and over, and $30 for children ages 3–12; 2- and 3-day passes are also available. Buy your pass online at www.visitsaltlake.com and download the pass to your smartphone or print a hard copy. For details, contact **Visit Salt Lake** (© **800/541-4955** or 801/534-4900; www.visitsaltlake.com).

including Brigham Young and Philo T. Farnsworth, the man whom we can all thank for bringing us television. The chandelier is astounding—it weighs 6,000 pounds and hangs from a 7,000-pound chain.

Other rooms include the State Reception Room, known as the **Gold Room** because the walls are made from locally mined gold-traverse marble; the offices of the governor and lieutenant governor; the **Hall of Governors,** a portrait gallery that honors all those who have served as governor of Utah since statehood in 1896; and the offices of Utah's attorney general. Downstairs are a small souvenir shop and additional exhibits, including a large topographical map of Utah.

The third floor houses the Senate, House of Representatives, and Supreme Court of Utah. You can either climb one of the two marble staircases or take the elevator. The state legislature meets for 45 days in January and February. In front of the House of Representatives is a replica of the Liberty Bell, one of 53 bronzed and cast in France in 1950. Allow at least an hour to explore here.

Capitol Hill, 350 N. State St., 120 State Capitol. www.utahstatecapitol.utah.gov. Ⓒ **801/538-1800.** Free admission and tours. Building Mon–Fri 7am–8pm; Sat–Sun 8am–6pm; guided tours Mon–Fri 9am–4pm, on the hour. Bus: 23 up Main St.

> ### Bigger than Texas?
>
> Brigham Young proposed the state of Deseret to the U.S. government in 1849. The vision included parts of modern-day California (including San Diego), Nevada, Utah, Idaho, Arizona, and New Mexico. Needless to say, the proposal didn't fly.

Council Hall Completed in 1866, Council Hall is a fine example of Federal Greek Revival architecture. Originally located downtown, it first served as City Hall and the meeting place for the Territorial Legislature; in the early 1960s, it was dismantled and reassembled—block by sandstone block, 325 of them—in its present location. Today, it houses the **Utah Travel Council** (www.utah.com) upstairs; the ground floor contains a bookstore and gift shop. Allow 45 minutes.

Capitol Hill, 300 N. State St. Ⓒ **800/200-1160** or 801/538-1030. Free admission. Mon–Fri 9am–5pm. Bus: 23 to the Capitol.

Governor's Mansion Silver magnate Thomas Kearns started building this palatial home in 1898, sparing no expense to make it as lavish as possible. African and Italian marble and exotic woods from around the world were used extensively throughout. Kearns's widow deeded it to the state in 1937, and the 36-room mansion is now the governor's residence. It suffered a devastating fire just before Christmas 1993, but has been fully restored to its appearance in 1902, the year the Kearns family moved in. The best time to see the mansion is in December, when it's elaborately decorated for Christmas. Allow about 30 minutes.

603 E. South Temple. Ⓒ **801/538-1005.** Free admission. June–Aug and Dec Thurs 2–4pm; call for hours at other times. TRAX: Trolley Square.

HOTELS ■

Comfort Suites Airport **2**
Residence Inn **14**
Salt Lake KOA/VIP **3**

RESTAURANTS ◆

Archibald's Restaurant **17**
Aristo's **5**
Cotton Bottom **12**
Crown Burgers **10**
Log Haven **11**
Market Street Cottonwood **15**
Market Street South Jordan **18**
Porcupine Bar & Grill **4**
Tuscany/Franck's **13**

ATTRACTIONS ●

Gardner Village **17**
Hogle Zoo **8**
International Peace Park **9**
Kennecot's Bingham Canyon Mine **19**
Salt Lake International Airport **1**
This is the Place Monument **7**
University of Utah and Medical Center **6**
Wheeler Farm **16**

Joseph Smith Memorial Building Between 1911 and 1987, this building served as the world-renowned Hotel Utah. Since renovated and converted into offices, meeting spaces, restaurants (www.diningattemplesquare. com), and reception areas (very popular for wedding receptions), the architectural details have been lovingly restored. The lobby retains its art-glass ceiling and massive marble pillars—it's worth a stop for a peek inside. The **Family-Search Center** (© 801/240-4085) has 100 computers and a staff to help you discover your family's roots. A big-screen 500-seat theater (© **801/240-4383**) offers free showings of an hour-long movie about the life of LDS founder Joseph Smith. Allow 30 minutes to 1½ hours.

15 E. South Temple. www.visittemplesquare.com. © **800/531-1000** or 801/240-1266. Free admission. Mon–Sat 9am–9pm. TRAX: Temple Square.

Museums

Clark Planetarium ★ This state-of-the-art planetarium presents laser light shows and big-screen movies in a 3D IMAX theater. It also contains a variety of interactive exhibits ranging from a display about the names of the planets to a Foucault pendulum, plus a rotating relief globe. Allow up to 3 hours.

110 S. 400 West. slco.org/clark-planetarium. © **385/468-7827.** Free admission to museum; show fees $7 before 5pm; $9 5pm and later; $7 children 12 and under. Sun–Wed 10:30am–7pm; Thurs 10:30am–10pm; Fri–Sat 10:30am–11pm. TRAX: EnergySolutions Arena.

Gallivan Plaza Some call this Salt Lake City's outdoor living room, with its intimate spaces, performances, food offerings, all kinds of characters and activities, and good vantage points for watching the goings-on. The Plaza also hosts live entertainment at its amphitheater, and there's an outdoor ice-skating rink (call or visit the website for hours and rates). Allow 30 minutes—more if you plan to skate or dine here.

239 S. Main St. (the entire block btw. Main and State sts., and 200 and 300 South). www. thegallivancenter.com. © **801/535-6110.** Free admission (fees for some special events). Daily 7am–10pm. TRAX: Gallivan Plaza.

The Leonardo "The Leo" (named for Leonardo da Vinci) is a science and technology museum with a wide range of exhibits dedicated to innovation. Cutting-edge displays compellingly meld art and science, showcasing technological advancements in prostheses, biofuels, and architecture. (The building is a contemporary work of art in itself.) Philip Beesley's "Hylozoic Veil," an evolving environmental sculpture that subtly responds to outside factors, is a particularly captivating installation.

209 E. 500 South. www.theleonardo.org. © **801/531-9800.** Admission $12.95 adults, $9.95 seniors (65+), $8.95 kids 3–12. Daily 10am–5pm. Closed July 4.

Natural History Museum of Utah ★ Moved to a stunning new building in 2011, this museum covers more than 200 million years of natural history with a focus on Utah. All-new exhibits—including intriguing dinosaur exhibits—describe the geologic and natural history of Utah right up to the present. Allow 2 hours.

At the University of Utah, 301 Wakara Way. www.umnh.utah.edu. ⓒ **801/581-6927.** Admission $14.95 adults, $12.95 seniors (65+) and ages 13–24, $9.95 ages 3–12. Daily 10am–5pm (Wed until 9pm). TRAX: S. Campus Dr.

Pioneer Memorial Museum   Operated by the Daughters of Utah Pioneers, this museum, housed in a Grecian-style building, contains an immense collection of pioneer portraits and memorabilia, 200,000 artifacts in all. All six stories are packed with relics of Utah's history, such as paintings, photos, and the personal effects of church leaders Brigham Young and Heber C. Kimball. The collection also includes exhibits on spinning, weaving, railroading, mining, and guns; a restored 1902 steam fire engine; and a few unusual relics like hair wreaths, temple replicas, and a stuffed two-headed calf. Explore on your own or with the aid of a guide sheet; tours are also available with advance arrangements. A short film is shown throughout the day. Allow 1 hour.

300 N. Main St. www.dupinternational.org. ⓒ **801/532-6479.** Free admission; contributions welcome. Mon–Sat 9am–4pm. Closed major holidays. TRAX: Temple Square.

Utah Museum of Contemporary Art (UMOCA) ★   Changing exhibits feature contemporary works by local, regional, and national artists. There are generally several simultaneous exhibitions in a variety of mediums, including paintings, photographs, sculptures, and ceramics. Allow at least 1 hour, and check the schedule for lectures, poetry readings, concerts, workshops, and other art-centric events.

20 S. West Temple. www.utahmoca.org ⓒ **801/328-4201.**. Free admission; donations welcome. Tues–Thurs and Sat 11am–6pm; Fri 11am–9pm. TRAX: Temple Square.

Utah Museum of Fine Arts ★★   This is among the very best art museums in the state, housing a permanent collection of more than 18,000 objects. Changing displays might include Greek and Egyptian antiquities, Italian Renaissance works, art by European masters, Early American art, 20th-century lithographic prints and photography, and art objects from Southeast Asia, China, Japan, and African and pre-Columbian cultures. Exhibits highlight shows from other institutions and private collections. Recently renovated and painted, the 74,000-square-foot museum has over 20 galleries, a bookstore, a cafe, and a community education center. Allow 2 to 4 hours.

At the University of Utah, 410 Campus Center Dr. www.umfa.utah.edu. ⓒ **801/581-7332.** Admission $12.95 adults, $9.95 seniors and ages 6–18, free for children 5 and under. Tues–Sun 10am–5pm (Wed until 9pm). Closed major holidays. TRAX: S. Campus Dr.

Organized Tours

City Sights Tours (www.saltlakecitytours.org; ⓒ **801/364-3333**) offers several tours of the city and surrounding areas, including the Rocky Mountains. The 4-hour Salt Lake City Deluxe tour, which includes an organ recital in the

Mormon Tabernacle is $49 for adults, $25 ages 10 and under. The seasonal 4- to 5-hour tour to Kennecott's Bingham Canyon Mine, which includes a stop at the beach on the Great Salt Lake, is $79 adults, $40 kids. A Sunday city tour that includes a Mormon Tabernacle Choir concert also costs $59 adults, $30 ages 10 and under. Check the website for details and additional tours.

Parks & Gardens

Gilgal Garden ★ Folk-art aficionados won't want to skip this collection of ornate, bizarre, and often abstract sculptures, the handiwork of the late Thomas Child, a mason and devout Mormon. Child's beliefs shine through in his works, which include a sphinxlike Joseph Smith, and his Monument to the Trade, in honor of bricklaying. The sculptures almost went the way of the dodo before locals fought to restore the property and turned it into a city park in 2000. Allow about 1 hour.

749 E. 500 South. www.gilgalgarden.org. ℂ **801/582-0432.** Free admission. Daily Apr–Sept 8am–8pm; rest of year daily 9am–5pm. Closed Thanksgiving, Dec 25, and Jan 1. Bus: 209.

International Peace Gardens ★ Begun in 1939 by the Salt Lake Council of Women, the Peace Gardens have expanded over the years and now belong to the city. Take a stroll along the Jordan River, through the gardens, and past statuary and displays representing different countries (such as Buddha statues, windmills, and Viking tomb replicas). Benches are scattered about for moments of rest and contemplation. Allow about 1 hour.

Jordan Park, 1000 S. 900 West. www.internationalpeacegardens.org. ℂ **801/938-5326.** Free admission. May–Sept daily dawn–dusk. Bus: 209.

Liberty Park ★★ This big, delightful city park has trails for walking and jogging, tennis and bocce courts, a small lake with ducks and paddle-boat rentals, picnic facilities, a playground, a children's garden, a children's amusement park, a museum, and an excellent aviary. Covering 100 acres, this is a favorite gathering spot for locals, as well as one of the best dog-walking areas in the city (dogs must be leashed and owners must clean up after them). In the park, the **Chase Home Museum of Utah Folk Arts** (https://heritage.utah.gov/arts-and-museums/chasehome; ℂ **801/533-5760**), in the historic Brigham Young/Chase home, contains exhibits of pioneer art, American Indian art, and folk art. Allow 30 minutes. **Tracy Aviary** (www.tracyaviary.org; ℂ **801/245-7285**), in the southwest section of the park, has more than 400 birds, including a number of endangered species. There are special exhibits of cuckoos and pelicans (you can feed the latter with a keeper for $3), and free-flying bird shows are presented during the summer (call for schedule). Allow at least 1 hour.

Btw. 500 and 700 East, and 900 and 1300 South. Entrances from 900 and 1300 South. ℂ **801/972-7800** for the city parks department. Park and museum free admission; Tracy Aviary admission $11.95 adults, $9.95 seniors (65+) and students, $7.95 ages 3–12. $5 after 5pm on Mon, June–Aug (open late). Park daily 6am–11pm (dawn–dusk in winter). Museum Tues and Thurs–Sat 11am–4pm and Wed 11am–8pm (summer); Wed–Sat 11am–4pm (rest of year). Tracy Aviary daily 9am–5pm, and summer Mon until 8pm.

Concerts at **Red Butte amphitheater** (www.redbuttegarden.org; © **801/585-0556**) are one of the highlights of a Salt Lake summer. Starting in May and running into September, the series features music as diverse as David Byrne, Weird Al Yankovich, and Death Cab for Cutie, as well as up-and-coming acts. On-site food and beverage is available, but most people bring their own portable feast and some wine and picnic on the grass. The sun setting behind the Wasatch is a backdrop to the stage that makes this an unforgettable experience. Catch a show if you can.

Red Butte Garden and Arboretum ★★   This Arboretum on the University of Utah campus features 18 acres of display gardens and 450,000 springtime blooming bulbs with 5 miles of nature trails. Located in the foothills of the Wasatch Mountains, this is a terrific spot to take a break or catch a summer concert. Allow 2 hours.

300 Wakara Way. www.redbuttegarden.org. © **801/585-0556.** Admission $14 for adults, $12 seniors (65+) and military, $7 ages 3–17. May–Aug daily 9am–9pm; reduced hours the rest of the year. From downtown, drive east on 400 South, past the university entrance, continuing until 400 South becomes Foothill Dr.; turn left on Wakara Way.

This Is The Place Heritage Park   Brigham Young and the Mormon pioneers got their first glimpse of the Salt Lake Valley at the site of this historic park. A tall granite and bronze sculpture was erected in 1947 to commemorate the centennial of their arrival. The park, which covers more than 1,600 acres, offers hiking along part of the trail used by the pioneers, with opportunities for cross-country skiing in winter. This is a good place for wildlife viewing and birding in winter and spring, with additional songbirds and raptors present in summer and fall. There's a picnic area, but no camping, and a visitor center contains exhibits depicting the Mormon pioneers' trek from Illinois to the Great Salt Lake Valley in 1847.

Also in the park, Heritage Village is a pioneer village comprising original buildings from across the state along with some reproductions. In summer and during special events, it becomes a living-history museum of the period from 1847 to 1869, with costumed villagers and a variety of demonstrations and activities, including wagon rides. For a week each December the village re-creates a pioneer Christmas celebration. Allow 1 to 2 hours.

2601 E. Sunnyside Ave. www.thisistheplace.org. © **801/582-1847.** Free admission to park and visitor center. Admission to Heritage Village $12.95 adults, $10.95 seniors (65+), $8.95 children 3–11 (reduced admission Sun). Daily 10am–5pm. Bus: 228.

Utah's Hogle Zoo ★   This 42-acre, modern zoo near the entrance to Emigration Canyon is home to over 800 animals representing over 250 species. Take a stroll through a solarium with exotic plants and birds, tropical gardens, rare Grévy's zebras, and a giraffe house with a balcony so you can look eye-to-eye with the tall-necked creatures. In summer, rides on a small

5

SALT LAKE CITY

More to See & Do

replica of an 1869 steam train are offered for $2.50, or you can ride a hand-carved animal on the Conservation Carousel for $2.50. As with any zoo, it's best to visit in a cooler season, or at least the coolest part of the day, when more animals are out and about. If you have an all-adult group, check the Hogle Zoo events calendar to find out the dates of ZooBrew, an evening set aside to enjoy adult beverages and see the animals at night. Allow 1 to 2 hours.

2600 E. Sunnyside Ave. www.hoglezoo.org. © **801/584-1700**. Admission summer $18.95 adults, $16.95 seniors (65+), $14.95 children 3–12; winter $16.95 adults, $14.95 seniors (65+), $12.95 children 3–12. Mar–Oct daily 9am–6pm; Nov–Feb daily 10am–5pm Closed Sept 6, Christmas, and New Year's Day. Special hours for Zoo Lights Dec 1–31.

Especially for Kids

In addition to what's listed below, the Clark Planetarium (p. 70), Utah's Hogle Zoo (p. 73), Liberty Park (p. 72), Natural History Museum of Utah (p. 70), and Kennecott's Bingham Canyon Mine (see below) are great places to visit with kids.

Discovery Gateway ★★ With eight permanent exhibits, this 60,000-square-foot, three-story facility in the Gateway development on the west side of downtown is the place for kids of all ages to explore: Children can play a marimba, make a stop-motion animated video, or engineer a paper plane to throw in a wind tunnel. The museum also features a child-size grocery store where kids can be both shoppers and checkers, and an outdoor "flight to life" exhibit with a real helicopter now serving as a simulator. Allow 1 to 3 hours.

444 W. 100 South. www.discoverygateway.org. © **801/456-5437**. Admission $12.50 adults (Sun $10), $10 seniors (65+). Mon–Thurs 10am–6pm; Fri–Sat 10am–7pm; Sun noon–6pm. Call for holiday hours. TRAX: EnergySolutions Arena.

Wheeler Historic Farm This living-history dairy farm, where you can see demonstrations of farming and daily activities from the late 19th century, features hundred-year-old farm buildings, a small petting zoo, and a nature preserve. Activities include experiencing various farm chores (such as egg gathering and cow milking), farmhouse tours, and tractor-driven wagon rides. A variety of annual events is also offered, including story time at the farm, a farm festival in May, and a summer camp week. Allow 1 to 2 hours.

In Cottonwood Regional Park, 6351 S. 900 East (just north of I-215 exit 9). https://slco. org/wheeler-farm. © **385/468-1755**. Free admission to farm; 50¢–$3 for tours and special activities. Daily dawn–dusk. Bus: 209.

NEARBY ATTRACTIONS

Gardner Village This quaint village is a cluster of restored historic homes and buildings surrounding Gardner Mill, a flour mill built by Scottish immigrant Archibald Gardner in 1877. Brass plaques tell the stories of each of the historic structures. The mill, which is on the National Historic Register, now houses a large store specializing in country furniture and gift items, as well as **Archibald's Restaurant** (ℭ 801/566-6940), serving classic American dishes. Close to two dozen shops in the other historic buildings that sell a wide range of items, including art, crafts, clothing, candy, quilts, dolls, and home furnishings. The village also has a spa, a bakery, and a picturesque duck pond. Plan to spend at least an hour here.

1100 W. 7800 South, West Jordan. www.gardnervillage.com. ℭ **801/566-8903.** Free admission. The village is 12 miles south of downtown. From I-15, take exit 297 and head west on 7200 South, turn left (south) onto Redwood Rd. and left again on 7800 South; it's on the left (north) side of the road. From I-215, take exit 13 for Redwood Rd. and follow directions above. TRAX: Midvale Center.

Kennecott's Bingham Canyon Mine ★ From most places in Salt Lake City, you can't help seeing this mammoth open pit mine, first dug in 1906. Because of several landslides in 2014, the Visitor's Center is currently closed. Call or check the website for updates and a virtual tour.

Utah 48 (7200 South), about 25 miles southwest of Salt Lake City outside Copperton. www.kennecott.com. ℭ **801/204-2000.** Take I-15 south to exit 297 for Midvale; head west on Utah 48 to the mine.

OUTDOOR PURSUITS

Salt Lake City is an excellent base for skiing and snowboarding (see chapters 6 and 7), and plenty of opportunities for hiking and other warm-weather activities lie just outside the city in the 1.3 million acres of the Wasatch-Cache National Forest. For maps and detailed trail information, contact the **Uinta-Wasatch-Cache National Forest** (www.fs.usda.gov/detail/uwcnf/; ℭ **800/999-2103**). Another good source of information is the nonprofit **Public Lands Interpretive Association** (http://publiclands.org), located in the REI building (see below).

Renting equipment instead of hauling it with you often makes the most sense for outdoor vacations—lots of places that a offer rentals in Utah. **Recreational Equipment, Inc. (REI),** 3285 E. 3300 South (www.rei.com; ℭ 801/486-2100), offers a wide range of sporting goods, both sales and rentals. A good source for sales and rentals of ski and golf equipment, bikes, and in-line skates is **Utah Ski & Golf,** 134 W. 600 South, in downtown Salt Lake City (www.utahskigolf.com; ℭ **801/355-9088**) with three other locations in Utah. **Canyon Sports,** at 517 S. 200 West in Salt Lake City (www.canyon sports.com; ℭ **801/322-4220**), rents winter and summer equipment.

BIKING A number of bikeways are strung along city streets, some separate from but running parallel to the road, some a designated bike lane on the road, and others sharing the road with motor vehicles. From mid-May through September, City Creek Canyon, east of Capitol Hill, is closed to motor vehicles. It's open to hikers and in-line skaters at any time, and bicyclists can use the road on odd-numbered days. For information on the best places to bike, as well as rentals and repairs, stop at **Canyon Sports,** 1844 E. Fort Union Blvd. (www.canyonsports.com; ℭ **800/736-8754**).

THE BIGGEST LITTLE ski town IN THE WORLD

Drive less than an hour from downtown Salt Lake City and you can be skiing the resorts in Big and Little Cottonwood Canyons: Alta, Snowbird, Brighton, and Solitude. Although you can stay in lodges and hotels in and around the canyons, many visitors base themselves in Salt Lake City proper to cut costs. If you're looking to ski several of the resorts, get a **Ski Salt Lake Super Pass** (www.visitsaltlake.com/ski/superpass), offered by the Salt Lake Convention and Visitors Bureau. It's good at all four of

the resorts in the canyons and is a value. Prices range according to age and duration. For more on activities in the canyons, see chapter 7.

But the outdoor opportunities extend beyond Big and Little Cottonwood Canyons. For the record, 11 of 14 of Utah's ski resorts are within 70 miles of Salt Lake City International Airport. You can easily spend the day skiing Alta, not to mention Ogden and/or Park City, and be back downtown for dinner and a Jazz game.

BOATING   The Great Salt Lake has marinas on the south shore and on Antelope Island (p. 82).

DIVING & SNORKELING   South of the Great Salt Lake in Grantsville, **Bonneville Seabase,** 1600 North SR 138 (www.seabase.net; © **435/884-3874**), has four diving bays up to 60 feet deep. All have exotic sea life, and one has a boat wreck. Rentals and classes are available; day use fees are $20.

FISHING   Trout populate the rivers feeding into the Great Salt Lake, although fish can't live in the lake itself. Popular spots include Big and Little Cottonwood creeks and Mill Creek. Fishing licenses are required; you can get one, along with maps and suggestions, at most sporting-goods stores.

GOLFING   Salt Lake City has ranked number-one U.S. golf city in "Golf Digest" in years past. For general information and to reserve a tee time contact **Salt Lake City Golf** (www.slc-golf.com; © 801/485-7730). Rates range from $14 to $19 for 9 holes and $30 to $38 for 18 holes; all courses require reservations. The 18-hole, par-72 **Bonneville,** 954 Connor St. (© 801/583-9513), has hills, a large ravine, and a creek. The 9-hole, par-36 **Forest Dale,** 2375 S. 900 East (© 801/483-5420), is a redesigned historic course with huge trees and challenging water hazards. The 18-hole, par-72 **Glendale,** 1630 W. 2100 South (© 801/974-2403), features fine bent grass greens and splendid mountain views. Two 18-hole courses are located at **Mountain Dell** (© 801/582-3812), in Parley's Canyon, east on I-80: the par-71 lake course and the par-72 canyon course, provide breathtaking views and a strong likelihood of seeing deer, elk, moose, and other wildlife. The 9-hole, par-34 **Nibley Park,** 2730 S. 700 East (© 801/483-5418), is a good beginner course. The 18-hole, par-72 **Rose Park,** 1386 N. Redwood Rd. (© 801/596-5030), is flat but challenging.

JOGGING   **Memory Grove Park** and **City Creek Canyon** are both great options for walking or jogging. The park is on the east side of the Capitol, and the canyon follows City Creek to the northeast. In town, you can go to one of the city parks, such as **Liberty Park** (p. 72).

SPECTATOR SPORTS

The National Basketball Association's **Utah Jazz** (www.nba.com/jazz; ✆ 801/325-2500) usually packs the house, so get your tickets early. They play at the **EnergySolutions Arena,** 301 W. South Temple.

The **Utah Grizzlies** (www.utahgrizzlies.com; ✆ **801/988-8000)** of the East Coast Hockey League, play in the Maverik Center, 3200 S. Decker Lake Dr., West Valley City (off I-215 exit 20).

Real Salt Lake (www.rsl.com; ✆ **801/727-2700)**, the city's professional soccer team, plays at Rio Tinto Stadium, 9256 S. State St., in Sandy.

If you want to take in a minor league baseball game, the Pacific Coast League's **Salt Lake Bees** (www.slbees.com; ✆ **801/325-2337)**, a Triple-A affiliate of the Anaheim Angels, play at Smith's Ballpark, at 77 W. 1300 South.

The **Utah Blaze** (www.utblaze.com; ✆ **888/992-5293)** plays Arena Football League opponents March through July indoors at EnergySolutions Arena.

The University of Utah's **Runnin' Utes and Lady Utes** (www.utahutes.com; ✆ **801/581-8849)** compete in the Pac-12 Conference. The women's gymnastics team is phenomenal, and men's football and basketball have been growing in stature nationally. Tickets are usually available on fairly short notice, although it's best to call far in advance for football games.

SHOPPING

Salt Lake City offers plenty of retail opportunities, both in big malls and quaint neighborhood shopping areas. Many Salt Lake City stores are closed on Sundays (the influence of the LDS Church); typical store hours are Monday through Saturday from 9am to 6pm. Shopping malls are often open Sunday afternoons from noon to 5 or 6pm, and also stay open a few hours later on weeknights.

The most popular shopping destination in the city is **City Creek Center,** a major undertaking of the real estate arm of the LDS Church. City Creek Center, right across from Temple Square, covers almost 20 acres of downtown, swallowing two older shopping centers. An outdoor mall with a retractable roof, pedestrian skybridge, and meandering landscape creeks, it holds more than 110 stores and restaurants (mostly mall staples), from Apple and Anthropologie to Tiffany and West Elm. To get the lay of the land inside the sprawling mall, pay attention to the many way-finding signs. If you're in downtown Salt Lake City, it's hard to miss City Creek—it's right on Main Street (50 S. Main; ✆ **801/521-2012)**.

The Gateway, on the west side of downtown at 18 N. Rio Grande St. (www.shopthegateway.com; ⓒ 801/456-0000), is a large, open-air shopping mall and entertainment and dining center. It covers 2 city blocks near EnergySolutions Arena and features restaurants and entertainment venues as well as Dave & Buster's, plus a megaplex theater, museums and other attractions, and restaurants. The historic Union Pacific Railroad Depot serves as the main entrance. The Gateway is a favorite place for festivals, so check the website for up-to-date info.

Nearby, off an eclectic block of Broadway (E. 300 South) **Ken Sanders Rare Books,** 268 S. 200 East (www.kensandersbooks.com; ⓒ **801/521-3819**), is the bookstore of your dreams, piled with used and antiquarian books, posters and ephemera. Ken Sanders himself is a beloved figure (you may have seen him on PBS's "Antiques Roadshow"). Take time to browse his collection of books about Utah by the legendary Edward Abbey, and if Ken's there's by chance, have a word with the man himself.

Another central shopping destination is **Historic Trolley Square,** 600 South at 700 East (www.trolleysquare.com; ⓒ **801/521-9877**), with modern shops, galleries, and restaurants in an old-fashioned setting. You'll also see two of the city's original trolley cars, a historic water tower, and two of the city's first street lamps.

Movie buffs will like the **Jordan Commons** complex, encompassing 2 city blocks at 9335 S. State St., south of downtown Salt Lake City in Sandy. The complex boasts 17 movie theaters surrounding a food court offering cuisines from Chinese to Mexican, plus a deli, coffee shop, and, of course, popcorn. The theaters are equipped with chairs large enough to accommodate food trays, so you can bring your dinner in with you! Call ⓒ **801/304-4577** or check www.megaplextheatres.com for movie information and tickets.

Although you couldn't yet call Salt Lake City an arts center, it does have a growing arts community, along with 20 or so galleries. On the third Friday of each month, there is an evening **Gallery Stroll.** One of the oldest galleries in Salt Lake City, the **Phillips Gallery,** 444 E. 200 South (www.phillips-gallery. com; ⓒ **801/364-8284**), represents over 100 artists, most of whom are Utahns, and exhibits everything from traditional to contemporary paintings, sculptures, and ceramics.

Modern West Fine Art, 177 E. 200 South (www.modernwestfineart.com; ⓒ **801/355-3383**) owned by an eminent local art collector, specializes in art of the west, from traditional tribal arts to modern masters. Visit the website for current exhibits.

The **"A" Gallery,** 1321 S. 2100 East (www.agalleryonline.com; ⓒ **801/583-4800**), is a 10-square-foot, long-standing contemporary art gallery featuring a sculpture garden. The **Hope Gallery,** 151 S. Main St. (www.hopegallery.com; ⓒ **801/532-1336**), is a 15,000-square-foot facility focusing on late-19th- and early-20th-century European and Scandinavian fine art, with an emphasis on religious works.

SALT LAKE CITY AFTER DARK

Salt Lake City has left behind its image as a quiet town where the sidewalks are rolled up at night. Check "Salt Lake" magazine, the free publications "City Weekly," "SLUG," and "Catalyst" or go to visitsaltlake.com, produced by Visit Salt Lake, for the latest events and concerts. VSL also publishes a print guide.

Utah's Drinking Laws

The cumbersome private-club-membership requirements for entry into bars, nightclubs, and some restaurants are a thing of Utah's past, thanks to legislation that went into effect on July 1, 2009. Tipplers no longer need to pay membership fees or fill out applications before entering an establishment to buy an alcoholic drink. However, that didn't clear away all confusion about the state's complicated and convoluted liquor laws.

Much of the confusion comes from the terms used to define the different types of liquor licenses held by different businesses. Liquor, wine, full-strength beer, and regular beer (3.2% alcohol) are available by the glass at licensed restaurants and clubs. Wine is also available by the bottle in these establishments. Beer may also be purchased in many places that have a "beer only" type license. These include taverns, beer bars, smaller restaurants or cafes, snack bars, etc. Alcohol beverage service in a licensed restaurant requires that you order food with your drink and that your beverage be delivered to your table or counter by your server. You can buy 3.2 Beer in convenience and grocery stores, but heavy beer, wine, and liquor can only be sold in a state-owned store. However, you can buy beer directly from most local breweries. Where and how drinks are mixed and served in restaurants, where kids are allowed and not, are complicated subjects that even many Utahns aren't quite clear about. Go to **https://abc.utah.gov** for the endless details.

THE PERFORMING ARTS

Tickets for performances at a variety of venues can be obtained from **Art Tix** (arttix.artsaltlake.org; ✆ **888/451-2787** or 801/355-2787).

The highly acclaimed **Utah Symphony & Opera** ★★★ (www.usuo.org; ✆ **801/533-6683**) combines one of the country's top symphony orchestras and the well-respected Utah Opera Company. It presents four operas a year plus a year-round symphony season at Abravanel Hall, 123 W. South Temple, an elegant 2,800-seat venue known for its excellent acoustics and the towering sculpture by Dale Chihuly in the lobby.

Dance is one of the art forms most appreciated by Utahns, largely due to its approval by the LDS church. The nationally acclaimed **Ballet West** ★★ (www.balletwest.org; ✆ **801/869-6900**) performs at the historic Capitol Theatre, 50 W. 200 South. The October-to-May season usually brings four or five productions, ranging from classical to contemporary, as well as holiday stagings of *The Nutcracker.* Modern dance is presented by the **Repertory Dance**

Theatre (www.rdtutah.org; ℂ 801/534-1000) and the **Ririe-Woodbury Dance Company** (www.ririewoodbury.com; ℂ 801/297-4241), with performances at the Rose Wagner Performing Arts Center, located at 138 W. 300 South, and other venues. For an edgier approach to modern dance, keep your eyes open for performances by **SB Dance**. Billed as "theater art for curious minds," its performance schedule can be found at www.sbdance.com

The **Pioneer Theatre Company**, 300 S. 1400 East (www.pioneertheatre. org; ℂ 801/581-6961), is Utah's resident professional theater. Located on the university campus, the Pioneer has a repertoire that ranges from classical to contemporary plays and musicals. Recent productions have included *Next to Normal* and *Annie*. Producing edgier contemporary fare, the **Salt Lake Acting Company**, 168 W. 500 North (www.saltlakeactingcompany.org; ℂ 801/363-7522), stages about six plays by local and national playwrights annually. The family-oriented **Hale Centre Theatre**, 3333 S. Decker Lake Dr., West Valley City (www.hct.org; ℂ 801/984-9000), features locally produced and performed plays and musical comedies.

THE CLUB & MUSIC SCENE

Salt Lake City is shedding its strait-laced image and beginning to develop a party crowd distinctly its own in a collection of bars and taverns that never require ties or jackets. **Downtown UnderCurrent**, 279 E. 300 South (ℂ 801/574-2556) and **Copper Common**, 111 E. Broadway (http://copper common.com; ℂ 801/355-0543), each next to their sister restaurants, are slightly upscale and usually crowded but offer sophisticated bar bites alongside well-crafted cocktails. Spirits and brews from the city's thriving local liquor business are prominent behind the bars of most establishments.

One of the city's star bars is **Water Witch**, 163 W. 900 South (ℂ 801/462-0967), a small neighborhood watering hole that attracts visitors and guests from around the state. The bartender/owners here are knowledgeable pros who have great fun shaking drinks and chatting with customers. Check the BarFly section of *Salt Lake* magazine for more bars.

Squatters Pub Brewery, 147 W. Broadway (www.squatters.com; ℂ 801/363-2739), has combined with Wasatch Brewery to form Utah Brewers cooperative—each has their own brewpub and both brew top-notch suds and thumbs its their collective noses at local conservatism with such beer names as Provo Girl and Chasing Tail. Check out **Squatters Pub Brewery** downtown at 147 Broadway (ℂ 801/363-2739) and **Squatters Roadhouse Grill** in Park City (1900 Park Ave., Park City; ℂ 435/649-9868) and **Wasatch Brew Pub,** also in Sugarhouse (2110 South Highland Drive; ℂ 801/783-1127) and Park City (250 Main St.; ℂ 435/649-0900).

The **Red Rock Brewing Company**, 254 S. 200 West (www.redrockbrew ing.com; ℂ 801/521-7446), is another solid downtown brewpub, and a good spot to eat if you're looking for pub grub. The **Beerhive**, 128 Main St., (ℂ 801/364-4268), doesn't brew its own, but has a mind-boggling selection of beers and ales from all over the world, served on a unique ice bar.

Copper Common (see above), a sister establishment of new Americana restaurants Copper Onion and Copper Kitchen, serves excellent and innovative food and has a staff of knowledgeable bartenders. A few blocks away, **Undercurrent,** 279 E. 300 South (www.undercurrentbar.com; ℂ **801/574-2556**) sibling of seafood restaurant Current, is also an upscale establishment with good food and drinks and a (not too) sophisticated atmosphere.

You don't need to do the full-meal deal at **Spencer's for Steaks & Chops,** 255 S. West Temple, in the Hilton Hotel (ℂ **801/238-4748**), just pop into the cozy bar for a well-made drink and a chef-made nosh in the clubby bar. On the other end of the cultural spectrum, **Junior's Tavern** at 30 E. 300 South (ℂ **801/322-0318**) is a classic dive with a steady clientele of long-time Salt Lakers. **Urban Lounge,** 241 S. 500 East (www.theurbanloungeslc.com; ℂ **801/746-0557**), books local and national indie and hip-hop acts. For dueling pianos, hit **Keys on Main** at 242 S. Main St. (www.keysonmain.com; ℂ **801/363-3638**).

On the east side, the **Porcupine Pub & Grill,** 3690 Fort Union Blvd. (www.porcupinepub.com; ℂ **801/942-5555**), is an après-ski hot spot, with hearty food and 24 beers on tap. Over in Sugarhouse, near I-80, **The Ruin**, 1215 Wilmington Ave. (ℂ **801/869-3730**) is a comfortable lounge with good bartenders.

THE GREAT SALT LAKE & ANTELOPE ISLAND STATE PARK

You wouldn't expect to come across what is essentially a small ocean in the middle of the desert, but there it is: the Great Salt Lake. The lake is all that's left of ancient Lake Bonneville, which once covered most of western Utah and parts of Idaho and Nevada. Unlike its mother lake, the Great Salt Lake has no outlet, so everything that flows into it—some 2 million tons of minerals annually—stays here until someone or something—usually brine flies, brine shrimp, birds, or humans—removes it. Minerals, including salt, potassium, and magnesium, are mined here; don't be surprised to see front-end loaders moving huge piles of salt to the Morton Salt facility along I-80, on the lake's south shore.

Antelope Island is not super popular with Salt Lake City residents, who mostly think of the lake as a place for "lake stink" and seasonal biting gnats. The "stink" disappears by the time you get to the island proper from the causeway, but do check to see if those pesky flies are in season. And skip your visit if they are. Facilities are limited, but the unpopulated mountains and prairies of Antelope Island give you a beautiful glimpse of what this landscape was like before white men arrived. Don't miss it. Boaters should bring their own boats, as no rentals are available. Despite its salinity, this is a relatively flat lake—kind of like a big puddle—so don't pack your surfboard. Pack a hat, water, sunscreen, and binoculars.

Antelope Island State Park ★

The largest of 10 islands in the Great Salt Lake, measuring about 5 miles wide and 15 miles long, Antelope Island was named by Kit Carson and John Frémont in 1843 for the many pronghorns (which resemble, but technically aren't antelope) that they found here. Hunting wiped out the herd by the 1870s, but buffalo (bison) were introduced in 1893—500 to 700 of them now make the island their home—and pronghorn now number in the hundreds. The beaches of Antelope Island don't have the fine-grained sand and shells of an ocean beach; rather, they're a mixture of dirt and gravel. But the water is a great place to relax; because of its high salinity, you don't have to work hard to stay afloat.

ESSENTIALS

GETTING THERE   Antelope Island is about 30 miles northwest of Salt Lake City and about 16 miles southwest of Ogden. Take I-15 to exit 332, go 6½ miles west to the park entrance, and cross the 7½-mile causeway to the island.

VISITOR INFORMATION   Antelope Island State Park (www.state parks.utah.gov) is open from 6am to 10 pm daily; the **visitor center** (☏ **801/725-9263**) is open daily from 9am to 6pm, and has exhibits and information on the Great Salt Lake and the island's wildlife and migratory birds. The historic **Fielding Garr Ranch** is open daily from 9am to 6pm.

FEES & REGULATIONS   Day-use fees are $10 per vehicle up to 8 people (seniors 62 and over, $5 per vehicle) and $3 for pedestrians, bicyclists, or in-line skaters. The marina offers dock rental overnight. Pets are welcome in the park but must be leashed.

OUTDOOR PURSUITS

BIKING, HIKING & HORSEBACK RIDING   More than 30 miles of hiking trails and bike and horse paths traverse the island, most of which are closed to vehicular traffic. Although generally unmarked, trails follow old ranch roads. Check at the visitor center or talk with a ranger before heading out; they can fill you in on current conditions and tell you where you're most likely to spot wildlife.

The 3-mile **Lake Side Trail** leaves the Bridger Bay Campground and follows the beach around the northwestern tip of the island to the group camping area on White Rock Bay. The walk is magnificent at sunset. Other trails take you away from the crowds, where you might catch a glimpse of a buffalo or other wildlife.

BOATING   Boaters will find a marina with restrooms, docks, and fresh water for cleaning boats, but little else.

SWIMMING   The largest beach is at **Bridger Bay,** with picnic tables and restrooms with outdoor showers to wash off the salt.

WILDLIFE-WATCHING   You can drive to the **buffalo corral** and see these great shaggy creatures, impressive as anything on the African veldt— fairly close-up. If you head into the less-traveled areas, you might spot **pronghorns, deer, buffaloes, bobcats, elk, coyotes,** and **bighorn sheep.**

The annual **bison roundup** takes place in late November and early December. You can usually see wranglers herding the bison into corrals on the last weekend of November (binoculars are helpful) and get a close-up view the next weekend as the bison receive their annual checkups. Call for exact dates.

CAMPING

The park has four campgrounds: **Bridger Bay Campground, White Rock Bay Campground, Lakeside Group Campsite,** and **Ladyfinger Campground.** Although none of them offer hookups, each area does have pit toilets and Bridger Bay Beach has flush toilets and showers; Bridger Bay Beach has picnic tables as well. The cost at Bridger Bay Campground is $15 the first night, $12 each additional night. Reservations are available by calling ⓒ **800/322-3770** or visiting www.stateparks.utah.gov.

MORE TO SEE & DO

Ten miles south of the visitor center, down a paved road, is the **Fielding Garr Ranch House.** The original three-room adobe house, built in 1848, was inhabited until the state acquired it in 1981. Besides the ranch house, the small spread contains is a small building that served as a schoolroom by day and sleeping quarters for the farmhands at night, plus a spring house, the only freshwater source.

Check with the visitor center for current ranch hours as well as schedules and rates for wagon rides.

Great Salt Lake State Marina

This is usually a good spot to launch your boat (assuming you brought one; there are no rentals here), but not what one would call a great destination. Because of excess usage, the lake's level is decreasing every year. A less-than-exciting stretch of muddy/sandy beach greets you, but the expanse of water and distant islands can be lovely, especially at dusk or early in the morning. Prickly pear cactuses bloom along the shore in the late spring. And for those susceptible to the lure of the sea, this huge inland ocean is mysteriously irresistible any time of year. Sailing and watersports are the main attractions here—although you can also laze on the beach. Facilities include picnic tables, open showers for washing off salt and sand, and restrooms.

Be forewarned, though. The air can be heavy with the stench of rotting algae at times, making even a brief stroll on the beach quite unpleasant. At other times, when the wind is right or the lake is high enough, trekking out to the water's edge is downright enjoyable.

ESSENTIALS

Great Salt Lake State Park is 16 miles west of Salt Lake City. Take I-80 west to exit 104; head east on the frontage road about 2 miles to the park entrance. The marina is open year-round, and the beach is open daily in summer from dawn to dusk (8am–5pm Oct–Mar), with admission fees of $3 per car ($1 seniors). Boat slips and a launching ramp are available, but there are no boat rentals. Contact **Great Salt Lake State Marina** at ⓒ **801/250-1898** or visit www.stateparks.utah.gov. Park headquarters are located at the marina.

THE NORTHERN WASATCH FRONT: UTAH'S OLD WEST

Salt Lake City was founded for religious reasons; Ogden grew in response to the rowdy railroad boom. Their different origins explain why the neighboring cities are still so different. In contrast to staid Salt Lake City's Mormon history, Ogden's past is filled with shoot-em-ups and gangsters. The Golden Spike National Historic Site, commemorating the completion in 1869 of the first transcontinental railroad, is a good starting point for thinking about Ogden—the mammoth endeavor brought hundreds of Chinese laborers to the area. Historic 25th Street was the center of the action then and now.

Ogden is another great home base for outdoor recreation: You can ski at nearby resorts in the winter, or hike, fish, and ride horses in the summer. Mandatory for all history buffs is the surprisingly poignant pilgrimage to Golden Spike National Historic Site, the point at which the East and West coasts of the United States were joined by rail in 1869. North of Ogden is the pretty little town of Logan, home to Utah State University and a similarly bountiful outdoor-recreation hot spot. For a color map of the Wasatch Front, see the inside back cover of this book.

OGDEN: UTAH'S WEST AT ITS WILDEST

Ogden has always been a city apart from the rest of Utah. Officially founded by Mormon pioneers, Ogden really began as a meeting place for mountain men and fur trappers. In the 1820s, Jim Bridger, Peter Skene Ogden, Jedediah Smith and Etienne Provost, and Hugh Glass gathered annually to trade furs for supplies; to eat, drink, and tell stories and demonstrate their skills and generally raise some Cain. Later, in the 1870s—much to the chagrin of the

HOTELS ■
Best Western
   High Country Inn **1**
Days Inn **10**
Hampton Inn & Suites **6**
Motel 6 **4**
Sleep Inn **1**

RESTAURANTS ◆
Bistro 258 **7**
Farr Better Ice Cream **5**
The Greenery **2**
Jeremiah's **1**
Prairie Schooner **3**
Roosters 25th Street
   Brewing Co. **8**
Union Grill **9**

ⓘ Information

church—Ogden grew into a seriously rowdy railroad town. It retains some of that devil-may-care attitude today.

But Ogden's current popularity has little to do with its wild beginnings. The bustling city of about 86,000 has some good museums and historic sites, and the bar and restaurant scene is booming with a whole different and edgier vibe than Salt Lake City. At an elevation of 4,300 feet, Ogden is a perfect base for enjoying the surrounding mountains for skiing, snowboarding, snowmobiling, hiking, mountain biking, horseback riding, or boating. Mt. Ben Lomond Peak, which lies to the north of the city, may look familiar—it's said to have inspired the famous Paramount Pictures logo.

Essentials

GETTING THERE   Ogden is easily accessible from the north and south via I-15, and from the east and northwest on I-84. Shuttle service to and from Salt Lake International Airport is $30 to $40 one-way; try **Xpress Shuttle** (www. xpressshuttleutah.com; ✆ **801/596-5555**) For the best service, call at least 24 hours in advance. The commuter train, UTA **FrontRunner** (www.rideuta. com; ✆ **801/743-3882**) runs from Salt Lake City to Ogden. A one-way fare from Salt Lake to Ogden is about $5.

VISITOR INFORMATION   The **Ogden/Weber Convention & Visitors Bureau** maintains an information center at Union Station, 2438 Washington Blvd. (www.visitogden.com; ✆ **801/778-6250**). From I-15 North/I-84 West, take exit 341 and head east to Washington Boulevard; turn north (left) and continue for about 6 blocks. The information center is open Monday through Friday 8am to 5pm.

For information on the area's national forests, contact the **Ogden Ranger District,** Uinta-Wasatch-Cache National Forest, 507 25th St. (www.fs.fed.us/ r4/uwc; ✆ **801/625-5112**). You can also inquire at the forest's visitor center at Union Station, 2501 Wall Ave. (✆ **801/625-5306**).

GETTING AROUND   Driving is the easiest way to explore Ogden. The streets are laid out in typically neat Mormon-pioneer fashion, but with a slightly different nomenclature than Salt Lake City. The streets running east to west are numbered from 1st Street in the north to 47th in the south, and north–south streets are named for U.S. presidents and other historical figures. Most people define the city center as the intersection of 25th Street and Washington Boulevard, an area that is a mix of historic and modern buildings.

For car rentals, try **Enterprise** (www.enterprise.com; ✆ **801/399-5555**) or **Hertz** (www.hertz.com; ✆ **800/654-3131** or 801/614-5005).

The **Utah Transit Authority** (www.rideuta.com; ✆ **800/743-3882** or 801/743-3882) provides bus transport throughout greater Ogden daily with limited service on Sunday. Exact fares are required; schedules are available at the information center. Of course, there's always Uber and Lyft.

FAST FACTS   The **McKay-Dee Hospital Center,** 4401 Harrison Blvd. (✆ **801/627-2800),** has a 24-hour emergency room. The main post office is at 3680 Pacific Ave. (www.usps.com for other locations and hours; ✆ **800/275-8777**). The local newspaper is the "Standard Examiner." Sales tax is 7.1%.

What to See & Do

Eccles Community Art Center   Built in 1893, this two-and-a-half-story turreted mansion was the home of David and Bertha Eccles—a philanthropic name that you'll see often in Utah. Bertha made it known to her family that she wished the house to be used for education and cultural enrichment. It became the home of the Ogden Community Arts Council in 1959.

Changing exhibits in the Main House feature works by local, regional, and national artists in a variety of mediums. The Carriage House gallery offers local arts and crafts, such as paintings, pottery, fabric art, and jewelry. The Renaissance Complex presents ongoing educational programs and houses the ticket office for the Ogden Symphony and Ballet West. Outside is a sculpture and flower garden with a fountain and benches where you can sit and enjoy the view. Allow an hour and a half, and call ahead for a schedule of events and information on classes in the visual arts and dance.

2580 Jefferson Ave. www.ogden4arts.org. ℭ **801/392-6935.** Free admission. Mon–Fri 9am–5pm; Sat 9am–3pm. Closed major holidays. From I-15, take exit 342 and head east on 24th St. to Jefferson Ave.; turn right (south) and go 2 blocks.

Fort Buenaventura ★ With a replica of an 1846 fort and trading post, and exhibits depicting the local mountain men and fur trade of the 1820s, this park shows what life was like back in the day. Built in 1846 by fur trapper and horse trader Miles Goodyear, the fort was the first permanent Anglo settlement in the Great Basin. The Mormons bought the fort when they arrived in 1847, and Ogden grew up around it.

Rangers lead tours of the reconstructed fort (included in the admission fee), and the park has ponds, canoes for rent ($5 per hour), a picnic area, and a pleasant campground ($18–$23 per night). There's a disc golf course, a 2-mile hiking trail that meanders around the park, and fishing in the Weber River is permitted with a license. The park also has a kids' fishing pond, open only to children 12 and younger, no license required. The visitor center has exhibits of American Indian artifacts typical of the area. Allow at least 1 hour.

Fort Buenaventura hosts several traditional mountain-man rendezvous each year, with music, Dutch-oven food, and a variety of contests that typically include a tomahawk throw, a canoe race, a shooting competition, and foot-races, with all competitors in pre-1840s dress. The rendezvous are usually scheduled on Easter (with a nondenominational sunrise service and egg hunt) and Labor Day weekends. A Pioneer Skills Festival takes place on Pioneer Day, July 24. Mountain-man supplies are available in a shop at the fort every Saturday.

444 24th St. www.co.weber.ut.us/parks/fortb. ℭ **801/399-8099.** Admission $2 per person; free for children 4 and under. Apr–Sept daily 7am–9pm; call for hours Oct–Mar. From downtown Ogden, take 24th St. west across the railroad tracks.

George S. Eccles Dinosaur Park ★ Dinosaurs were everywhere in prehistoric Utah and they still are. Wander among life-size reproductions of more than 100 prehistoric creatures from the Cretaceous and Jurassic periods in this 5-acre fantasyland playground. The smallest is about the size of a turkey, and the enormous Tyrannosaurus rex is 30 feet high, 49 feet long, and weighs about 7 tons. Other cold-blooded friends include a 33-foot-long Parasaurolophus (a duck-billed dinosaur), a Triceratops, and a winged lizard, or Pteranodon. There's even a replica of a 65-million-year-old volcano. Also on-site is the Elizabeth Dee Shaw Stewart Museum, with exciting hands-on exhibits of the latest dinosaur finds from Utah and around the world. It includes a sand pit where budding paleontologists can excavate real dinosaur bones. Other activities include gold-panning (fool's gold) and hunting for gems in a cave (real gems). There is a basic restaurant here as well. Allow 2 hours.

1544 E. Park Blvd., Ogden River Pkwy. www.dinosaurpark.org. © **801/393-3466.** Admission $7 adults, $6 seniors (62+), students with IDs, and children 2–12, free for children 1 and under. Memorial Day to Labor Day Mon–Sat 10am–7pm, Sun 10am–5pm; check for winter hours. Closed Easter, Thanksgiving, and Christmas, as well as Sun Nov–Mar. From exit 344, take 12th St. east 5 miles.

Hill Aerospace Museum ★   Get a close-up view of more than 90 planes, missiles, and aerospace vehicles at this museum. Aircraft on display include the rare B-17G "Flying Fortress," one of the few P-38s around, the SR-71C "Blackbird" spy plane, a Soviet MiG-21 fighter, and two aircraft that are still flyable: a JN-4 "Jenny" and a Piper L-4J "Grasshopper," painted and marked to look like one that flew in support of the Allied invasion of North Africa in November 1942. Other exhibits include a World War II chapel with the 384th Bomb Group Memorial Stained Glass Window, an exact duplicate of a memorial stained glass window donated by the 384th Bomb Group to the Parish Church of St. James the Apostle in the village of Grafton Underwood, near Kettering, England. The window depicts a B-17 Flying Fortress over the cliffs of Dover. An exhibit of historic Air Force uniforms, a fire truck, a Gatling gun, thermonuclear missiles (decommissioned, thankfully), and a Norden bombsight bring the reality of wartime to life. Displays illustrate the history of the Air Force, how aircraft fly, and what the Air Force does today. The gift shop offers a wide range of very cool Air Force–related items. Allow 1 hour.

7961 Wardleigh Rd., Hill Air Force Base. www.hill.af.mil/library/museum. © **801/777-6868** or 777-6818. Free admission; donations welcome. Daily 9am–4:30pm. Closed New Year's Day, Thanksgiving, and Christmas. From I-15, take exit 338 to the museum.

Salomon Center ★★   Opened in 2007, this one-of-a-kind, $19-million facility has become the centerpiece of downtown Ogden, featuring a Gold's Gym as a second-floor anchor. The highlights here are the three stand-alone training grounds for extreme sports: the Flowrider (a wave simulator for surfers), a 50-foot climbing wall, and iFly (a skydiving simulator). The complex also houses an arcade and two restaurants (Mexican and pizza), and a 13-screen cinema complex is right next door. Prices vary for activities—2 minutes in the iFly costs $55; an hour on the Flowrider is $20.

2261 Kiesel Ave. www.salomoncenter.com. © **801/399-4653.** Free admission; fees for skydiving, wave simulators, and other activities. Open daily; hours vary by activity.

Treehouse Museum ★★   In this excellent reading-oriented museum you can climb into a two-story faux tree with a spiral staircase in its trunk, participate in daily arts and crafts activities, or "step into stories" by authors from near and far. The American Dream exhibit boasts an impressive giant floor map of the United States and a kid-size Oval Office with exhibits on U.S.

presidents. In the Utah Heritage area, kids explore a pioneer schoolhouse and store, and try their hands at creating American Indian pictographs. Events include hourly storytelling programs and seasonal plays in the 132-seat theater; call for showtimes. Allow at least 1 hour.

347 22nd St. www.treehousemuseum.org. ℂ **801/394-9663.** Admission $5 adults and kids 13–15; $8 ages 12 and under. Mon 10am–3pm (until 5pm June–Aug and holidays); Tues–Thurs and Sat 10am–5pm; Fri 10am–8pm. Closed New Year's Day, July 4, July 24, Thanksgiving, and Christmas. Located just north of the Salomon Center.

Union Station This stately depot faces historic 25th Street, with colorful flower beds and a fountain gracing the cobbled courtyard in front. Built in 1924 to replace the original depot, which was destroyed by fire, the station now houses the Utah State Railroad Museum, John M. Browning Firearms Museum, the Browning-Kimball Classic Car Museum and the Utah State Cowboy and Western Heritage Museum. You'll also find some restaurants and a Forest Services information center, and the Ogden/Weber Convention and Visitor's Bureau. Plan to spend an hour or two here.

The restored lobby is the place to start. The immense room is graced with murals at each end commemorating the building of the railroad and the linking of east and west. Both 12×50-foot murals were done in the late 1970s by Edward Laning, based on works he painted in 1935 for New York's Ellis Island Immigration Building.

The **Utah State Railroad Museum** displays gas-turbine locomotive designs and has an extensive HO-gauge layout that depicts the construction and geography of the 1,776-mile transcontinental route. Wander around on your own, or let a railroad buff guide you through, describing the whys and wherefores of what you're seeing. The **Browning Single Shot Rifle** was designed and produced in Ogden and the town is proud of its connection with "the gun the won the west." The **Browning Firearms Museum** displays Browning guns from 1878 to present, a replica of an 1880s gun shop, and a film describing the Browning legacy. The **Browning-Kimball Car Museum** features beautiful examples of classic cars, mostly luxury models. You can see about a dozen vehicles from the early 1900s, including a 1901 curved-dash Oldsmobile, Pierce-Arrows from 1909 and 1931, and a 1932 Lincoln. The **Gallery at the Station** exhibits a variety of art through invitational and competitive shows. Outside, the **Eccles Rail Center** pays tribute to the Goliaths of the rails—locomotives designed to pull long trains through the steep mountains of the West. On display are a burly "Big Blow," a gas turbine rated at more than twice the horsepower of typical modern locomotives (one of only two on display anywhere), and a commemorative car used in the torch relay for the 2002 Winter Olympics.

2501 Wall Ave. www.theunionstation.org. ℂ **801/393-9886.** Admission to museums $5 adults, $4 seniors 64 and over and teens 13–17, $3 children 11 and under, $12 family. Mon–Sat 10am–5pm. Closed New Year's Day, Thanksgiving, and Christmas. Take exit 341A off I-15 and follow 31st St. east to Wall Ave.; go north 6 blocks.

WALKING TOUR: **HISTORIC DOWNTOWN OGDEN—A WALK THROUGH THE HISTORY OF THE AMERICAN WEST**

START: **2148 Grant Ave.**

FINISH: **2539 Washington Blvd.**

TIME: **1–2 hours.**

BEST TIMES: **Any.**

WORST TIMES: **None, although windy days in winter can be biting cold.**

Begin your tour at 2148 Grant Ave., on Tabernacle Square, where you'll find:

1 Miles Goodyear Cabin & Daughters of Utah Pioneers Museum

This cottonwood log cabin was built in 1845 on the Weber River at Fort Buenaventura, which is now a county-run park (p. 87). The cabin is believed to be the first permanent pioneer home in Utah. Next door, the 1902 Gothic-style brick Relief Society Building now houses the **Daughters of Utah Pioneers Museum** (www.weberdupmuseum.org; ✆ **801/393-4460**), containing pioneer photographs, artifacts, and memorabilia. Both the museum and cabin are open during summer only.

Now head south on Grant Avenue for 3 blocks to 298 24th St., the:

2 Ogden Post Office

This is one of two fine examples of Classical Revival Federal architecture in Utah (the other is the Salt Lake City post office). This building, constructed between 1905 and 1909, held a post office, a courthouse, and offices until 1974. The lobby, elevator, second-floor courtroom, and much of the beautiful woodwork have been lovingly restored. The building now houses a reception center and other offices.

Turn east on 24th Street; a block down the street, at 385 24th St., is the:

3 Eccles Building

Now the Hampton Inn & Suites (p. 98), this steel-framed, brick-faced, boxlike 1913 building with "Chicago-style" windows combines elements of Prairie style with classical details, evident in the terra-cotta figurines and geometric motifs along the second- and eighth-floor cornices.

Turn south onto Washington Boulevard, and continue to 2415 Washington Blvd. to see:

4 Peery's Egyptian Theater

Built as a movie theater in the Egyptian Revival style in 1924, the cinema reopened in 1997 after extensive renovation. The facade has four fluted columns, with two sculpted pharaohs between each, plus two sculptures of deities perched on the roof. The interior is equally exotic: The proscenium is decorated with paintings of Egyptian figures and colorful columns and the Mighty Wurlitzer Pipe Organ was restored in 2004. The best way to see the theater is to attend a performance. The theater doesn't show movies regularly, but hosts live productions and film festivals and is a screening venue for the Sundance Film Festival.

Cross the street to 2510 Washington Blvd., where you'll find the:

5 Ben Lomond Hotel

This Italian Renaissance Revival hotel, built in 1927 (by the same firm that built the Egyptian Theater) on the remains of the 1890 Reed Hotel, is a handsome reminder of the opulent 1920s, and is listed on the National Register of Historic Places.

Cross again to 2539 Washington Blvd., to see the:

6 Municipal Building

One of the finest representations of the Art Deco style of architecture in Utah, this building is also an excellent example of a WPA project. Built in 1939, the building comprises a series of rectangular brick blocks with glazed terra-cotta trim, symmetrically tapered to the tall central mass—grand and awe-inspiring.

Walk down Adams Street to:

7 Historic 25th Street

Finally, take a few minutes to walk along Historic 25th Street, once known nationwide as "Two-Bit Street" because of its rowdiness. There are still rumors of underground tunnels supposedly used as opium dens and secret passages for bootleggers. The largest remaining group of turn-of-the-20th-century storefronts in the state has been renovated over the last decade and boutiques, independent restaurants, and pubs now line the avenue.

What to See & Do Nearby
A TASTE OF HISTORY IN HUNTSVILLE

Founded in 1860, tiny Huntsville is about 15 miles east of Ogden and some-what removed from the civilization of Ogden. The town is known best as the home of the **Shooting Star Saloon** ★★, 7350 E. 200 South (https://shooting-star-saloon.business.site; © **801/745-2002**), established in 1862 and said to be the oldest continuously operating saloon in Utah. The Shooting Star looks like a wild West Hollywood set, but it's the real deal. The rustic watering hole pretends to be nothing else. Dollar bills are pinned to the ceiling; the walls are decorated with animal-head trophies, steer skulls, the famous and inexplicable stuffed St. Bernard's head (Buck), and cowboy art; the handsome oak back bar was built in 1895. Stop in for a draft beer and one of the best, sloppiest and most challenging hamburgers in the state, the knockwurst-topped Star Burger. Wear your cowboy boots, put some money in the jukebox, and shoot a game of pool. The saloon is open Monday through Thursday 11am to 9pm, Friday and Saturday from 11am to 10pm, and Sunday 11am to 8pm. To get there from Ogden, head east on Utah 39. It'll take you 20 to 25 minutes to get there, but it's well worth the drive.

Visit the **Ogden Nature Center,** 966 W. 12th St. (www.ogdennaturecenter.org; ☏ **801/621-7595),** a 152-acre wildlife sanctuary and rehabilitation center where injured birds are treated and released back into the wild. There are trails (including one fully accessible trail) for warm-weather strolling or, when snow blankets the ground, snowshoeing and cross-country skiing. Watch for golden eagles, prairie falcons, goshawks, red-tailed hawks, great horned owls, and long-eared owls. The Learning and Visitors Center houses hawks, ravens, and other birds, plus a variety of exhibits and a gift shop. The center sponsors naturalist-led educational programs; call ahead or check online for a schedule. Admission is $5 for ages 12 and up, $4 seniors 65 and over, $3 for children 2 through 11, and free for children 1 and under. Hours are Monday through Friday 9am to 5pm and Saturday 9am to 4pm. To get here from I-15, take exit 344 and head east on 12th Street. Allow at least 2 hours.

AN HISTORIC FAMILY-FUN CENTER

About 22 miles south of Ogden, **Lagoon,** 375 N. Lagoon Dr., Farmington (www.lagoonpark.com; ☏ **800/748-5246** or 801/451-8000), in contrast to the Shooting Star, is a family affair. A summer tradition for Utah kids since 1906, when the original attraction of swimming was augmented by an early version of a roller coaster. Next came a carousel of 45 hand-carved animals (still in operation today). Today Lagoon is a combination amusement park, water park, and historical park filled with more than 125 rides and attractions, including **Wicked,** a twisting coaster that rockets riders to the top of the first hill at 40mph—not for the faint of heart. There are plenty of gentler rides, too, such as the more recent additions such as Ruka Safari and Flying Tigers, which are designed to allow adults to ride with their kids or grandkids.

The big news was 2017's major redesign of **Terroride,** a 50-year-old attraction designed by Bill Tracy and one of only eight of its type remaining across America. The park worked to restore Tracy's wax and papier-mâché figures and the entrance mural while coming up with a new storyline and collaborating with Utah Opera's scenic department for updated sets.

Lagoon has a **midway** with games, shops, food courts, and the inevitable-in-Utah **Pioneer Village,** outfitted with one of the country's finest collection of horse-drawn carriages, plus a gun collection and American Indian artifacts. Lagoon's water park, **Lagoon A Beach,** is the center of midsummer activities, with a 65-foot twisting, enclosed tube ride, three serpentine slides, and whitewater rapids. The less intrepid can enjoy a lazy river with waterfalls, tunnels, steamy hot tubs.

Admission costs $55.95 for adults and children 51 inches and taller, $49.95 for seniors 65 and over, $39.95 for children under 48 inches tall, and $28 for ages 3 and under. The parking fee is $10, or you can buy a season pass. The park is open daily, usually from 10 or 11am, between Memorial Day and Labor Day, and weekends from mid-April to May and the month of September; hours vary so call or go online for the current schedule. The park is closed in winter, but opens for a special Halloween event for 3 or 4 weeks in October. To get here, from I-15 northbound, take exit 322; southbound, take exit 325.

Lagoon has an RV park and campground with more than 200 shady sites, both pull-through with hookups and grassy tent sites. The campground has a mini-store, and campers receive Lagoon admission discounts. Rates range from $34 for tent and no-hookup RV sites up to $48 for pull-through RV sites with full hookups.

Sports & Outdoor Pursuits

The nearby **Uinta-Wasatch-Cache National Forest** offers plenty of opportunities for outdoor recreation (see "Visitor Information," on p. 110). For camping and other equipment and supplies, stop by **GEAR:30**, 1931 Washington Blvd., Ogden (www.gearthirty.com; ✆ **801/732-5870**).

BIKING The **Ogden River Parkway** ★★ (www.weberpathways.org) is a 3.4-mile paved, wheelchair-accessible path along the Ogden River, extending from the mouth of Ogden Canyon west to Washington Boulevard. It's excellent for walking, jogging, and bicycling; it also leads to **Big D Sports Park** (with playground and sporting fields), **Lorin Farr Park** (p. 96), and **George S. Eccles Dinosaur Park** (p. 87).

East of Ogden are two strenuous but spectacular road rides. The **Trappers Loop Road** winds 9 miles along Utah 167 from Mountain Green (exit 92 off I-84) north to Huntsville. This route alternates between wide-open meadows backed by high mountain peaks and forests of tall evergreens and aspens.

The second ride, along Snowbasin Road, climbs more than 2,000 feet over 10 miles from Pineview Reservoir. Your efforts will be rewarded with stunning views of the ski runs and towering peaks. Also open in summer, **Snowbasin,** 3925 E. Snowbasin Rd. (www.snowbasin.com; ✆ **801/520-1000**), is a mountain-biking destination—the single-track trails are well maintained and wind through scenic groves of aspens and pines. All levels of riding are available from the base including gondola-accessed trails. More than 26 miles of trails connect to additional Forest Service trails for nearly 50 miles of fun. For the true "gearhead," Snowbasin offers gondola bike access to challenging uphill climbs and extreme downhill switchbacks. The truly adventurous will want to try the "Top to Bottom and More" Mountain Bike Adventure. Novice and moderate trails are the perfect choices for a scenic family ride or picnic. The resort is open from the last Sunday in June through the first Sunday in October, on Saturday and Sunday, from 9am to 6pm. Trail passes are $14 for hikers and $25 for bikers daily.

The 3 Bs of Snowbasin

Snowbasin's free weekly summer Sunday concert series, **Blues, Brews & BBQ,** is a summertime tradition. Enjoy live music (past acts have included Los Lobos and Yarn), beer and margaritas, and barbecue on Earl's Patio, from noon to 5:30pm.

You can get additional trail information at the Forest Service visitor center in Union Station (p. 89)—ask for the excellent **Pathways in Weber County** map and brochure. For bike repairs and accessories, stop at **Bingham Cyclery,** 1895 Washington Blvd. (www.binghamcyclery.com; ⓒ **801/399-4981**). In Eden, **Diamond Peak Mountain Sports,** at the junction of Utah highways 158 and 162 (www.peakstuff.com; ⓒ **801/745-0101**), offers rentals, repairs, and sales of bikes, boards, and skis.

CLIMBING   Ogden was a rock-climbing mecca, but many popular routes in and around Ogden Canyon have been closed. At the Salomon Center (p. 88), the **iRock climbing wall** (ⓒ **801/399-4653;** www.irockutah.com) costs $10 adults, $7.50 for kids 11 and under. Rental equipment is available.

FISHING   Brown, rainbow, cutthroat, brook, and lake trout thrive in the waters of the Uinta-Wasatch-Cache National Forest around Ogden. You might also find perch, bass, catfish, whitefish, and crappie. Popular spots to wet your line are **Pineview Reservoir, Causey Reservoir,** and the **Ogden** and **Weber rivers.** For supplies, licenses, and tips on where they're biting, stop at **Anglers' Den,** 5348 S. 1900 West, Roy (ⓒ **801/773-1166**). The shop can also refer you to local guides.

GOLF   Golfers will find an abundance of opportunities in the Ogden area, which boasts challenging courses with spectacular views of the surrounding mountains. Public courses include the **Mount Ogden Golf Course,** 1787 Constitution Way (ⓒ **801/629-0699),** an 18-hole, par-71 championship course located on the east side of the city against the mountains, which charges $28 for 18 holes, with cart rental $14, and **El Monte Golf Course,** 1300 Valley Dr. (ⓒ **801/629-0694),** a scenic 9-hole, par-35 course of rolling hills and old-style greens in Ogden Canyon, with fees of $13 for 9 holes, and an extra $7 for a cart.

For one of the finest practice areas around, try **Toad's Fun Zone,** 1690 W. 400 North, exit 346 off I-15 (www.toadsfz.com; ⓒ **801/392-4653**), with two 18-hole miniature golf courses (one indoor and one outdoor), a year-round driving range, and a 9-hole par-3 course. An indoor glow-in-the-dark minigolf course is located at **Fat Cats** in the Salomon Center (p. 88).

HIKING   The **Ogden River Parkway** ★★ (p. 93) is great for walking. Several hiking trails are accessible from the east side of downtown Ogden. **Indian Trail** ★ takes off from the parking area at 22nd Street and Buchanan Avenue, and the narrow path winds about 4.3 miles through thick stands of oak, spruce, and fir trees. The trail offers some of the finest views of Ogden Canyon from above—particularly of the waterfall at the mouth of the canyon—before dropping down to the parking area on Utah 39. This moderately difficult trail takes about 4 hours one-way.

A little over a half-mile along Indian Trail, **Hidden Valley Trail** cuts off sharply to the south. The route is difficult, climbing steadily through the old Lake Bonneville terraces, and is surrounded by dense stands of oak, maple, and aspen. After a mile and a half, you reach a turnaround; from here, enjoy a clear view of the rugged face of Mt. Ogden to the southeast. The hike takes about 2 hours one-way.

An easy 1½-hour hike is the **Mt. Ogden Park Trail,** linking the parking lots at 29th and 36th streets. It's mostly flat and surfaced with bark chips. The trail follows the east edge of a golf course much of the way, encountering splashing streams and even occasional wildlife. The views are inspiring at sunrise and sunset.

For additional trail information, ask for the **Pathways in Weber County** brochure at the Forest Service's visitor information center in Union Station (p. 89) or visit the excellent website www.weberpathways.org.

ICE-SKATING & CURLING The **Ice Sheet,** 4390 Harrison Blvd., in the southeast part of the city (www.co.weber.ut.us/icesheet; ✆ **801/778-6300**), offers year-round ice-skating, a learn-to-skate program, hockey and figure-skating clinics, clinics on curling (this was the curling venue for the 2002 Olympics), and skate rentals. Call for current rates and schedules.

WATERSPORTS **Willard Bay State Park** and **Pineview Reservoir** (p. 96) are your destinations for boating, water-skiing, and swimming. Also check out the kayak parks on the **Ogden River Parkway** (p. 93), at **Lagoon** (p. 92), and in **Lorin Farr Park** (p. 96).

WINTER SPORTS Deep snow turns the mountains surrounding Ogden into a winter playground, with four family-oriented ski resorts (see "Ogden Valley & the Northern Wasatch Front," later in this chapter) and seemingly unlimited forest trails for cross-country skiers, snowshoers, and snowmobilers.

If you want more excitement (and are a good skier) get away from the groomed trails, lift lines, and parking lots and take to the skies with **Diamond Peaks Heli-ski Adventures** (www.diamondpeaks.com; ✆ **801/745-4631**), based in Ogden. Helicopters fly you to the tops of several privately owned mountains where there are no developed trails, just pure snow. A six-run heli-ski tour, with lunch, costs $1,150; ask about one-drop packages at Powder Mountain.

Parks & Recreation Areas

For boating and water-skiing, head 10 miles north to **Willard Bay State Park,** 900 W. 650 North, No. A, Willard (www.stateparks.utah.gov; ✆ **435/734-9494**). In addition to watersports, the 9,900-acre **Willard Reservoir** offers birding and wildlife viewing. There are two marinas, restrooms with showers, 131 campsites (some with RV hookups), and an RV dump station. A trail leads to a wide, sandy beach for swimming and sunbathing. Some campsites are along the waterfront, but most are along a meandering access road among the abundant cottonwoods and willows along Willard Creek. Fees run from $10 to $40, depending on type of vehicle, number of people, and date. Take I-15 exit 351 to South Marina, or exit 357 for North Marina.

In the Ogden Ranger District of the **Uinta-Wasatch-Cache National Forest** (ww.fs.fed.us/r4/uwc; ✆ **801/625-5112**), **Pineview Reservoir** is 6 miles east of Ogden via Utah 39. Surrounded by towering mountains and forested hillsides, the 2,874-acre reservoir is a popular watersports destination. Created by the construction of an earth-and-rock dam in 1937, Pineview has two boat ramps and two designated swimming areas. Anglers catch smallmouth and largemouth bass, black bullhead catfish, crappie, bluegill, yellow perch, and tiger muskie. The **North Arm Wildlife Viewing Trail,** accessible from Utah 162 where the North Fork of the Ogden River enters the reservoir, is an easy .7-mile round-trip walk through a riparian wetland, where you're likely to see northern orioles, yellow warblers, and white-crowned sparrows, plus ducks, geese, hawks, and mule deer. Bring your binoculars. The best viewing times are spring and early summer.

The Forest Service's **Anderson Cove Campground,** at 5,000-feet elevation along the south edge of the reservoir, has paved roads and 68 sites, and costs $24 per night. It's usually open from May through September, and has vault toilets and drinking water. For reservations, contact the **National Recreation Reservation Service** (www.recreation.gov; ✆ **877/444-6777**).

If you need to cool off, head to **Lorin Farr Park,** 769 Canyon Rd., Ogden River Parkway (✆ **801/629-8284,** or 801/629-8259 for pool). Facilities include water slides, a swimming pool, a playground, a skateboard park, and a picnic area with grills. The park is open year-round, but the pool is open in summer only. Admission to the park is free, but there are charges for swimming (call for current rates and schedules).

MTC Learning Park, 1750 Monroe Blvd. (✆ **801/629-8284),** is home to a nice botanical garden featuring indigenous plants and wildflowers and includes a stretch of the trail that's part of the Ogden River Parkway.

Spectator Sports

Weber State University, southeast of downtown, belongs to the Big Sky Athletic Conference and the Mountain West Athletic Conference. Football games kick off at Stewart Stadium at the south end of campus with the Salt Lake shimmering in the distance, while basketball and women's volleyball take place at **Dee Events Center,** 4400 Harrison Blvd. Contact the school's athletic department (www.weberstatesports.com; ✆ **801/626-6500**) for schedules.

America is waking up to the delights of minor league baseball and Ogden has a minor league baseball team. A short-season "A" team affiliate of the Los Angeles Dodgers, the **Raptors** play from mid-June to early September at Lindquist Field, 2330 Lincoln Ave. (www.ogden-raptors.com; ✆ **801/393-2400**).

Shopping

At one time a bawdy collection of saloons, rooming houses, brothels, and opium dens, Ogden's 25th Street has become one of the best shopping—and eating—strips in Utah. Historic buildings house antiques shops, specialty and vintage stores, restaurants, and bars. Among the best stops here is **IndigoSage Furniture Gallery,** 195 25th St. (✆ **801/621-7243),** for unique and unusual furniture design ideas and home accessories. Browse in **Booked on 25th,** 147 25th St. (www.bookedon25th.com; ✆ **801/394-4891),** an independent bookstore with lots of volumes by local writers. **Lavender Vinyl,** 123 25th St. (✆ **385/240-0336),** is an old-fashioned record store—adults can buy some nostalgia while their kids search for the latest cutting-edge music. Everyone will get a kick out of **Queen Bee,** 270 25th St. (✆ **801/791-0241),** which specializes in books, gifts, and fine chocolate. Also worth a look is **Gallery 25,** 268 25th St. (www.gallery25ogden.com; ✆ **801/334-9881),** a cooperative gallery featuring the work of local artists.

At the mouth of Ogden Canyon is a historic Victorian spa, reworked into **Rainbow Gardens,** 1851 Valley Dr. (www.rainbowgardens.com; ✆ **801/621-1606).** Dubbing itself as Utah's largest gift shop, it has everything from flowers and Olympic souvenirs to a restaurant (p. 100) and a trailhead out back.

Those searching for their favorite stores will enjoy **Newgate Mall,** 36th Street and Wall Avenue (www.newgatemall.com; ✆ **801/621-1161),** with all the expected mall delights—department stores, abundant fast eateries, and a 14-screen movie theater. The mall is open Monday through Saturday from 10am to 9pm, and Sunday from noon to 6pm.

Where to Stay

In addition to the choices below, the Ogden area is home to a number of affordable chain motels. **Motel 6,** 1206 W. 21st St. (www.motel6.com; ✆ **801/393-8644); Days Inn,** 3306 Washington Blvd. (www.daysinn.com; ✆ **801/399-5671);** and **Sleep Inn,** 1155 S. 1700 West (www.sleepinn.com; ✆ **801/731-6500),** usually charge $90 to $105 double.

Pets are not allowed unless otherwise noted.

Alaskan Inn ★★ Discover the wilds of Alaska in this enchanting B&B, where the unique rooms and cabins whisk you to a land of tundra, snow-capped peaks, tall pines, grizzly bears, and cascading waterfalls. Stay in the handsome 12-room log lodge or one of the 11 cabins. All units have whirlpool tubs for two; the cabins also have freestanding showers, and one has a kitchenette. In the popular Northern Lights room, you can enjoy a light show of the Aurora Borealis while lounging in bed or soaking in the tub. Or perhaps you'd prefer the Bears' Den, with a cozy cavelike atmosphere. Cabins are more simply furnished, but maintain the Alaska theme; you can dwell in a trapper's cabin or listen to the call of the bull moose along the Kenai River.

Located some 15 minutes from downtown Ogden, the inn is nestled among tall pines along the Ogden River, with easy access to hiking trails in the national forest. Full breakfasts are served in your room or cabin. Free tours of the inn are offered daily at 1pm. Smoking is not permitted and neither are children.

435 Ogden Canyon Rd. www.alaskaninn.com. ✆ **801/621-8600.** 23 units. $140 and up double. Rates include full breakfast. **Amenities:** Free Wi-Fi.

Best Western Plus High Country Inn ★ Located just off I-15, this above-average motel offers comfortable rooms with a modern mission-style decor. Guests have a choice of one or two queen-size beds or one king-size. Amenities include Wi-Fi, ski lockers and ski tuning, and the popular Jeremiah's restaurant.

1335 W. 12th St. www.bestwestern.com. ℂ **800/594-8979** or 801/394-9474. 109 units, including 4 suites. $95–$190, depending on season. Just off I-15 exit 344. Pets accepted with deposit. **Amenities:** Restaurant; exercise room; indoor Jacuzzi; outdoor heated pool.

Hampton Inn & Suites ★★ This eight-story Art Deco–style structure, built in 1913, was renovated in 2002 for the Olympics. More like a boutique hotel than a chain, its standard rooms have a comfortably refined atmosphere. The junior one-room "suites" are much more spacious, with upgraded amenities and sleeper sofas, and the 12 two-room executive suites are top of the line, with just about every amenity you might want. The hotel has secure covered parking, same-day dry cleaning, a business center, and a nice balance of historic architecture and reliable modernity.

2401 Washington Blvd. www.ogdensuites.hamptoninn.com. ℂ **801/394-9400.** 124 units. $99–$175 double, depending on room and season. Rates include continental breakfast. **Amenities:** Fitness center, free Wi-Fi.

HUNTSVILLE

Atomic Chalet ★★ Growing up in the shadow of a nuclear power plant in Orange County, California, gave Wes Welch the inspiration for his inn's name, but his experience as a professional volleyball player in the European Alps inspired its style and service. The Atomic Chalet, which housed the U.S. Ski Team during the 2002 Winter Olympics, is a two-story, cedar-clad lodge with a pool table in the parlor and a hip sensibility throughout. The rooms have one king-size or queen-size bed, plus a ladder up to a loft with one or two twins. The contrast of unfinished pine furnishings, with marble-laden bathrooms gives an idea of this inn's combination of comfort and rusticity. Rooms do not have phones. There are boot warmers and glove driers, and you can rent cruiser bicycles and kayaks. Breakfast includes home-baked bread, yogurt, granola, and fresh fruit. Other perks: Avid skier Welch has insider's tips for the slopes and he's known for throwing parties during ski season.

6917 E. 100 South. www.atomicchalet.com. ℂ **801/745-0538.** 4 units. $115–$139 double in winter; lower rates rest of year. Rates include continental breakfast and après-ski specialties. **Amenities:** Outdoor Jacuzzi; bike and kayak rentals.

Jackson Fork Inn ★ A delightful alternative to standard hotels, this unique little (7 rooms) inn was formerly an old family barn, believed to have been constructed in the 1930s. It is now in its third location. Five units have a spiral staircase leading to an upstairs bedroom loft; two rooms have whirlpool tubs. The charming Jackson Fork Inn restaurant serves dinner and Sunday brunch; next door is Chris Cafe, a low-key beer bar that serves three meals a day. The inn is completely nonsmoking.

7345 E. 900 South (Utah Hwy. 39). www.jacksonforkinn.com. ② **800/255-0672** or 801/745-0051. 7 units. $110–$150 double, depending on season. Rates include continental breakfast. Pets accepted ($20 1-time fee). **Amenities:** Restaurant; room service; DVD library; free Wi-Fi.

EDEN

Basinview Lodging (www.basinviewlodging.com; ② **877/686-4733**), which manages a wide variety of condos and vacation homes, is a good one-stop shop for ski-oriented lodging in the Ogden Valley.

Snowberry Inn Bed & Breakfast ★ The Snowberry, built in 1992, is a large log-cabin-style inn within 15 minutes of three ski areas and convenient to outdoor activities in the surrounding national forest. Each room is accented with antiques and collectibles related to its theme (Canyons, Wasatch Winter, Pioneer, and so on), but no phone. The Pioneer room is wheelchair accessible, and the Sundance Suite is the best family option. Each room has its own bathroom, some with shower only; the Monte Cristo has a claw-foot tub with a shower. Amenities include a game room with a pool table, foosball, and darts. The inn has an open, friendly atmosphere and great breakfasts—a signature dish is crème brûlée French toast. Smoking is not permitted inside.

1315 N. Utah Hwy. 158. www.snowberryinn.com. ② **888/746-2634** or 801/745-2634. 8 units. $109–$150 double. Rates include breakfast. Pets accepted with prior approval. **Amenities:** Outdoor Jacuzzi; free Wi-Fi. From Ogden, follow Utah 39 east about 8 miles and turn north on Utah 158; the inn is about 2½ miles up on the west side of the road.

CAMPING

In addition to the following options, the national forest offers camping in the **Pineview Recreation Area,** discussed above under "Parks & Recreation Areas," which also covers camping at **Willard Bay State Park.** Additional camping is found at **Fort Buenaventura** (p. 87) and at **Lagoon** (p. 92).

Century RV & Mobile Home Park This campground, conveniently located near the interstate and downtown Ogden, has shade trees, grass, and pull-through and back-in gravel sites. There's also a large tent-camping area, a bathhouse with hot showers, a dump station, a convenience store, a coin-operated laundry, a playground, free Wi-Fi, and a heated outdoor pool and hot tub. Cable TV hookups are available.

1399 W. 2100 South (1 block west of I-15 exit 343), Ogden. www.centuryparkrv.com. ② **801/731-3800.** 166 sites. $28–$38.

Cherry Hill Camping Resort ★ This immaculately maintained, remarkably comprehensive campground is part of a large complex containing a water park, miniature golf course, and batting cages. You'll find manicured lawns, shade trees, and paved interior roads, along with a heated pool, recreation hall, and game room. The campground offers complete RV hookups, a dump station, a convenience store, and loads of sites for tent camping. Note that some recreational and camping services are limited from November to April. Call ahead.

1325 S. Main St. (2 blocks south of I-15 exit 328), Kaysville. www.cherry-hill.com. ✆ **888/446-2267** for reservations, or 801/451-5379.182 sites. Tent spaces $36, full hook-up $44; lower rates Nov–Apr.

Where to Eat

The Greenery ★ AMERICAN   A local lunch favorite, this pleasant eatery has a green-and-white color scheme, checkerboard floors, nice canyon views, and—of course—plenty of greenery inside and out. The menu (while the same for lunch and dinner) is diverse, and the food is good. Try the fresh-baked Mormon Muffin, made from a pioneer recipe and served with Utah honey butter. Other house specialties include Chinese chicken salad, the Fowl Play sandwich (turkey, avocado, and melted mozzarella), and caramel apple pie. Bottled beer is available.

In Rainbow Gardens, 1851 Valley Dr. www.rainbowgardens.com. ✆ **801/392-1777** or 801/621-1606. Main courses $7–$15. Mon–Thurs 11am–9:30pm; Fri–Sat 11am–10pm; Sun 11am–9pm. From downtown, take Washington Blvd. north to 12th St. and head west to the mouth of Ogden Canyon.

Hearth on 25th ★★ AMERICAN   Chef-conceived, from-scratch food focusing on live-fire cooking, and craft cocktails in a surprising second floor location looking out over 25th Street. Some of the menu is daring, but go ahead, try the yak meatballs and the watercress Caesar with romaine, mizuna, asparagus, radish, and pea shoots tossed in a burnt-lemon Caesar dressing. The burrata starter—house-made burrata, wood-fired grapes, charred spring onion puree, arugula, strawberry balsamic, cilantro-roasted onion evoo, candied nuts, Utah red salt, and crostini could be a meal in itself. Definitely one of the most adventurous places to eat in Ogden.

195 25th Street, Suite 6. www.hearth25.com. ✆ **801/399-0088.** Main courses $20–$40. Day menu: Mon–Sat noon–5pm; dinner menu: Mon–Thurs: 5–9pm; Fri–Sat 5–10pm. Enter the lobby from 25th street and take the stairs or elevator to the second floor.

The Oaks ★ AMERICAN   This restaurant's unbeatable location—tucked among the pines in Ogden Canyon, with patio dining directly over the bubbling and crashing Ogden River—is unique and totally Utah. The Oaks moved to its present spot way back in 1933, when it evolved into a hamburger and hot dog takeout joint. In 1981, Keith and Belinda Rounkles turned it into a full-service sit-down eatery and ice-cream parlor. Today, the family-friendly, home-style eatery has a rugged Western decor, accented by old photos, maps, and postcards. Food is good, solid, American fare, made mostly from scratch. Breakfast, served until noon, features the usuals, along with huevos rancheros and some exotic omelets. The lunch and dinner menus bring a variety of burgers and sandwiches, including the house specialty: sliced sirloin smothered with mushrooms, onions, and green peppers and topped with mozzarella and

American cheese, served on a French bun. Dinner specials, such as charbroiled steak, chicken, or salmon, are also available; the pasta of the day is available at lunch and dinner. Utah microbrews and other beer and wine are served with meals.

750 Ogden Canyon (Utah Hwy. 39). www.theoaksinogdencanyon.com. © **801/394-2421.** Main courses breakfast & lunch $5–$12, dinner $15–$25. Summer daily 8am–10pm; shorter hours rest of year.

> ### Farr Better Ice Cream
>
> Choose from over 50 flavors of ice cream and a wide range of malts, shakes, sundaes, frozen yogurt, and homemade fudge at **Farr Better Ice Cream—Utah's Original Ice Cream Shoppe ★,** 274 21st St. (© **801/393-8629,** ext. 20), in business since 1920. Cones start at $3. It's open Monday through Saturday from 10am to 10pm; in summer they open at 9am and scoop until 11pm on Friday and Saturday.

Prairie Schooner ★ STEAK On the south side of the Ogden River, the Prairie Schooner is so named because every dining table is modeled after a prairie schooner—that's a covered wagon for you Eastern folk. The Western theme doesn't end there; the dining room features life-size campfire dioramas, a stuffed wolf, and a facade modeled after Old West storefronts. But what's kept the place in business for decades are the steaks, including a monster 24-ounce porterhouse and a 16-ounce T-bone, as well as those of the chicken-fried, sirloin, and prime-rib varieties. There is also a full selection of seafood and surf-and-turf combos, and a smattering of chicken. Lunch is composed of sandwiches and a few items from the grill. Full liquor service is available.

445 Park Blvd. www.prairieschoonerrestaurant.com. © **801/392-2712.** Main courses $8–$22 lunch, $10–$50 dinner. Mon–Fri 11am–3pm, dinner Mon–Thurs 3–9pm; Fri–Sat 3–10pm. From downtown, drive north on Washington Blvd. and turn right (east) just before the arch at Park Blvd.

Ramen Haus ★★ JAPANESE/RAMEN Sergei and Shani Oveson waited 6 years to start Ramen Haus, their first restaurant. The couple had worked for years in some of the state's best Japanese restaurants and Sergei did a stint at Izakaya Suki Asian Gastropub in Washington, D.C. Their menu boasts small plates of uncommon Japanese fare, like *enoki shoyu bataa* (seared enoki mushrooms with butter and soy) and *tsukemono* (pickled bites), but the centerpiece is the ramen—healthy, nutrient-dense bone broths and fresh (never frozen) authentic ramen noodles. While you're there, do yourself a favor and order the pork buns. And no matter whether you think you want dessert or not, order the Honey Toast—Japanese brioche filled with ice cream and drizzled with honey.

2550 Washington Blvd. © **801/393-0000.** $4–$10 per dish—you are expected to order several small dishes. Wed–Sat 11:30am–2pm and 5–8:30pm, Sun 3:30–8:30pm.

Roosters 25th Street Brewing Co. ★ AMERICAN This two-story, redbrick brewpub, with its prominently displayed brewing vats and intriguing metal and wood tables, is popular for both its eclectic menu and its beers.

Pizza comes in several varieties, including a vegetarian option with mushrooms, peppers, asparagus, spinach, and sun-dried tomatoes. The beer-battered fish and chips is light and crisp. For an appetizer, try the crunchy Onion Loops, onion slices fried in a homemade beer batter. Fish tacos, turkey enchiladas, pasta, steaks, great soups, and excellent specialty sandwiches are also available. Weekends bring a brunch menu that includes a killer chili verde omelet. Request patio seating if the weather is nice. As you might expect, freshly brewed beer is served—try the Junction City Chocolate Stout—and full liquor service is available.

253 25th St. www.roostersbrewingco.com. ⓒ **801/627-6171.** Reservations not accepted. Main courses $7–$15 brunch and lunch, $9–$22 dinner. Mon–Thurs 11am–10pm; Fri 11am–11pm; Sat 10am–11pm; Sun 10am–10pm.

Slackwater Pizzeria & Pub ★★ PIZZA   As beloved for its vast beer selection as the quality of its pizza and other food, Slackwater's irreplaceable charm is its riverside location. The Slackwater also has one of the largest assortments of specialty beers in Ogden, including limited availability local brews. Its menu of bizarre to classic pizzas—curry pizza? mac & cheese pizza? ceviche-topped pizza?—hits the mark, even when the combo sounds unlikely. Take a chance; there's plenty of liquid courage on tap and in the bottle. Sandwiches, soups, salads, and small plates round out the menu. Slackwater hosts live music and other events as well, check the website for details.

1895 Washington Blvd. https://slackwaterpizzeria.com. ⓒ **801/399-0637.** Pizza $12–$15, sandwiches about $10. Mon–Thurs 11am–10pm, Fri–Sat 11am–11pm, Sun 10am–9pm.

Sonora Grill ★★ MEXICAN   A remarkably fine Mexican restaurant, Sonora Grill is not your usual tacos and tamales joint—it offered Utah's first ceviche bar, tableside guacamole, and hand-made flour and corn tortillas. The dining rooms are spacious, comfortable, and beautifully decorated with Mexican furniture and copper. The menu focuses on regional Mexican specialties like *cochinita pibil*, a slow-roasted pork marinated in achiote, citrus, and cinnamon with coconut almond rice, red enchilada sauce, pineapple, cilantro, and black beans. Full liquor service is available and the margaritas are excellent.

2310 S. Kiesel Ave. www.thesonoragrill.com. ⓒ **801/393-1999.** Main courses $12–$15. Sun 10am–9pm; Mon–Thurs 11:30am–9pm; Fri 11am–10pm; Sat 10am–11pm.

HUNTSVILLE & EDEN

In addition to the recommendation below, don't forget the burgers at Huntsville's Shooting Star Saloon (p. 91).

Carlos and Harley's Fresh-Mex Cantina ★ MEXICAN   This funky little Mexican joint, located in the old (built in 1880) Eden General Store building, is fun for all ages, with an inviting bar and eclectic—meaning colorful and eccentric—decor. The log cabin atmosphere is homey and social, perfect for enjoying south-of-the-border specialties such as spicy poblano chicken, seafood enchiladas, and fajitas. Tuesdays bring all-you-can-eat tacos. In the Historic Eden General Store 5510 E. 2200 North, Eden. www.carlosandharleys. com. © **801/745-8226.** Main courses $9–$21. Daily 11:30am–9pm.

Ogden After Dark

All summer long, Monday through Saturday, the outdoor **Ogden Amphitheater,** 343 25th St. (www.ocae.org; © **801/393-3866**), hosts free and paid events, including movies, community theater, open-mic nights, and concerts. Events at the historic **Peery's Egyptian Theater,** 2415 Washington Blvd. (www.peerysegyptiantheater.com; © **801/395-3200**), include ballet and performances on the restored Mighty Wurlitzer organ. During the school year, **Weber State University's Department of Performing Arts** (www.weber. edu/performingarts/default.html; © **801/626-6437**) presents regular live entertainment at various venues; call © **800/978-8457** for tickets or check the website for a schedule.

For classical offerings, contact the **Ogden Symphony and Ballet,** 638 E. 26th St. (www.symphonyballet.org; © **801/399-9214**), which presents a variety of performances, ranging from solo violin recitals and pops concerts to ballets, such as "The Nutcracker," at various venues.

The **Golden Spike Event Center,** 1000 N. 1200 West (www.golden spikeeventcenter.com; © **801/399-8798**), has surround seating for more than 6,000 people and hosts concerts, rodeos, horse races, demolition derbies, circuses, auctions, and other special events. Call for current events. If you're lucky, you might get to see a chariot race—remember "Ben Hur"?—or a monster-truck rally.

There are more bars per capita in Ogden than any city in Utah. (It's sometimes called "Utah's liver.") For after-hours entertainment, the **City Club,** 264 25th St. (www.thecityclubonline.net; © **801/392-4447**), offers good eats and walls plastered with Beatles memorabilia, while **Brewski's,** 244 25th St. (www.brewskisonline.net; © **801/394-1713**), features lots of local bands and rock 'n' roll. **Lighthouse Lounge** features live music and cold beer, 130 25th St. (© **801/392-3901**).

You can catch live comedy at **Wiseguys Comedy Cafe,** 269 25th St. (www. wiseguyscomedy.com; © **801/622-5588**), with shows on Friday and Saturday nights. **Diamond Lounge,** in the Hotel Ben Lomond (2510 Washington Blvd.; © **801/627-1900**) offers a dueling piano bar.

WHERE EAST MET WEST: GOLDEN SPIKE

50 miles NW of Ogden, 90 miles NW of Salt Lake City

You don't have to be a train buff to be impressed by the **Golden Spike National Historic Site ★★.** Something about the site where America's East and West coasts were finally joined by rail is a thrilling glimpse of history. On

May 10, 1869, the Central Pacific met the Union Pacific at Promontory Summit. The nation's second transcontinental telegraph had been strung along the track as it was laid, and as the final spike was driven home, the signal "Done" raced across the country—and jubilation erupted from coast to coast. A ragged town of tents quickly sprang up along the track at Promontory Summit, but within 8 months the railroads moved their terminal operations to Ogden. In 1904, the Lucin Cutoff bypassed Promontory altogether, and in 1942 the rails were torn up for use in military depots.

Although today less than 2 miles of track are here, they are laid on the original roadbed, where you can see fully functional replicas of the two engines, the Central Pacific's "Jupiter" and Union Pacific's "119," that met here in 1869. From mid- to late spring into early October, the magnificent machines are on display and make short runs (inquire at the visitor center for a schedule). Presentations are given trackside.

Essentials

Admission for up to a week is $7 per vehicle ($4 per pedestrian/bicyclist/motorcyclist) from May through mid-September and $5 per vehicle ($3 per pedestrian/bicyclist/motorcyclist) the rest of the year. There are no camping facilities. Outside attractions are open daily during daylight hours.

GETTING THERE From Ogden, head north on I-15 to exit 365, turn west on Utah 83 for 29 miles to a sign for Golden Spike, turn south, and go 7½ miles.

INFORMATION/VISITOR CENTER The **Golden Spike National Historic Site** (www.nps.gov/gosp; © **435/471-2209,** ext. 29) visitor center is at 6200 North 22300 West, Promontory Summit; it's open daily year-round from 9am to 5pm (closed Thanksgiving, Christmas, and New Year's Day). Restrooms, picnic areas, and a bookstore are located at the visitor center, which also offers slide programs, films, and museum exhibits detailing the linking of the nation. Ranger programs take place daily; check at the visitor center for the current schedule.

SPECIAL EVENTS The park has several special events throughout the year, many with free admission. On May 10 is a reenactment of the original **Golden Spike Ceremony,** with food, souvenirs, and handicrafts. Reenactments are also held on Saturdays and holidays from May into October. On the second Saturday in August, the **Annual Railroaders' Festival** features reenactments of the Golden Spike ceremony, a spike-driving contest, and handcar races and rides. Hot food, crafts booths, and live music add to the festivities. Although not free (regular entrance fees apply), the **Annual Railroaders' Film Festival and Winter Steam Demonstration,** held during the Christmas season, is a lot of fun, with classic Hollywood railroad films and a special appearance by one of the two resident steam locomotives.

Exploring the Historic Site
BY CAR

Die-hard railroad buffs can drive the self-guided **Promontory Trail Auto Tour** along 7 miles of the historic railroad grades. A booklet explaining the markers along the tour is available at the visitor center. Notice the two parallel grades laid by the competing companies (see box below), clearings for sidings, original rock culverts, and many cuts and fills. Allow about 1¼ hours.

ON FOOT

The **Big Fill Trail** is a 1½-mile loop along part of the original rail beds to the Big Trestle site and the Big Fill. The Big Fill was created when some 250 dump-cart teams and more than 500 workers—mostly Chinese immigrants—dumped load after load of rock and dirt into a ravine to create the 170-foot-deep, 500-foot span of fill required to lay the Central Pacific's track. The Union Pacific built their trestle just 150 feet away. It was never intended to be a permanent structure; speed was the goal, rather than strength. Constructed by hand by Irish and Mormon crews in 1869, the last spike went into the 85-foot-high, 400-foot-long trestle on May 5, just 36 days after it was begun.

You can hike on either the Central Pacific or Union Pacific rail bed, although the Central Pacific rail bed is an easier walk. Markers along both grades point out cuts and fills, quarries, vistas, and caves.

This is the desert, so bring water, wear a hat, and be prepared for mosquitoes and ticks. Rattlesnakes are rare, but be alert and stay clear if you see one. And be glad that you weren't one of the workers in that backbreaking effort of 1869.

OGDEN VALLEY & THE NORTHERN WASATCH FRONT

You'll find splendid powder skiing, low prices, few lift lines, and friendly people in abundance at the relatively undeveloped ski areas of northern Utah. Don't expect fancy lodges (at least not yet), but do be prepared for breathtaking scenery, a wide variety of fine terrain, and a relaxed family atmosphere.

The Ogden Valley Resorts

These resorts are just northwest of Ogden; to reach any of them, take I-15 exit 344 onto 12th Street and follow Utah 39 east. Wolf Mountain and Powder Mountain are just off Utah 158, and Snowbasin is off Utah 226.

NORDIC VALLEY SKIING & TUBING

Family-oriented **Nordic Valley Ski Resort,** 3567 Nordic Valley Way, Eden, (www.nordicvalley.com; © **801/745-3511**), formerly Wolf Mountain Ski Resort, is Utah's smallest and least expensive ski area; it has among the best night-lighting systems in the state. Refreshingly informal and casual, this ski resort—whatever the name—has long been a favorite of Ogden-area families because it's a good place to learn to ski, with enough variety to keep everyone satisfied. The terrain is rated about 30% beginner, 40% intermediate, and 30% advanced. Annual snowfall averages 300 inches. At the time of writing the resort's future plans included a new gondola, new lifts, and a retail village to accommodate year-round activities. Check the website for the most up-to-date details.

The short double chairlift Wolfdeedo Chair and the longer Wolf's Lair Triple Chair access the beginner slope and the Wolf's Lair Terrain Park. Howling Wolf Chair, a longer double chairlift with a midway unloading station, provides the only access to most of the resort's terrain as it runs up the center of the hill; it also accesses the beginner slope and terrain park. A short surface lift, the Magic Carpet, is also available for beginners. The vertical drop is 1,000 feet from the top elevation of 6,400 feet.

The ski area is generally open from the end of December to mid-March, with four lifts operating from 10am to 9pm Monday through Thursday and 9am to 9pm Friday and Saturday.

GETTING THERE From I-15, follow Utah 39 east about 11 miles, turn north (left) onto Utah 158 for about 3 miles, then turn west (left), following signs to the ski area.

LIFT TICKETS Day passes (9am–8pm) for adults cost $50 ($35 for kids); half-days and night skiing passes are $35 apiece ($22 for kids). Combination day and night passes are available.

LESSONS & PROGRAMS The ski school offers private and group lessons; call for rates and information. The ski shop has equipment for rent and accessories for sale. No child-care facilities are available.

WHERE TO STAY & EAT The mountain has no overnight lodging; see "Where to Stay," in the Ogden section earlier in this chapter, for nearby accommodations. The lodge serves hot sandwiches, homemade soups, pizza, and hot and cold beverages. You can relax around the fireplace on a cold day or outside on the deck when it's sunny and warm.

POWDER MOUNTAIN RESORT

Powder Mountain Resort, 6965 E. Powder Mountain Rd., Eden (www.powdermountain.com; ✆ **801/745-3772,** or 801/745-3771 for snow info) is a family ski area in two respects: It was founded in 1972 by the Cobabe family, who still own and run it, and it's aimed at providing a variety of skiing opportunities to suit everyone in your family. Among the 8,000 skiable acres—the most of any resort in the country—are plenty of beginner runs, which seem to grade upward in difficulty as you move from the Sundown area to the Timberline area and then the Hidden Lake area; so by the time you're skiing Three Miles, you can consider yourself an intermediate and try cruising over the big, swooping blue fields. There's no dearth of expert and powder skiing in the wilds, either. Powder Mountain uses snowcats and shuttle buses to transport skiers to more than 2,000 acres of spectacular powder that is not served by lifts—it's an out-of-bounds, backcountry skier's dream come true. Powder Mountain is also is a favorite among snowboarders, as boarding is allowed everywhere.

The elevation at the summit is 9,422 feet so a bonus is the view: On a clear day, you can see across the Great Salt Lake and sometimes all the way to Park City. With more than 500 inches of snowfall annually, Powder Mountain doesn't have—or need—any snow-making.

GETTING THERE   From I-15, follow Utah 39 east about 11 miles, turn north (left) onto Utah 158, and drive about 8 miles to the ski area.

LIFT TICKETS   Day passes (9am–8pm) for adults cost $50 ($35 for kids); half-days and night skiing passes are $35 apiece ($22 for kids). Combination day and night passes are available.

LESSONS & PROGRAMS   The ski school offers a full range of ski and snowboarding lessons and other activities, both group and private, from half-day to multiday. These include children's lessons, a program designed especially for and taught by women, and guided Alpine tours. Private lessons (1 or 2 people) start at $160 for an hour; semi-private half-day lessons cost $400 per person. The resort's Timberline Lodge and Sundown Lodge both have ski shops where skis and snowboards are available for rent and accessories are for sale. No child-care facilities are available.

WHERE TO STAY & EAT   Most skiers stay in Ogden or Ogden Valley (see "Where to Stay," in the Ogden section earlier in this chapter), but for those who want to sleep slope-side, the **Columbine Inn** (www.columbineinnutah. com; © **801/745-1414**) has five rooms with a pleasant ski-chalet atmosphere, as well as a number of adjacent condo units that sleep as many as a dozen people. Rooms are located next to the lodge, off the main parking lot. Doubles cost $125 to $175 in ski season, with condominiums going for $350 to $680. Smoking is not permitted.

As for dining, the **Powder Keg** in the basement of Timberline Lodge serves sandwiches and draft beer around a cozy fireplace; there is also a cafeteria. Hidden Lake Lodge serves lunch at the summit. Sundown Lodge offers pizza, burgers, sandwiches, and soups.

SNOWBASIN ★★

All the powderhounds' attention was directed at Park City resorts until Snowbasin hosted the downhill and Super G competition at the 2002 Olympics. Although it's among America's oldest ski areas (it opened in 1939), Snowbasin had remained a local secret. Skiers have been flocking to the resort ever since word of the area's great terrain got out. Particularly popular for its top-to-bottom intermediate runs, Snowbasin offers plenty of untracked powder; long, well-groomed trails; and Utah's third-largest vertical drop. Beginners have plenty of terrain on which to develop their ski-legs, and some great transitional runs off the Wildcat lift will help them graduate from novice to intermediate status. With its wide-open powder bowls and Olympic downhill courses, expert skiing at Snowbasin has been growing by leaps and bounds.

Snowbasin Resort, 3925 Snow Basin Rd., Huntsville (www.snowbasin. com; ✆ **801/620-1000,** or 801/620-1100 for snow conditions), has 108 runs, rated 20% beginner, 50% intermediate, and 30% advanced. Included in its 3,000 acres are beautiful powder bowls and glade skiing. Snowbasin has two high-speed quads, one handle tow, one Magic Carpet, and four triple chairlifts, plus two high-speed eight-passenger gondolas and a tram that serves the starting point for the downhill racecourses. The lift-served vertical drop is 2,950 feet from the 9,350-foot summit. All lifts are open to snowboarders, with retaining devices required. With about 400 inches of annual snowfall, Snowbasin has not really needed snowmaking equipment, although snowmaking has been added to assure an early season opening. The ski season generally runs from Thanksgiving to mid-April, with lifts operating daily from 9am to 4pm. The resort is also now open in summer, when it transforms into a hiking, biking, and horseback-riding mecca (p. 114) and serves as a venue for events like Blues, Brews & Barbecue (see box p. 93).

GETTING THERE   Take I-15 to exit 324, then go north on U.S. 89 for about 10 miles. At the mouth of Weber Canyon, merge onto I-84 eastbound, which you take several miles to exit 92 for Mountain Green. Head east about 2 miles and turn north (left) onto Utah 167 (Trapper's Loop). Go about 5 miles to Utah 226, where you turn left and drive 3 miles to the resort.

LIFT TICKETS   All-day adult lift tickets cost $109, half-day tickets are $85; for ages 7 to 12, an all-day ticket is $59, a half-day ticket is $45; seniors over 65 pay $85 for a full day and $70 for a half-day, while ages 75 and above pay $39 for a full day, $30 half-day. Kids 6 and under can ride the lift free.

LESSONS & PROGRAMS   Snowbasin's ski school (✆ **801/620-1015**) offer skiing and snowboarding lessons for all ages and abilities, with rates starting at $129 for a full-day group lesson and $399 for a private half-day lesson. A unique women's program, the Diva program, is highlighted by women teaching women. Children's lessons are also available. The Grizzly Center at the base offers ski and snowboard equipment rental and repair, plus clothing and accessories for sale. No childcare facilities are available.

WHERE TO STAY & EAT   No lodging is available at the ski area itself; most skiers stay near Ogden (see "Where to Stay," in the Ogden section, earlier in this chapter). In preparation for the Olympics, Snowbasin built three handsome restaurants—one at the base and two on the mountain. All serve American fare in a mountain lodge atmosphere; the on-mountain restaurants are preferable for their wondrous views.

Northern Wasatch Front (Near the Idaho Border)

BEAVER MOUNTAIN SKI AREA ★

Skiing at Beaver Mountain Ski Area is like going home to see the folks. Located at the top of beautiful Logan Canyon in the Uinta-Wasatch-Cache National Forest, this small resort has been operated by the Seeholzer family since 1939. The emphasis is on friendliness, personal attention, and, as Ted

Seeholzer puts it, "helping skiers find the right runs for them." Beaver Mountain gets plenty of snow and has a good mix of terrains, well-maintained slopes, and a northeast exposure that makes morning runs a warm, sunny experience. Snowboarders are welcome. Both bump skiers and snowboarders like the steep Lue's Run (named for Ted's mother, Luella), while hot-doggers are directed to Harry's Hollow (named for Ted's father), which has plenty of bumps—and is located right under a lift so everyone can see you showing off.

Beaver Mountain Ski Area, 40000 East Hwy. 89, Garden City (www.ski thebcav.com; (C) **435/753-0921**, or 435/753-4822 for ski reports), receives an average of 400 inches of snow annually and has a top elevation of 8,800 feet and a vertical drop of 1,600 feet. One double chairlifts, a surface lift, and three triple chairlifts service 828 total skiable acres. The terrain is 35% beginner, 40% intermediate, and 25% advanced, and there are 30 runs. The season runs from early December through March, with the lifts operating daily from 9am to 4pm. The mountain is closed on Christmas Day.

GETTING THERE   Take I-15 to exit 362, then go east on U.S. 89 about 50 miles through Logan and Logan Canyon, and take the turnoff to the ski area.

LIFT TICKETS   All-day adult lift tickets cost $50; $40 for seniors and children 11 and under. No half-day lift tickets are offered.

LESSONS & PROGRAMS   The ski school offers group and private lessons for adults, children, and girls-only groups in a range of expertise, from beginner to expert. Prices vary from year to year, so check the website, lessons are also available. The lodge is the place to find ski rentals, lockers, and a small shop that sells clothing and accessories. No child-care facilities are available.

WHERE TO STAY & EAT   Most lodging and restaurants can be found 27 miles west in Logan (see "Logan," below). A cafeteria at the day lodge sells hamburgers, sandwiches, and soft drinks.

Nearby places to stay include **Beaver Creek Lodge,** 12800 E. Hwy. 89, Logan (www.beavercreeklodge.com; (C) **435/946-3400**), a half-mile east of the ski area along U.S. 89. Open year-round, this 11-room log lodge offers all the modern conveniences in a spectacular mountain setting surrounded by the national forest. Spacious guest rooms contain log furnishings, handmade bed quilts, TVs and DVD players, and whirlpool tubs with showers. A large common room offers a stone fireplace and big-screen TV with DVD players, and the decks offer panoramic views. Hiking, mountain biking, horseback riding, and snowmobiling are all available on the property and in the surrounding national forest (see "Sports & Outdoor Pursuits," later in this chapter). Room rates are $169 in winter and $149 in summer, with Friday- and Saturday-night rates the highest; meals are available during ski season at an additional charge. No smoking is permitted.

A small **RV park** ((C) **435/563-5677**) with 23 sites for RVs and tents is open at Beaver Mountain Ski Area in summer, with showers and lots of trees. RV sites with hookups cost $25; tent sites are also available. A large tent and a yurt are available from April through November (call for details).

6 | LOGAN

46 miles N of Ogden, 81 miles NE of Salt Lake City

Nestled in the fertile Cache Valley, at an elevation of 4,525 feet, Logan is flanked by the rugged Wasatch and Bear River mountains. Once part of prehistoric Lake Bonneville, then home to the Blackfoot, Paiute, Shoshone, and Ute Indians, the valley is now a rich farming area known for its cheeses and high-tech businesses. Mountain men arrived in the 1820s to trap beaver in the Logan River, caching (hence the valley's and county's name) the pelts in holes they dug throughout the area. Then, in 1856, Mormon pioneers established several villages in the valley.

With a population of about 50,000, Logan is a small city, but with many of the attractions of its larger neighbors to the south. Particularly worthwhile are visits to the LDS Church's Tabernacle and Temple, both handsome 19th-century structures, and a drive out to the American West Heritage Center for a trip through 100 years of Western history: 1820 to 1920. Thanks in part to Utah State University, Logan offers lots of culture—art exhibits, live music, or theater.

But nobody who comes to Logan really wants to spend much time indoors. Beautiful Logan Canyon and the nearby mountains are a delightful escape for hikers, mountain bikers, equestrians, anglers, and rock climbers.

Essentials

GETTING THERE   From Salt Lake City and Ogden, take I-15 north to exit 362, then follow U.S. 89/91 northeast about 24 miles to downtown Logan. Those flying to Salt Lake City can arrange transportation with the **Salt Lake Express Shuttle** (www.saltlakeexpress.com; © 208/656-8824). Two days' notice is recommended; fares vary according to time and day.

VISITOR INFORMATION   The Cache Valley Visitors Bureau has a **Visitor Information Center** located in a beautifully restored 1883 courthouse at 199 N. Main St. (www.tourcachevalley.com; © 800/882-4433 or 435/755-1890). It's open Monday through Friday from 8am to 5pm; June through August, it's also open Saturday from 9am to 1pm. Check out the Explore Logan app.

GETTING AROUND   As with most Utah cities, Logan is laid out on a grid, with the center at the intersection of Main Street (north to south) and Center Street (east to west). Tabernacle Square is the block to the northeast of the intersection. U.S. 89/91 enters town on a diagonal from the southwest, along the golf course at the south end of town. Utah State University is located on the northeast side of town, north of U.S. 89 between 700 and 1400 East.

The **Cache Valley Transit District,** or CVTD (www.cvtdbus.org; © 435/752-2877), is a free citywide bus service. Buses run Monday through Friday 5am to 7:10pm and Saturday 10:15am to 7:10pm, except major holidays. A route map is available at the visitor center on Main Street (see above) or on the website. For a cab, call **Logan Transportation** (© 435/753-3663).

Car-rental agencies in Logan include Enterprise, 2026 N. Main St. (www.enterprise.com; ℭ 800/261-7331 or 435/755-6111), and Avis, 900 N. Main St. (www.avis.com; ℭ 800/331-1212 or 435/753-3575).

FAST FACTS The Logan Regional Hospital, 500 E. 1400 North (ℭ 435/716-1000), has a 24-hour emergency room. The main post office is at 75 W. 200 North (www.usps.com; ℭ 800/275-8777).

What to See & Do

Although, like all LDS Temples, the Logan temple is not open to the general public, you can still view the outside 175 N. 300 East (ℭ 435/752-3611), and its beautiful grounds. The temple was completed in 1884, and its octagonal towers give the four-story limestone structure the appearance of a medieval castle. Because it sits on a slight rise, it can be seen from just about anywhere in the valley.

American West Heritage Center This living history museum, covering 160 acres, tells the story of the Old West from 1820 to 1920. It includes the Jensen Historical Farm, an authentic 1917 farm where visitors can learn about farming in the early 20th century, and the Pioneer Era Area (1845–70), which describes homesteading and life in a dugout or log cabin. There are also depictions of life in Shoshone Indian villages and mountain-man encampments. Allow 2 hours. Seasonal festivals (special fees apply), held several times a year, feature arts and crafts demonstrations, corn mazes, baby animal days, and Western reenactments, competitions, music, and food.

4025 South U.S. 89/91 (6 miles south of Logan), Wellsville. www.awhc.org. ℭ 800/225-3378 or 435/245-6050. Admission $7 adults, $6 children 3–11, military, and seniors 55 and over, free for children 2 and under; festival admission varies. Historic sites June–Aug Tues–Sat 11am–4pm. Welcome Center June–Aug Mon 9am–3pm, Tues–Fri 9am–5pm; rest of year Mon–Fri 9am–3pm. Some seasonal variations. Closed Jan 1, Thanksgiving, and Dec 25.

Cache Museum—Daughters of Utah Pioneers This small museum displays pioneer—mostly Mormon—artifacts from 1859 to 1899—basically the first 40 years of Mormon settlement in the area. You can see guns, musical instruments (including the first organ used in the LDS Tabernacle), handmade pioneer furniture, clothing, and kitchenware. On exhibit are several pieces of furniture made by Brigham Young for his daughter Luna Young Thatcher, who lived in Logan. Allow 30 minutes.

160 N. Main St. ℭ 435/752-5139. Free admission. May–Sept Tues–Fri 10am–4pm; by appointment rest of year.

LDS Tabernacle The Tabernacle was built from locally quarried stone in a style that's a mash-up of Greek, Roman, Gothic, and Byzantine architecture. The main stone, quartzite, is from Green Canyon, 8 miles northeast of Logan; the white limestone used for the corners and trimmings came from Idaho. Construction started in 1865 and took almost 27 years to complete. The main hall and balcony can accommodate about 1,800 people, and the pipe organ is a work of art. The pillars are made of wood that has been expertly painted to simulate marble, a technique widely used throughout pioneer Utah. The extensive genealogical library is open to the public. Allow 30 minutes.

50 N. Main St. ℂ**435/755-5598.** Free admission. June–Aug daily 9am–5pm.

Utah State University Founded in 1888, Utah State University (USU) is situated on a beach that was once the shore of the great prehistoric Lake Bonneville. Established through the Federal Land Grant Program as the Agricultural College of Utah, USU has about 28,000 students and an international reputation for research and teaching.

Old Main was the first USU building, and is the oldest building in continuous use on any Utah college campus. At various times, it has housed nearly every office and department of the school. Its tall bell tower is a campus landmark.

The **Museum of Anthropology,** Room 252, Old Main (http://anthromuseum.usu.edu; ℂ **435/797-7545**), has exhibits on the early inhabitants of the Great Basin as well as on the peoples of Polynesia and other areas around the world. It's open Tuesday through Friday from 10am to 4pm and on the first Saturday of the month from 10am to 2pm year-round; admission is free. Allow 45 minutes.

The **Nora Eccles Harrison Museum of Art,** 650 N. 1100 East (http://artmuseum.usu.edu; ℂ **435/797-0163**), displays a fine collection of ceramics and offers changing multimedia exhibits. It's usually open Tuesday through Saturday from 11am to 4pm; at the time of this writing it was closed for renovation and expansion but is still presenting offsite exhibits and events. Check the website. Allow 1 hour. Admission is free; there is a suggested donation of $5.

The **Nutrition & Food Science Building,** 750 N. 1200 East (ℂ **435/797-2112**), sells locally famous **Aggie Ice Cream** (more than 21 flavors) as well as Utah cheese. Call the store (http://aggieicecream.usu.edu; ℂ **888/586-2735** or 435/797-2109) for more information.

102 Old Main. www.usu.edu. ℂ**435/797-1000.** The 400-acre campus lies north of U.S. 89 and mostly east of 800 East. To get to the campus, drive north on I-15 and take exit 362. Drive east through Brigham City and the Canyon. The highway turns into Main St. Turn right on 500 North. When you get to the hill, turn left up the slope. Parking is just past the traffic light on the right.

Zootah This small but intriguing zoo, formerly the Willow Park Zoo, is home to a variety of animals, from lemurs to elk to bobcats, plus one of the best collections of birds in the region, with about 100 species (including wild avians who nest here). Children are invited to feed the ducks, geese, and trout. The attractive grounds have a lovely, grassy play and picnic area shaded by tall trees. Allow 1½ hours.

419 W. 700 South. https://willowparkzoo.wixsite.com/home. ℂ**435/716-9265.** Admission $4 adults, $3 children 2–11, and free for kids 2 and under. Daily 9am–dusk. Closed Jan 1, Thanksgiving, and Dec 25, with possible seasonal closures. From Main St., head west on 600 South for 3 blocks, turn south (left) onto 300 West for 1 block, then west (right) onto 700 South.

Sports & Outdoor Pursuits

The Wasatch-Cache National Forest, which covers almost 2 million acres of northern Utah, offers many opportunities for outdoor recreation. For maps and other information, contact the **Logan Ranger District office,** 1500 E. U.S. 89 (www.fs.fed.us/r4/uwc; ✆ **435/755-3620**). For outdoor equipment and supplies, as well as knowledgeable staff to help you find the best spot for your activity, stop by **Al's Sporting Goods,** 1617 N. Main (www.alssports.com; ✆ **435/752-5151**).

Excellent water sports, fishing, and wildlife viewing can all be had at **Bear Lake State Park** (www.stateparks.utah.gov; ✆ **435/946-3343**), along the Utah-Idaho border about 40 miles northeast of Logan via U.S. 89. The state's second-largest freshwater lake (20 miles long and 8 miles wide), Bear Lake is known for the azure blue of its water, caused by the suspension of calcium carbonate (limestone) particles in the lake. Facilities include boat ramps and rentals, a marina, picnic areas, campgrounds, and a 4.2-mile paved walking and biking trail. Deer are often seen in the park, and bird-watchers may spot ducks, geese, white pelicans, herons, and sandhill cranes, among other species. Anglers catch lake trout and huge cutthroat trout; an alleged Loch Ness–style monster, 90 feet long and dating back to local tribal legend, is said to inhabit the lake. Elevation is 5,900 feet. The day-use fee is $6 per vehicle, May through October 31; November 1 to April 30, $5 per vehicle. Camping costs vary according to campground, but generally cost $12 to $25. Contact the marina at **Cisco's Landing** in Garden City (www.ciscoslanding.com; ✆ **435/946-2717**) for boat rentals and lake tours.

Tip: In Utah, Bear Lake and raspberries are synonymous. With the rise in land values, agriculture is being squeezed out, but locals still take pride in their fruit—Bear Lake Raspberry Days are celebrated every August. A must-try in Bear Lake in the summertime is the famous raspberry milkshake from **La Beau's Drive-in** (✆ **435-946-8821**).

BIKING Cache Valley's patchwork of farms and villages offers excellent road biking through the countryside on well-maintained roads, and mountain bikers have plenty of opportunities in the Uinta-Wasatch-Cache National Forest. For tips on the best biking spots, contact the visitors' bureau or the ranger district office (above). Each June the **Utah Multiple Sclerosis Society** (http://bikeutu.nationalmssociety.org; ✆ **801/424-0113**) sponsors the 2-day **Harmons Best Dam Bike Ride,** in which more than 1,500 participants pedal up to 150 miles a day along Cache Valley's back roads. Funds support the battle against multiple sclerosis.

BIRDING Northern Utah has great birding, especially from spring through early fall in the area's wetlands. Two particularly good spots are along the Bear River west of Logan, and Cutler Marsh. These spots offer opportunities to see great blue herons, snowy egrets, white pelicans, western grebes, and a variety of other wetlands species.

FISHING   Logan River and Bear River offer wonderful fly-fishing, and streams throughout the area are popular for rainbow, albino, cutthroat, and brook trout. **Bear Lake** (p. 113) offers great lake fishing (including ice-fishing in winter) for trophy cutthroat and lake trout.

HIKING   Numerous hiking possibilities abound in the **Wasatch-Cache National Forest** east of Logan, and Logan Canyon in particular offers spectacular scenery. Among the easy hikes is the **Spring Hollow Trail,** about 6½ miles up Logan Canyon, which leads a half-mile to one of the area's most photographed rivers. Stop at the visitors' bureau or the Logan Ranger District office (p. 113) for a free brochure and other information.

HORSEBACK RIDING   The **Beaver Creek Lodge** (p. 109), in Logan Canyon (www.beavercreeklodge.com; ✆ **800/946-4485**), is about 25 miles northeast of Logan on U.S. 89, just east of Beaver Mountain Ski Resort (see "Ogden Valley & the Northern Wasatch Front," earlier in this chapter). One- to 4-hour guided rides are available for beginner through expert levels, costing from $45 to $89. Trails include a wide range of terrains, from mountaintops to rolling hills covered with aspens, pine trees, and wildflowers. The challenging rides to the top of a mountain reward you with panoramic views of the forest and Bear Lake. Reservations are recommended.

ROCK CLIMBING   The sheer rock walls of Logan Canyon make this one of the most challenging climbing areas in the West. An abundance of vertical and overhanging limestone and quartzite faces wait for eager climbers, and more than 400 routes have been developed—most are bolt-protected sport climbs. For practice, classes, information, and climbing advice visit **Elevation Rock Gym,** 1780 N. 200 East, North Logan (www.elevationrockgym.com; ✆ **435/799-3902**).

SNOWMOBILING & OTHER WINTER FUN   Snowmobiling opportunities can be found throughout the Uinta-Wasatch-Cache National Forest. Rentals are available at Beaver Creek Lodge (p. 109), which offers access to more than 300 miles of groomed snowmobile trails. Full-day rental rates are $209 to $279 for one rider, and $30 more for two riders. Guided day trips run an additional $395. Another popular activity is taking a sleigh ride among a herd of about 400 elk at the **Hardware Ranch Wildlife Management Area** (www.hardwareranch.com; ✆ **435/753-6206**), about 20 miles southeast of Logan ($5 adults, $3 kids; cash only). Information on snowmobiling, snowshoeing, and cross-country skiing can be obtained from the Uinta-Wasatch-Cache National Forest's Logan Ranger District office (p. 113). Downhill skiing is at Beaver Mountain Ski Area (p. 108).

Spectator Sports

A member of the Western Athletic Conference, **Utah State University** (www.utahstateaggies.com; ✆ **888/878-2831** or 435/797-0305) competes in all major sports, winning conference championships in football, men's basketball, and women's outdoor track in recent years.

Where to Stay

Among the reliable, moderately priced chains in Logan (around $120–$150 per double) are **Best Western Baugh Motel,** 153 S. Main St. (www.bestwestern. com; ☏ 435/752-5220), and the **Holiday Inn Express,** 2235 N. Main St. (www. hiexpress.com; ☏ 435/752-3444). On the campus of Utah State, the **University Inn & Conference Center,** 650 N. 875 East (www.usu.edu/univinn; ☏ 435/797-0017), offers hotel-style rooms and suites with double rates starting at $89. In nearby Providence (just south of Logan), the **Old Rock Church** (www.oldrockchurch.com; ☏ 435/752-3432) is a standout B&B located in a Latter Day Saints meeting hall that dates back to 1871; rates run $125 to $175 for a double.

Rates are highest in summer and lowest usually during the first 3 or 4 months of the year.

Seasons at the Riter Mansion ★★   This 1899 Greek Revival mansion, built by a prominent Logan pharmacist, has long been central to the area population's social life. As a lodging, it's a splendid alternative to the motels on Main Street, and features a nice variety of unique rooms such as the Library Suite (with 500 books and a four-poster queen bed) and the Parlor Suite (with hardwoods and a jetted tub in the bathroom).

168 N. 100 East. www.theritermansion.com. ☏ **800/478-7459** or 435/752-7727. 6 units. $99–$169 double. **Amenities:** Free Wi-Fi.

Where to Eat

Two words: Kitchen Sink. **Angie's,** 690 N. Main St. (☏ **435/752-9252**), is famous for its Kitchen Sink sundae, which is literally a kitchen sink filled with a scoop of every flavor of ice cream in the house covered with every imaginable topping. You can have a family-oriented, value-priced meal at Angie's, but leave room for the sink. Also recommended is **Elements,** serving contemporary American cuisine from wood-fired pizza to steaks to filet-mignon quesadillas. 35 E. 640 South (www.theelementsrestaurant.com; ☏ **435/750-5171**),

The Beehive Grill ★ AMERICAN   Touting itself as "Logan's only root beer brew pub," the Beehive Grill is just that—and a lot more. It also serves draft beers from the Moab Brewery, makes gelato in-house, and offers a diverse selection of food, ranging from fish tacos to barbecue and burgers. It also has a nice slate of vegetarian specials, including a burrito stuffed with walnuts, pineapple, and artichoke hearts. It has two distinct seating areas in the bar and dining room, and the atmosphere is casual but contemporary, attracting a cross section of Loganites: Utah State students and faculty, families, and blue-collar types. The bar has some great nightly specials and full liquor service.

255 S. Main St. ☏ **435/753-2600.** www.thebeehivegrill.com. Main courses $7–$22. Sun–Thurs 11:30am–10pm; Fri–Sat 11:30am–11pm.

The Bluebird ★★ AMERICAN   One of the last survivors of its kind, Bluebird opened in 1914 as a candy shop and soda fountain. That's what it still does, with the addition of real food. The decor, reminiscent of the 1920s, features the original marble behind the soda fountain and a mural depicting Logan from 1856 to modern times. The lunch menu offers sandwiches, such as a patty melt and barbecue pork, plus several full meal offerings, including a 6-ounce sirloin steak, pineapple chicken, and a filet mignon. In addition to a few sandwiches, the dinner menu brings such options as vegetarian pasta primavera, chicken-fried steak, and the popular slow-roasted prime rib. No alcohol.

19 N. Main St. ⓒ **435/752-3155.** Main courses $7–$16. Mon–Thurs 11am–9:30pm; Fri–Sat 11am–10pm. Just north of Center St.

Tandoori Oven ★ INDIAN   This unpretentious restaurant started out in 2007 in a gas station and gained such an avid following that it's expanding by almost 900 square feet. Some folks think Tandoori Oven might be the best restaurant in town–certainly this is Indian food that could compete anywhere. The menu is full of standards like chicken masala, spicy lamb vindaloo, vegetable coconut korma (mixed vegetables cooked with coconut milk, onions, tomatoes, cashew nuts, golden raisins and, of course, spices), and assorted Indian breads and meats cooked in a tandoor oven. Oh, and a great strawberry lassi.

720 E. 1000 North. www.tandoorivenlogan.com. ⓒ **435/750-6836.** Main courses around $10. Mon–Sat 11am– 2:30pm and 4–9:30pm.

Logan After Dark

Logan was once known as "the Athens of the West" for the extent of its cultural offerings and while that is certainly overstating the case, the city's love of the arts endures. The **Utah Festival Opera & Musical Theatre** Company, 59 S. 100 West (www.ufoc.org; ⓒ **800/262-0074** or 435/750-0300, ext. 106), presents a summer series of grand operas, light operettas, and musicals at the historic **Ellen Eccles Theatre,** 43 S. Main St. (www.centerforthearts.us; ⓒ **435/752-0026**), a dazzling piece of restoration. Recent productions have included "Into the Woods," "Tosca," and "The Barber of Seville." The theater stages other productions, too, ranging from modern dance performances to big band concerts. Call or visit the website for the current schedule.

One of the few true professional repertory companies around, the Old **Lyric Repertory Company,** 28 W. Center St. (https://lyricrep.usu.edu; ⓒ **435/752-1500** or 797-8022 for the box office), founded at Utah State University in 1967, presents a variety of comedies, dramas, and musicals, with equity actors, during its 8-week summer season.

THE SOUTHERN WASATCH FRONT: WORLD-CLASS SKIING & MORE

7

This is the heart of Utah's terrific ski country. Set amid majestic mountain scenery southeast of Salt Lake City, nestled between some of the country's top ski resorts—including Deer Valley, Snowbird, and Alta—is an abundance of natural wonders, such as Timpanogos Cave National Monument and Provo Canyon. The towns in this area run the gamut from Park City—aka "Sin City" to some—to Provo, one the most conservative cities in the state, and the home of Brigham Young University. Over the mountains from Park City, the Heber Valley is a spectacular sight from land or air (take a balloon ride for the latter), and more than a hint of Hollywood even glitters in this remarkable mountain landscape, thanks to Robert Redford's Sundance Resort near Provo and the annual hullabaloo in Park City, the Sundance Film Festival.

This chapter is arranged geographically from north to south, from the Cottonwood Canyons and Park City resorts to Provo and nearby Timpanogos Cave National Monument, with a few stops in between, including pristine Strawberry Reservoir, Sundance Resort and Institute, and even an antique train.

For a **map** of the Wasatch Front, see in the inside front cover of this book.

THE COTTONWOOD CANYONS RESORTS

30 miles SE of downtown Salt Lake City

You say you want some snow? Here it is, some 500 inches of it piling up every year, just waiting for you powder-hungry skiers to make that short drive from Salt Lake City. Brighton and Solitude ski resorts are in Big Cottonwood Canyon, and Alta and Snowbird ski resorts are in its sister canyon, Little Cottonwood.

If you're skiing on a budget, stay at the more affordable Salt Lake City lodgings rather than at the resorts themselves. The resorts are so close—less than an hour's drive—that city dwellers sometimes even hit the slopes before or after a day (okay, make that a half-day) at the office.

But this area is more than just a winter playground. Big Cottonwood Canyon, cut by ancient rivers over more centuries than you can imagine, is a spectacular setting for warm-weather picnicking, camping, mountain biking, and hiking. Rugged, glacier-carved Little Cottonwood Canyon is filled with lush fields of summer wildflowers (in summer, don't miss the hike up to Albion Basin and Cecret Lake) the brilliant hues of autumn, and then a winter blanket of powder snow.

Getting There

BY CAR   From Salt Lake City, take I-215 south to exit 7, then follow Utah 210 south. Turn east onto Utah 190 to reach Solitude and Brighton in Big Cottonwood Canyon; continue on Utah 210 south and east to Snowbird and Alta in Little Cottonwood Canyon. From Salt Lake City International Airport, it'll take about an hour to reach any of the four ski areas.

BY BUS   The **Utah Transit Authority (UTA;** www.rideuta.com; ✆ **801/743-3882**) provides bus service from downtown Salt Lake City hotels and various park-and-ride lots throughout the city into Big and Little Cottonwood Canyons. UTA ski buses have special racks and compartments to securely hold ski gear and are equipped with chains to traverse canyon roads in the snow. Check current prices at www.rideuta.com.

Big Cottonwood Canyon

Each turn along your drive to the summit of this 15-mile-long canyon brings you to yet another grand, dizzying vista. Rock climbers love these steep, rugged canyon walls—watch for them as you drive.

BRIGHTON SKI RESORT ★

In operation since 1936, the low-key, family-friendly **Brighton Ski Resort,** 12601 Big Cottonwood Canyon Rd., Brighton (www.brightonresort.com; ✆ **801/532-4731**), unpretentious and a tad scruffy compared to the luxury of other resorts, is where many Utahns first learn to ski and snowboard. Credit for that goes to the highly regarded ski and snowboard school and the lower lift-tickets prices. Children 10 and under stay and ski free with their parents, and teens particularly enjoy the bumps of Lost Maid Trail as it winds through the woods. But don't let its reputation as a beginner's mountain fool you: Brighton's slopes have a full range of terrain, all the powder you can imagine, and virtually no crowds. More Utahns than out-of-staters hit the slopes here—Brighton is located just 35 miles from downtown Salt Lake City at the top of Big Cottonwood Canyon, and visitors tend to stay away because of the

Ski City Super Pass

If you want to experience all of the Cottonwood Canyons resorts, your best deal is the **Ski City Super Pass,** which allows you to mix and match a set of days at your choice of Alta, Snowbird, Brighton, and Solitude, and includes transportation on UTA ski buses. Pass prices vary based on the number of days you choose (from 3 to 14 days) and optional lodging packages, beginning with a ski-only 3-day pass costing $276 for adults and $156 for ages 12 and under. Visit **www.ski city.com/skicity/super-pass** for more info or to buy a pass.

paucity of area lodgings. Elbow room is plentiful on the intermediate and advanced slopes, even on the weekends, and you may have them all to yourself on weekdays. Brighton is one of the state's top snowboarding destinations. Plus, you needn't leave after dark: Brighton lights up 200 acres for night skiing.

Brighton has seven lifts serving over 1,050 acres in the Wasatch-Cache National Forest. The lift-served vertical drop is 1,745 feet, accessible by hiking. Base elevation is 8,755 feet. Lifts are open daily from 9am to 4pm, mid-November to mid-April, with night skiing and snowboarding Monday through Saturday from 4 to 9pm from early December to March. Brighton has a beautiful day lodge, with ticket windows, restrooms, a common area, a ski rental and repair facility, and a convenient bus depot.

LIFT TICKETS Adult all-day passes cost $85; seniors (65+) cost $57; youth passes (ages 11–13) cost $53; and children 10 and under ski free with an adult (with a maximum of two kids per paying adult). Night skiing (4–9pm) is $45 for adults, $29 for youth.

Tip: The **Sol-Bright Day Pass** ($115, all ages 11 and up) enables day access to both Brighton and neighboring Solitude Mountain.

LESSONS & PROGRAMS **Brighton Ski & Snowboard School** (© 800/873-5512) offers both private and group lessons for adults. Kids' lessons range from $65 for 2 hours to $135 for the whole day, including lunch. Group lessons start at $55 for adults and night skiing lessons cost $55, and include the lift ticket. But the ski and snowboard school offers a variety of workshops and clinics, including a telemark series as well as adult parallel, senior, children's, and women's workshops. Check the website to find a lesson tailored to you.

WHERE TO STAY & EAT **Brighton Lodge,** at the ski resort (www.brigh tonresort.com; © 855/201-7669, ext. 120), is a ski in/ski out facility with 20 units, ranging from dorm-style rooms (which sleep up to four) to luxurious suites. Prices change seasonally, but are generally lower than most other resorts. Expect to pay about $139 for a dorm room and $19 for a suite. The lodge's large outdoor Jacuzzi will help loosen those sore muscles for your next day of skiing. You'll find cafeteria-style dining for all three meals and a bar that opens for lunch and stays open through après-ski and dinner. Another option is **Mount Majestic Properties** (www.mountmajestic.com; © **801/824-4700**), which rents all manner of mountain homes and condominiums. Rates begin at about $250 per night and minimum-night stay requirements may apply.

WARM-WEATHER FUN Mountain biking and hiking are popular activities, but note that lifts are not open in summer. The **Silver Lake Loop Trail** is an easy .8-mile walk around the lake. Watch out for moose and pika.

SOLITUDE MOUNTAIN RESORT

Solitude, 12000 Big Cottonwood Canyon, Solitude (www.skisolitude.com; © **800/748-4754** or 801/534-1400; snow report 801/536-5777) is a friendly, family-oriented resort that hasn't garnered the publicity of some of the others, so lift lines are shorter. The snow is terrific, and it's easy to reach—it's in Big Cottonwood Canyon, just 28 miles from downtown Salt Lake City. Like its next-door neighbor, Brighton—which is connected to Solitude via the Sol-Bright Trail—Solitude enjoys excellent powder and few crowds. Its 1,200-plus acres of skiable terrain range from well-groomed, sunny beginner and intermediate trails to gently pitched bowls and glades. The mountain is well designed, with runs laid out so beginners won't suddenly find themselves in more difficult terrain. Intermediates have wide-open bowls in which to cruise and practice their powder skiing, several excellent forest runs, and some great bumpy stretches on which to hone their mogul skills. Advanced skiers have many long fall lines, open powder areas, and steeply graded chutes.

Solitude is the state's only downhill ski area with a world-class Nordic center out its back door: The University of Utah and U.S. Olympic teams train here. The resort also has an ice-skating rink.

Four high-speed quad lifts, two fixed-grip quads, one triple, and one double service 77 runs and three bowls. The resort is open from early November to late April, daily from 9am to 4pm. With a summit elevation of 10,035 feet and a vertical drop of 2,047 feet, Solitude receives an average yearly snowfall of more than 500 inches.

LIFT TICKETS All-day passes cost $92 for adults, $65 for seniors 70 and older, $59 for kids 7 to 14, and those 6 and under ski free. Afternoon half-day adult lift tickets are $75.

Great Cross-Country Skiing

Solitude Nordic Center ★★ is Utah's oldest cross-country ski area. It has about 12 miles of groomed trails, including a children's trail, and offers rentals and lessons. The center is located between Solitude and Brighton at 8,700 feet and connects the two downhill resorts. Trails pass through alpine forests and meadows and around frozen Silver Lake. The Silver Lake Day Lodge offers rentals, equipment for sale, lessons, and light snacks. Trail passes for ages 11 to 69 cost $20 for a full day, $16 for a half-day. Those 10 and under or 70 and over ski free.

The Cottonwood Canyons Resorts | THE SOUTHERN WASATCH FRONT: WORLD-CLASS SKIING & MORE

LESSONS & PROGRAMS   Solitude's **ski school** offers group and private lessons. Adult group classes include a lift ticket and cost $135 for a half-day, $210 for the whole all day; call Ⓒ **801/536-5730** for additional rates and for customized private lessons. The **Moonbeam Kid's Program** offers an all-day learn-to-ski program for ages 7 to 13, and includes lunch, lift ticket, and rental, for $147. The ski school offers programs and classes for every age and experience level.

WHERE TO STAY & EAT   The **Inn at Solitude** (www.innatsolitude.com; Ⓒ **877/517-7717**) is a full-service luxury hotel, with 46 rooms and nightly rates from $277 to $370 during ski season (lower in summer). Its restaurant, **St. Bernard's,** offers fine dining with a menu from Europe's Alpine regions. Breakfast and dinner are served.

The resort also manages numerous **condo units and private homes,** with ski season prices ranging from a few hundred dollars to over $1,000.

Adjacent to the Apex Chairlift and with terrific views of the mountain, the day lodge **Last Chance Mining Camp** offers hearty lunches, and après-ski refreshments. The **Moonbeam Lodge** has a cafeteria for breakfast and lunch and a pub for dinner and libations. **Honeycomb Grill,** nestled on the canyon floor, adds amazing mountain views to its gourmet dinner and weekend brunch. The **Thirsty Squirrel** is a pub in the base village with an in-house sushi bar open weekend nights. Also in the village is **Stone Haus,** open for lunch and dinner serving pizza and ice cream.

For an unusual experience, reserve dinner at the **Yurt** (Ⓒ **801/536-5709**), in the forest above the main lodge. You can either cross-country ski or snowshoe through the evergreens to get to your elegant five-course gourmet meal served at a table set with linen, silver, and crystal. Closed in summer.

WARM-WEATHER FUN   Solitude remains open in summer, offering chairlift rides, mountain bike and scooter rentals, 18-hole mountainside disc golf, and a place to hike or just kick back and watch the wildflowers grow.

Little Cottonwood Canyon

With towering peaks rising 11,000 feet above the road on both sides, Utah 210 takes you on a lovely scenic drive through the canyon. Located at the junction of Utah 209 and Utah 210, the mouth of Little Cottonwood Canyon is where pioneers quarried the granite used to build the LDS Church's Salt Lake City Temple.

Bonus: On the way up to Brighton, consider a stop at an authentic log lodge, the **Silver Fork Lodge,** 11332 Big Cottonwood Canyon Road, Brighton (www.silverforklodge.com; Ⓒ **801/533-9977**). This is the real deal—a log lodge built in 1947. There are a few rustic rooms, starting at $135, but the restaurant is the destination, with a double deck looking out over the mountains for summer and a roaring stone fireplace inside for winter. It's open for dinner nightly from 5 to 9pm (main courses $32–$40); be sure to try the smoked trout and brie appetizer. The restaurant is also open for lunch and breakfast, when the star is the sourdough pancake plate made with the lodge's 50-year-old sourdough starter. Open year round.

ALTA SKI AREA ★★★

Alta (www.alta.com; © **801/359-1078;** snow report 801/572-3939), is a skier's legend—famous for its snow—over 500 inches per year of some of the lightest powder in the world—and at $139 for an all-day lift ticket, it's an excellent value. Located about 45 minutes southeast of Salt Lake City, at the top of Little Cottonwood Canyon, Alta is an excellent choice for serious skiers of all levels. Beginners have their share of runs, and the more adventurous novices can even try a bit of easygoing tree skiing through the woods. Intermediates will find plenty of open cruising ground, forested areas, and long, arcing chutes to glide through, plus opportunities to work on their bumps technique (try Challenger for a moderately pitched set) or practice their turns in the powder. Experts will find an abundance of the Cottonwood Canyons' famous powder and spectacular runs, like steep, long Alf's High Rustler. Alta offers much for the expert and the extreme skier—far too much to cover here—but hard-core skiers should know that you have to step out of the bindings and do a bit of hiking to get to some of the longest drops and best powder-laden runs. And this is a true skier's mountain: Alta is one of the few Western ski areas left that forbids snowboarding.

Alta's fans are many and loyal. That's because the emphasis here is on quality skiing, and to protect that quality, Alta has chosen to limit its uphill capacity. This is a classic ski resort, with both European-style terrain *and* sensibilities. This means that people are turned away on those occasions when the ski gods determine there are already enough skiers on the mountain. An announcement is made on 530 AM radio about a half-hour before the closure.

More than 116 runs are served by a new arrangement of lifts, including the new Supreme Lift. Alta has 2,200 skiable acres, with snow-making on 50 acres. Although it's famous for its expert runs, Alta also has fine beginner and intermediate trails. The breakdown is 25% beginner, 40% intermediate, and 35% advanced, with a base elevation of 8,530 feet rising to 10,550 feet at the top, yielding a vertical drop of 2,020 feet. Alta is generally open from mid-November to mid-April, with lifts operating daily from 9:15am to 4:30pm.

Alta Ski Lifts Company owns and operates only the ski area; all other businesses and services are privately run. At the base of Albion and Sunnyside lifts is a day lodge with a cafeteria, lift-ticket sales, day care, the ski school, and rentals. Two more cafeterias are located on the mountain. A transfer tow connects the Albion and Wildcat lift areas; in this base area, there are four lodges with dining facilities, ski rentals, and kids' programs.

LIFT TICKETS All-day, all-lift tickets cost $139, all-day children's tickets are $88. The area also has a "Ski Free After 3" ticket, which allows beginners to test out some of the easiest terrain in Albion Basin for an hour and a half at the end of the day.

LESSONS & PROGRAMS   Founded in 1948 by Alf Engen, the highly regarded **ski school** (📞 **801/799-2271**) is recognized for its contribution to the development of professional ski instruction. Two-hour group lessons cost $70; private and specialized instruction is also available. The **Children's Ski Adventures** program, for ages 4 to 12, offers fun skill development, and lessons in ski etiquette. Choose either a half- or all-day program.

Alta's **day-care program** (www.altachildrenscenter.com; 📞 **801/742-3042**) is open to children ages 2 months to 10 years old; reservations are encouraged. Call for current rates.

WHERE TO STAY & EAT   The best places to stay in Alta are slope-side. The following accommodations add a 15% service charge to your bill in lieu of tipping.

Alta Lodge (www.altalodge.com; 📞 **800/707-2582** or 801/742-3500) is perhaps the quintessential mountain ski lodge—simple and rustic, with a touch of class. The lodge has Jacuzzis, saunas, a general store, a kids' program, a bar, and a restaurant with superb food. The comfortable units range from small and basic dormitory rooms to handsome corner rooms with fireplaces and a balcony. Rates during regular season range from $456 to $594, but rates change do change seasonally so check the website or as the resort prefers, call.

Rustler Lodge (www.rustlerlodge.com; 📞 **888/532-2582** for reservations, or 801/742-2200) is elegant yet relaxed, with a great mountain-lodge ambience, a spa, and rooms that range from basic to deluxe (suites available). Rates, including full breakfast and dinner, range from $144 to $1,029 for two; a bed for one in a dorm room, with breakfast and dinner, costs $159 to $227.

The big value here is the **Alta Peruvian Lodge** (www.altaperuvian.com; 📞 **800/453-8488** or 801/742-3000), featuring lodging and three meals for $107 to $132 in dorms, $339 for a double with shared bathroom, and $409 to $599 double with private bathroom. The funky bar here is the best après-ski spot on the mountain.

Dining Near Alta

Rustic and unpretentious, the 50-year-old **Shallow Shaft,** 10199 E. Hwy 210, Sandy (www.shallowshaft.com; 📞 **801/742-2177**), is a local favorite, serving some of the finest food in the area. The menu of haute-American food is complemented by an excellent wine list. Dinner prices top out at $65 for buffalo tenderloin.

SNOWBIRD SKI & SUMMER RESORT ★★

The combination of super skiing and snowboarding plus excellent facilities lures both hardcore enthusiasts seeking spectacular powder, and those who enjoy the pampering that accompanies a stay at a full-service resort. Consistently rated among America's top-10 ski resorts, **Snowbird,** 9385 S. Snowbird Center Dr., Snowbird (www.snowbird.com; 📞 **800/232-9542** or 801/933-2222, and 801/933-2100 for snow conditions), is Alta's younger, slicker sister. The same wonderful snow falls here, but this resort has a wider range of amenities, including Snowbird's extremely popular spa and salon—worth the trip even if you don't ski. Some, however, find Snowbird's dense, modern village and resort atmosphere less welcoming than Alta's historic, European-style lodges and classic, ruggedly Western atmosphere and attitude, but once you're inside, it's all about comfort.

Many expert skiers absolutely worship Snowbird, however, with plunging cliff runs like Great Scott, one of the steepest runs in the country. Mogul-meisters will want to take the Peruvian or Gad II lifts to a great variety of fall lines on some steep and sinuous runs.

But beginners and intermediates haven't been forgotten, and their runs are also top-notch. There are even some "family-only" ski zones. Novices might want to head over to explore West Second South, set in a woodsy glade, or the less crowded Baby Thunder area. Intermediates will enjoy the excellent runs coming off the Gad II lift; if you decide to take the tram, wait around a bit at the top while your fellow riders take off so that you'll have these blue runs all to yourself—the next tramload won't get dumped off for another 5 minutes.

The entire mountain is open to snowboarders, and the resort also provides snowmobile adventures and cat skiing and snowboarding.

Snowbird has 168 runs on 2,500 acres, rated 27% beginner, 38% intermediate, and 35% advanced. The ski season generally runs from mid-November to mid-May, although the record 783 inches—that's over 60 feet—of snow that fell in 2010–11 allowed Snowbird to keep the lifts running through the Fourth of July—the latest lift-served skiing ever in Utah. From a base elevation of 7,760 feet, the vertical rise of 3,240 feet reaches Hidden Peak at 11,000 feet.

An aerial tram transports 125 skiers and boarders at a time up 2,900 vertical feet to Hidden Peak in about 7 minutes. It's quick, but can feel like a crowded New York City subway car. Snowbird also has four high-speed detachable quads, six doubles, and two conveyor lifts, giving it a total uphill capacity of 17,400 skiers per hour. The tram and lifts operate between 9am and 4:30pm daily, except for one that operates until 8:30pm for night skiing Wednesdays, Fridays, and Saturdays.

LIFT TICKETS Adult lift tickets cost $129 and $61 for kids. Children 6 and under can ride the lifts for free and the tram for $15. Combination lift tickets are available for both Snowbird and Alta. It gets complicated, so check the website for the combination that works best for you.

LESSONS & PROGRAMS The **ski and snowboarding school** (© **801/947-8222**) offers an all-day class (which includes lunch); a package

---

Off the Slopes at Snowbird

Don't miss the popular **Cliff Spa** (www.snowbird.com/spa; © **801/933-2225**), which offers a lap pool and huge whirl-pool, aerobic and weight-training rooms, and individual treatment rooms for massages, body wraps, mud baths, and hydrotherapy. Snowbird provides a variety of facilities for children, including a state-licensed day-care center and a youth camp; call for details.

for first-timers; and specialized workshops for racers, women, snowboarders, half-pipe riders, and seniors. Two-and-a-half-hour workshops start at $130, while a full-day private lesson is $785.

Established in 1977, Snowbird's **Wasatch Adaptive Sports Program** (www.wasatchadaptivesports.org; *©* **801/933-2188**) is among the best special-needs sports programs in the country. Using state-of-the-art adaptive ski devices and a team of specially trained instructors, the program is available to children and adults alike. Sit-skis, mono-skis, and outriggers are available at no extra cost.

HELI-SKIING Between December 15 and April 15, helicopter skiing is available on more than 40,000 acres from **Wasatch Powderbird Guides** (www.powderbird.com; *©* **800/974-4354** or 801/742-2800). Daily rates (seven runs, a continental breakfast, and lunch) are $1,260 per person for individual seating and up to $18,000 for a private charter.

WHERE TO STAY & EAT The approximately 900 rooms at Snowbird range from standard lodge units to luxurious condominiums with kitchens and fireplaces; almost every unit has a terrific view. **Snowbird Central Reservations** (*©* **800/453-3000**) books all lodging for the resort and can also arrange ground transportation. This resort is a world in itself—the spa and several on-property restaurants mean you never have to get in your car.

The **Cliff Lodge & Spa** is located in a ski-in, ski-out pedestrian mall. Practically all of the 511 rooms, with mission-style furnishings, have splendid views of the mountain or canyon. Choose a standard or extra-large room, or a one- or two-bedroom suite. You'll find a splendid spa, restaurants, shops, and practically anything else you might want. Rooms start at $230 for a double in ski season.

The **Lodge at Snowbird,** the **Inn,** and **Iron Blosam Lodge** are condominium properties, offering privately owned rooms, efficiencies, studios, and one-bedroom and one-bedroom-with-loft units. Many have Western decor with Murphy beds and/or sofa beds. All units have access to the amenities—spa, dining, skiing—at Snowbird. Rentals are arranged through a property company but are fixed by the owners and will fluctuate based on the season, and can run anywhere from $1,000 to $14,000 for a week's stay. Visit the Snowbird website for more details.

The **Aerie Restaurant** (*©* **801/933-2160**), on the top floor of the Cliff Lodge, features New American dining with spectacular views, and serves a skier's breakfast buffet in the winter, and sushi and "gastro-pub" specialties for dinner year-round. Entree prices range from $23 to $44, but there's also a menu of small plates and sandwiches. Also in the Cliff Lodge, **El Chanate** (*©* **801/933-2025**), a Mexican restaurant, was closed at press time but scheduled to reopen during 2018–19 winter season, after a serious renovation. On level B of the Cliff Lodge is the **Atrium** (*©* **801/933-2140**), with tremendous alpine views. The Atrium features a buffet lunch in winter and a light breakfast buffet in summer, with prices from $12 to $22. The Atrium Espresso Bar is open daily.

For steak and seafood, try **Steak Pit** (📞 801/933-2260), in the Snowbird Center, open for dinner daily. Prices range from $19 to $48. Also in the Snowbird Center is **Forklift Restaurant** (📞 801/933-2440), serving breakfast and lunch daily. Prices at Forklift range from $7 to $11.

The **Lodge Bistro** (📞 801/933-2145) is on the pool level in the Lodge at Snowbird, offering an eclectic dinner menu in an intimate setting. Italian fare is offered for dinner daily at Iron Blosam's **Wildflower** (📞 801/933-2230). Entrees at both restaurants range from $10 to $35.

WARM-WEATHER FUN   After the skiers go home for the season, Snowbird is still active with hikers and mountain bikers. A lift hauls mountain bikers up the slopes. Snowbird's summer music program includes several annual festivals and in the fall the resort hosts its famous Oktoberfest; call or visit the website for details.

PARK CITY: UTAH'S PREMIER RESORT TOWN ★★

31 miles E of Salt Lake City

Utah's most sophisticated resort community, **Park City,** is reminiscent of Aspen, Colorado, and Taos, New Mexico—other historic Western towns that have made the most of excellent ski terrain while evolving into popular year-round vacation destinations, offering a casual Western atmosphere with a touch of elegance.

A silver boom brought thousands to Park City in the 1870s, and that boom continued for 50 years, giving Park City a population of 10,000 at its height, with more than 30 saloons along Main Street and a flourishing red-light district. Then came the Depression and plummeting mineral prices, leaving Park City to doze in the summer sun and under a blanket of winter snow. In 1963, the area's first ski lift was built (rates were $2.50 for a weekend of sledding and skiing), and Park City was on the road to becoming one of the West's most popular ski towns. The 2002 Olympics helped cement its reputation internationally.

Today's visitors will find three separate ski areas, lodgings that range from moderate to luxurious, some of the state's most innovative restaurants and best shops, an abundance of fine performing arts events, many of Utah's liveliest nightspots, and plenty of hiking, mountain biking, fishing, and other outdoor opportunities.

In 2015, two of the Park City area resorts—Park City Mountain Resort and Canyons Resort—were bought by Vail and combined into Park City, the largest single ski and snowboard resort in the United States.

As in many tourist towns, prices here can be a bit steep; if you're watching your wallet, avoid visiting during the Christmas season or the Sundance Film Festival in mid- to late January, when Hollywood takes over. Those who are really pinching pennies might want to stay in Salt Lake City and drive to Park City in the morning for a day of skiing, exploring, or adventuring.

The Park City Area

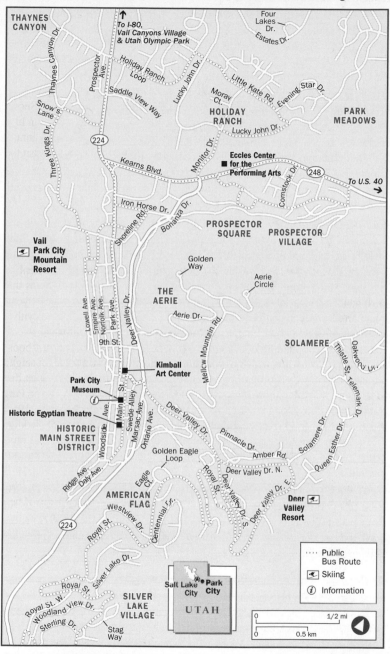

THAYNES CANYON

To I-80, Vail Canyons Village & Utah Olympic Park

Four Lakes Dr.

Estates Dr.

Prospector Ave.

Holiday Ranch Loop

Thaynes Canyon Dr.

Saddle View Way

Lucky John Dr.

Little Kate Rd.

Evening Star Dr.

PARK MEADOWS

Snow's Lane

Moray Ct.

HOLIDAY RANCH

Three Kings Dr.

224

Kearns Blvd.

Monitor Dr.

Lucky John Dr.

Eccles Center for the Performing Arts

Comstock Dr.

248

To U.S. 40

Iron Horse Dr.

Shoreline Rd.

Bonanza Dr.

PROSPECTOR SQUARE

PROSPECTOR VILLAGE

Vail Park City Mountain Resort

Golden Way

Aerie Circle

THE AERIE

Aerie Dr.

SOLAMERE

Oakwood Dr.

Thistle St.

Telemark Dr.

Lowell Ave.

Empire Ave.

Norfolk Ave.

Park Ave.

Deer Valley Dr.

Mellow Mountain Rd.

9th St.

Kimball Art Center

Park City Museum

Historic Egyptian Theatre

Main St.

Swede Alley

Marsac Ave.

Ontario Ave.

Deer Valley Dr.

Pinnacle Dr.

Solamere Dr.

Queen Esther Dr.

HISTORIC MAIN STREET DISTRICT

Woodside

Ridge Ave.

Daly Ave.

Golden Eagle Loop

Eagle Ct.

Centennial Pk.

Amber Rd.

Deer Valley Dr. N.

Royal St.

Deer Valley Dr. E.

Deer Valley Dr. S.

Deer Valley Resort

AMERICAN FLAG

Westview Dr.

224

Royal St.

Silver Lake Dr.

Royal St. W.

Royal St.

Woodland View Dr.

SILVER LAKE VILLAGE

Sterling Dr.

Stag Way

Salt Lake City

Park City

UTAH

.... Public Bus Route

Skiing

(i) Information

0   1/2 mi
0   0.5 km

Essentials

GETTING THERE   Most visitors fly into Salt Lake City International Airport and drive or take a shuttle to Park City. Driving time from the airport is about 35 minutes. At I-80 exit 145, take Utah 224 into Park City. Family-operated **My Shuttle** (myshuttleparkcityutah.com; ✆ **435/605-4710**) offers private shuttles from the Salt Lake City airport and hotels as does **M&L Park City Shuttle** (www.mlparkcityshuttle.com; ✆ **801/699-3403**).

VISITOR INFORMATION   The **Park City Chamber of Commerce Visitors Center,** 1794 Olympic Pkwy., Park City (www.visitparkcity.com; ✆ **435/658-9616**), is open Monday through Saturday from 9am to 6pm. It operates a visitor information center in Kimball Junction near the entrance to the Utah Olympic Park near I-80, open Monday through Saturday from 9am to 6pm and Sunday from 10am to 6pm, and another at 333 Main St., which is open Monday through Saturday from 10am to 7pm and Sunday from noon to 6pm. Both locations have shorter hours in the off season.

GETTING AROUND   Parking in Park City is limited, to put it mildly, and it is one of the town's ongoing problems. Parking is scarce in the historic Main Street area, and almost impossible if you're driving a motor home or pulling a trailer. If you've arrived by car, the best plan is to park it and ride the free city bus. Main Street has metered parking (in effect daily 11am–8pm) and fairly large parking lots (all of which charge a fee) are situated near both the upper and lower ends of Main Street.

If you still want to rent a car, try **Enterprise,** 1776 Park Ave. Ste. 12 (www.enterprise.com; ✆ **435/655-7277**).

Park City's very efficient free transit system offers several routes throughout Park City and the surrounding area, daily from 7:30am until 10:30pm. The **Main Street Trolley** links Main Street and Park City Mountain Resort, and **public buses** travel to the outlying areas. Pick up the *Transit System Guide* brochure for a good route map and specific schedules. The weekly booklet *This Week in Park City* contains helpful info plus several area maps, including one of Main Street. Both are available at the visitor centers and many lodgings.

FAST FACTS   To take care of injury or illness, go to **Park City Healthcare,** 1665 Bonanza Dr. (www.parkcityclinic.com; ✆ **435/649-7640**). The main **post office** is at 450 Main St. (www.usps.com; ✆ **800/275-8777**). The local **newspaper** is the "Park Record" (www.parkrecord.com), published twice weekly.

Skiing the Park City Area Resorts

The three area ski resorts, all within a few minutes' drive of each other, are vastly different. There's something for everyone here: Posh **Deer Valley** is Utah's upscale resort, famous for its amenities and dining, and big and lively **Park City,** now owned by Vail, is the party resort. The **Canyons Village,**

Sixty-four of Park City's buildings are listed on the National Register of Historic Places. During the summer months the **Park City Main Street Historic Walking Tour,** led by the Park City Museum, brings the town's lively past to life. Tours are offered Monday through Friday at 2pm; the cost is $7 (http://parkcityhistory.org/events-old/historic-walking-tours; © **435/649-7457**). From another point of view, **Park City Ghost Tours** (www.parkcityghost-tours.com; © **435/615-7673**) introduce you to the famously haunted places around town, nightly at 8pm ($20 adults, $10 kids).

owned by Vail, is casual and friendly with good food. Snowboarders are welcome at Park City and Canyons Village, but not Deer Valley.

Many skiers try all three resorts, and if you're going to do so, it will pay to do a bit of advance planning. There are multiple levels and types of season passes with different requirements and restrictions—the Silver Pass, The Gold Pass, the Ikon Pass, the Yeti Pass, etc. It's best to visit www.skiutah.com/passes to find the one that's right for you.

DEER VALLEY RESORT ★★★

If you're looking for a first-class experience *in every way,* this is your place. Unquestionably Utah's most elegant and sophisticated resort, **Deer Valley,** 2250 Deer Valley Dr., Park City (www.deervalley.com; © **800/424-3337** or 435/649-1000, or 435/649-2000 for snow conditions), offers perfectly manicured slopes, guest service attendants, heated sidewalks, and some of the state's finest dining and lodging. Along with all this, you get fantastic skiing—especially if you crave long, smooth, perfectly groomed cruising runs that let you enjoy the spectacular mountain scenery around you. Although half of the terrain is rated intermediate, beginners love Success, a long run that gives them the feeling they're actually getting somewhere. In addition, much of the intermediate terrain is fit for advancing novices, as the entire mountain is kept very skiable. Experts will find some steep, exhilarating-enough trails on top, through majestic aspen and evergreen glades, plus plenty of woodsy terrain to explore. Deer Valley is primarily a pampering resort experience, meant for cruising wide lanes of impeccably groomed snow all day, then hobnobbing all evening with the rich—and often famous—over gourmet meals in the plush lodges.

Six bowls and 100 runs are spread over Empire Canyon, Deer Crest, Flagstaff, Bald, and Bald Eagle mountains, served by a more than 20 lifts. The base is at 6,570 feet with the summit at 9,570 feet. The ski season generally runs from early December to mid-April, with lifts operating daily from 9am to 4:15pm. The 2,026 skiable acres are rated 15% beginner, 50% intermediate, and 35% advanced. Deer Valley very rarely needs its snowmaking equipment.

GETTING THERE   From Utah 224, head southeast on Deer Valley Drive to the resort.

LIFT TICKETS   All-day lift tickets cost $169 for adults, $118 for seniors 65 and up, $105 for "juniors," aged 5 to 12, and $40 for children 4 and under. Half-day and multiday packages are available and prices may be higher during holidays.

LESSONS & PROGRAMS   The **ski school** (✆ **435/645-6648**) at Deer Valley offers private and group lessons, workshops, and clinics. The unique Max 4 Instruction offers a chance to improve your skiing in the comfort of a small-group setting with a maximum of four students. Max 4 lessons are $200 for beginners (morning sessions) and all abilities (afternoons). Youth lessons range from $257 to $270, depending on age and ability. A full-day private lesson for an adult can cost $965. The licensed **child-care center,** open daily from 8:30am to 4:30pm, costs $154 per day for kids ages 2 months to 12 years, and includes lunch; it's $159 per day for infants.

WHERE TO EAT ON THE MOUNTAIN   Snow Park Lodge (✆ **435/ 645-6632**), at the base, has a bakery, two restaurants, and a lounge. The **Seafood Buffet,** open Monday through Saturday evenings, offers a mammoth salad and seafood buffet (with non-seafood choices) and fancy desserts. **Snow Park Lounge** serves hors d'oeuvres after 3:30pm.

Silver Lake Lodge (✆ **435/645-6715**), midway up the mountain, serves a variety of quick-and-easy food all day, including continental breakfasts (with fresh-baked pastries), salads, grilled fare, and pizzas. You can also choose from two fine-dining rooms, the **Mariposa,** open evenings only, and **Royal Street Café,** open for lunch, après-ski, and dinner. **Fireside Dining** at Empire Canyon Lodge (✆ **435/645-6632**) is a unique alpine dining room offering Continental lunch and dinner menus, while also serving as a base for moonlight sleigh rides and snowshoe treks.

For picnics, a meal at the condo, or a simple waterside supper on the deck, **Deer Valley Grocery** (✆ **435/615-2400**) serves prepared and packaged foods from 7:30am to 8:30pm daily. And the newest eatery at Deer Valley, **The Brass Tag** (✆ **435/615-2410**), offers a grab-and-go menu, along with lunch and dinner fare, a vegan menu, and a bar menu.

THE MEGA-RESORT: PARK CITY MOUNTAIN RESORT

Park City Mountain Resort, a complex made up of two former resorts—Park City and Canyons Village—is one of the largest ski areas in North America. The resort now has 41 lifts 348 trails, eight terrain parks, both a super and a mini-pipe on 3,300 acres, plus two Magic Carpet people movers in the children's learning area. Still, the former Park City and Canyons Village resort retain much of their pre-Vail atmosphere and culture. The two resort centers are connected and each offers a constellation of restaurants and amenities. For this section, we'll treat them as two properties.

PARK CITY MOUNTAIN RESORT ★★

Park City Mountain Resort, 1345 Lowell Ave. Park City (www.parkcity mountain.com; ℂ **435/649-8111**), historically one of Utah's largest and liveliest resorts, is where the U.S. Ski and Snowboard Olympic team comes to train. The U.S. Ski and Snowboard Association's Center of Excellence is here as well—and who could blame them? There's plenty of dependable, powdery snow and a variety of terrain and runs that offers something for everyone. Surveys continually rank Park City among the country's top resorts for both its terrain and its challenging runs. And, because it's located right in the heart of Park City, what more could you ask for in terms of amenities?

Beginners will find plenty of great training ground, blessedly free of that frequent mountain problem—hordes of advanced skiers whizzing their way right through the green runs on their way to the bottom. After they have a good handle on the sport, beginners and novices can head up the lift to Summit House and then glide down their own scenic 3½-mile green run. Intermediates will find good cruising ground and powder runs; experts can delight in some 750 acres of wide-open bowls and hair-raising narrow chutes. After a good storm, the locals know to rise early, race to the top of the Jupiter Bowl, and carve their way back down through fresh powder.

And the local roots are evident: There's a triple-chair access lift directly from Park City's Old Town Main Street onto the mountain, as well as two runs (Quit 'n' Time and Creole) that lead back into town. So those staying in Park City proper don't have to ride back and forth to the base resort every day. With a base elevation of 6,900 feet and summit of 10,000 feet, the vertical drop is 3,100 feet. Park City's season generally runs from late November to mid-April, with lifts operating daily between 9am and 4pm. Night operations usually run from Christmas through late March from 4 to 7:30pm, and include a snowboard park.

The **Resort Center,** at the base of the mountain, houses the ski school, equipment sales and rentals, a restaurant and bar, lockers, and a ticket office.

GETTING THERE   The resort is off of Main Street, Park City.

LIFT TICKETS   All-day lift ticket fees vary throughout the season and there are a number of packages available for the giant resort. Best to check the website to make sure your skiing and lodging are compatible. Single day lift tickets for adults are about $110; 2-day tickets are $216.

LESSONS & PROGRAMS   The **Park City Mountain Resort Ski and Snowboard School** (ℂ **800/227-2754**) offers a wide variety of choices for every level. Customized packages are available and the entire resort is undergoing massive changes, so check the website for details. A full-day adult group lesson here (or at Canyons Village) will run about $209.

WHERE TO EAT ON THE MOUNTAIN   In addition to the wide variety of options in Park City (see "Where to Eat," later in this chapter), you'll find the following slope-side facilities. Only Viking Yurt requires reservations.

ski THEM ALL IN JUST 1 DAY

Ski Utah's **Interconnect Adventure Tour** is unique. Six full-time guides take a dozen skiers on journeys to the slopes of four to six of Utah's renowned resorts—and about 20 miles of untracked backcountry in between.

"If you're a good skier and looking for a day of adventure, come out with us," says Deb Lovci, one of the guides and owner of the Old Town Guest House in Park City (see "Where to Stay" in Park City, below). "It's an awesome way to see how the whole Wasatch is connected."

Tours visit the Deer Valley, Park City Mountain, Solitude Mountain, Brighton, and Snowbird resorts, the Alta Ski Area, and use the backcountry routes to navigate between the resorts. These rarely used routes offer incredible views of some of the most majestic terrain in the Rockies.

Interested skiers should know a few things before making reservations. Skiers should be advanced, comfortable with skiing a variety of terrains and snow conditions, and in good physical condition. "It's a long day," Lovci notes. Be sure to make reservations in advance—these popular tours fill up around holidays and on weekends. Tours are done completely with alpine gear.

The trip is offered daily from mid-December to mid-April, weather permitting, departing from either Deer Valley Resort (Sun–Mon, Wed, and Fri; p. 129) or Snowbird Ski & Summer Resort (Tues, Thurs, and Sat; p. 123), and costs $395, including lunch, lift tickets at all resorts, guide service, and transportation—and a much-deserved finisher's pin. Participants must be at least 16, and snowboarding is not permitted.

For additional information, call **Ski Utah** at $\textcircled{C}$ **801/534-1907,** or visit www.skiutah.com/interconnect.

The **Legacy Cafe,** at the Legacy Lodge, offers homemade breakfast and dinner buffets. For lunch, Legacy serves soups and stews, sandwiches, pizza, a salad bar, and fresh roasted meats. **Legends Bar & Grill** offers lunch and après-ski refreshments.

The iconic **Mid-Mountain Lodge** is at the base of Pioneer Lift on the Mid-Mountain Ski Run, at 8,700 feet. Built around 1898, the lodge may be the oldest original mine building in Park City. At press time the lodge was undergoing renovations but was expected to re-open in time for the 2018–19 ski season.

Summit House, at the top of the Bonanza chairlift, serves lunch and boasts an outdoor deck with magnificent panoramic views and a cozy fireplace inside. The **Snow Hut,** at the bottom of the Silverlode six-passenger lift, serves breakfast and lunch daily, winter only.

The most refined and recommended eatery here is the **Viking Yurt,** accessible by a 20-minutes sleigh ride, and so only open in the winter. The six-course menu cost $140 per person (more at Christmastime), excluding alcoholic beverages. Advance reservations are required. Call $\textcircled{C}$ **435/615-9878** or visit www.vikingyurt.com for additional information.

CANYONS VILLAGE

Canyons Village, 4000 Canyons Resort Dr., Park City (www.vailresorts.com; $\textcircled{C}$ **435/649-5400**), part of Utah's largest ski area, offers a wide variety of terrain on eight distinct mountains, with an excellent people-moving system to get you to the ski runs quickly and efficiently. In the past few years, intermediate and expert terrains have been greatly expanded. The large beginners' area offers gentle slopes and grand views.

The resort receives an average of 355 inches of snow a year, but also has snowmaking capability. The lift-served vertical drop is 3,190 feet, from a base elevation of 6,800 feet. You're up there. The summit elevation is 9,990 feet. The season usually runs from early December to mid-April, with lifts operating daily from 9am to 4pm.

The resort offers ski and snowboard rentals and a day-care center.

GETTING THERE   The Canyons is on the west side of Utah 224 a few miles south of I-80.

LIFT TICKETS   Again, there are multiple options for lift tickets at Park City Mountain Resort, both at Park City and at Canyons Village. Single day lift tickets for adults are about $110, and 2-day tickets are $216. Multiple packages can be purchased for the whole resort, so shop online for your exact travel/ski needs.

LESSONS & PROGRAMS   The **ski school** (© **877/472-6306**) offers lessons for both skiing and snowboarding. Rates and offerings are the same as those outlined Park City Mountain Resort (above).

WHERE TO STAY & EAT ON THE MOUNTAIN   You'll find a nice range of lodging options at the resort proper, including the **Grand Summit Hotel, Sundial Lodge,** and **Waldorf Astoria Park City.** The ski-season rates range from $340 for a double room at Sundial to $1,758 for a four-bedroom suite at the Waldorf Astoria. Among the ski area's restaurants are the **Red Pine Lodge,** featuring lunches of pizza, fresh grilled entrees, hearty soups, and a salad bar; **Lookout Cabin,** specializing in Rocky Mountain cuisine for lunch and featuring spectacular views from its perch atop Lookout Peak; and the **Farm,** featuring New American cuisine at the foot of the Red Pine Gondola.

More Winter Fun

CROSS-COUNTRY SKIING   **White Pine Nordic Center** (www.white pinetouring.com; © **435/649-6249**) operates Park City's cross-country ski center, with more than 12 miles of groomed trails on the Park City Golf Course on Utah 224, on the north side of town. The center offers rentals, instruction (including skating and telemark lessons), guided tours, and sales and service. The terrain is rated 60% beginner, 20% intermediate, and 20% advanced. Full-day trail passes cost $18 for adults, $10 for kids 6 to 12; children 5 and under and seniors 65 and over ski free. White Pine is usually open from mid-November through March.

SNOWMOBILE & SLEIGH RIDES   Guided snowmobiling tours and sleigh rides are available at the scenic Rockin' R Ranch, east of Park City in Weber Canyon, from **Rocky Mountain Recreation** (www.rockymtnrec.com;

The Olympics Live On

Park City's $100-million **Utah Olympic Park,** 3000 Bear Hollow Dr. (www.utaholymplclegacy.org; © **435/658-4200**), constructed for the 2002 Olympics, has six state-of-the-art ski jumps, a 1,335m bobsled/luge track, a freestyle aerials training and competition hill, a day lodge, a ski museum, and an exhibit on the 2002 games. The **U.S. Ski Team** uses the facility regularly, and it's open year-round for guided and self-guided tours. In summer, daring types can try riding the Extreme Zipline—one of the steepest in the world—or an alpine slide, the first on the continent made of stainless steel. On summer Saturdays, national team members demonstrate freestyle aerials and ski jumping. The Olympic Park also offers piloted bobsled runs and skeleton rides and schedules workshops on freestyle aerials and ski jumping, even for amateurs. Call for schedules and rates. Besides the fees for the assorted activities, admission is free.

© **800/303-7256** or 435/645-7256). A sleigh ride, with dinner, costs about $89 for adults, $79 for children 12 and under. Snowmobile trips range from $109 to $209 for the driver ($25–$60 for a passenger), depending on length.

Warm-Weather Fun In & Around Park City

ALPINE SLIDE In addition to the stainless steel slide at the Utah Olympic Park (see above), a plastic bobsled-like track over a half-mile long is housed at **Park City Mountain Resort** (p. 130). Riders control the speed of their sleds. The resort also has an alpine coaster, ziplines, and other adrenaline-pumping amusements. Visit the resort's website for details.

BALLOONING Call **Park City Balloon Adventures** (www.pcballoon adventures.com; © **800/396-8787** or 435/645-8787) for a bird's-eye view of the mountains. Prices start at $250 per person for a 1-hour flight.

FLY-FISHING Anglers have plenty of opportunities for fishing in the streams in the mountains around Park City, either on their own or with local guides. For tips on where they're biting, as well as equipment and information on guided trips, check with **Jans Mountain Outfitters,** 1600 Park Ave. (www.jans.com; © **435/649-4949**), or **Park City Fly Shop,** 2065 Sidewinder Dr., Prospector Square (www.pcflyshop.com; © **435/645-8382**).

HIKING & MOUNTAIN BIKING With hundreds of miles of trails crisscrossing the mountains around Park City, opportunities abound for hiking and mountain biking. For a short hike with a variety of terrains and good views of both mountains and town, try the 1.5-mile **Sweeny Switchbacks Trail,** accessible from near the base of the town lift.

The 30-mile **Historic Union Pacific Rail Trail State Park** hiking and biking path follows the old Union Pacific railroad bed from Park City to Echo Reservoir. It offers wonderful views of meadows, the volcanic crags of Silver Creek Canyon, the Weber River, Echo Reservoir, and the steep walls of Echo Canyon. You might spot deer, elk, moose, and bald eagles along the trail.

Elevation ranges from 6,900 to 5,280 feet. An end-of-the-trail pickup service is available from **Daytrips** (www.daytrips.com; ✆ **888/649-8294**).

Dirt roads and single-track trails at **Park City** (p. 126) are open to hikers and mountain bikers, who can ride the PayDay chairlift up, and then bike or hike down. Tickets cost $24 for an adult and 21 for a child.

Deer Valley Resort (p. 129) offers more than 50 miles of panoramic trails for both hikers and bikers, with chairlift access in summer ($12–$48, depending on the number of rides and lifts). As you might expect, the terrain is steep and beautiful. **Canyons Village** (p. 132) also has hiking trails and runs the Red Pine Lift during its summer season; tickets are $24 for adults, $21 for kids 5 to 12.

For bike rentals, guided rides and hikes (as well as climbs), and even mountain biking clinics, get in touch with **White Pine Touring Center,** 1790 Bonanza Dr. (www.whitepinetouring.com; ✆ **435/649-8170**). For a good description of area trails, pick up a copy of the free *Park City Hiking & Biking Trail Map* at either visitor center and at sporting-goods shops. The website of the **Mountain Trails Foundation** (www.mountaintrails.org) is another good resource.

HORSEBACK RIDING   Guided trail rides are available from several outfitters in the area. **Rocky Mountain Recreation** (p. 133) operates stables at Park City Mountain Resort, at Deer Valley Resort, 2,300-acre Rockin' R Ranch and Stillman Ranch. It operates daily from late May to late October. Rates start at $66 for adults and $56 for children for a 1-hour ride. Rides with meals and overnight trips are also offered; call for details.

More to See & Do in Park City

Kimball Art Center ★   This highly respected center for visual arts is housed in a historic 1929 building but will be moving to a new space in 2022. Exhibits include classic and contemporary, national and international art, well as works by local artists. This nonprofit community art center also sponsors classes, workshops, and seminars throughout the year. Each summer, on the first weekend in August, it produces the Park City Arts Festival, an outdoor exhibit featuring works by about 200 fine artists, and is open daily leading up to and during the event. Allow about 45 minutes.

1401 Kearns Blvd. www.kimballartcenter.org. ✆ **435/649-8882.** Free admission; donations accepted. Tues–Fri 10am–5pm; Sat–Sun noon–5pm.

Park City Museum   Following a major 2-year expansion and renovation, the museum reopened in fall 2009. The original territorial jail downstairs is a must-see—the dark, tiny cells were state of the art in 1886. The upstairs is a bit more civilized, displaying a stagecoach, 19th-century mining equipment, vintage photographs, and early ski gear. Allow about 1½ hours.

528 Main St. www.parkcityhistory.org. ✆ **435/649-7457.** Admission $12 adults, $10 seniors, $5 children 7–17, free for children 6 and under. Mon–Sat 10am–7pm; Sun noon–6pm. Main St. Trolley.

Shopping

A typical old west mining town street that runs straight up the hill in the middle of town, historic Main Street is becoming less historic all the time. Formerly lined with galleries, boutiques, and an array of local shops, more and more this is becoming another prime space for national brands (Marmot, Gorsuch, lululemon, for example), though there are still a few treasure troves to be found (see below). Take the Main Street Trolley up and down—you won't find a place to park and it's a fairly steep slope. You won't find many bargains on Main Street, but prices aren't too far out of line for a tourist and ski town.

ON MAIN STREET   Get reading material of all kinds at **Dolly's Bookstore,** 510 Main St. (www.dollysbookstore.com; © **435/649-8062**).

The venerable **Burns Cowboy Shop,** at 363 Main (www.burnscowboyshop.com; © **800/453-1281,** ext. 431), specializes in high-end boots and hats for ladies and gents. Several locally owned boutiques offer women's fashion, such as **Cake,** 577 Main St. (© **435/649-1256**); **Flight,** 545 Main St. (© **435/604-0806**); and **Mary Jane's,** 613 Main St. (© **435/645-7463**), which specializing in very cool shoes.

OFF MAIN STREET   **No Place Like Home** (1685 Bonanza Dr., Park City Plaza (© **435/649-9700**), is the place to go for kitchen and home accessories. Choose from glassware, gadgets, gourmet coffee beans, bed and bath items, and lots more.

Park City continues to expand, offering new places to shop just out of town, such as **Newpark Town Center** at 1456 Newpark Blvd. (© **435/658-2695**).

IF YOU MUST   The **Tanger Factory Outlets** is located at 6699 N. Landmark Dr. (www.tangeroutlet.com; © **435/645-7078**). From downtown Park City, take Utah 224 north to I-80, but don't get on; instead, go west on the south frontage road to the mall. Among the best outlet malls around, this place houses more than 60 stores, including Banana Republic, Carter's, Gap, Levi's, Nike, Old Navy, Polo Ralph Lauren, Samsonite, and Tommy Bahama.

Where to Stay

Park City is all about its tourists so there are dozens of places to stay, including nearly all the state's luxury accommodations. Even some of the most luxurious properties, however, lack air-conditioning, but at this elevation—6,900 feet in Park City and higher in the mountains—it's seldom needed—though the hot days are increasing. For skiers interested in renting a condo, check out the offerings online at **www.parkcitylodging.com** or **www.resortproperty management.com.** For central reservations at Deer Valley, call © **800/558-3337.**

Among the franchise properties in Park City are the **Best Western Plus Landmark Inn,** 6560 N. Landmark Dr. (www.bwlandmarkinn.com; © **435/649-7300**), with ski-season rates for two from $233 to $259, and **Hampton Inn and Suites,** 6609 N. Landmark Dr. (www.hamptoninn.com;

A Helping Hand for Room Reservations

Although it's possible to book reservations directly with individual lodges, many people find it more convenient to go the one-stop-shopping route, making all their arrangements directly with one of the resorts. See the contact information earlier in this chapter under "Skiing the Park City Area Resorts."

© **435/645-0900),** with ski-season rates of $198 to $209 double. You can save some money by staying in Kimball Junction and taking the free shuttle into Park City. Try the **Newpark Resort,** 1456 Newpark Blvd. (www.newpark resort.com; *©* **877/649-3600** or 435/649-3600) or **Holiday Inn Express Hotel & Suites,** 1501 W. Ute Blvd. (www.holidayinn.com; *©* **888/465-4329** or 435/658-1600).

Note: Listed rates indicate rack rates for peak seasons, excluding special events. Rates are almost always higher—sometimes dramatically so—during ski season, and rates during Christmas week and the Sundance Film Festival can be absurd. The best bargains are in spring and fall. Pets are not allowed, unless otherwise noted.

DEER VALLEY RESORT

Goldener Hirsch Inn ★★   This château-style inn, the most charming hotel in Deer Valley, combines warm hospitality with European charm reminiscent of the inn's sister hotel in Salzburg, the Hotel Goldener Hirsch. It deviates beautifully from the typical log-and-stone decor of most Park City resorts. Austrian antiques adorn the common areas and walls, and the feeling is echoed in the guest rooms, elegantly furnished with hand-painted, carved Austrian furniture, wood-burning fireplaces, and small private balconies. King-size beds with down comforters, and minibars stocked with snacks and nonalcoholic beverages bring in 21st century comfort. The excellent restaurant is Austrian in decor and features European/New American–inspired fare. In summer, you can dine outdoors on the flower-filled deck.

7570 Royal St. E., Silver Lake Village. www.goldenerhirschinn.com. *©* **435/649-7770.** $650 and up. **Amenities:** Restaurant; free Wi-Fi.

Montage Deer Valley ★★★   New in 2010, the monumental Montage Deer Valley (the first outside Southern California) is banked into the mountainside like a fortress. The views are staggering: You can see all the way to Wyoming from many rooms and from the terrace where they saber a bottle of champagne every day at sunset. Interiors are likewise impressive, featuring art of local flora and fauna (including several original Remingtons) and superlative furnishings and decor. The bedding is plush and marshmallow-soft; the bathrooms have soaking tubs and rain shower heads. The facilities are also a cut above, from Utah's largest spa (35,000 sq. ft.!) to the kid's art program to the zinc bar in the lounge. The incredible game room features a commercial Wii installation, pool tables, foosball tables, bowling lanes, and vintage arcade games. This is a true ski-in, ski-out experience: There are three lifts right out the door.

9100 Marsac Ave. www.montagedeervalley.com. © **435/604-1300.** 220 units, including 66 suites and residences. Rates range from $400 double to $1,890 3-bedroom residence. Check the website for specials. **Amenities:** 4 restaurants; concierge; exercise room; 3 outdoor and 3 indoor Jacuzzis; outdoor heated pool; room service; sauna; spa, Wi-Fi ($15/day).

Stein Eriksen Lodge ★★★ Opened in 1982 under the direction of Stein Eriksen, the Norwegian 1952 Olympic gold medalist, this standout hotel retains both the striking decor and the intimate charm of Eriksen's original plan. It's considered the "classiest" resort in Park City. The lobby has a magnificent three-story stone fireplace fronted by an elegant seating area. The main lodge has 13 rooms, with the remaining units in nearby buildings. The connecting sidewalks are heated, and the grounds are beautifully landscaped. Spacious deluxe rooms contain one king- or two queen-size beds, a whirlpool tub, and solid wood furniture; suites have full kitchens. Each of the three large mountain chalet–style townhouse suites has a stone fireplace, full kitchen with service for eight, and private deck. The lodge has two dining venues: the famed **Glitretind Restaurant** (reviewed below), serving three meals daily, and the more casual Troll Hallen Lounge. The **Chateaux Deer Valley** (www. the-chateaux.com; © **435/658-9500**), a full-service less-expensive condo property in Silver Lake Village (with rates starting at $149), is under the same management.

Stein Way. www.steinlodge.com. © **800/453-1302** or 435/649-3700. 180 units. $355–$1,100 double. **Amenities:** 2 restaurants; babysitting; concierge; exercise room; outdoor Jacuzzi; outdoor heated pool; room service; sauna; spa; free Wi-Fi.

PARK CITY

Chateau Après Lodge For budget-minded travelers this lodge is a good option close to the slopes—150 yards away, to be exact. It looks like a Swiss Alps–style lodge from the outside—simple but attractive—and has a large central fireplace in the lobby. Rooms include a queen, double, or single bed, plus a private shower-only bathroom. The single-sex dorms have a shared bathroom and start at $40. The entire facility is nonsmoking.

1299 Norfolk Ave. www.chateauapres.com. © **435/649-9372.** 32 units. $40 dorm room; $150 and up private room. Rates include continental breakfast. **Amenities:** Free Wi-Fi.

Hotel Park City ★★★ Drawing inspiration from the grand lodges of the national park system, the designers of Hotel Park City made sure all the Western-style rooms have sublime mountain views. Half of the suites are in the main lodge, with the rest located on the Park City Golf Course (the clubhouse is in the hotel and becomes a cross-country center come winter). Rooms feature king-size beds, two TVs, kitchenettes, and washers and dryers; the luxurious bathrooms have big jetted tubs and separate three-head showers. The on-site spa is top-rate and the central courtyard boasts a year-round pool.

The Silver Star lift to Park City Mountain Resort is easily accessible from the hotel.

2001 Park Ave. www.hotelparkcity.com. ℭ **435/200-2000**. 100 suites. Winter $399–$3,000 double; summer $179–$1,500 double. **Amenities:** Restaurant; lounge; concierge; outdoor Jacuzzi; outdoor heated pool; room service; sauna; spa; free Wi-Fi.

Main & Sky ★★★ This LEED-certified hotel and residence offers posh contemporary style. Located in a historic spot just off Main Street, the hotel exudes outstanding attention to detail in everything from the timbers recycled from a trestle over Salt Lake to the underwater surround sound in the lap pool to the bathroom doors, which are fitted with copper weavings made in Africa to help fund AIDS research. Most units in this all-suite hotel feature a deck and a hot tub; some add a billiards table and/or gas fireplace. The penthouse suites are spectacular—this is one of the only luxury hotels right on Main Street so besides the mountain views, you have excellent people-watching. The Sugati wellness spa uses holistic treatments reflecting Eastern and Western traditions.

201 Heber Ave. www.skyparkcity.com. ℭ **435/658-2500**. Winter $325–$1,999 for 1- to 3-bedroom units, $1,500–$3,000 penthouse suite; lower rates spring–fall. **Amenities:** 2 lounges; concierge; outdoor Jacuzzi; small indoor lap pool; spa; free Wi-Fi.

Treasure Mountain Inn ★ A Park City original, built in 1963 when the ski industry was just beginning, the renewed Treasure Mountain Inn has won accolades as Park City's most environmentally conscious lodging (thanks to its green supplies, recycling program, and salt-based hot tub). Contemporary studios and one- and two-bedroom condominium units feature flatscreen TVs, iPod docking stations, full kitchens, and a king-size bed or two queens. The courtyard is especially attractive, centered on the hot tub with a faux waterfall.

255 Main St. www.treasuremountaininn.com. ℭ **800/344-2460** or 435/655-4501. $379 double in season; from $139 off-season 2-night minimum stay in winter. **Amenities:** Outdoor Jacuzzi; fitness center; free Wi-Fi.

Washington School House ★★★ Nestled against the Wasatch Mountains, this 1889 limestone schoolhouse turned inn has been reborn as a boutique hotel. The exterior has been faithfully restored to its late-19th-century appearance, but the interior was gutted and reinvented with a classic feel rarely found in Park City. Rooms are decorated with antiques and reproductions, as well as modern American art. Facilities include ski storage and heated pool and Jacuzzi.

543 Park Ave. www.washingtonschoolhouse.com. ℭ **435/649-3800**. 12 units. Winter rates $500–$700 double; $1,000–$6,100 suite; lower rates spring to fall. Rates include full breakfast. **Amenities:** Outdoor heated pool and Jacuzzi; ski storage; free Wi-Fi.

Where to Eat

Park City is well known for its restaurants, though they're not all on Main Street. Several menu guides are available free at the visitor centers. Check the

"Park Record" for information and coupons for two-for-one entrées at some restaurants, and especially in the off-season. For coffee, baked goods, and Internet access, try **Park City Coffee Roaster,** 1764 Uinta Way (www. pcroaster.com; ℂ **435/647-9097**). **El Chubasco,** 1890 Bonanza Dr. (www. elchubascopc.info; ℂ **435/645-9114**), is beloved by local mountain bikers and ski bums—and everyone—for its great Mexican food and one of the best salsa bars in Utah. Modern **Vinto Pizzeria,** 900 Main St. (www.vinto.com; ℂ **435/615-9990**), is family-friendly and serves wood-fired pies and great gelato. Another local favorite, **Good Karma,** 1782 Prospector Ave. (www. goodkarmarestaurants.com; ℂ **435/658-0958**), offers Indo-Persian cuisine and American breakfasts.

Note that hours may change in the off season, so call ahead to confirm opening times.

Cafe Terigo ★ EUROPEAN/CONTINENTAL   This upscale eatery is a good choice when you want innovative cuisine in a classy atmosphere. In fine weather, you can eat outdoors; otherwise, dine in the simple European-style cafe, wit fresh flowers on the tables and wrought-iron chandeliers overhead. The lunch menu offers burgers and a variety of sandwiches, such as a grilled vegetable sandwich with sweet onions, zucchini, mushrooms, roasted red peppers, and provolone cheese on homemade focaccia. Dinner involves such main courses as herb-encrusted Utah rainbow trout; beef tenderloin with gorgonzola polenta, shiitake mushrooms, and red chard; and almond-crusted salmon, served with green beans and a shallot salad. A variety of pastas and pizzas (with toppings such as shrimp and artichoke hearts) are also available, not to mention a delectable bread pudding for dessert. The cafe sells espresso and has full liquor service.

424 Main St. www.cafeterigo.com. ℂ **435/645-9555.** Main courses $11–$15 lunch, $16–$29 dinner. Daily 11:30am–2:30pm and 5:30–10pm. Closed Sun spring and fall. Main St. Trolley.

The Eating Establishment ★ AMERICAN   Probably the oldest continuously operating restaurant on Park City's historic Main Street, the Eating Establishment is casual and comfortable and a solid choice for families or anyone who wants a Utah-size serving of comfort food at a reasonable price. The dining room and enclosed courtyard have a southwestern feel. The extensive menu famously features breakfast until 3:30pm. Lunch choices include charbroiled burgers, fish and chips, salads, sandwiches, and barbecued pork, beef, or chicken. Dinners feature salads, excellent barbecued baby back ribs, certified Kansas City Angus strip steak, several pasta selections, and fresh seafood specials. Desserts, such as the mud pie and New York–style cheesecake, are made in-house. Full liquor service is available.

317 Main St. www.theeatingestablishment.net. ℂ **435/649-8284.** Main courses $7–$14 breakfast and lunch, $9–$23 dinner. Sun–Thurs 8am–9pm, Fri–Sat 8am–10pm. Main St. Trolley.

Glitretind Restaurant ★★★ REGIONAL AMERICAN   Located in the elegant Stein Eriksen Lodge, this equally stylish restaurant is a top pick for fine dining. Chef Zane Holmquist serves innovative, seasonal, impeccably presented meals in a charming and airy dining room with views of the spectacular Wasatch Mountains. Breakfast offerings include French toast, pancakes, a fruit plate, and omelets; for lunch choose a soup, salad, sandwich, or full meal. At lunch and dinner, Stein's Wild Game Chili, with wild boar, buffalo, and elk, is a stalwart, but influences range from Asian (salmon with pickled beet noodles, cucumber, and Thai basil-cucumber sauce) to American (Double D Ranch filet of beef, grilled fingerling potatoes and baby tomatoes with basil and white balsamic.) Vegetarian options are available. The restaurant has an excellent wine list and also offers full liquor service.

Stein Eriksen Lodge (p. 138), Deer Valley. ⓒ **435/645-6455.** www.steinlodge.com. Reservations requested. Main courses $12–$20 breakfast, $14–$22 lunch, $29–$50 dinner. Daily 7am–10pm (dinner served 6–9pm); Sun jazz brunch 11am–2:30pm. Bus: Deer Valley Loop.

Handle ★★★ NEW AMERICAN   Chef-owner Briar Handly has made his name—he's twice been named a James Beard award semi-finalist. Handley, along with his wife, Melissa Gray, and partners have created a modern, casually elegant restaurant at the top of Heber Avenue. The menu specializes in small plates with big flavor such as the biscuit slider with pulled pork, slaw, pickled red onion, and chipotle brown sugar or green gazpacho with blue crab. Famous dishes include Handly's fried chicken breast, served with changing sides, and General Tso cauliflower. Be prepared to be surprised. Full liquor service.

136 Heber Ave. www.handleparkcity.com. ⓒ **435/502-1155.** Plates run $3–$38, except the 25-oz. $70 prime ribeye. Sun–Thurs 5:30– 9pm; Fri–Sat 5:30–10pm.

High West Distillery ★★ NEW AMERICAN   This was Utah's first new distillery since the Church of Latter-day Saints shuttered a few church-owned stills a century ago. With a rollicking barroom and more refined dining areas in an attached historic house, the space is a converted livery (1907) that served as a garage for most of the 20th century. Both the design and the whiskey at High West have won numerous awards. Reimagined as an eatery, it's one of the most charming spaces in Park City and one of the tastiest, though be aware it's an over-21 facility. Tour the distillery, order one of the original cocktails, and dig into gourmet mac and cheese, bacon-wrapped shrimp, and bourbon-bacon-cashew-caramel popcorn for a start. Mains are designed to match with whiskey, not wine (though wine is available.) Grilled Tomahawk pork chop, pan-fried trout, and steak are standouts. Distillery tours are free, and a flight of whiskey will run $18.

703 Park Ave. www.highwest.com. ⓒ **435/649-8300.** Reservations recommended. Small plates $8–$13; large plates $14–$55. Daily 11am–9pm.

Purple Sage ★★ AMERICAN   Serving what they call "American Western cuisine," this upscale dinner restaurant is owned and operated by the same people who do such a great job at nearby Cafe Terigo (above). The atmosphere could be described as "refined casual Western," and the menu offers innovative and sometimes fascinating variations on American favorites. Buffalo short ribs, corn-battered Utah trout, and fried chicken with mashers and bacon-pepper gravy are highly recommended. Full liquor service.

434 Main St. www.purplesageparkcity.com. © **435/655-9505.** Main courses $18–$29 dinner. Sun–Thurs 5:30–9:30pm. Fri–Sat 5:30–10pm. Main St. Trolley.

350 Main ★★ CONTEMPORARY GLOBAL   A rich, romantic setting for an excellent meal, 350 Main is one of Park City's most reliable eateries. That's not to say it isn't creative— preparations are adventurous and bold, dabbling in French and Asian traditions while coming up with distinct and bold flavors. Utilizing primarily local, organic, and antioxidant-rich ingredients; many items on the menu are gluten-free. The main courses run the gamut from a grilled 16oz. pork chop with white bean cassoulet to Brazilian *pao de queijo*. Goat and elk are also on the menu—this is a place to eat adventurously, but there are familiar dishes as well. Full liquor service (including a wine list beloved by "Wine Spectator") is available.

350 Main St. www.350main.com. © **435/649-3140.** Reservations recommended. Main courses $23–$40. Daily 5:30–10pm. Main St. Trolley.

Tupelo ★★★ SOUTHERN/AMERICAN   Despite the Deep South name, Executive Chef/owner Matt Harris cooks globally inspired food, artisanally (and locally) sourced, and stunningly prepared. There is a Southern slant in many dishes, however—from Harris' own Southern roots and influences from his mentor, renowned Atlanta chef Kevin Rathbun. The buttermilk biscuits, as one would expect, are extraordinary and there are other homey dishes elevated by the kitchen: deviled eggs with crème fraîche and country ham, for instance, or roasted bass with corn chowder, smoked andouille sausage, and marble potatoes. But not all his dishes reflect his roots. Rigatoni is served carbonara style with proper prosciutto and Parmesan and a local egg. Lunch is served only in winter, but Sunday brunch is served all year long.

508 Main St. www.tupeloparkcity.com. © **435/615-7700.** Dinner main courses $26–$38. Dinner daily (winter) from 5:30; off-season (Wed–Sat only) 5:30–9:30pm. Sun brunch (year-round) 11am–2pm. Main St. Trolley.

Wasatch Brew Pub ★ AMERICAN   Views of the brewing area and Main Street dominate the scene in this popular brewpub, the first in Utah back in 1988, which courts controversy with such beers as Polygamy Porter (tag line: "Why have just one?"). Beyond the liquid refreshments, you can get well-prepared pub grub for lunch or dinner, including fish and chips, burgers, pulled pork sliders, various pizzas, and a mean pastrami Reuben melt.

250 Main St. www.wasatchbeers.com. © **435/649-0900.** Reservations not accepted. Main courses $10–$18. Mon–Fri 11am–10pm; Sat–Sun 10am–10pm; Sun brunch 11am–2pm. Main St. Trolley.

Movies, Music & More in the Mountains: Sundance & the Performing Arts

For 10 days every January, the Hollywood glitterati and the paparazzi who trail them descend on Park City in droves for the star-studded **Sundance Film Festival** ★★★ (www.sundance.org/festival; ✆ **435/776-7878**). The slate includes cutting-edge indies as well as blockbuster premieres, and the event has grown into the top festival of its kind in the country. There are screenings in Park City as well as Sundance Resort, Kimball Junction, Salt Lake City, and even Ogden. (*Skiers note:* Festival time is actually a great time to hit the slopes, as everyone else is jammed like sardines into the theaters or thronging Main Street looking for celebrities.) The festival is so popular now (and, yes, mainstream) that tickets can be difficult and expensive to score. Attending the festival requires considerable advance planning. Tickets go on sale (and sell out) during a slim window of time at the end of October, although a handful of tickets are made available the day of a screening, and more comprehensive packages go on sale in September. Go online or call the film festival for details.

Also during festival time—and easier to get tickets for—the **Slamdance Film Festival** (www.slamdance.com) focuses on emerging artists and low-budget independent films, like Sundance did originally. Visit the website for details and schedules. Also, and under the official Sundance program, **New Frontier** features avant-garde and experimental films; check the Sundance website for details.

Throughout the summer, **concerts** are presented at a variety of venues around Park City. Past **Sundance films** are screened for free in City Park on summer Thursday nights. The **Park City Film Series** (www.parkcityfilm series.com) screens independent movies at the Park City Library for $8; there are also free screenings and a package price for the series.

The **Deer Valley Music Festival** ★★ (www.deervalleymusicfestival.org; ✆ **801/533-66833**) is the summer home of the Utah Symphony and takes place in July and August. The program includes classical masterpieces like Tchaikovsky's *1812 Overture,* plus jazz and popular works by composers such as Gilbert and Sullivan and John Philip Sousa. There are also concerts by pop acts of all stripes. The stage faces the mountainside; bring a chair or blanket and relax under the stars. Call the box office for schedule and ticket information.

The 1,300-seat **George S. and Dolores Doré Eccles Center for the Performing Arts,** 1750 Kearns Blvd., and the outdoor **Snow Park Amphitheatre** at Deer Valley (www.ecclescenter.org; ✆ **435/655-3114**), present a wide variety of top national arts acts. Recent productions and concerts have included Willie Nelson, Joss Stone, Trisha Yearwood, and the New Chinese Acrobats.

The **Historic Egyptian Theatre,** 328 Main St. (www.egyptiantheatrecom pany.org; ✆ **435/649-9371**), was built in 1926 in the popular Egyptian Revival style. Originally used for vaudeville and silent films, this was the first theater in Park City to offer the "new talking pictures." Today, the Egyptian is the home of the Egyptian Theatre Company, which presents an array of dramas, comedies, musicals, and other productions throughout the year, along with popular musicians and lecturers.

7 | Park City After Dark: The Club Scene

Park City has some of the best nightlife in a state not known for it. Most venues are busiest during ski season, and generally have fewer nights of live music at other times.

The **Spur Bar & Grill,** 350½ Main St. (www.thespurbarandgrill.com; ✆ **435/615-1618**), is a contemporary Western joint that has regular live music and is open until 1am. **O'Shucks,** 427 Main St. (✆ **435/645-3999**), is one of those low-key places where beers are available in 32-ounce schooners and you can chuck your peanut shells on the floor. The burgers are pretty good, too. "Helping people forget their name since 1903," the **No Name Saloon** at 447 Main St. (www.nonamesaloon.net; ✆ **435/649-6667**) is another fun place to drink, an old redbrick with lots of TVs, a constant crowd, and a nice rooftop patio. An outlaw bar with craft cocktails and live music downstairs on Main Street, **O. P. Rockwell** is named after Brigham Young's "Avenging Angel" pal, Porter Rockwell. It's at 268 Main St. (✆ **435/565-4486**); open daily from 5pm to 1am.

AN HISTORIC RAILROAD, FRESHWATER PLAYGROUNDS & SOME GREAT STATE PARKS

It doesn't snow all the time in the southern Wasatch Front—when warm weather finally arrives, the area becomes a whole new kind of playground. The wonderful lakes and parks near Park City become more and more popular by the year. To the northeast is **Rockport State Park,** a man-made lake that attracts watersports enthusiasts, from swimmers to ice-fishermen, year-round. Not far from Park City is **Jordanelle State Park,** a great boating lake, and **Wasatch Mountain State Park,** which is Utah's second-largest state park and a major golf destination. Heading southeast from Park City, you'll reach **Heber City,** whose main claim to fame is its historic steam train. A bit farther afield along U.S. 40 is pristine Strawberry Reservoir, a favorite water playground.

Heber Valley Railroad

Those who love old trains, who want to see firsthand some of the history of the American West, or who simply enjoy beautiful scenery, should go for a ride on the **Heber Valley Railroad ★★**. This 100-year-old excursion train provides an exciting step back into the past, while also offering a fun ride through a delightful diversity of landscapes. Excursions ranging from 1½ to 3 hours are offered on both steam and vintage diesel trains, and a number of special-event trips are scheduled, including murder mysteries, sunset excursions, and the "Polar Express" Christmas trip. Train cars have restrooms, snack bars, and souvenir shops.

The views along the shores of Deer Creek Lake and through beautiful Provo Canyon are wonderful at any time, but fall is one of the prettiest seasons to ride the train, when the mountainsides show the rich hues of changing leaves.

The train depot is in Heber City, 20 miles south of Park City via Utah 248 and U.S. 40. Round-trip tickets cost $15 to $30 for ages 13 and up, and $16 to $20 for children 3 to 12. Rates are higher for special events and meal and entertainment excursions; one-way tickets are also available (call for rates). There are combination rafting and horseback riding train expeditions, Star Wars–themed rides and a trip that ends with a zipline ride. The ticket office is open daily from 9am to 5pm. For information, contact **Heber Valley Railroad,** 450 S. 600 West, Heber City (www.hebervalleyrr.org; 🕾 **435/654-5601** or 801/581-9980 from Salt Lake City).

Rockport State Park

Rockport, one of the Utah State Park system's man-made lakes, is a great destination offering a full range of outdoor activities, from windsurfing to wildlife watching. In the winter, add ice fishing and cross-country skiing. Facilities at the half-mile-wide, 3-mile-long lake include a marina, a boat ramp and courtesy docks, a picnic area, and camping spots in a variety of settings. The Wanship Dam, at the north end of the lake, is an important water-storage and flood-control dam on the Weber River, which has its headwaters high in the Uinta Mountains.

ESSENTIALS
GETTING THERE From Park City, head east on I-80 for about 11 miles to exit 156, then go 5 miles south on Utah 32 along the western bank of Rockport Lake to the access road. The park entrance is at the lake's southern tip. Turn east to the park entrance, and then follow the road around to the north along the eastern bank.

INFORMATION, FEES & REGULATIONS Contact **Rockport State Park,** 9040 N. Utah 302 (www.stateparks.utah.gov; 🕾 **435/336-2241**). Open year-round, the park has a day-use fee of $12 per vehicle. Pets are allowed, but must be confined or leashed.

OUTDOOR PURSUITS
CROSS-COUNTRY SKIING Groomed cross-country ski trails run through the open sagebrush, and these offer a better chance of seeing wildlife than the more forested areas in the surrounding national forest.

HIKING & WILDLIFE-WATCHING A 4-mile round-trip hike takes off from Juniper Campground. This easy, relatively flat walk among juniper and sagebrush, offers an opportunity to glimpse mule deer, yellow-belly marmots, badgers, raccoons, weasels, skunks, and ground squirrels. Less visible are elk, moose, coyotes, bobcats, and cougars. Birds abound, and sometimes you can spot Western grebes, Canada geese, whistling swans, great blue herons, and golden and bald eagles. More frequently seen are ducks, red-tailed hawks, magpies, scrub jays, and hummingbirds.

WATER ACTIVITIES The day-use area, located about 3½ miles north of the park entrance, offers the best swimming. The lake is also popular for boating, windsurfing, water-skiing, sailing, kayaking, and fishing. Both the lake and river are home to rainbow and brown trout, yellow perch, and smallmouth bass. Unfortunately, there are no equipment outfitters nearby.

CAMPING A number of RV and tent campsites are located in five areas around the lake. The first campground is to the right of the access road, along the Weber River rather than the lake. Sites are shady and provide easy access to a trail along the river, handy for fishermen. The remainder of the sites lies between the road and the lake, along its eastern bank, and most have vault toilets only. One campground, Juniper, has sites with water and electric hookups, a dump station, and modern restrooms. Sites cost $15 to $30; yurts are $80; cabins are $90, and solar-powered glamping tents, with fireplaces and fairly luxurious beds, are $85. The park generally fills on weekends, but reservations can be made through the state parks' website (www.stateparks.utah. gov) or by calling ✆ **800/322-3770.**

Jordanelle State Park ★★

Two recreation areas provide access to **Jordanelle Reservoir** in the beautiful Wasatch Mountains. Both areas are great for boating, fishing, picnicking, and camping. The reservoir is shaped rather like a boomerang, with the dam at the elbow. The Perimeter Trail connects the highly developed **Hailstone Recreation Site** to the more primitive **Rock Cliff Recreation Site.** Hailstone is on the terraced peninsula poking into the upper arm just above the dam; Rock Cliff is at the southeastern tip of the lower arm of the reservoir. Hailstone's camping and picnicking areas face the widest part of the reservoir, which is perfect for speedboats, water-skiing, and personal watercraft. The narrow arm reaching down to Rock Cliff is designated for low-speed water use. Trails circle the reservoir and connect to other area trails. They're open to hikers, mountain bikers, horseback riders, and cross-country skiers.

ESSENTIALS

GETTING THERE To get to Hailstone from Park City, head east on Kearns Boulevard (Utah 248) for about 3¾ miles; at U.S. 40, go southeast 4 miles to exit 8 and follow the entrance road east into Hailstone. From Heber City, take U.S. 40 northwest about 6 miles.

For Rock Cliff, from Park City, continue southeast on U.S. 40 past Hailstone for about 2 miles to Utah 32, then east about 6 miles to the entrance. From Heber City, follow U.S. 40 northwest for about 4 miles, then head east onto Utah 32 for about 6 miles to the entrance.

INFORMATION, FEES & REGULATIONS Contact **Jordanelle State Park** (https://stateparks.utah.gov/parks/jordanelle; ✆ **435/649-9540** for

Hailstone or **435/782-3030** for Rock Cliff) for their rather complicated open hours, and stop at the **visitor center** at Hailstone or the **Nature Center** at Rock Cliff, a nature-oriented visitor center, for information and trail maps. The exhibit room in the visitor center at Hailstone presents an overview of human history in the area.

Note: In order to protect the abundance of wildlife, particularly birds, pets are not allowed at Rock Cliff. They're welcome at Hailstone, but must be confined or leashed. Bicycling is permitted on established public roads, in parking areas, and on the Perimeter Trail.

HAILSTONE RECREATION SITE

Hailstone has three camping areas—a total of 200 sites—and a group pavilion, along with a swimming beach and a picnic area available for day use. The 76-slip marina offers camping, picnicking supplies, boat rentals, a small restaurant, an amphitheater, boat ramps, a wheelchair-accessible fishing deck, and a fish-cleaning station.

OUTDOOR PURSUITS A concessionaire at **Jordanelle Marina** (www. jordanellemarina.com; ☏ **435/655-9919**) rents ski boats, jet skis, and fishing boats.

CAMPING Hailstone's three camping areas have walk-in tent sites, RV/ tent sites without hookups, and RV sites with water and electric hookups. Facilities include modern restrooms, showers, a small coin-op laundry, and a playground. Cost is $16 to $25 to camp; $10 for day use. For reservations, log onto the Utah State Parks' website (www.stateparks.utah.gov) or call ☏ **800/322-3770.**

ROCK CLIFF RECREATION SITE

Rock Cliff contains three walk-in camping areas; picnic tables; the **Nature Center,** which offers maps, environmental programs, and exhibits on the various habitats of the area and how man's activities impact them; and the **Jordanelle Discovery Trail,** a boardwalk interpretive trail that winds through the Provo River riparian terrain.

BIRDING **Rock Cliff** offers great opportunities for **birding ★**, with more than 160 species either living here or passing through, and eagles and other raptors nesting in the area. Situated as it is among numerous riparian wetlands, Rock Cliff is designed to protect these sensitive habitats. Trails and boardwalks traverse the area, and bridges cross the waterways at four points, enabling you to get quite close to a variety of wetland life without inadvertently doing any harm to their habitats.

CAMPING The recreation area has three walk-in campgrounds with a total of 50 sites and two modern restrooms with showers. These sites are more nature-oriented than those at Hailstone and are scattered over 100 acres, providing great privacy. Cost is $16. The site doesn't have any areas for RVs. For reservations, call ☏ **800/322-3770** or log on to the Utah State Parks' website, **www.stateparks.utah.gov**.

Wasatch Mountain State Park

Wasatch mountain state park is Utah's most developed state park, and among its most popular. This year-round destination is well maintained and well serviced, though it's not exactly a wilderness experience. There are four very popular 18-hole golf courses, for example, the lake and mountain courses at Wasatch mountain, and Soldier Hollow. Trails are continually being expanded to meet the demands of hikers and mountain bikers. In winter, a network of groomed cross-country skiing and snowmobiling trails lead from the park into the surrounding forest, and both cross-country-ski and snowmobile rentals are available. Wasatch Mountain's rangers offer a variety of instructive and interpretive programs. Fall is the best time to visit: the incomparable juxtaposition of rich reds, ochers, and deep evergreens will exceed your expectations.

ESSENTIALS

GETTING THERE It's about 5½ miles from Heber City to the park: From downtown, turn west on Utah 113 (100 South) to Midway; following signs for the state park, jog north on 200 West, then west on 200 North, and finally north again on Homestead Drive. The visitor center is located on Homestead Drive (where it becomes Snake Creek Rd.), in the park.

INFORMATION/VISITOR CENTER For advance information, contact **Wasatch Mountain State Park** (www.stateparks.utah.gov; ℂ **435/654-1791**). The visitor center, on Homestead Drive (where it becomes Snake Creek Rd.), also serves as a lounge for golfers. It's open daily from 8am to 5pm and includes a large mountain-lodge-style room with comfortable seating. Rangers are on hand to discuss park activities and provide trail maps and other information.

FEES & REGULATIONS The day-use fee is $7 per vehicle. Pets are welcome in the park, but must be confined or leashed.

RANGER PROGRAMS Interpretive programs take place most Friday and Saturday summer nights at the amphitheater, and a junior ranger program is offered Saturday mornings. The stocked pond adjacent to the visitor center provides fishing fun for children 15 and under in summer; call for details.

OUTDOOR PURSUITS

CROSS-COUNTRY SKIING A 7½-mile Nordic ski track, with both diagonal stride and skating lanes, is laid out on the golf course in winter. Neither dogs nor snowmobiles are allowed on the track, which is open from 8am to 5pm. At the southern end of the park, **Soldier Hollow** (www.soldierhollow.com; ℂ **435/654-2002**) was the 2002 Olympics site for biathlon and cross-country-skiing competitions, and its open for cross-country skiing, snowshoeing, tubing, and other nonmotorized winter sports; in summer, mountain biking and horseback riding are popular. Day passes are $10 for ages 13 and up, $5 for kids 12 and under. Rent equipment at the **Rossignol Demo Center** (ℂ **435/709-3469**).

GOLF With the USGA-sanctioned 36-hole, par-143 **Lake** and **Mountain** courses, golfing is the most popular pastime here. Ten lakes are scattered throughout the tree-lined fairways, and the views of the lovely Heber Valley are grand. Another 36 holes (the Gold and Silver courses) are at the **Soldier Hollow Golf Course** at the southern end of the park. Facilities include a full-service pro shop, driving range, practice greens, and a cafe. Fees for adults are $45 to $50 for 18 holes with lower fees for juniors and seniors, twilight, shoulder season and late times. Contact the course (www.soldierhollowgolf. com; ✆ **435/654-7442**) for details and tee times (reserve up to a week in advance).

HIKING & WILDLIFE-WATCHING **Pine Creek Nature Trail** is just over a mile in length and encompasses three smaller loops. Many songbirds make their homes in the trees along the trail, so watch for Steller's jays, chickadees, wrens, robins, and Western tanagers. You might also see the tracks of mule deer along the creek, where they come to forage. From the large parking area in Pine Creek campground, follow the half-mile trail to the Pine Creek trailhead, which lies just north of the Oak Hollow loop. The trail begins at an elevation of 6,100 feet and climbs 220 feet, crossing Pine Creek four times and traversing several boulder ridges. The trail guide describes some of the plants you'll see on this hike. Don't attempt the trail after a rain, as it becomes quite muddy and slick. No bikes or motorized vehicles are allowed. Be sure to take water, a sun hat, and binoculars. Literature describing the plant and animal life of the park is available at the camp manager's office near the entrance to the campground and at the visitor center.

MOUNTAIN BIKING An 18-mile loop affords great fun for mountain bikes. The road leaves the visitor center and heads west, winding through magnificent wooded country and offering occasional breathtaking views of the valley.

SNOWMOBILING The park's 90 miles of groomed trails, very popular among snowmobilers, take you into Pine Creek, Snake Creek, and American Fork canyons. Warming stations are located at the clubhouse and visitor center.

CAMPING Four camping loops in the **Pine Creek Campground** provide a total of 139 sites, including about 80 that are off-limits to tenters. All have modern restrooms, and all except Little Deer Creek, the smallest loop, have showers. Some sites are nestled among trees and are quite shady; others are more open. All except Little Deer Creek have paved parking pads, water, electricity, picnic tables, and barbecue grills; some also have sewer hookups. A dump station is located near the entrance to the campground. Camping fees are $15. Reservations are advised and can be made by calling ✆ **800/322-3770,** or through the state parks website (www.stateparks.utah.gov).

An Historic Railroad

Strawberry Reservoir ★★

Located along U.S. 40 in the eastern portion of the Uinta National Forest, the jewel-like Strawberry Reservoir is a terrific water playground offering amazing fishing, as well as boating, hiking, and mountain biking. It's also great for cross-country skiing, ice-fishing, and snowmobiling in winter.

Utah's premier trout fishery—indeed, one of the premier trout fisheries in the West—Strawberry Reservoir is home to huge cutthroat and rainbow trout and kokanee salmon, so it's no surprise that fishing is the number-one draw. Fishing boats with outboard motors are available at **Strawberry Bay Marina** (www.strawberrybay.com; ℂ **435/548-2261**); call for current rates.

Strawberry Reservoir has four marinas, with the largest at Strawberry Bay. This is the only one that provides year-round services, including a restaurant and lodging at **Strawberry Bay Lodge** (www.strawberrybay.com; ℂ **435/548-2261**), with rooms for $80 for one full-size bed to $320 for a suite with four queens; the others offer limited services.

Campgrounds are located at each of the four marinas on the reservoir. Sites in the Strawberry Bay campgrounds have hookups; Soldier Creek, Aspen Grove, and Renegade do not. The fee is $20 per vehicle. Boat ramps and fish-cleaning facilities are located adjacent to each campground. Reservations can be made for a limited number of designated campsites in summer through the **National Recreation Reservation Service** (www.recreation.gov; ℂ **877/444-6777**).

To get to Strawberry Reservoir from Heber City, drive 22 miles southeast on U.S. 40 and turn south onto the access road. After about a half-mile, you'll come to the USFS visitor center for Strawberry Reservoir.

For information, contact the **Heber-Kamas Ranger District** (www.fs.fed.us/r4/uwc; ℂ **435/654-0470**), or stop by the **Strawberry Visitor Center** (ℂ **435/548-2321**). Day use is free in some parts of the complex, but there's a $5 fee in most areas.

WHERE TO STAY & EAT

Heber City has a number of motels and inns, including **Holiday Inn Express,** 1268 S. Main St. (www.hiexpress.com; ℂ **435/654-9990**), with rates from $89 to $129 for two people. The Swiss-themed **Zermatt Resort & Spa,** 784 W. Resort Dr., Midway (www.zermattresort.com; ℂ **866/643-2015**), targets the convention crowd but has terrific facilities for weekend visitors. Rates start around $172 for a double room and go north of $1,000 a night for three-bedroom suites. The **Homestead Resort,** 700 N. Homestead Dr., Midway (www.homesteadresort.com; ℂ **888/327-7220**), has a wide variety of options (doubles are typically $149–$199 and suites, condos, and cottages are $250 and up) in myriad buildings on a golf course, as well as the 55-foot volcanic Homestead Crater, its interior developed for soaking, diving, or snorkeling in the 90°F (32°C) water. Combined crater and room rates are available.

In downtown Midway, the **Café Galleria,** 101 W. Main St. (www.cafegalleriapizza.com; ℂ **435/657-2002**), serves wood-fired pizza, bagel sandwiches, and salads. Home to a terrific model railway, the classic 50s **Dairy Keen,** 199 S. Main St., Heber City (𝒞 **435/654-5336**), is a good bet for families, focusing on juicy burgers and thick milkshakes.

Blue Boar Inn ★★★ Winner of the prestigious Utah's "Best of State" award in the B&B category every year it's been given, the Blue Boar Inn is tucked into an upscale neighborhood under the beautiful mountain vista of Wasatch Mountain State Park. Owned by Adobe Systems founder John Warnock, this is a special property, with a dozen attractive and plush guest rooms named for poets and authors. All of the rooms have their own unique charms, from the elephant-embroidered pillows in the Rudyard Kipling room to the leather sleigh bed in the Charles Dickens; the William Shakespeare room is very European with a rococo hand-carved king-size bed from Italy. Each room has a fireplace and a jetted tub. Named for a watering hole in Robin Hood lore, the Blue Boar Inn is also home to one of the region's best restaurants, with contemporary chef Eric May's Continental menu that's heavy on fresh seafood (main courses typically $30–$40) and has a superlative 3,000-bottle wine cellar. Through the entire property, every detail, from the fascinating antiques (including 600-year-old crossbows) to the impeccable landscaping, hits the mark.

1235 Warm Springs Rd., Midway. www.theblueboarinn.com. 𝒞 **435/654-1400.** 12 units. $175–$295 double. Rates include full breakfast. **Amenities:** Restaurant; bar; free Wi-Fi.

SUNDANCE RESORT

14 miles NE of Provo, 50 miles SE of Salt Lake City

Situated in beautiful Provo Canyon, at the base of 12,000-foot Mt. Timpanogos, Sundance is a year-round resort that emphasizes its arts programs as much as its skiing and outdoor activities. That should come as no surprise—it's owned by actor/director Robert Redford, who bought the original property in 1969 and named it after his character in the classic film "Butch Cassidy and the Sundance Kid." You might recognize the area: Redford and director Sydney Pollack set their 1972 film "Jeremiah Johnson" here. It's more heavily forested than many of the Wasatch Front resorts.

The goal for Sundance was to create a place where the outdoors and the arts could come together in a truly unique mountain community, and it seems to be a success. The rustic yet elegant, environmentally friendly retreat is a full-service ski resort in winter. During the summer, you can explore great hiking trails and participate in other warm-weather outdoor activities.

Essentials

GETTING THERE Sundance is less than an hour's drive from Salt Lake City via I-15. From Park City, take U.S. 189 south to Sundance. From Provo, take I-15 to exit 272, go east on Utah 52 for 5½ miles, turn north on U.S. 189

YOU WANNA BE IN PICTURES: THE sundance FILM FESTIVAL

Forget California—Hollywood is here. If you want to be (or at least be up on) the next art-house cinema sensation, visit Utah.

Originally conceived as a creative nexus for American independent film-makers, the festival has outgrown its original venue at Park City's historic Egyptian Theater a thousand-fold. Now films are shown on several Park City screens, as well as in Salt Lake City and Ogden. Alas, many feel that the festival's original "independent" focus has been overshadowed by the presence of big film promoters and distributors. Still, many of the hottest independent films have been discovered at this 10-day January event, hosted by Robert Redford's Sundance Institute. The festival doesn't actually take place at Sundance Resort; it's held 30 miles away, in Park City (p. 126). There are screenings here during the festival, however, as well as lodging packages and shuttles that take guests back and forth to Park City.

The festival has seen the rise to glory of many pictures, including *sex, lies, and videotape*; *Reservoir Dogs*; *Slacker*; *Like Water for Chocolate*; *Hoop Dreams*; *The Station Agent*; *The Aristocrats*; and *Napoleon Dynamite*—and that's just the short list.

Hosting the nation's premier annual film festival is only part of the Sundance Institute's role in the world of American cinema. Since Redford founded the Insti-tute, it has brought some of the finest and most well-respected directors, actors, and producers to Utah to serve as advisors while students rehearse, shoot, and edit their works.

Admission to the festival—as a film-maker or as an audience member—is nonexclusive; that means you can rub shoulders with the rich and famous and up-and-coming. To receive a free guide, or to learn how to purchase tickets, contact the **Sundance Institute** (www. sundance.org; ✆ **435/658-3456** or 435/776-7878).

up Provo Canyon for 7 miles, and turn north on Utah 92 for about 2 miles to Sundance. In winter, the road beyond Sundance is often closed by snow.

A van shuttle service connects Sundance with both Salt Lake International Airport and Provo Airport. Call **Sundance Resort** (see below) for information and to arrange for pickup.

VISITOR INFORMATION   For information on all facilities and activities, plus lodging reservations, contact **Sundance Resort,** 8841 Alpine Loop Rd., Sundance (www.sundanceresort.com; ✆ **800/892-1600** or 866/259-7468).

Skiing Sundance

Sundance is known for its quiet, intimate setting and lack of lift lines. It offers runs for all levels—some quite challenging—including several delightfully long cruising trails for novices. The area is gaining a reputation as a good place to learn to ski or snowboard. The two levels of skiing are pretty well separated from each other: The beginner areas and some of the intermediate terrain are on the front mountain, whereas the prime blue runs and all of the expert slopes are on the back mountain. The expert crowd will be pleased with the steep glades, precipitous bump runs (due to the general lack of traffic, the mountain never really bumps up too high, though), and untracked snow on the back mountain, where you'll have to work at it to run into another skier.

The terrain is rated 20% beginner, 40% intermediate, and 40% advanced, with a total of 44 runs over 450 skiable acres. Three quad and one triple chairlift, plus a handle tow, serve the mountain, which has a vertical drop of 2,150 feet, from a base elevation of 6,100 feet to the top at 8,250 feet. Sundance is usually open from mid-December to early April, and has state-of-the-art snowmaking equipment on the entire front mountain. Lifts operate daily from 9am to 4:30pm and, additionally on Monday, Wednesday, Friday, and Saturday 4:30 to 9pm.

Bearclaw's Cabin, the only mountaintop day lodge in Utah, offers snacks and hot drinks, as well as stupendous views. **Creekside** day lodge, at the base of the ski area, serves excellent quick lunches during ski season. Equipment rental and sales are available.

LIFT TICKETS   Adult (13+) all-day lift tickets cost $80, children 6 to 12 are $53, 5 and under ski free, and seniors 65 and over pay $30. Night skiing is $40 for adults, $31 for children. If you're staying at the resort, the lift ticket is included in your room rate.

LESSONS & PROGRAMS   The **ski school** (✆ **801/225-4140**) offers private and group lessons daily, as well as specialized workshops. Three-hour private lessons start at $350; group lessons start at $85 for 2½ hours.

Sundance Kids ski school offers several programs, including group lessons and all-day programs that include supervision, lunch, and instruction. The resort has no day-care facility.

CROSS-COUNTRY SKIING & SNOWSHOEING   Sundance's excellent **Nordic Center ★★★** is 1½ miles north of the main Sundance entrance. It has about 21 miles of groomed Nordic and snowshoe trails. Classic, skating, and telemark rentals and lessons are available. Trail passes for adults cost $18 for a full day, or $14 after 2pm; juniors (age 7–17) cost $9; kids 6 and under and seniors 65 and over ski free.

Warm-Weather Fun

An abundance of warm-weather activities and spectacular scenery make Sundance just as popular a destination in the summer as during the winter. A quad ski lift operates in warm weather (usually from late May through late Oct), carrying hikers and bikers to upper trails, and offering scenic rides to anyone. Lift rides cost $20, $18 for kids 6 to 12, $17 for seniors 65 and older, and are free for children 5 and under accompanied by an adult.

FLY-FISHING   The **Provo River** provides great fly-fishing just 10 minutes away for rainbow, cutthroat, and German brown trout. Licenses and information are available at Sundance's **General Store** (p. 154). Sundance offers guided fishing trips, including equipment rentals. Rates start at $200 per person for group, $300 for private, half-day fly-fishing trips.

HIKING & MOUNTAIN BIKING Sundance is home to a terrific network of close to a dozen trails, some of which connect to the Uinta National Forest, 88 W. 100 North, Provo (http://fs.usda.gov/uwcnf; ✆ **801/342-5100**). The resort's trails range from hour-long nature walks to all-day affairs, and include three routes to the summit of Mt. Timpanogos.

The **Sundance Nature Trail,** a 1- to 1½-hour round-trip hike, winds through groves of spruce, oak, and maple and across alpine meadows before reaching a cascading waterfall. The **Great Western Trail,** one of the Wasatch Front's most spectacular trails, climbs nearly 4,000 feet to some amazing scenic vistas. It starts at the base of Aspen Grove, winds to the crest of North Fork and American Fork canyons, and ends at the top of Alta ski area. This is an 8- to 10-hour round-trip hike.

Mountain bikers will find the mountain trails at Sundance fun and challenging. Bikers can minimize some of the work by taking their bikes up the lift and pedaling down. The mountain biker's trail-use fee is $12, which includes one lift ride; a full-day pass, including unlimited use of the lift, costs $28.

Contact the resort for a comprehensive trail guide.

HORSEBACK RIDING The **Sundance Stables** offer guided mountain rides of 1 hour and up, starting at $65 per person. Call the main number at Sundance for information.

Shopping

The **General Store** (✆ **801/223-4250**) in the Sundance Resort was the inspiration for the Sundance catalog; it may have come to you in the mail at some time or another. If so, you may recognize the American Indian art and jewelry, local crafts, and high-end Southwest-style clothing and outdoor wear that line the shelves. You can also browse through hiking and fishing apparel and gear (including licenses and rentals) in warm weather, ski accessories in winter, and fresh-baked goodies year-round. At **Sundance Mountain Outfitters** (✆ **801/223-4121**), you can also check out hiking and fishing apparel and gear (including licenses and rentals) in warm weather, and ski accessories in winter.

Where to Stay

Sundance offers standard rooms, studios, and cottage suites that range from $288 to $600 per night, as well as larger mountain suites and several luxury mountain homes that can cost over $1,000 per night. Each suite is outfitted with well-crafted handmade furnishings that match the rustic luxury of the entire resort, as well as American Indian crafts, stone fireplaces, and outdoor decks; most have fully equipped kitchens. All units include two free lift passes per bedroom; complimentary yoga, wellness classes, and guided nature walks; and free Wi-Fi. Contact the **Sundance Resort** (www.sundanceresort. com; ✆ **801/225-4100**) for more information and reservations.

Where to Eat

The Sundance restaurants' culinary approach stresses the use of natural, seasonal ingredients, and dishes are often prepared with such locally raised products as lamb, fresh trout or chicken, and lots of seasonal fruit and vegetables. Dinner reservations are recommended, particularly in season. Full liquor service is available.

The **Tree Room** ★★ (© 801/223-4200 for reservations), the resort's most elegant dining room for over 30 years, is the place for relaxing, romantic dinners with wine and candlelight in a room decorated with American Indian rugs and kachinas artifacts from Redford's private collection. (When it opened, a tree grew in the middle of the dining room; it has since died and been removed.) Seasonal menus might include wild Alaskan salmon with collard greens and roasted beets, grilled buffalo tenderloin with wild mushroom au gratin, and a signature pepper steak with buttermilk mashed potatoes and mango chutney. It's open Tuesday through Thursday from 5 to 9pm, Friday and Saturday from 5 to 10pm. Dinner entree prices from $32 to $56.

The **Foundry Grill** (© 801/223-4220), a less formal eatery offering seasonal ranch-style cuisine, serves three meals Monday through Saturday and brunch and dinner on Sunday. Wood is the predominant feature in both decor and food—a wood oven and wood-fired grill and rotisserie are the main cooking methods. Lunch main courses range from $14 to $24; dinner entrees run $24 to $44.

The **Owl Bar** (© 801/223-4222) is just next door. This is the same 1890s bar frequented by Butch Cassidy's Hole-in-the-Wall Gang, moved here from Thermopolis, Wyoming, stripped of shag, and refinished—but now locals and resort guests belly up to the Victorian rosewood bar to order their favorite tipple and listen to live music. A full grill menu is available, from popcorn to filet mignon, ($5–$44); it's open from 5pm weekdays and noon weekends.

PROVO & ENVIRONS

45 miles S of Salt Lake City, 258 miles NE of St. George

The second-largest metropolitan area in Utah, **Provo** (elevation 4,500 ft.) and its adjacent communities have a population of over 500,000. The main draw here is Brigham Young University, with its museums, cultural events, and spectator sports. Provo also makes a good base for exploring the nearby mountains, Timpanogos Cave National Monument, and the quite spectacular gardens and other attractions at Thanksgiving Point, in nearby Lehi. The Ute Indian tribe reigned here until Mormon leader Brigham Young sent 30 families south from Salt Lake City in March 1849 to colonize the area. Today, the city remains primarily Mormon; many restaurants, stores, and attractions are closed Sundays.

South of Provo lies **Springville,** a town of about 30,000 that likes to refer to itself as "Utah's Art City." Although not a major tourist destination, it is home to the **Springville Museum of Art,** one of the state's finest art museums. **Orem,** which abuts Provo on the northwest, is a tech industry hub. Utah Lake State Park, just west of downtown Provo, is great for boating, and the surrounding Wasatch Mountains abound with natural beauty and recreational opportunities.

7 Essentials

GETTING THERE Provo and Orem are easily accessible from the north or south by I-15. If you're driving in from the east on I-70, take exit 156 at Green River and follow U.S. 6 northwest to I-15 north.

Amtrak (www.amtrak.com; *℗* **800/872-7245**) offers passenger service to Provo on the Chicago-to-Emeryville California Zephyr line. The train station is located at 600 South and 300 West.

The **Utah Transit Authority** runs about a dozen bus routes in and around the Provo area, with connections to Salt Lake City, Lehi, and Springville. For schedule information, call *℗* **801/743-3882** or check the web, **www.rideuta. com.** Route maps and schedules are also available at the visitor center in the county courthouse. The FrontRunner train runs south to here from Salt Lake City—check the website for schedules and fares.

VISITOR INFORMATION The **Utah Valley Convention and Visitors Bureau** runs a visitor center at 220 W. Center St., Provo (www.utahvalley.org/cvb; *℗* **800/222-8824** or 801/851-2100). The visitor center is open 9am to 5pm Monday through Friday.

For information on the surrounding national forest, contact the **Uinta National Forest,** 88 W. 100 North, Provo (http://fs.usda.gov/uwcnf; *℗* **801/342-5100**).

GETTING AROUND The easiest way to get around is by car. The streets are organized in a numbered grid pattern, beginning at the intersection of Center Street and University Avenue in Provo. From here, the blocks increase by 100 in all four directions, such as 100 South, 200 West, 700 North, and so forth. University Parkway cuts diagonally northwest across the grid from Brigham Young University to connect with 1300 South (I-15 exit 269) in Orem. The center of Orem is the intersection of Center Street (I-15 exit 271) and Main Street. State Street (U.S. 89) crosses the city diagonally.

Major car-rental agencies include **Avis** (www.avis.com; *℗* **800/238-4898** or 801/494-1529) and **Enterprise** (www.enterprise.com; *℗* **800/261-7331** or 801/375-7755).

FAST FACTS The main hospital in Provo is **Utah Valley Regional Medical Center,** 1034 N. 500 West (*℗* **801/357-7850**), with a 24-hour emergency room. The main **post office** is at 95 W. 100 South (www.usps.com; *℗* **800/275-8777**). The local newspaper is the "Daily Herald" (www.heraldextra.com). The **sales tax** totals 6.25%.

Where to Stay & Eat in Downtown Provo

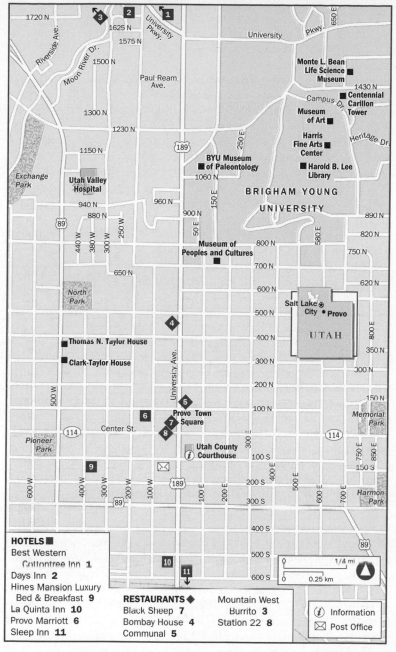

1720 N
1625 N
1575 N
University Pkwy.
University Pkwy.
1500 N
Riverside Ave.
Moon River Dr.
Paul Ream Ave.
1300 N
1230 N
1150 N
189
Exchange Park
Utah Valley Hospital
940 N
880 N
960 N
440 W
380 W
300 W
250 W
89
650 E
Monte L. Bean Life Science Museum
1430 N
Centennial Carillon Tower
Campus Dr.
Museum of Art
Harris Fine Arts Center
Heritage Dr.
250 E
Harold B. Lee Library
BYU Museum of Paleontology
1060 N
150 E
50 E
BRIGHAM YOUNG UNIVERSITY
890 N
820 N
750 N
580 E
Museum of Peoples and Cultures
800 N
700 N
650 N
North Park
600 N
500 N
620 N
Salt Lake City
Provo
UTAH
800 E
350 E
Thomas N. Taylor House
Clark-Taylor House
400 N
300 N
300 N
200 N
University Ave.
500 W
100 N
150 N
Memorial Park
Provo Town Square
Center St.
114
114
Pioneer Park
Utah County Courthouse
750 E
850 E
150 S
Harmon Park
89
600 W
400 W
300 W
200 W
100 W
189
100 E
200 E
100 S
200 S
300 S
400 S
300 E
400 E
500 E
600 E
700 E
89

HOTELS ■
Best Western Cottontree Inn **1**
Days Inn **2**
Hines Mansion Luxury Bed & Breakfast **9**
La Quinta Inn **10**
Provo Marriott **6**
Sleep Inn **11**

RESTAURANTS ◆
Black Sheep **7**
Bombay House **4**
Communal **5**
Mountain West Burrito **3**
Station 22 **8**

1/4 mi
0   0.25 km

(i) Information
✉ Post Office

Exploring Brigham Young University

Founded in 1875 by Brigham Young, Brigham Young University is the nation's largest church-owned private university, sponsored by the Church of Jesus Christ of Latter-day Saints. Home to more than 30,000 students, the beautiful 638-acre campus is located on the east side of Provo at the base of the Wasatch Mountains.

For information, contact **Brigham Young University, Public Affairs and Guest Relations** (www.byu.edu; ✆ **801/422-4678**). To get to the university from I-15 north, take exit 269, University Parkway, and travel east through Orem into Provo to the northwest entrance of the campus.

Free 40-minute **tours** of the campus, beginning at the visitor center, are offered Monday through Friday on the hour from 9am to 4pm. Allow at least 1 hour. Admission to campus museums is free unless otherwise noted; allow 1 to 2 hours for each of the BYU museums.

The 112-foot-tall **Spencer W. Kimball Tower,** a campus landmark, houses 52 bells that toll at intervals throughout the day.

The **Monte L. Bean Life Science Museum,** 645 E. Phillips Lane, just east of the Marriott Center (http://mlbean.byu.edu; ✆ **801/422-5051**), houses extensive collections of insects, plants, reptiles, fish, shells, mammals, and birds from around the world, with an emphasis on Utah's wildlife. It's open Wednesday through Friday from 10am to 9pm and Saturday and Monday from 10am to 5pm. Admission is free.

The **BYU Museum of Paleontology,** 1683 N. Provo Canyon Rd., west of LaVell Edwards Football Stadium (✆ **801/422-3680**), houses one of Utah's largest collections of dinosaur bones from the Jurassic period. Guided tours are available by appointment. Hours are Monday through Friday from 9am to 5pm and there is no admission charge.

The **Harris Fine Arts Center,** Campus Drive (✆ **801/422-2981** or 801/422-4322 for the ticket office), houses galleries featuring American and European artists. The B. F. Larsen Gallery and Gallery 303 feature student and faculty exhibitions. The center also hosts theatrical and musical performances in its five theaters; call for the schedule and ticket prices.

The state-of-the-art **BYU Museum of Art** ★★, north of the Fine Arts Center at 492 E. Campus Dr. (http://moa.byu.edu; ✆ **801/422-8287**), is one of the largest museums in the West. Its 17,000-plus-piece collection includes ceramics, sculpture, paintings, and pottery—everything from etchings by Rembrandt and Monet to jade and ivory from Asia. The museum also contains a gift shop and a cafe that serves lunch. Hours are Monday, Thursday, and Friday from 10am to 9pm; and Tuesday, Wednesday, and Saturday from 10am to 6pm. Admission is charged for special exhibitions only.

The **Museum of Peoples and Cultures** in Allen Hall, 2201 N. Canyon Road (http://mpc.byu.edu; ✆ **801/422-0020**), focuses on the cultures of the Western Hemisphere, but also looks at Colombian, Egyptian, Israeli, Polynesian, and Syrian societies. It's open Monday through Friday from 9am to 5pm; admission is free.

The **Harold B. Lee Library** (http://lib.byu.edu; © **801/422-2927**) is the largest library in Utah, with more than three million bound volumes. Library hours are Monday through Friday from 7am to midnight and Saturday from 8am to midnight. The second floor houses one of the world's largest **genealogical libraries** (© **801/422-6200**), with free services to all.

More to See & Do in the Provo Area

Here in Provo, home of Brigham Young University, are a number of stately homes that once belonged to well-to-do church officials, as well as commercial buildings constructed to serve the growing community. Stop at the **visitor center** (p. 128) for a booklet describing the city's dozens of historic buildings. Nearby, the **Utah County Courthouse** is well worth a visit. This magnificent structure was built of Manti limestone in the 1920s. Notice the marble floors and detailing, the fine collection of artwork displayed on the walls, and the overall feeling of grandeur emanating from the classical balance of the design.

The **Provo Town Square,** at the intersection of University Avenue and Center Street, contains the core of Provo's business community, which began to develop and grow in the 1890s. Here you'll see the 1900 **Knight Block,** a big red building with a large clock; the **Gates & Snow Furniture Co.,** to the east of the Knight Block, with one of Utah's best pressed-tin fronts; and the **Zion Bank,** at the northwest corner, situated in what was originally the Bank of Commerce building. West along Center Street sits a row of period storefronts, with the newer businesses now occupying them.

An interesting historic home is the **Thomas N. Taylor House,** 342 N. 500 West. "T.N.T.," as he was known, was manager of the Taylor Brothers Store and served as mayor of Provo and president of the Utah Stake of the LDS Church. His home, built in the first decade of the 20th century, exemplifies the kind of house most second-generation Utahns aspired to have. Nearby is the **Clark-Taylor House,** 310 N. 500 West, thought to be the oldest home in Utah Valley still standing on its original site. The adobe structure was built in 1854, with later additions of the two-story front, the trim around the windows, and the gables. Neither of these houses is open for tours.

Heading out of town, a turnout on U.S. 189, about 4 miles north and east of Provo, affords awe-inspiring views of **Bridal Veil Falls,** a double cataract waterfall that drops 607 feet to the Provo River. This is also a good spot to begin hikes into Provo Canyon.

Hutchings Museum Born in 1889, John Hutchings had an insatiable curiosity about the world around him. He collected and studied numerous objects, discussing his observations with friends and family. His collections are the core of this museum, which houses mineral displays and rare specimens of variscite and crystal aluminum, and describes their links to mining districts of the region. Also on display are dinosaur bones, flamingo tracks from Spanish Fork Canyon, a piece of tusk from a woolly mammoth, tools and pottery from early man, and artifacts from Utah's early residents, including a shotgun owned by famed outlaw Butch Cassidy. Allow 45 minutes.

55 N. Center St., Lehi. www.hutchingsmuseum.org. © **801/768-7180.** Admission $4 adults; $3 seniors, students, and children 3–12; free for children 2 and under. Tues–Sat 11am–5pm. From I-15 exit 279, take Main St. west to Center St. and turn right.

Provo Beach Resort ★ If you're craving water on your desert visit, come here for a mind-boggling array of diversions (indoor surfing to outdoor beach cruiser bicycles, laser tag, not to mention Pinewood Derby, minigolf, and a boardwalk complete with a carousel). It's located at an upscale mall on the north side of Provo proper. Allow at least an 1 hour.

4801 N. University Ave. www.provobeachresort.com. © **801/224-5001.** Admission varies by activity; Flowrider surfing $20/hour, laser tag $7/game, carousel rides $1. Mon–Thurs 11am–10pm; Fri 11am–11pm; Sat 10am–11pm. Closed legal holidays.

Springville Museum of Art ★★ The art of Utah is the cornerstone of the oldest art museum in Utah, housed in part in a 1937 Spanish Colonial Revival–style building. The museum contains one of the finest displays of Utah art available, arranged in chronological order to illustrate the development of art in the state. Of its nine galleries, four are reserved for changing exhibits of historical and contemporary art of Utah. The museum also has an excellent (and little-known) collection of Russian and Soviet Socialist Realism. The museum contains a research library and bookstore, and offers a series of lectures. Allow about 1 hour for your visit.

126 E. 400 South, Springville. © **801/489-2727.** www.sma.nebo.edu. Free admission; donations accepted. Tues–Sat 10am–5pm (Wed to 9pm); Closed holidays. From I-15 exit 260, go east to Springville, entering town on 400 South.

Thanksgiving Point ★★ This huge complex, developed by the cofounders of WordPerfect software as an expression of gratitude to their community, includes a splendid dinosaur museum—the **Museum of Ancient Life.** Billed as the largest dinosaur museum in the world, it houses some of the longest and tallest dinosaur replicas ever put on display, plus fossils and related exhibits on paleontology. The museum contains a children's discovery room, a fossil lab where you can see paleontologists at work, a widescreen theater, and a museum store selling practically everything dinosaur related. Allow 2 hours.

Elsewhere at Thanksgiving Point are the delightful **Thanksgiving Point Gardens**—55 acres of themed gardens, including topiary, butterfly, fragrance, herb, and English rose gardens, plus an unusual waterfall garden, all connected by some 2 miles of landscaped brick pathways. The Children's Discovery Garden, designed to encourage children's imaginations, contains a large Noah's Ark, an underground exhibit area, and a hedge maze. Allow 2 hours. Kids will also enjoy **Farm Country,** with an animal park and exhibits on the farming life (allow 1–2 hr.). Other attractions include an amphitheater, a golf course (below), numerous shops, and several restaurants. Wagon and carriage rides are also offered.

3003 N. Thanksgiving Way, Lehi. www.thanksgivingpoint.com. (℃ **888/672-6040** or 801/768-2300. Admission to museum $20 adults (13+), $15 children 3–12 and seniors 65 and over, free for children 2 and under. Call for fees for gardens and other sites and activities. Grounds open Mon–Sat; call for hours for specific venues. Closed New Year's Day, Thanksgiving, and Christmas. From I-15 exit 284, go west to Thanksgiving Way.

Sports & Outdoor Pursuits

One of the top spots for fishing, boating, and swimming in this area is **Utah Lake State Park ★★**, 4400 W. Center St. (www.stateparks.utah.gov; (℃ **801/375-0731**), Utah's largest freshwater lake. The 96,600-acre lake is especially popular with owners of speedboats, personal watercraft, and sailboats, although the occasional canoe or kayak can be seen gliding by. Mountains dominate the view in all directions, and at night, the lights of the city illuminate the panorama to the east. Anglers catch channel catfish, walleye, white bass, black bass, and several species of panfish. While there are boat-launching ramps, there are no boat rentals. Although the park itself has no hiking or biking trails, the **Provo River Parkway Trail** leads from the edge of the park into Provo Canyon (see below).

The park's 54-site campground is open April through October only; the park is open for day use year-round. The campground has no RV hookups, but it does have a dump station as well as modern restrooms with showers. Day-use hours are 6am to 10pm in summer, 8am to 5pm in winter. Day use costs $10 per vehicle in summer, $5 in winter. Camping costs $30; reservations can be made by calling (℃ **800/322-3770,** or through the state parks website (www. stateparks.utah.gov). Take I-15 exit 268, Center Street west; it's about 3 miles to the park.

Outdoor recreation enthusiasts also head into the **Uinta National Forest,** which practically surrounds Provo and offers hundreds of miles of hiking, mountain biking, and horseback riding trails. Check with the **Forest Supervisor's office,** 88 W. 100 North (http://fs.usda.gov/uwcnf; (℃ **801/377-5780**), for maps and tips on where to go.

Right in town, the 15-mile **Provo River Parkway Trail** winds from Utah Lake to Provo Canyon, following the Provo River part of the way. This slag trail (slag is the rock left over when a metal is mined) is open to both bikers and hikers.

Among the public golf courses in the area are **Thanksgiving Point Golf Club** in Lehi (℃ **801/768-7400**), an 18-hole, par-72 championship course designed by golf pro Johnny Miller, with greens fees of $29 to $85 for 18 holes, cart included; **East Bay Golf Course,** 1860 S. Eastbay Blvd. ((℃ **801/373-6262**), on the south side of the city, which is an 18-hole, par-71 course with greens fees of $14 to $22 for 9 holes ($22 with a cart) and $28 for 18 holes, cart included.

Lehi is home to a huge (150,000-sq.-ft.!) **Cabela's** outpost, 2502 W. Grand Terrace Pkwy. (www.cabelas.com; ✆ **801/766-2500**), selling every kind of outdoor gear imaginable. They've even got a restaurant, horse corrals, and an indoor archery range.

Fun on the Ice

Peaks Ice Arena 100 N Seven Peaks Blvd. (www.provo.org/community/peaks-ice-arena; ✆ **801/852-7465**), built for the 2002 Olympics, contains two Olympic-size ice-skating rinks that are open to the public. Skate rental is available. The arena is open year-round; call for the current rates and schedule.

Spectator Sports

Brigham Young University is part of the Mountain West Conference. The **Cougars football** team plays at the 65,000-seat LaVell Edwards Football Stadium; tickets are hard to come by, so call as far in advance as possible. The **basketball** team plays in the 23,000-seat Marriott Center; you usually won't have too much trouble getting tickets. For general information on all BYU sports teams, call ✆ **801/422-2096,** or check the athletic department's website at www.byucougars.com. For tickets, call ✆ **801/422-2981,** or buy online at www.byutickets.com.

Where to Stay

In addition to the following listings, affordable chain and franchise motels in Provo include **Best Western Plus Cottontree Inn,** 2230 N. University Pkwy. (www.bestwestern.com; ✆ **801/373-7044**), **Days Inn,** 1675 W 200 North (www.daysinn.com; ✆ **801/375-8600**), and **Sleep Inn,** 1505 S. 40 East (www.sleepinnprovo.com; ✆ **801/377-6597**). Rates are typically $60 to $120 for a double at these properties.

Rates are highest in summer, lowest in late winter and early spring, and often significantly higher during Brigham Young University special events. Note that accommodations can be scarce at graduation time. Pets are not allowed unless otherwise noted.

Hines Mansion Bed & Breakfast ★★ Built in 1895 for pharmacist and mining magnate Russell Spencer Hines, this Victorian-style mansion is a true gem. It makes a wonderful spot to celebrate a special occasion or to simply relax and soak up some historical charm. Innkeepers Kati and Eric Lance have retained the mansion's historical ambience and integrity while adding numerous modern touches. Every room is unique, but each has a queen- or king-size bed, robes, and a two-person whirlpool tub plus a separate private bathroom. The penthouse, which occupies the entire top floor of the mansion, boasts a king-size bed, a 46-inch TV with a DVD player, and spectacular views of the city and nearby mountains from the tub. Fresh-baked cookies and fresh fruit are served each evening. Breakfasts feature fruit, yogurt, and a hot dish such as baked egg puffs or pecan pancakes. Smoking is not permitted.

383 W. 100 South. www.hinesmansion.com. ℂ **801/374-8400.** 9 units. $166–$225 double. Rates include full breakfast. No children under 12. **Amenities:** Free Wi-Fi.

Provo Marriott This well-regarded high-rise hotel in downtown Provo provides comfortable—even luxurious—accommodations with splendid views (especially from the upper floors) and all the amenities you could want. Public areas and bedrooms are handsomely appointed, decorated primarily in light earth tones. Some in-room fridges are available, and some units have whirlpool tubs. Allie's American Grille serves three meals daily.

101 W. 100 North. www.provomarriott.com. ℂ **801/377-4700.** 330 units, including 6 suites. $142–$189 double. **Amenities:** Restaurant; concierge-level rooms; fitness center; Jacuzzi; 2 heated pools (indoor and outdoor); room service; sauna; free Wi-Fi.

CAMPING

Lakeside RV Campground Situated along the Provo River, this campground offers the best of both worlds—it's close to the attractions and restaurants of Provo, and it offers a quiet camping experience with trees, flowers, grassy areas, ducks, and geese. In addition to the usual bathhouse, dump station, and RV hookups, the campground has a self-serve laundry, free Wi-Fi access, a heated pool, a nature walk, horseshoe pits, volleyball area, playground, dog park, and game room. A store sells groceries, and propane is available. You can fish in the Provo River, or head to Utah Lake, just a quarter-mile away.

4000 W. Center St. www.lakesidervcampground.com. ℂ **801/373-5267.** 130 sites (all RV sites, most with full hookups). $41.95 for 2 people. Tent sites $27. From I-15 exit 265B, go west 3 miles. Pets welcome.

Where to Eat

Provo is a conservative, family-oriented city. Many restaurants do not serve alcohol, and a number are closed on Sundays. But in recent years, the dining scene has grown a lot—the farm-to-table movement struck a chord with Utahns' pioneer heritage and there are now several excellent restaurants in Provo. In addition to the restaurants discussed below, try the recommended **Tree Room,** at the nearby Sundance Resort (p. 151).

Black Sheep Cafe ★★★ SOUTHWESTERN/NATIVE AMERICAN A brother and sister operation, this is a rare place that incorporates flavors of Navajo, Hopi, and Pueblo cuisines into their dishes. The stylish cafe looks out on to the busy street and inside is adorned with Native American art and objects. Locally sourced foods are emphasized—Utah honey, blue corn meal, farm vegetables and naturally raised meat. The Black Sheep Salad mixes greens with cactus pear and pomegranate vinaigrette, candied pecans, cranberries, and cojita cheese. Wedge salad has a touch of chipotle in the lime dressing and posole and green chile stew are staples. There is even a goat burger available and at dinner, and a hog jowl taco.

19 University Ave. www.blacksheepcafe.com. © **801/607-2485.** Lunch main courses $9–$15; dinner main courses $13–$22. Lunch Mon–Fri 11:30am–2:30pm; dinner Mon–Thurs 5–9pm, Fri–Sat 5–10pm.

Bombay House ★★ INDIAN

The Provo version of a revered Indian restaurant based in Salt Lake City, Bombay House Provo equals the original. All the classic sub-continental dishes are here—tikka masala, samosas, curries, korma, and saag paneer—and the tandoor oven turns out roasted meats and wonderful Indian breads. Biryani—the complicated rice dish that originated in Persia but was perfected in India—is particularly well executed in the Bombay House kitchen. Of course there are lots of vegetarian dishes as well as soothing milk-based drinks and desserts. There's a separate list of menu items containing gluten, because most of them don't.

463 N University Ave. http://bombayhouse.com. © **801/373-6677.** Main courses $15–$20. Mon–Sat 4–10pm.

Communal ★★★ AMERICAN

A groundbreaking restaurant in Provo (the "New York Times" wrote about it!) founded by Joseph McCrae and Colton Soelberg, a pair of chefs from Sundance's kitchens who have gone to form the Heirloom Restaurant Group, which owns several of Provo's finest eateries. Communal's intent was and is to serve locally sourced, imaginatively prepared food in a family atmosphere. The dining room has several communal tables and you can order family-style from a group menu. On the website is a list of farms and local purveyors where the food on your plate comes from—greens from Snuck Farms, eggs from Clifford Farms, cheese from Beehive Cheese. Imagine pork belly cooked for 48 hours, with pickled cucumber, mint, fresno chile, and fennel seed salsa verde. Rich, tart, sour, and sweet all at once. A roasted chicken breast comes with a fried leg and thigh with garlic cream sauce instead of cream gravy and a sweet/tart touch of apricot gastrique. To finish: butterscotch pudding with salted caramel sauce, cookie crumble, and whipped cream. You get the picture. Even though this is Provo, you can choose from a full list of beer and wine.

102 N University Ave. www.communalrestaurant.com. © **801/373-8000.** Lunch main courses $13–$15; dinner main courses $26–$28. Lunch Tues–Fri 11:30am–2pm; dinner Tues–Sat 5–10pm; Sat brunch 9am–2pm.

Mountain West Burrito ★★ MEXICAN

This is a small counter-service local chain specializing in fast Mexican food, but since it's owned by the Heirloom Group (see Communal) expect the emphasis to be on freshness as well as speed. The kitchen uses the same Double R Ranch beef you find in high-end restaurants, the chicken is from Red Bird, and Kurubota pork is from Snake River Farms in Idaho. The beans are organic; the rice is brown. And the menu couldn't be simpler: Choose your size of burrito or chimichanga or whether you want cheese, veg, or meat (including slow-roasted pork and grilled steak) for your quesadilla, nacho, or taco; vegan options are available.

1796 N 950 West. http://mountainwestburrito.com. © **801/805-1870.** Most dishes under $10. Mon–Sat 11am–9pm.

Station 22 ★★ AMERICAN Focusing on regional American cuisine, Station 22 also offers a craft soda menu, which included unusual and obscure bottled sodas from all over the world. Some you've heard of: Earp's Sarsaparilla is brewed by a descendant of Wyatt. Cream sodas, ginger sodas, colas—they're all here. Pair them with Station 22's American roots dishes like the Fry-Daddy basket (hushpuppies, sweet potato wedges, and French fries), chicken and waffles, fancy mac and cheese, or shrimp and grits. There is a selection of burgers and sandwiches range from "pulled pig" to a very luxurious grilled cheese. Fried cookie dough for dessert? It's up to you.

22 W. Center St. www.station22cafe.com. © **801/607-1803.** Main courses $5–$15. Mon–Thurs 11am–9pm; Fri–Sat 11am–10pm.

Provo After Dark

The **Brigham Young University Theatre,** on the BYU campus (www.byu arts.com; © **801/422-4322**), presents more than a dozen theatrical productions each year.

From summer through early fall, you can see live musicals and concerts under the stars at the **SCERA Shell Outdoor Theatre,** 699 S. State St., in SCERA Park, Orem (www.scera.org; © **801/225-2569**). The season usually includes several locally produced Broadway musicals, plus a variety of concerts, from pop to country to classical.

Provo has become a small center of alternative and cutting-edge music with several national acts getting their start in Provo clubs (Imagine Dragons, Neon Trees, Fictionist) like **Velour Live Music Gallery,** 135 N. University Ave., (http://velourlive.com; © **801/818-BAND**). Visit Velour's website for the current schedule. **A. Beauford Gifford's Libation Emporium,** 190 W. Center St. (www.abgsbar.com; © **801/373-1200**) is a downtown bar and rock venue.

TIMPANOGOS CAVE NATIONAL MONUMENT

20 miles N of Provo, 35 miles S of Salt Lake City

This national monument actually comprises three caves—Hansen, Middle, and Timpanogos—that are linked together by man-made tunnels. Martin Hansen discovered the first cavern in 1887 while tracking a mountain lion. The other two were reported in the early 1910s, and the connecting tunnels were constructed in the 1930s. The caves are filled with 47 kinds of formations, from stalactites and stalagmites to draperies and helictites. The caves aren't easy to reach, but their beauty and variety make them worth the rough 1½-hour trek to the mouth.

Essentials

The caves are accessible only on guided tours from early May to mid-October, daily from 7:30am to 4:30pm (8am–3:30pm after Labor Day). The caves close in winter because snow and ice make the access trail too hazardous. The steep trail is not navigable by wheelchair or stroller.

GETTING THERE/ACCESS POINTS   From Provo, head north on I-15 to exit 284, then east on Utah 92 to the visitor center, which is on the south side of the road. For a beautiful but slow drive when you leave the caves, continue east and then south on Utah 92 through American Fork Canyon, which is narrow and winding, and turn west on U.S. 189 back to Provo. From Salt Lake City, take I-15 south to exit 287, and proceed as above.

INFORMATION/VISITOR CENTER   The visitor center is on the south side of Utah 92. It is open daily from 7am to 6pm. Note that parking at the visitor center is limited for large vehicles, such as motor homes over 20 feet. Although small, the visitor center offers a short film about the caves, a few explanatory displays and booklets, and postcards for sale. A snack bar and gift shop are next to the center, as well as two picnic areas located along the shady banks of the American Fork River. One is across from the visitor center; a larger one, with fire grills and restrooms, is about a quarter-mile west. Contact **Timpanogos Cave National Monument** (www.nps.gov/tica; ✆ **801/756-5238** or 801/756-5239 in winter for information) for additional information.

FEES & REGULATIONS   Cave tours often sell out in advance. You must stop at the visitor center before starting your hike to the cave. Purchase tickets there or ahead of time through **www.recreation.gov.**

One-hour cave tours cost $8 for adults, $6 for children 6 to 15, $4 for children 3 to 5, and free for children 2 and under; 90-minute "Introduction to Caving" tours, available for ages 14 and up, cost $16 per person. The U.S. Forest Service also charges a $6 per vehicle fee to enter American Fork Canyon, where the national monument is located. Pets are not allowed on the trail or in the caves.

Exploring the Monument

The only way to see the caves is on a ranger-guided tour. Allow about 3 hours total for the basic cave tour—1½ hours hiking up, an hour in the caves, and 30 to 45 minutes hiking back down. The tours are limited to 20 persons and often fill up early in the morning, so it's best to call ahead and reserve your space with a credit card. The "Introduction to Caving" tours take you to less developed sections, and require some crawling through tight places. These tours are about a half-hour longer and are limited to five people. Reservations are required. The temperature inside the caves is around 45°F (7°C; about the same as a refrigerator), so take a jacket or sweatshirt.

THE HIKE TO THE CAVES   The change in elevation between the visitor center (at about 5,600 ft.) and the cave entrance is 1,065 feet, and the steep, albeit paved, trail is 1½ miles long; it's a physically demanding walk, but quite rewarding. The trail should not be attempted by anyone with breathing, heart, or walking difficulties. Wear good walking shoes and carry water and perhaps a snack.

This is a self-guided hike, so you can travel at your own pace, stopping at the benches along the way to rest and enjoy the views of the canyon, the Wasatch Range, and Utah Valley. A trail guide, available at the visitor center, will help you identify the wildflowers growing amid the Douglas fir, white fir, maple, and oak trees. You'll also spot chipmunks, ground squirrels, lizards, and myriad birds along the way. Restrooms are available at the cave entrance, but not inside the cave or along the trail.

TOURING THE CAVES   The basic ranger-guided cave tour is along a surfaced, well-lit, and fairly level route. You enter at the natural entrance to Hansen Cave and continue through Hansen, Middle, and Timpanogos Caves. The limestone chambers are festooned with delicately colored stalactites, forested with stalagmites, draperies, graceful flowstone, and helictites (unusual curvy formations for which the caves are famous), all in soft greens, reds, yellows, and white. The huge cave formation of linked stalactites at the Great Heart of Timpanogos is quite impressive, and the profusion of bizarre, brilliant white helictites in the Chimes Chamber of Timpanogos is stunning. Mirrorlike cave pools reflect the formations. Bring high-speed film or a flash if you're taking photos; tripods are not allowed. Remember that the formations are fragile and easily damaged, even by a light touch of your hand. Also note that the oils from your skin will change the chemical makeup of the formations, so please don't touch.

DINOSAURS & NATURAL WONDERS IN UTAH'S NORTHEAST CORNER

8

This region is indeed where the eternally fascinating dinosaurs once roamed, and it's one of the best places anywhere to learn about prehistoric creatures, but Northeast Utah is not all about giant reptiles. Still relatively undiscovered and unspoiled, more rugged and less developed and accessible, this is a playground of great scenic beauty, filled with fascinating geologic, historic (and prehistoric) sites. And, you know, dinosaurs.

VERNAL: GATEWAY TO DINOSAUR NATIONAL MONUMENT

175 miles E of Salt Lake City

A perfect base for exploring Dinosaur National Monument—just 20 miles from town—and Ashley National Forest, Vernal (at 5,280 ft. in elevation) is the largest community in the region. You'll find all the services you might need, as well as a few attractions that serve as a good introduction to the compelling geologic and natural history of the area. It's also emerging as a mountain-biking destination for those who have ridden southern Utah's slickrock and are looking for new terrain to pedal.

Essentials

GETTING THERE From Heber City, U.S. 40 leads east, past Strawberry Reservoir (there's world-class fishing here, if you have time to stop; p. 150) and through Duchesne and Roosevelt, each of which has a few motels, restaurants, and services, before reaching Vernal (158 miles from Heber City).

From I-70, take exit 157 west of Green River and follow U.S. 6/191 north 68 miles through Price and Helper, branching northeast above Helper to follow U.S. 191 for 44 beautiful, mountainous miles to Duchesne. Then take U.S. 40 east for 58 miles to Vernal.

The Northeast Corner

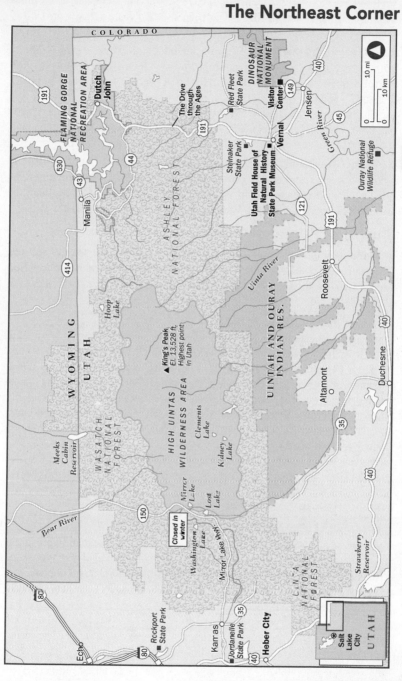

The **Vernal Regional Airport** (✆ 435/789-3400) is located about 1½ miles southeast of the center of town, with flights to and from Denver on **United Airlines** (www.united.com; ✆ 800/864-8331).

VISITOR INFORMATION   Information on area lodging, dining, and recreational facilities can be obtained from **Northeastern Utah's Dinosaurland Travel Board,** 134 W. Main St., Ste. 101, Vernal (www.dinoland.com; ✆ 800/477-5558 or 435/789-66932), open 24 hours every day. You can also get information at the **Utah Welcome Center** in Jensen, about 13 miles southeast of Vernal on U.S. 40 (✆ 435/789-6932), which is open daily (hours vary according to the season).

GETTING AROUND   Car rentals are available at the airport from **Enterprise** (www.enterprise.com; ✆ 800/261-7331 or 435/781-3008) and **Fox Rent A Car** (www.foxrentacar.com; ✆ 435/789-4777). Local transportation is available 24 hours a day from **Vernal City Cab** (✆ 435/790-1212).

Outdoor Pursuits

In addition to the outdoor recreation areas discussed here, see the sections "Dinosaur National Monument" and "Flaming Gorge National Recreation Area," later in this chapter. **Basin Sports,** 511 W. Main St., in Vernal (✆ 435/789-2199), is a good place to stock up on gear.

ASHLEY NATIONAL FOREST

This vast forest encompasses more than a million acres of beautiful mountain country, including **Flaming Gorge National Recreation Area** (p. 179) and the High Uintas Wilderness, which is home to **Kings Peak,** Utah's tallest mountain, at 13,528 feet. Throughout the national forest are numerous opportunities for hiking, backpacking, fishing, camping, cross-country skiing, and other activities. The Forest Service also rents out its guard stations and yurts, which make an excellent base for exploring the mountains north of Vernal (see "Where to Stay," below).

The two major access points are along U.S. 191 from Vernal and Utah 44 from Manila. Information is available from the **Ashley National Forest offices,** 355 N. Vernal Ave., Vernal (www.fs.fed.us/r4/Ashley; ✆ 435/789-1181), which is open Monday through Friday from 8am to 5pm.

OURAY NATIONAL WILDLIFE REFUGE

Hundreds of species of migratory birds and waterfowl make their home in this 11,987-acre wetlands refuge, which lies south of Vernal along the Green River. A 12-mile car tour route begins at the visitor contact station, which also has hiking trails and an observation tower. In addition to a variety of birds, you're likely to see mule deer. Be sure to bring binoculars and a bird guide.

To get here from Vernal, take U.S. 40 west about 14 miles and turn left (south) onto Utah 88 for about 14 miles to the refuge entrance. The visitor contact station is about a mile from the entrance. Entry is free. The refuge is open daily year-round, from an hour before sunrise to an hour after sunset;

A Drive Through the Ages

One of the most scenic drives in the state is the **Flaming Gorge–Uintas Scenic Byway**—U.S. 191 from Vernal up to Manila and Flaming Gorge National Recreation Area—one of the first designated national scenic byways in the United States. The 67-mile route climbs through foothills covered with pine and juniper trees into the Uinta Mountains; signs along the way explain the evolution of the intriguing geologic formations visible along the drive. Near Flaming Gorge, you pass the billion-year-old rock core of the Uinta Mountains. Stop at some of the many turnouts for scenic views, short walks, and wildlife viewing—watch for bighorn sheep, elk, mule deer, and moose, especially in spring.

camping is not allowed in the refuge. Contact the refuge office (http://ouray.fws.gov; © **435/545-2522**), for more information.

RED FLEET STATE PARK

Located 10 miles north of Vernal, at 4335 N. U.S. 191, this scenic park, which looks like a junior version of Lake Powell—only with 200-million-year-old dinosaur tracks—offers fishing, boating, swimming, and camping. The 750-acre **Red Fleet Reservoir** was named for three large, deep-red sandstone rock formations that resemble the hulls of ships. You'll encounter sandy beaches, rock cliffs, and plenty of open water; wildlife such as rabbits, ground squirrels, mule deer, and the occasional bobcat; and good fishing for rainbow and brown trout, bluegill, and bass. On chilly mornings, golden eagles are sometimes spotted sunning themselves on rock outcroppings; other birds that frequent the park include hawks, vultures, owls, and bluebirds.

The prehistoric **dinosaur tracks** can be found on a large slab of rock that slants down into the water and is located across the reservoir from the park's boat ramp. The greatest number of tracks can be seen when the water level is low, from late summer through winter. You can reach the tracks by boat or by swimming (wear a life jacket so you can return easily), or via a 1½-mile hike (one-way) from a Bureau of Land Management road. To reach the BLM road, continue north along U.S. 191 for 1 mile past the turnoff to Red Fleet. Turn right (east) just past mile marker 212, cross a cattle guard, and drive 2⅓ miles on the paved road to the trail head, a small turnout with a sign at the trail; a stock tank sits across the road, partly hidden by bushes and trees. Allow about 2 hours for the moderate hike over low, sandy hills.

Park facilities include the boat ramp, fish-cleaning stations, an RV dump station, and a 29-site campground. Although the campground is essentially a parking lot, it does offer splendid panoramic views across the lake. There are also five sites with full hookups, grassy areas for tents, plus tables and fire pits, and modern restrooms but no showers. Camping costs vary, from $11 for tents in the off-season to $30 in peak season; the day-use fee is $8 per vehicle. Gates are open daily from 6am to 10pm in summer, 8am to 5pm in winter.

Call ✆ **435/789-4432** for information and ✆ **800/322-3770** for campsite reservations. The Utah State Parks website is **www.stateparks.utah.gov.**

STEINAKER STATE PARK

Steinaker State Park offers a sandy swimming beach, good fishing for rainbow trout and largemouth bass, and an attractive campground, just 7 miles north of Vernal at 4335 N. U.S. 191. This reservoir, which covers 780 acres when full, is also popular with water-skiers and boaters. At the time of writing, water levels were dropping as the reservoir was drained for dam repairs. Construction on the dam will be carried out throughout 2019 and the reservoir is scheduled to begin refilling during the fall of 2019. Unfortunately, no rental facilities are nearby.

Wildlife here includes mule deer, jackrabbits, cottontails, ground squirrels, porcupines, and an occasional elk or bobcat. Migratory waterfowl are often seen in spring and fall, and the park also attracts American robins, pheasants, and golden eagles. The landscape is composed primarily of juniper and sagebrush, with cottonwoods and aspen trees near the lake. Spring usually brings out an abundance of wildflowers, such as Indian paintbrush, larkspur, and sego lily. Several unmarked hiking trails—ask a ranger for directions—and additional hiking opportunities are nearby on property managed by the Bureau of Land Management.

Facilities include a boat ramp, fish-cleaning station, and RV dump station. The tree-shaded campground contains 31 sites (five with RV hookups) and modern restrooms with hot showers. Picnic tables, barbecue grills, and fire pits are available. Camping costs $15 for tents or $28 for a site with full RV hookups; the day-use fee is $8. Cabins are available for $60 a night. Gates are open daily from 6am to 10pm in summer, from 8am to 5pm in winter. Call ✆ **435/789-4432** for information, 800/322-3770 for campsite reservations. The Utah State Parks website is www.stateparks.utah.gov.

What to See & Do in Town

Daughters of Utah Pioneers (DUP) Museum The DUP seems to have a presence in nearly every town in Utah; this Vernal outpost is located in a rock building erected in 1887 by the Uintah Stake of the LDS Church. The small museum offers a display of pioneer relics and photos, and a history of the settling of the area from the mid-1800s. Allow half an hour.

186 S. 500 West. www.dupinternational.org. ✆ **435/789-0352.** Donations requested. June–Aug Wed–Sat 10am–4pm. Closed rest of year.

Utah Field House of Natural History State Park Museum ★ Within an 80-mile radius of Vernal, much of the Earth's geologic history is visible—more than you can see in the Grand Canyon. This museum focuses on that history and, of course, dinosaurs. Visit the museum's theater first to watch a short film about paleontologists at work in the field. Then head outside to the park for a close-up look at a huge dinosaur skeleton and a number of exhibits on paleontology, geology, and the Fremont and Ute cultures. Kids will love the **Dinosaur Garden ★★**, with 18 life-size models of dinosaurs and other prehistoric creatures in a garden that simulates the dinosaurs' actual habitat. The gift shop sells dinosaur-related souvenirs and books. Allow at least 1 hour.

496 E. Main St. https://stateparks.utah.gov/parks/utah-field-house. Ⓒ **435/789-3799.** $7 adults, $3.50 children 6–12, free for children 5 and under. Mon–Sat 9am–5pm. Closed Thanksgiving, Christmas, and New Year's Day.

Western Heritage Museum ★ Western pre-history comes to life at this museum, which contains one of the country's best collections of Fremont Indian objects. It also has 1880s Ute artifacts and displays of historic rifles, fossils, and rocks. Pioneer life is depicted in a country store; a blacksmith shop with tack and saddles; a one-room schoolhouse; a barbershop; and a bedroom, kitchen, and parlor. Clothing from 1880 to 1930 is also on display. The museum features changing art exhibits, and early horse-drawn wagons and farm equipment are on display outside. Allow an hour.

Western Park, 328 E. 200 South. Ⓒ **435/789-7399.** Free admission. Memorial Day to Labor Day Mon–Fri 9am–6pm, Sat 10am–4pm; rest of year Mon–Fri 9am–5pm, Sat 10am–2pm.

Where to Stay

The best way to see Dinosaurland is to camp out in the middle of it. But if you must have an off-the-floor bed, the town of Vernal has more than a dozen motels, including chain and franchise properties like **Holiday Inn Express,** 1515 W. Main St. (www.hiexpress.com; Ⓒ 800/718-8466 or 435/789-4654), and **Super 8,** 1624 W. Main St. (www.super8.com; Ⓒ **800/800-8000** or 435/789-4326). Among the independents, the best option is the **Quality Inn** (formerly the Weston Plaza Hotel), 1684 W. Hwy. 40 (www.choicehotels.com; Ⓒ **435/789-9550**). Rates for double rooms range from $129 to $169, depending on the season. A good budget option is the **Sage Motel,** 54 W. Main St. (http://vernalmotels.com; Ⓒ **800/760-1442** or 435/789-1442), with extended stay suites available. There is also a B&B, the **Jensen Inn,** 5056 S. 9500 East, Jensen (www.thejenseninn.com; Ⓒ **435/789-5905**), not far from the boundary to Dinosaur National Monument. Doubles begin at $100 for two people, with a shared bath and include breakfast; family rooms and suites begin at $125. There's also a tepee and campground onsite. Another lodging option in this area is to stay at one of the **U.S. Forest Service's guard stations or yurts ★**, located in spectacular forest settings north of Vernal in the Ashley National Forest. Rates differ, and the facilities offer a range of amenities and sleeping capacities and are available year-round. For information, contact the **Vernal Ranger District** office (www.fs.fed.us/r4/Ashley; Ⓒ **435/789-1181**); for reservations, call Ⓒ **877/444-6777** or visit www.recreation.gov.

CAMPING

Among the area campgrounds with full RV hookups and hot showers is **Dinosaurland KOA,** 930 N. Vernal Ave., Vernal (Ⓒ **435/789-2148;** www.dinokoa.com).

com), which is open from April through October. It has RV sites, grassy tent sites, seven cabins, and two deluxe cottages. Both **Red Fleet State Park** (p. 171) and **Steinaker State Park** (p. 172) also have camping.

Where to Eat

Bakery and deli counters can be found at **Davis Jubilee**, 575 W. Main St. (✆ **435/789-2001**), and **Smith's**, 1080 W. Main St. (✆ **435/789-7135**).

Betty's Cafe ★ AMERICAN   This simple, down-home cafe is a local favorite, and it's easy to see why. It serves well-prepared homemade food at reasonable prices. Breakfast, which includes all the usual offerings, is served all day. Lunch fare is sandwiches, half- and quarter-pound burgers, plus such choices as chicken-fried steak, liver and onions, catfish, and hamburger steak. No alcoholic beverages are served, but the pie selection is great.

416 W. Main St. ✆ **435/781-2728.** Main courses $4–$13. Mon–Fri 6am–2pm; Sat–Sun 6am–noon.

Dinosaur Brew Haus ★ AMERICAN   A bare-bones beer joint with Salt Lake's Squatters microbrew on tap, the Dino Brew Haus isn't much to look at—with concrete walls, a pool table, and a slightly woodsy feel—but it serves reasonably good burgers and barbecue, as well as salads and sandwiches, including a portobello mushroom option. There's also a patio out back.

550 E. Main St. ✆ **435/781-0717.** Main courses $10–$23, Daily 11am–9pm.

7-11 Ranch Restaurant ★ AMERICAN   A good family restaurant offering home-style food in a comfortable, Western-style setting, the 7-11 Ranch Restaurant had its beginnings in 1933, when Warren "Fat" Belcher sold a cow and bought a hot dog stand. Now owned by Belcher's daughter Connie and her husband, Jerry Pope, the restaurant has changed a bit—you won't even find hot dogs on the menu—but you can count on friendly service and a wide range of American favorites. Choose from a variety of burgers—including a huge 1-pound killer—plus hot and cold sandwiches, deep-fried and grilled halibut and other seafood, excellent chef's salads, homemade chili, pork chops, and chicken in several variations. There are also steaks, barbecued beef or pork ribs, and prime ribs on Fridays. Breakfasts consist of the usual American favorites. The gift shop is loaded with dinosaur souvenirs.

77 E. Main St. www.7-11ranchrestaurant.com. ✆ **435/789-1170.** Main courses $6–$19. Mon–Sat 6am–10pm.

Vernal Brewing Company ★ BREWPUB   Just what you crave when you come off the river or trail, Vernal's first brewpub has the hearty menu of pizzas, burgers, sandwiches, and skillets that beer requires, plus an ever-changing menu of craft brews available by the pint, pitcher, or growler.

55 S. 500 East. www.vernalbrewing.com. ✆ **435/781-2337.** Sun–Thurs 11:30am–9pm; Fri–Sat 11:30am–10pm.

DINOSAUR NATIONAL MONUMENT

20 miles E of Vernal, 195 miles E of Salt Lake City

In some ways, this park offers two separate experiences: a look at the lost world of dinosaurs on one hand, and a scenic wonderland of colorful rock, deep river canyons, and a forest of Douglas fir on the other.

About 150 million years ago, the region was a warm land of ferns, conifers, grasses, ponds, and rivers, which made it a suitable habitat for dinosaurs, including vegetarians such as diplodocus, apatosaurus, and stegosaurus; and sharp-toothed carnivores, such as allosaurus, that hunted their vegetarian cousins. When these huge creatures died, most of their skeletons decayed and disappeared, but in at least one spot, floodwaters washed dinosaur carcasses into the bottom of a river. Here they were preserved in sand and covered with sediment, creating the largest quarry of Jurassic-period dinosaur bones ever discovered.

But visitors who limit their trip to the Dinosaur Quarry, fascinating as it is, miss quite a bit. Encompassing 325 square miles of stark canyons at the confluence of two rivers, the monument also offers hiking trails, pioneer homesteads, thousand-year-old rock art, spectacular panoramic vistas, wildlife-watching opportunities, and the thrills of white-water rafting.

The Yampa, Green, and smaller rivers are responsible for the area's fertility, creating microclimates that support hanging gardens of mosses and ferns, cottonwoods, and even an occasional Douglas fir—all just yards from the predominant landscape of sagebrush, cactus, and dwarfed piñon and juniper trees. Wildlife includes species that can survive the harsh extremes of the high desert climate—bighorn sheep, coyotes, rabbits, and snakes—as well as mule deer, beavers, and porcupines along the riverbanks. Birds that are occasionally spotted include peregrine falcons, sage grouse, and Canada geese.

Essentials

GETTING THERE/ACCESS POINTS/VISITOR CENTERS Straddling the Utah-Colorado state line, Dinosaur National Monument is accessible via two main roads—one from each state—that don't connect inside the monument.

The **visitor center** is 20 miles east of Vernal. To get here, take U.S. 40 to Jensen and head north on Utah 149 for 7 miles. The main visitor center at the Dinosaur Quarry closed in 2006 due to structural concerns and was replaced by a stunning new facility that opened in fall 2011. It is open daily from 9am to 5pm, with extended summer hours if staffing allows. It is closed New Year's Day, Thanksgiving, and Christmas.

Administrative offices and a small **visitor center** are located about 2 miles east of the town of Dinosaur, Colorado, at the intersection of U.S. 40 and Harpers Corner Drive. This visitor center offers a short slide program; hours are daily 9am to 4pm in summer (closed in winter). The center is closed for federal holidays.

Several other monument entrances exist, all without visitor centers: At the far eastern edge of the monument off U.S. 40, an entry road leads to Deerlodge Park (open in summer only); at the northern tip, off Colo. 318, a road goes to the Gates of Lodore; just inside the Utah border at Jones Hole Fish Hatchery, a road leads into the park via the Jones Hole Road from Vernal; and at the Rainbow Park section, you'll find a park entry road off Island Park Road (impassable when wet) from the monument's western edge.

INFORMATION   You can **Dinosaur National Monument** at ℂ **435/781-7700** or 970/374-3000 or visit www.nps.gov/dino. In addition, the nonprofit **Intermountain Natural History Association,** 1291 E. U.S. 40, Vernal (ℂ **800/845-3466;** www.inhaweb.com), offers numerous publications, maps, posters, and videos on the park and its geology, wildlife, history, and dinosaurs. Information on area lodging, dining, and recreational facilities can be obtained from the **Dinosaurland Travel Board** (p. 170).

FEES, BACKCOUNTRY PERMITS, REGULATIONS & SAFETY   The entry fee, charged only at the main Utah entrance, is $25 per vehicle or $20 per motorcycle, $15 per person for bicycle or walk-up, and is good for a week. Camping fees are extra (free to $12 per night); backcountry overnight camping permits, although free, are required and available from park rangers.

Regulations forbid damaging or taking anything, particularly fossils and other natural, historical, and archaeological items. Off-road driving is not permitted. Dogs must be leashed at all times. Pets are not allowed in buildings, on trails, more than 100 feet from developed roads, or on river trips.

Rangers warn that the rivers are not safe for swimming or wading; the water is icy cold, and the current is stronger than it appears.

SEASONS/AVOIDING THE CROWDS   Summer is the busiest and hottest time of the year at Dinosaur National Monument, with daytime temperatures often soaring into the upper 90s (30s Celsius). Winters are a lot quieter but can be cold, with fog, snow, and temperatures below zero (–18°C). The best times to visit are during what Utahns call the "shoulder season," what others call spring (although you should be prepared for rain showers) and fall—perhaps the very best time—when the cottonwood trees turn a brilliant gold.

RANGER PROGRAMS   Rangers present a variety of activities in summer, including evening campfire programs; check the schedules posted at either visitor center.

Seeing the Highlights

Those with only a short amount of time should make their first stop the shiny **Quarry Exhibit Hall,** accessible via shuttles departing from the Quarry Visitor Center. This is the only place in the monument where you can see dinosaur bones. This area is believed to be one of the world's most concentrated and accessible deposits of the fossilized remains of dinosaurs, crocodiles, turtles, and clams. The exhibit hall's fossil wall—which looks like a long slab of frozen pudding with bones sticking out of it—contains some 1,500 fossils. Models show what paleontologists believe these dinosaurs looked like when they still had their skin, and other exhibits detail life in the Jurassic.

After spending about an hour in the quarry area, drive the **Tour of the Tilted Rocks,** which takes an hour or two. If time allows, or if you're heading east into Colorado anyway, take another few hours to drive the scenic **Harpers Corner Drive** (see the next section for descriptions of both drives).

Exploring by Car

Drives in both the Utah and Colorado sections of the park allow motorists to see spectacular scenery in relative solitude. Brochures for each of the following drives are available at the visitor centers.

From the quarry area on the Utah side of the park, the **Tour of the Tilted Rocks** along Cub Creek Road is a 26-mile round-trip drive that's suitable for most passenger cars. This route takes you to 1,000-year-old rock art left by the Fremont people, a pioneer homestead, and views of nearby mountains and the Green River. Watch for prairie dogs both alongside and on the road. Although mostly paved, the last two miles of the road are dirt and narrow, and may be dusty or muddy. The last four miles are unplowed in the winter and may not be passable by car December to March. There is no food or services along the route. Allow 1 to 2 hours.

For the best scenic views, drive to Colorado and take the **Harpers Corner Drive.** This paved, 62-mile round-trip has several overlooks offering panoramic views into the gorges carved by the Yampa and Green rivers, a look at the derby-shaped Plug Hat Butte, and close-ups of a variety of other colorful rock formations. The drive also provides access to the easy, ¼-mile round-trip Plug Hat Nature Trail and the moderately difficult 2-mile round-trip **Harpers Corner Trail** (p. 178). Allow about 2 hours for the drive, more if you plan to do some hiking.

Outdoor Pursuits

BOATING To many people, the best way to see this beautiful, rugged country is from the river, where you can admire the scenery while crashing through thrilling white water and floating over smooth, silent stretches. About a dozen outfitters are authorized to run the **Yampa and Green rivers ★** through the monument, offering trips ranging from 1 to 5 days, usually from mid-May to mid-September. Among companies providing river trips are **Don Hatch River Expeditions** (www.donhatchrivertrips.com; ✆ **800/342-8243** or 435/789-4316) and **Dinosaur River Expeditions** (www.dinosaurriverexpeditions.com; ✆ **800/345-7238** or 435/781-0717). Prices start at about $90 for a 1-day trip. A complete list of authorized river-running companies is available from monument headquarters (see "Information," under "Essentials," p. 179).

FISHING The catch is mostly catfish in the Green and Yampa rivers, although there are also some trout. Several endangered species of fish—including the razorback sucker and humpback chub—must be returned unharmed to the water if caught. Either a Utah or Colorado fishing license (or both) is required, depending on where you plan to fish.

HIKING Because most visitors spend their time at the quarry and along the scenic drives, hikers willing to exert a little effort can discover spectacular and dramatic views of the colorful canyons while enjoying an isolated and quiet wilderness experience. The best times for hiking are spring and fall, but even then, hikers should carry at least a gallon of water per person, per day.

In addition to several developed trails, experienced backcountry hikers with the appropriate maps can explore miles of unspoiled canyons and rock benches. Ask rangers about the numerous possibilities.

In the Utah section of the park, you can search out extreme solitude along the **Sound of Silence Trail,** a moderate-to-difficult 3-mile hike that leaves Cub Creek Road about 2 miles east of the Dinosaur Quarry. This trail is designed to help you learn how to find your own way in the desert, and is not always easy to follow.

The **Desert Voices Nature Trail,** a self-guided nature trail near the quarry, offers sweeping panoramic views and a section with signs created by kids for kids. This 1½-mile hike (round-trip) is moderately difficult.

Visitors to the Colorado side of the park enjoy the **Cold Desert Trail,** which begins at the headquarters' visitor center. This easy ½-mile round-trip trail offers a good introduction to the natural history of this arid environment.

Panoramic vistas await visitors on the **Plug Hat Nature Trail,** an easy ¼-mile round-trip hike that introduces you to the interactions between plants and animals in the piñon juniper forest. It's located along the Harpers Corner Scenic Drive.

The very popular **Harpers Corner Trail ★** begins at the end of the Harpers Corner Scenic Drive. This 2-mile round-trip hike is moderately difficult but highly recommended for a magnificent view of the deep river canyons.

CAMPING The **Green River Campground,** 5 miles east of the Dinosaur Quarry and within park boundaries, has 80 RV and tent sites, modern restrooms, drinking water, tables, and fireplaces, but no showers or RV hookups. Park rangers often give campfire talks. The cost is $18 per night and it's open mid-April into October. Some sites can be reserved at www.recreation. gov or by calling 𝄐 **877/444-6777.**

Several smaller campgrounds with limited facilities are also available in the monument, with fees ranging from free to $8; check with the visitor centers.

FLAMING GORGE NATIONAL RECREATION AREA ★★

41 miles N of Vernal, 210 miles E of Salt Lake City

Tucked away in the far northeast corner of Utah and stretching up into Wyoming is **Flaming Gorge National Recreation Area,** one of Utah's most scenic areas. A dam was built on the Green River for flood control, water storage, and the generation of electricity, but the dam also created a huge and gorgeous lake—some 91 miles long, with more than 300 miles of shoreline—that has become one of the prime fishing and boating destinations of the region.

Here is some of the best fishing in the West, well over 100 miles of hiking and mountain-biking trails, and hundreds of camp and picnic sites. It's a boater's paradise, filled with everything from kayaks and canoes to ski and fishing boats to pontoons to gigantic houseboats with everything on board (including the kitchen sink).

Named by Major John Wesley Powell during his exploration of the Green and Colorado rivers in 1869, Flaming Gorge has a rugged, wild beauty that comes alive when the rising or setting sun paints the red rocks surrounding the lake in a fiery, brilliant palette. It's a land of clear blue water, colorful rocks, tall cliffs, dark forests, hot summer sun, and cold winter wind.

Essentials

Flaming Gorge National Recreation Area lies in the northeast corner of Utah, crossing into the southwest corner of Wyoming. The dam and main visitor center, in the southeast section of the national recreation area, are 41 miles north of Vernal (210 miles east of Salt Lake City via U.S. 40).

GETTING THERE From Vernal and other points south, take U.S. 191 north to its intersection with Utah 44 at the southern edge of the reservoir. U.S. 191 goes up the east side of the reservoir, leading to the dam and the community of Dutch John; Utah 44 goes around the reservoir on the west side, eventually ending at the village of Manila. Both of these towns offer accommodations, restaurants, fuel, and other services.

From I-80 in Wyoming, follow U.S. 191 south around the reservoir's east side to the dam; or Wyo. 530 and Utah highways 43 and 44 to Manila and the west and south sides of the reservoir.

INFORMATION/VISITOR CENTER The recreation area is administered by the Ashley National Forest. For information, contact the **Flaming Gorge National Recreation Area** (www.fs.usda.gov/r4/Ashley; ✆ **435/784-3445**). The **Intermountain Natural History Association,** 1291 E. U.S. 40, Vernal (www.inhaweb.com; ✆ **800/845-3466**), sells maps, books, and other publications.

The **Flaming Gorge Dam Visitor Center** (www.flaminggorgecountry. com/Flaming-Gorge-Dam-Visitor-Center; © **435/885-3135**), along U.S. 191 on the east side of the recreation area, is open daily from April 15 to October 15, from 9am to 5pm. You can get information on the geology, history, flora, and fauna of the area; the construction of the dam; and facilities and recreation possibilities. Free dam tours lasting 45 minutes to an hour are conducted from 9am to 3pm in summer only; a new tour starts every 20 minutes or so.

FEES & REGULATIONS Entry to the recreation area is $5 for 1 day or $15 for up to 7 days. Administered by the U.S. Forest Service, regulations here are based mostly on common sense, and are aimed at preserving water quality and protecting the forest and historic sites. Utah and Wyoming fishing and boating regulations apply in those states' sections of the recreation area, and the appropriate fishing licenses are required. Dogs are allowed on hiking trails but are not permitted in buildings and should be leashed at all times.

SEASONS/AVOIDING THE CROWDS As one would expect, summer is the busy season at this major boating destination, when both the air and water are at their warmest. This is the best time to come for watersports, and with elevations from 5,600 to over 8,000 feet, it never gets as hot here as it does in many other parts of Utah. Although summer is the busiest time of year, this remains a relatively undiscovered destination, and you will likely have no trouble finding campsites, lodging, or boat rentals. Hikers enjoy the area in the fall; during the cold, snowy winter, this is a popular snowshoeing, cross-country skiing, and ice-fishing destination.

Exploring Flaming Gorge by Car

Numerous viewpoints are situated along U.S. 191 and Utah 44 in the Utah section of Flaming Gorge; especially dramatic is the **Red Canyon Overlook** on the southern edge, where a rainbow of colors splashes across 1,000-foot-tall cliffs. Another great overlook is **Dowd Mountain.** In Wyoming, highways are farther from the lake, offering few opportunities to see the river and its canyons.

Sheep Creek Canyon, south of Manila on the western side, has been designated a special geological area by the Forest Service because of its dramatically twisted and upturned rocks. A mostly paved 11-mile loop road cuts off from Utah 44, offering a half-hour tour of this beautiful, narrow canyon, with its lavish display of rocks that have eroded into intricate patterns, a process that began with the uplifting of the Uinta Mountains millions of years ago. This loop may be closed in winter; check at the visitor center before heading out.

Outdoor Pursuits

BIKING A number of mountain-biking trails provide splendid views of the recreation area's scenery, especially in the Utah section. Bikes are permitted in most of Flaming Gorge and adjacent Ashley National Forest, except in the High Uintas Wilderness, where all wheeled vehicles are prohibited. Bikes are also restricted from Memorial Day to Labor Day on a section of the Little Hole National Recreation Trail along the Green River below the dam, due to very heavy use by anglers and hikers. Keep in mind that mountain bikers here often share trails with hikers, horses, and four-wheelers. A free mountain-biking brochure is available at area visitor centers.

For a scenic and fairly easy ride, try the 5-mile one-way **Red Canyon Rim Trail.** This single track gains very little elevation but follows the south rim of the canyon, providing terrific views of the lake 1,700 feet below. Deer and elk are frequently seen in the forested areas. Watch also for interpretive signs on area wildlife and the ecosystem. Trailheads and parking are located at Red Canyon Visitor Center, Red Canyon Lodge, and Greendale Overlook.

> ## Impressions
>
> *The river enters the range by a flaring, brilliant red gorge, that may be seen from the north a score of miles away . . . We name it Flaming Gorge.*
> —Explorer Major John Wesley Powell, May 26, 1869

Death Valley Trail, a moderately difficult 15-mile round-trip ride, offers good views of the Uinta Mountains and ends with a fine view of the lake from the top of Sheep Creek Hill. The trailhead is located along Utah 44, south of Manila, at mile marker 16.5.

Rentals of full-suspension mountain bikes are available at **Red Canyon Lodge,** in Dutch John (www.redcanyonlodge.com; ✆ **435/889-3759**), at rates of $12 for 1 hour, $20 for a half-day, and $36 for a full day. The lodge also sponsors a mountain-bike festival each year in August. In Vernal, head to **Altitude Cycle,** 580 E. Main St. (www.altitudecycle.com; ✆ **435/781-2295**), for gear, service, and advice.

BOATING & HOUSEBOATING   As at Lake Powell, boaters on Flaming Gorge reservoir get to enjoy the incredible, colorful scenery from a unique perspective. Magnificent fiery red canyons surround the lake in the Utah section, and the wide-open Wyoming badlands farther north.

Three marinas on **Lake Flaming Gorge** provide boat rentals, fuel, launching ramps, and boating and fishing supplies. **Cedar Springs Marina** (www.cedarspringsmarina.com; ✆ **435/889-3795**) is located 2 miles west of Flaming Gorge Dam; **Lucerne Valley Marina** (www.flaminggorge.com; ✆ **435/784-3483**) is on the west side of the lake, 7 miles east of Manila; and **Buckboard Marina** (www.buckboardmarina.com; ✆ **307/875-6927**) is also on the west side of the lake, off Wyo. 530, 22 miles north of Manila.

Nine boat ramps serve those who bring their own craft; boat and water-ski rentals are available at all three marinas. Although types of boats and costs vary, a 14-foot fishing boat with a small outboard motor usually costs about $145 per day, a 17- or 18-foot ski boat with a powerful outboard motor costs about $250 to $350 per day, and a 24-foot pontoon boat with a 50-horsepower outboard motor will run you about $225 to $250 per day. Partial-day rentals are available. At Lucerne Valley Marina, a 36-foot houseboat costs about $1,280 for 3 nights during the summer, with discounts in spring and fall; a

8

UTAH'S NORTHEAST CORNER

Flaming Gorge National Recreation Area

Flaming Gorge is one of the best places in Utah to see a wide variety of wildlife. Boaters should watch for **osprey, peregrine falcons, swifts**, and **swallows** along the cliffs. **Bighorn sheep** are sometimes spotted clambering on the rocky cliffs on the north side of the lake in spring and early summer. On land, be on the lookout for **pronghorns** (technically, they're not antelope) year-round along the west side of the lake, particularly in Lucerne Valley and In the campground. Hikers on the Little Hole National Recreation Trail should keep their eyes peeled for a variety of birds, including **bald eagles** in winter.

52-footer is also available for about $1,950 for 3 nights in the summer. For all boat rentals, life jackets are included but fuel is extra.

Non-motorized boating is permitted on a 20-acre private lake at **Red Canyon Lodge** (p. 185), where you can rent canoes, rowboats, and paddle boats. **Dinosaur River Expeditions** (www.dinoadv.com; ℂ **800/345-7238** or 435/781-0717), in Vernal, offers a 1-day raft trip for $90 for adults and $55 for kids 7 to 12.

FISHING   You might want to bring along a muscular friend if you plan to fish Lake Flaming Gorge, which is famous for its record-breaking trout catches, such as the 57-pound lake trout caught in 2017, the 26-pound, 2-ounce rainbow caught in 1979; and the 33-pound, 10-ounce German brown caught in 1977. You'll encounter other cold-water species such as smallmouth bass and kokanee salmon. Fishing is popular year-round, although ice-fishermen are warned to make sure the ice is strong enough to hold them.

Cedar Springs and Lucerne Valley marinas (see "Boating & Houseboating," above) offer a variety of fishing guide services. Typical rates for one or two people in a guided trip aboard a sportfishing boat vary, but many require a hefty deposit and cash or check may be preferred. Also providing guided fishing trips, in a 28-foot sportfishing boat with state-of-the-art fish-finding and GPS equipment, is Kyle Edwards of **Conquest Expeditions** ★★ (www.conquestexpeditions.com; ℂ **801/244-9948**). Rates for a 4-hour fishing trip, with all equipment (but not fishing licenses), are $350 for one or two people and $450 for three or four people. Rates for an 8-hour fishing trip are $550 for one or two people, $650 for three or four.

Trout fishing on the Green River below the dam is also outstanding. **The Dutch John Resort,** based in Dutch John (https://dutchjohnresort.com; ℂ **435/885-3191**), offers guided fishing trips for one or two people, with rates of $525 for an 8- to 10-hour trip A complete list of guides is available at the Flaming Gorge Dam Visitor Center (p. 180).

Two private stocked lakes are also at **Red Canyon Lodge** (p. 185), one with a fully accessible fishing pier, and both open to catch-and-release fishing only. No state fishing license is needed, but a Red Canyon Lodge permit is required (free for guests, $5 for nonguests). A free kids' fishing pond is in front of the lodge's restaurant.

HIKING Many of the trails here offer spectacular scenic views of the reservoir and its colorful canyons. Remember, though, that in most cases the trail is shared with mountain bikers and in some cases horses and 4WD vehicles as well.

The **Red Canyon Rim Trail** runs 5 miles (one-way) from the Red Canyon Visitor Center to the Greendale Rest Area, accessible from either of those points or at Green's Lake or Canyon Rim campgrounds. The trail wanders through a forest of Douglas fir and pine, with stops along the canyon rim providing outstanding views of the lake far below (see also "Biking," above).

For an easy 3-mile round-trip hike to an overlook offering a fine view of the lake, try the **Bear Canyon Bootleg Trail,** which starts just off U.S. 191 opposite Firefighters Memorial Campground, 3 miles south of the dam.

One trail popular with hikers is the **Little Hole National Recreation Trail,** which runs about 7 miles from the dam spillway downstream to Little Hole, with its fishing platforms and picnic areas. The trail is easy to moderate and offers splendid vistas of the Green River, which appears to be a mere ribbon of emerald when seen from the cliffs above. This is a good trail for birders, who may spot osprey in summer and bald eagles in winter.

Hikers can also use the mountain-biking trails listed above. A free hiking-trails brochure is available at the visitor centers.

HORSEBACK RIDING Many of the more than 100 miles of trails in Flaming Gorge are open to riders. Guided rides are available from **Red Canyon Stables** at Red Canyon Lodge (p. 185), with options ranging from one-hour rides to half- and whole-day adventures. Children must be at least 6 years old to go on rides.

SWIMMING Sometimes you've just got to dive right in, even though the water is pretty cold. Lake Flaming Gorge has two designated swimming areas: **Sunny Cove,** just north of the dam, and **Lucerne Beach,** a mile west of Lucerne Campground. Neither has a lifeguard.

WINTER SPORTS Ice-fishing is popular, but check with rangers first for ice conditions. Also popular from mid-January until the snow melts are cross-country skiing, snowshoeing (an excellent way to see wildlife), and snowmobiling. At Red Canyon Lodge, you can rent snowshoes (poles are extra), and Flaming Gorge Resort (p. 184) rents cross-country ski packages in winter.

Man-Made Attractions
FLAMING GORGE DAM & POWER PLANT

Water is what Westerners obsess about. The history of the West is the history of its water supply and debates over water rights, pipelines, and appropriate use still rage. Completed in 1963 at a cost of $50 million for the dam and another $65 million for the power plant, Flaming Gorge is part of the Colorado River Storage Project, which also includes Glen Canyon Dam on the Colorado River along the Arizona-Utah border, Navajo Dam on the San Juan River in New Mexico, and a series of three dams on the Gunnison River in

Colorado. At full capacity, the lake is 91 miles long and holds almost 4 million acre-feet of water. The dam, constructed in an arch shape for strength, is 1,285 feet long and stands some 450 feet tall; its three turbine generators can produce 152,000 kilowatts of electricity, enough to satify the needs of 210,000 people. On the down side, the dam and reservoir fragmented the upper Green River, blocking fish migration and significantly impacting many native species. Water released from the dam is generally cold and clear, as compared to the river's natural warm and silty flow, further changing the local riverine ecology.

The dam and power plant are open for free guided tours 9am to 5pm daily from mid-April to mid-October. The total round-trip walking distance is just under half a mile. Check at the visitor center for opening hours and times of the hour-long guided tours. You'll walk along the crest of the dam, then take an elevator ride to the power plant below, where you get to see the inner workings of the hydroelectric plant, with its huge transformers, generators, and turbines.

SWETT RANCH HISTORIC SITE

Sometimes you need help imagining what it was really like to settle the West. Homesteaders toiled endlessly doing backbreaking work to create a sustainable home in the arid desert. The Sweet homestead, listed on the National Register of Historic Places, gives a glimpse into those challenges. Constructed by Oscar Swett starting in 1909, the site contains two cabins, a five-room house, a meat house, a root cellar, sheds, a granary, and a barn, built and improved upon over a period of 58 years. Swett and his wife, Emma, raised nine children here, running the 397-acre ranch using only horse and human muscle power, before selling the property in 1968. From Utah 44, take U.S. 191 north for a half-mile and turn west (left) onto Forest Road 158, which you follow 1½ miles to the ranch. The unpaved Forest Road is muddy when wet and not recommended for large RVs or trailers at any time. The ranch is open daily 10am to 5pm from Memorial Day to Labor Day; guided tours are available. Admission is free. Allow about an hour.

Where to Stay

In addition to the lodging suggestions below, see the "Where to Stay" section in "Vernal: Gateway to Dinosaur National Monument," earlier in this chapter.

Flaming Gorge Resort   A location close to everything you'll want to do makes this well-maintained property a good choice for those seeking a modern motel room or a one-bedroom condominium with all the adventures just outside your door. Motel rooms come with two queen-size beds and an optional rollaway; condo units contain one queen bed, a single, and a hide-a-bed, plus a fully equipped kitchen. There is also a "trailer suite" and a four-bedroom suite for those needing a little more room. Facilities include a restaurant that serves three meals daily, a gas station, a liquor and convenience store, and a fly and tackle shop. Guided fishing and rafting trips on the Green River are available, and the lodge offers non-motorized watercraft rentals and mountain-bike rentals in the summer.

155 Greendale, U.S. 191 (4 miles south of Flaming Gorge Dam), Dutch John. www. flaminggorgeresort.com. © **877/348-7688** or 435/889-3773. 48 units, including 27 suites. Apr–Oct $115–$155 double, $159–$269 condo or suite; rates change according to season, so check the website. **Amenities:** Restaurant; bike rentals; free Wi-Fi.

Red Canyon Lodge ★ Open since 1930, this secluded cabin resort offers a variety of delightful handcrafted log cabins. All have private bathrooms, two queen-size beds, a separate living room, minifridges, limited cooking facilities, vaulted ceilings, and covered porches. Some also have freestanding woodstoves (firewood provided), kitchenettes, and custom wood furniture. Lower-priced units have showers only while the pricier rooms offer tub/shower combos. The lodge has two private lakes plus a kids' fishing pond, boat and mountain-bike rentals, hiking and mountain-biking trails, horseback rides (p. 183), a restaurant, and a gift shop.

2450 W. Red Canyon Lodge (turn off Utah 44 at milepost 3.5), Dutch John. www.redcanyonlodge.com. © **435/889-3759.** 18 units. $159 double, $169 for three or four people in the Ponderosa-Style cabins. Other styles have different rates. Dogs allowed (free). **Amenities:** Restaurant (reviewed below); bike rentals; free Wi-Fi; kitchenettes in some units; no phones.

CAMPING

U.S. Forest Service campgrounds are located throughout Flaming Gorge Recreation Area and range from primitive sites to modern facilities with showers (open in summer only) and flush toilets, but no RV hookups. Some are open year-round, others in summer only. Most sites cost $10 to $20. The more developed (and expensive) sites, including a favorite campground, **Deer Run,** include use of the showers (those camping in the cheap spots have to pay for a shower—bring quarters). Campsite reservations are available through the **National Recreation Reservation Service** (www.recreation.gov; © **877/444-6777**). Dispersed forest camping (with no facilities) is free; check with forest service personnel for suggested locations. RV dump stations are located in several locations in the recreation area (check at the visitor center).

Commercial campgrounds with full RV hookups are located in Vernal (see p. 168). A **KOA campground** (www.utahidahokoa.com; © **800/562-3254** or 435/784-3184), located in Manila, is open from mid-April through mid-October, and charges about $22 to $27 for tent sites and $32 to $37 for RV sites. It also has cabins at $45 to $65 per night double.

Where to Eat

Red Canyon Lodge Dining Room ★★ AMERICAN For locals and visitors alike, this is a popular spot—especially the patio on nice summer days. The dining room maintains a classic mountain-lodge atmosphere, along with views of tall pines and a small lake. Top choices here include the buffalo rib-eye and the elk medallions with black cherry–burgundy sauce. The menu also features pastas, salads, steaks, chicken (try the mildly spicy Szechuan chicken pasta), fish, and slow-roasted prime rib. Nightly fine-dining specials include a broiled salmon filet with hollandaise sauce. You'll also find standard American breakfasts, and burgers and sandwiches at lunch. Full liquor service is available.

In Red Canyon Lodge, 2450 W. Red Canyon Lodge (turn off Utah 44 at milepost 3.5), Dutch John. ⓒ 435/889-3759. Reservations accepted for large parties only. Main courses $9–$12 lunch, $16–$25 dinner. Hours change with the season so check the website.

UTAH'S DIXIE & THE COLORFUL SOUTHWEST CORNER

Small lakes and big rocks, golf courses and ski areas, Shakespeare and the latest special effects—you'll find it all in the southwest corner of Utah, dubbed "Color Country" by the locals for its numerous and colorful rock formations. In addition to the attractions, another reason to visit is the warm winter weather: The region's largest city, **St. George,** and its immediate surroundings are known as "Utah's Dixie" for the mild climate as well as the area's previous life as a Civil War–era cotton-growing region. Color Country is a terrific winter playground; there's no need to ever put away the golf clubs or swimsuits in this neighborhood.

The range of elevations here means you can often lounge around the pool in the morning and build a snowman that same afternoon. From the scorching desert at St. George, it's only 74 miles—and almost 7,500 feet up—to the cool mountain forest at Cedar Breaks National Monument. Home to a variety of scenic and recreation areas (including a ski resort), a surprising number of historic attractions, and excellent performing arts events (such as the Utah Shakespearean Festival in Cedar City), this region also serves as the gateway to several of the area's spectacular national parks. For a detailed **map** of the Southwest Corner, please see the inside front cover.

Here, you can step back more than a hundred years at Mormon leader Brigham Young's winter home or cheer on the Dixie State College Red Storm football team. Of course, the favorite stops are all outdoors: the rugged red-rock cliffs at Snow Canyon State Park, the ruddy sands of Coral Pink Sand Dunes State Park, and the panoramic views from Cedar Breaks National Monument. This area is also a good base for those visiting the area's national parks, including Grand Canyon (pick up a copy of "Frommer's Arizona and the Grand Canyon"), Great Basin, and Zion (see chapter 10).

In recent years, St. George has been booming, with Washington County's population jumping over 50% from 2000 to 2010; the metropolitan area is now home to about 155,000 people. More than a few Californians have retired here after falling in love with the climate—and the real estate prices. But the growth hasn't changed everything: The space is still wide open, the winters still mild, and the surroundings still starkly beautiful.

GETTING OUTDOORS IN UTAH'S COLOR COUNTRY

This is (another) of Utah's playgrounds, a year-round mecca for hikers, mountain bikers, golfers, boaters, anglers, and anybody else who just wants to get outdoors. Among the top spots for experiencing nature at its best are Cedar Breaks National Monument, a high-mountain oasis of towering pines and firs, with wildflowers galore, and state parks such as Snow Canyon, Coral Pink Sand Dunes, and Quail Creek.

The best seasons for outdoor activities here are based on elevation. In St. George and other lowlands, spring and fall are best, winter's okay, and summer is worst, because temperatures soar well over 100°F (38°C). However, not everyone says no to St. George in summer: Its desert climate makes it the golfing capital of Utah. The Sunbrook is considered one of the state's best courses, with a challenging layout and spectacular views of the White Hills, but you can stay a week in St. George and play a different course each day. On the other side of the seasonal coin, don't try to drive up the mountains to Cedar Breaks until June at the earliest or mid-October at the latest; the roads will be closed by snow.

A good way to see this part of Utah is on foot. Hiking trails abound throughout the Dixie and Fishlake national forests north of St. George. Several of the best trails are in state parks, particularly Snow Canyon State Park near St. George, and in the nearby national parks.

Biking here generally means mountain biking. Even when riding in the city, you never know when you're going to discover a great little trail turning off into the red-rock desert or up into alpine meadows. The best mountain biking is at Brian Head Resort. Both road and mountain bikes can take you to beautiful areas in and around Snow Canyon State Park near St. George.

For an area with so much desert, there's a lot of boating here: Utahns have created reservoirs to provide the desert and its residents with drinking and irrigation water. The best boating is at Quail Creek State Park near St. George; for a bit more solitude try the relatively undeveloped Gunlock State Park, also near St. George, or Minersville State Park, west of Beaver. The top fishing hole in these parts is Quail Creek State Park, but there are plenty of smaller lakes and hidden streams in the national forests.

The Southwest Corner

Ski Area

Grand Staircase–Escalante
National Monument
Original Boundary

Off-road vehicles can simply be a means to get to an isolated fishing stream or hiking trail, or the adventure itself. The old mining and logging roads in the national forests are great for four-wheel exploring. Visitors with dune buggies will want to challenge the shifting dunes at Coral Pink Sand Dunes State Park, just outside Kanab.

An abundance of wildlife makes its home in this part of the state. Sure, you'll encounter deer, squirrels, chipmunks, and other furry creatures at Cedar Breaks National Monument and the area's national parks, but there's also animal life in the desert, including everyone's favorites: the luminescent scorpions at Coral Pink Sand Dunes State Park and the Gila monster at Snow Canyon State Park, also home to numerous songbirds.

It may be hot down in the desert, but there's plenty of snow on those mountaintops, and the skiing is great at Brian Head Resort and Eagle Point. In winter, cross-country skiers and snowshoers will want to head to nearby Cedar Breaks National Monument after the snow closes the roads to cars.

ST. GEORGE: GATEWAY TO THE WONDERS OF THE SOUTH

120 miles NE of Las Vegas, Nevada; 305 miles SW of Salt Lake City

In the fall of 1861, Brigham Young sent 309 families to establish a cotton-growing community in the semiarid Virgin River Valley. Today, the city of St. George, at an elevation of 2,800 feet, has more than 70,000 inhabitants, not to mention its seasonal snowbirds who descend upon St. George for thee region's gentle winters. Life in St. George, known as one of Utah's more conservative communities, is still strongly influenced by the Mormon church. Despite the climate, this desert city appears quite green, with tree-lined streets and lovely grassy areas. St. George also has more than a half-dozen golf courses, along with recreational and cultural facilities to suit most every taste.

St. George is also the gateway to some of the most spectacular scenery in the West. Zion, Bryce, and Grand Canyon national parks are within relatively easy driving distance, as are Cedar Breaks and Pipe Springs national monuments and Snow Canyon, Gunlock, and Quail Creek state parks. Depending on your itinerary, St. George may be the largest town that you stop in en route to Lake Powell and Glen Canyon National Recreation Area, Capitol Reef National Park, and the prehistoric Indian sites in the Four Corners area.

Essentials

GETTING THERE The closest major airport is McCarran International Airport, in Las Vegas (www.mccarran.com; ✆ **702/261-5211**). Most major airlines fly into McCarran, where you can rent a car from most major car-rental companies and drive the 120 miles northeast on I-15 to St. George.

The **St. George Shuttle** (www.stgshuttle.com; ✆ **800/933-8320** or 435/628-8320) provides daily van service to and from the Las Vegas airport ($20–$50

St. George & Environs

Central St. George

SANTA CLARA

WASHINGTON

DIXIE DOWNS

ST. GEORGE

Salt Lake City
UTAH
St. George

Golf Course
Airport

To Quail Creek State Park
Exit 10

To Pine Valley, Snow Canyon State Park and Red Mountain Spa

To Gunlock State Park

To Las Vegas and Virgin River Gorge

St. George Municipal Airport

See "Central St. George" inset

HOTELS ■
Best Western Abbey Inn **15**
Best Western Coral Hills **16**
Crystal Inn-St. George **17**
Dixie Palm Motel **8**
Green Gate Village Historic
Bed & Breakfast **21**
Inn at Entrada **21**
McArthur's Temple View
RV Resort **14**
Seven Wives Inn
Bed & Breakfast **3**

RESTAURANTS ◆
Bear Paw Cafe **6**
Judd's General Store **11**
Painted Pony **5**

ATTRACTIONS ●
Brigham Young Winter Home
Historical Site **4**
Daughters of Utah Pioneers
Museum **7**
Jacob Hamblin Home **1**
St. George Dinosaur
Discovery Site at Johnson
Farm **19**
St. George Tabernacle **10**
St. George Temple **13**

GOLF COURSES ●
Dixie Red Hills Golf Course **2**
Green Spring Golf Course **20**
Southgate Golf Course **17**
St. George Golf Club **18**
Sunbrook Golf Course **12**

each way) and also offers transportation between St. George and Salt Lake City ($48–$60); reservations are required).

The **St. George Municipal Airport**, 4550 S. Airport Pkwy., south of the city (www.sgcity.org/airport; © **435/627-4080**) opened in 2011 and is served by multiple carriers. Airline websites are listed in chapter 16.

St. George is on I-15. Take exit 2 (Airport Pkwy.).

VISITOR INFORMATION   Before your trip, contact the **St. George Area Chamber of Commerce** (© **435/628-1658;** www.stgeorgechamber.com) for a visitor's guide. When you get into town, stop in at the information center operated by the chamber in the historic Pioneer Courthouse, 97 St. George Blvd.; it's open Monday to Friday 9am to 5pm.

For information on the state and national parks in the area, as well as Dixie National Forest and land administered by the National Park Service and the Bureau of Land Management, stop by the **Interagency Office and Visitor Center,** 345 E. Riverside Dr. (www.fs.fed.us/r4, www.nps.gov, or www. ut.blm.gov; © **435/688-3246**). This is a good place to ask questions about the area's public lands, get trail recommendations, and pick up backcountry permits for the Grand Canyon. Free brochures are available, and maps, books, posters, and videos are for sale. To get there, take I-15 exit 6 and turn east. The center is open Monday through Friday 7:45am to 5pm and Saturday from 10am to 3pm.

GETTING AROUND   Like most Utah towns, this one is organized on the street grid system, and it's centered on the point at which Tabernacle Street (running east-west) crosses Main Street (running north-south), with numbered streets increasing in each direction by hundreds. St. George Boulevard takes the place of 100 North, Bluff Street runs along a bluff at the western edge of the city, I-15 cuts through in a northeast direction (from exit 6 at the south end of Bluff St. to exit 8 at the east end of St. George Blvd.), and River Road lies at the eastern edge, becoming Red Cliffs Road north of St. George Boulevard. Other than that, the system stays true to the grid.

Car-rental agencies with offices in St. George include **Avis** (www.avis.com; © **435/627-2002**), **Budget** (www.budget.com; © **435/673-6825**), and **Hertz** (www.hertz.com; © **435/652-9941**), all at St. George Municipal Airport, and **Enterprise**, 289 E. St. George Blvd. (www.enterprise.com; © **435/634-1556**).

Free on-street parking is available in much of the city, and many streets are tree-lined and shady.

For a taxi, call **AAA Quality Cab** (© **435/656-5222**) or **Taxi USA** (© **435/656-1500**).

FAST FACTS   One of the larger hospitals in this part of the state is **Dixie Regional Medical Center,** 1380 E. Medical Center Dr. (www.intermountain healthcare.org; © **435/251-1000**), which provides 24-hour emergency care. The **post office** is located at 180 N. Main St. (www.usps.com; © **800/275-8777**). The regional newspaper is the "Spectrum" (www.thespectrum.com).

What to See & Do

Most visitors head to St. George for rest and relaxation at the spas, golf courses, and area parks, but there's also a good deal of history in these parts, not to mention more prehistory: Yep, there were dinosaurs here too. The **St. George Dinosaur Discovery Site at Johnson Farm**, 2180 E. Riverside Dr. (www.utahdinosaurs.com; © **435/574-3466**) not only showcases 2,000 fossilized tracks left by dinosaurs of all kinds when the area sat on the edge of a vast lake, it's an active research center. It's open daily from 10am to 6pm; admission is $6 adults, $3 kids ages 4 to 11, and those 3 and under are free. In Kayenta in Coyote Gulch Art Village, outside Ivins north of St. George, is the **Desert Rose Labyrinth and Sculpture Garden** (© **435/674-2306**), featuring a labyrinth made of local red rock and intriguing outdoor art. Admission is free; it is open dawn to dusk.

MORMON HISTORY IN & AROUND ST. GEORGE

Because the LDS Church was the primary driving force in the settlement of St. George, it should come as no surprise that most of the sightseeing in town is church-related. At the town's historic buildings, staffed by knowledgeable church members, you'll learn about the church as well as the specific sites; expect a little sales pitch on the benefits of Christianity in general and the Mormon faith in particular. If you accept a free Book of Mormon, expect a missionary visit when you get home.

Brigham Young Winter Home Historical Site Church leader Brigham Young was one of St. George's original snowbirds. He escaped the Salt Lake City cold during the last few winters of his life by coming south to this house. In addition to its obvious religious importance, this home is a handsome example of how the well to do of the late 19th century lived. Allow 30 minutes for the guided tour.

67 W. 200 North. www.stgeorgetemplevisitorscenter.org. © **435/673-5181**. Daily 9am–9pm. From I-15 exit 8, head west on St. George Blvd., turn right (north) onto Main St., and then left (west) onto 200 North.

Daughters of Utah Pioneers Museum Many towns in Utah have a DUP museum in part because Mormons hold a powerful reverence for their own past. Like its sister museums, this DUP location contains an eclectic collection of items that belonged to the pioneers—including its showpiece, a bed used by Brigham Young, plus spinning wheels, an 1894 loom, guns, tools, musical instruments, and other relics from bygone days. Vintage photos, mostly of pioneer families, are on display, and copies are available for purchase. DUP volunteers lead guided tours. Allow at least a half-hour.

145 N. 100 East. www.dupstgeorge.org. © **435/628-7274**. Free admission; donations accepted. Fall and spring Mon–Tues and Thurs–Sat 10am–5pm. Closed Dec. From I-15 exit 8, head west on St. George Blvd. and turn right (north) at 100 East.

Jacob Hamblin Home ★ This stone-and-pine house, built in 1862, is closer to what you'd think of as a pioneer home than most of the refined houses of St. George, and it's typical of pioneer homes throughout the West—except for one aspect that is definitively Mormon: It has two identical bedrooms, one for each of Hamblin's wives. Note also that the dining table is set in typical Mormon fashion, with plates upside down and chairs facing away from the table to facilitate kneeling for before-meal prayers. The guided tour lasts about a half-hour.

3325 Hamblin Dr., Santa Clara. www.stgeorgetemplevisitorscenter.org. © **435/673-5181.** Free guided tours. Summer Mon–Sat 9am–7pm; rest of year Mon–Sat 9am–5pm; Sun 1–5pm. From St. George, go 3 miles west on Sunset Blvd. to the community of Santa Clara; watch for sign.

Pine Valley Chapel   You may have to look at Pine Valley Chapel awhile before you realize it resembles an upside-down boat—and that's because it is an upside-down boat. The eccentric, attractive white chapel was built in 1868 by Ebenezer Bryce (for whom Bryce Canyon National Park was named) and Lorenzo and Erastus Snow (for whom Snow Canyon State Park was named). The settlers of the Pine Valley logging and saw-milling community wanted to build a church that would also function as a school and community center. Unfortunately there was no architect or builder in the frontier town so Bryce, who had experience as a shipbuilder, was the best they could do. Bryce laid out the structure as an upside-down boat: Each of the walls was constructed flat on the ground, then lifted up and tied at the corners with strips of rawhide. The chapel was constructed of local pine and ponderosa and set on a foundation of granite and red limestone. Today it is the oldest LDS chapel in continuous use.

50 W. Main St., Pine Valley. www.lds.org. © **435/574-3202.** Free guided tours. Daily 10am–5pm, but closed Sun 10am–1pm for services. From St. George, go north on Utah 18 to Central and head east on Forest Rd. 035.

St. George Tabernacle ★   This is the most beautiful building in St. George—an excellent example of fine old-world craftsmanship, from the hand-quarried red stone walls to the intricate interior woodwork. The woodwork is done exclusively in pine, which is what they had on hand, but it was meticulously painted to look like exotic hardwoods and even marble. Completed in 1876 after 13 years of work, the Tabernacle served as a house of worship and town meeting hall. During the 1880s, when a nearby silver strike brought many Catholics to the area, the Tabernacle was used for a Roman Catholic High Mass led by a Roman Catholic priest, but with music from the liturgy sung by the local Mormon choir—in Latin. Today, the Tabernacle functions as a community center, presenting free weekly concerts and other cultural events (see "St. George After Dark," later in this chapter). The guided tour takes about half an hour.

18 S. Main St., at Tabernacle St. www.stgeorgetemplevisitorscenter.org. © **435/673-5181.** Free guided tours. Daily 10am–5pm; last tour at 4:30pm. From I-15 exit 8, head west on St. George Blvd. and turn left at Main St.

St. George Temple   Completed in 1877, St. George Temple was the first Mormon temple built in Utah, and is the world's oldest still in use today. The majestic white temple is not open to the public, but you can walk among the beautiful gardens and stop at the visitor center south of the temple for a tour of the center's exhibits and a multimedia program on the beliefs of the Church of Jesus Christ of Latter-day Saints.

490 S. 300 East. www.stgeorgetemplevisitorscenter.org. © **435/673-5181.** Temple not open to the public; free guided tours of visitor center exhibits. Daily 9am–9pm. From I-15 exit 8, head west on St. George Blvd. to 200 East, turn left (south) and go about 6 blocks.

Snow Canyon State Park ★★★

Snow Canyon is one of the prettiest state parks in a state where there's a surfeit of natural beauty; it's surrounded by rock cliffs and walls of Navajo sandstone in shades of red, layered with white and black from ancient lava flows. Hike the trails and discover shifting desert sand dunes, mysterious lava caves, colorful desert plants, and a variety of rock formations. You can also hike to a cactus garden and several ancient petroglyphs (ask park rangers for directions).

Because the summers here are hot—well over 100°F (38°C)—the best time to visit is any other time of the year. Winters are mild, but nights can be chilly. Spring and fall are usually perfect weather-wise, and therefore the busiest. By the way, don't come looking for snow—Snow Canyon was named for pioneers Lorenzo and Erastus Snow, who discovered the canyon.

ESSENTIALS
GETTING THERE   The park is 11 miles northwest of St. George, off Utah 18.

INFORMATION, FEES & REGULATIONS   For a copy of the park's brochure, contact **Snow Canyon State Park,** 1002 Snow Canyon Dr., Ivins (www.stateparks.utah.gov; © **435/628-2255**). Day-use fee is $10 per vehicle; $5 per senior vehicle, pedestrian, or cyclist. As in most state parks, dogs are welcome, even on trails, but must be leashed. The park is open from 6am to 10pm.

OUTDOOR PURSUITS
HIKING   Like most of Utah's parks, the best way to see Snow Canyon is to get out in the middle of it. Several short trails make for easy full- or half-day hikes that allow you to be surrounded by nature instead of viewing it from your car window. The **Hidden Piñon Trail** ★ is a 1½-mile round-trip self-guided nature trail that wanders among lava rocks, through several canyons, and onto rocky flatlands, offering panoramic views of the surrounding mountains. The trail begins across the highway from the park's campground; you can pick up a brochure at the park office/entrance station. The walk is fairly easy, but allow at least an hour, especially if you're planning to keep an eye

out for local vegetation such as Mormon tea, prickly pear cactus, and banana yucca.

An easy 2-mile round-trip is the **Johnson Canyon Trail,** which begins just south of the campground, passes the popular rock-climbing wall (see below) and some low sand dunes, and then leads into Johnson Canyon and a view of Johnson Arch (both named after pioneer wife Maude Johnson), spanning 200 feet high above.

The **Lava Flow Overlook Trail,** a 1½-mile round-trip, starts just north of the campground. Caves can be found for about a half-mile along the trail, but watch carefully—it's easy to miss them. The caves were formed from liquid lava, and Native American tribes, at times, have occupied the large rooms. Another quarter-mile past the caves is the **West Canyon Overlook,** with a breathtaking view into West Canyon.

Several longer and steeper trails lead to spectacular views of the canyons and distant vistas; check with park rangers for details.

MOUNTAIN BIKING   Bicycling is only allowed on the 7-mile round-trip **Whiptail Trail** and the unpaved **West Canyon Road.** The latter 8-mile round-trip road lies just west of the park; ask park rangers for directions. You can rent bikes at **Bicycles Unlimited** (p. 197).

ROCK CLIMBING   Climbers love the tall wall of rock on the east side of the road just south of the campground. Check with the park office for information.

WILDLIFE-WATCHING   You're pretty sure to see the usual cottontail rabbits, ground squirrels, and songbirds; luckier visitors may also spot desert mule deer, bobcats, coyotes, kit foxes, eagles, and owls. Although it's unlikely, you may see a desert tortoise (a federally listed threatened species) or a Gila monster. Snow Canyon is also home to some rattlesnakes.

CAMPING   Snow Canyon's 36-site campground is one of the best in the state. One section has rather closely spaced sites with electric hookups. If you don't require electricity you can set up camp in delightful little side canyons, surrounded by colorful red rocks and Utah juniper. The views are spectacular no matter where you set up. Facilities include hot showers, modern restrooms, and an RV dump station. Campsites cost $20 to $25. Reservations are recommended from February through May and September through November; call ☏ **800/322-3770** or visit www.stateparks.utah.gov.

More Outdoor Pursuits in the St. George Area

In addition to the outdoor opportunities that Snow Canyon State Park offers, great hiking, biking, and fishing can be enjoyed in the Dixie National Forest and on nearby lands administered by the Bureau of Land Management. For information, contact the Interagency Office (p. 192).

FISHING   **Quail Creek** and **Gunlock** state parks are the local fishing holes. For equipment, licenses, and tips on where they're biting, visit **Hurst Ace Hardware,** 160 N. Bluff St. (www.hurststores.com; ☏ **435/673-6141**).

GOLFING Utah's golf capital attracts golfers from around the country to a variety of public courses, known for their challenging designs, well-maintained fairways and greens, and spectacularly scenic settings. Rates given below are for winter; summer rates are usually lower. The area's best course, encompassing three 9-hole, par-36 courses, is the 27-hole **Sunbrook Golf Course,** 2366 W. Sunbrook Dr. (www.sgcity.org/golf; © **435/627-4400**), tops in both design and magnificent scenery. Greens fees are $18 to $26 summer for 9 holes and $56 fall to spring for 18 holes, cart included. Also highly rated, and considered by many to be the area's second-best course, is **Green Spring Golf Course,** 588 N. Green Spring Dr., Washington (www.golfgreenspring. com; © **435/673-7888**), several miles northeast of St. George. Challenging Green Spring is an 18-hole, par-72 course, with fees of $24 to $64 for 18 holes, cart included, with the lowest fees in the summer.

Other 18-hole courses include the par-73 municipal **St. George Golf Club,** 2190 S. 1400 East (© **435/627-4404**), and the par-70 **Southgate Golf Course,** 1975 S. Tonaquint Dr. (© **435/627-4440**). Fees at these city-owned courses are $19 to $33 for 18 holes, cart included. The par-34, 9-hole **Dixie Red Hills Golf Course,** 645 W. 1200 North (© **435/627-4444**), charges $13 to $21 for 9 holes.

You can play the renowned private Entrada at **Snow Canyon Country Club,** 2537 Entrada Trail (www.golfentrada.com; © **435/986-2200**), if you stay at the Inn at Entrada (see "Where to Stay," later in this chapter). Greens fees are $110 (winter and summer) to $150 (spring and fall) on the 18-hole Johnny Miller–designed course. The marketing cooperative called the **Red Rock Golf Trail** (www.redrockgolftrail.com; © **888/345-5551**) offers golfers a number of play-and-stay packages that start at about $139 per day for 18 holes and a room in an area hotel, based on double occupancy.

HIKING Some of the best hiking in the area is at Snow Canyon State Park (p. 195) and in the Dixie National Forest to the north, which has some 200 miles of trails. Check with forest rangers for current trail conditions and be sure to carry detailed maps on any long hikes, especially if you're venturing into the Pine Valley Wilderness Area. Stop at the Interagency Office and Visitor Center (p. 192) for maps and details.

MOUNTAIN BIKING & ROAD BIKING With hundreds of miles of trails in the St. George area, mountain biking continues to grow in popularity. For information on the best mountain-biking areas, plus maps, mountain-biking trail guides, bike repairs, bike accessories, and rentals, stop at **Bicycles Unlimited,** 90 S. 100 East (www.bicyclesunlimited.com; © **888/673-4492** or 435/673-4492) it's open Monday through Saturday 9am to 6pm. Top-quality road and mountain bikes rent for $69 to $85 per 24-hour period; ask about multiday rates.

A popular road-biking trip is the scenic **24-mile loop** from St. George through Santa Clara, Ivins, and Snow Canyon State Park. The route follows paved roads with narrow shoulders but generally little traffic. Allow 2 to 3 hours. Head north out of St. George on Bluff Street (Utah 18) and follow it to its intersection with U.S. 91. Turn west (left) and go about 6 miles to the village of Santa Clara, where you can visit the Jacob Hamblin Home (p. 193). From Santa Clara, continue west about a mile before turning north (right); follow the signs to Ivins and the Tuacahn Amphitheater. At Ivins, turn east (right) onto the Snow Canyon Road, following signs for Snow Canyon State Park, where you can easily spend several hours or several days exploring the red-rock formations, lava pools, and sand dunes. From the park, continue east to Utah 18, turn south (right), and pedal back into St. George.

Spectator Sports

The **Dixie State College Red Storm** are the ones to root for in St. George. The football, women's volleyball, women's soccer, men's and women's basketball, men's baseball, men's golf, and women's softball teams at this community college are often nationally ranked. You're not likely to have any trouble getting tickets to join the 5,000 students in Hansen Stadium or Burns Arena. Tickets are available at the **Athletic Department** offices (www.dixie athletics.com; ℭ **877/546-7327** or 435/879-4295).

Where to Stay

St. George has a compact center with a good selection of lodgings within easy walking distance of restaurants and attractions. Most are on St. George Boulevard and Bluff Street. Summer is the slow season here—people tend to head to the mountains when the temperature hits 115°F (46°C)—so prices are lowest then. High seasons are spring and fall. Golf packages may be available.

Reliable chain properties in the area, almost all clustered around exits 6 and 8 off Hwy. 15, include a pair of top-notch Best Westerns: the **Best Western Plus Abbey Inn,** 1129 S. Bluff St. (www.bwabbeyinn.com; ℭ **435/652-1234**), with rates of $88 to $124 double and $114 to $169 suite, and the **Best Western Coral Hills,** 125 E. St. George Blvd. (www.coralhills.com; ℭ **800/542-7733** or 435/849-8507), with rates of $79 to $138 and up, depending on the season.

Also in town near I-15 is **Crystal Inn,** 1450 S. Hilton Dr. (www.crystal innstgeorge.com; ℭ **435/688-7477**). There are numerous inexpensive chain properties, including **Motel 6,** 205 N. 1000 East (www.motel6.com; ℭ **435/628-7979**), and **Quality Inn,** 1165 S. Bluff St. (www.qualityinn.com; ℭ **435/628-4481**). Room prices at these properties vary—always check—and are higher during special events.

Pets are generally not accepted unless otherwise noted.

MODERATE TO EXPENSIVE

Green Gate Village Historic Bed & Breakfast ★★   You enter the eponymous gate and can't help wondering why the green gate is significant. Here's the story: It seems Brigham Young ordered white paint for the St. George Temple in 1877, but got a shipment of green instead. He couldn't send

it back, so Young gave the green stuff to locals for their gates and fences. Only one original green gate remains: It's on display in the inn's garden. The B&B offers 32 units throughout 10 separate buildings—all restored pioneer homes from the late 1800s, sitting in their own flower-filled little "village" across the street from Town Square. Each has a different floor plan, though most have one king bed. Breakfast is served in the central 1876 Bentley House. Quaint period authenticity is what it's all about here.

76 W. Tabernacle St., St. George. www.greengatevillageinn.com. © **435/628-6999.** 32 units. $139–$179 double. Rates include full breakfast. From I-15 exit 8, head west to Main St., turn left (south) 1 block to Tabernacle St., and turn right (west) to Green Gate Village. **Amenities:** Outdoor Jacuzzi; small outdoor heated pool; free Wi-Fi.

The Inn at Entrada ★★★

Although the rooms are separate casitas like Green Gate, the Inn at Entrada isn't quaint—this is pure modern luxury. Located on an exclusive Johnny Miller–designed golf course north of downtown St. George, the gated Inn offers a place to get away from it, even though it's part of a residential development. The high-tech units feature automatic shades and touch-control lighting as well as plenty of Southwestern-inspired style. But it's the recreational facilities that are the real draw: Besides access to the Entrada at Snow Canyon Country Club with purchase of a golf package (see above), guests have the run of a rec center with a full gym, pools, and sand volleyball courts. All units have kitchens; all but the studios have washers and dryers.

2588 W. Sinagua Trail, Ivins. www.innatentrada.com. © **435/634-7100.** 54 units. $179–$1,000 and up. Rates include access to gym, pool, and golf course. **Amenities:** Restaurant; exercise room; 18-hole golf course; 1 indoor and 1 outdoor Jacuzzi; 1 indoor and 1 outdoor heated pool; tennis courts; free Wi-Fi.

Red Mountain Resort ★★★

The big geodesic dome is your first clue that this resort has some different intentions. The dome houses the spa, which bills itself as a "wellness and adventure retreat" indicating that health is a big part of Red Rock's mission. One of the largest destination spa resorts in the country, Red Mountain is also among the best, and it serves as an excellent base for all sorts of adventures beyond facials and yoga in southwestern Utah. Guests can stay in either stylishly chic hotel-style rooms or condo-like villas, all done in earth tones with a contemporary style. The geodesic dome spa has a sublime view of adjacent Snow Canyon State Park and a terrific staff. Other on-site activities include fitness classes, guided hikes on nearby trails, and a terrific restaurant, also with views, that's focused on healthy cuisine.

1275 E. Red Mountain Circle, Ivins. www.redmountainresort.com. © **435/673-4905.** 106 units, including 24 villas. $535 and way up. Packages available. Located about 7 miles north of St. George via Utah 18 and Utah 8. **Amenities:** Restaurant; bike rentals; exercise room; Jacuzzi; indoor pool; 2 outdoor pools; spa; free Wi-Fi.

Seven Wives Inn Bed & Breakfast ★★

Polygamy is the only thing many people know about Mormons—shows like "Sister Wives" and "Big Love" have rekindled curiosity. But no polygamists are currently hiding in the attic of Seven Wives Inn anymore—as there were in the 1880s after polygamy was outlawed. One of these polygamists was Benjamin F. Johnson, an ancestor of the innkeepers, who really did have seven wives (hence the name for the B&B). It's fascinating to imagine what things must have been like in those days. Decorated with antiques, mostly Victorian and Eastlake, the inn consists of two historic abodes: the main house, built in 1873, where the polygamists hid, and the president's house next door, a four-square Victorian built 10 years later that played host to many of the LDS Church's early presidents. Each room has a deck or balcony, and private bathroom; most units have DVD players, four have a functioning fireplace, and four have two-person whirlpool tubs—one of which is installed in a Model T Ford. A separate wheelchair-accessible cottage furnished with replica pioneer furniture, an extra-large shower, a two-person whirlpool, a king-size bed, a kitchenette, and a gas fireplace is also available. Tours are offered by appointment; smoking is not permitted.

217 N. 100 West, St. George. www.sevenwivesinn.com. ℂ **800/600-3737** or 435/628-3737. 13 units, including 2 suites. Rates begin at $250. Rates include full breakfast. Pets allowed with deposit. **Amenities:** Outdoor pool; free Wi-Fi.

INEXPENSIVE

Dixie Palm Motel ★ Travelers on tight budgets should head to the Dixie Palm for basic lodging at bargain-basement rates. Located right in the center of town, within walking distance of several restaurants and attractions, this motel is clean and well maintained—and the price is right. All rooms have fridges and microwaves, some even have full kitchens, and some are "family suites" with plenty of room and up to three beds.

185 E. St. George Blvd., St. George. www.dixiepalmmotel.com. ℂ **435/673-3531.** 15 units. Rooms from $50. **Amenities:** Restaurant; free Wi-Fi.

CAMPING

Snow Canyon, Quail Creek, and Gunlock state parks also have campgrounds.

McArthur's Temple View RV Resort This large RV park is right in town and has an attractive outdoor pool and hot tub, as well as an exercise room, a shuffleboard court, Wi-Fi near the clubhouse, and a putting/chipping green.

975 S. Main St., St. George. www.templeviewrv.com. ℂ **800/776-6410** or 435/673-6400. 260 sites. About $40 per site. Just off I-15 exit 6.

Where to Eat

In addition to the restaurants discussed below, the **Bear Paw Coffee Company**, 75 N. Main St. (www.bearpawcafe.com; ℂ **435/634-0126**), serves great breakfasts ranging from steak and eggs to French toast. Also don't miss **Judd's General Store,** a century-old business at Green Gate Village (see

"Where to Stay," earlier in this chapter), with sandwiches and soups for lunch as well as ice cream, candy, and one of the widest selections of bottled soft drinks in the state.

Painted Pony ★★★ STEAK/AMERICAN   Randall Richards's excellent eatery is easily the best restaurant in St. George—it has been for decades—and it's also the best between Vegas and Salt Lake. In a lively, second-story contemporary space overlooking Ancestor Square, the Pony's food and attitude is infused with a sensibility that's more California than Utah. Richards's creative menu has some constants— like the excellent bacon-wrapped duck with apple stuffing and purée of celery root. There are some standard well-cooked steaks and inventive sides—Stilton fritter, for example or blue cheese-stuffed pear. The room, with a curving bar and a colorful equine motif, nicely complements the menu. Lunch offerings include gourmet sandwiches and salads. Full liquor service is available.

The Tower at Ancestor Square, 1 W. St. George Blvd., No. 22. www.painted-pony.com. ⓒ **435/634-1700.** Main courses $9–$11 lunch, $26–$34 dinner. Mon–Sat 11:30am–10pm; Sun 4–9pm.

Xetava Gardens Cafe ★★ NEW AMERICAN   The courtyard is the prize. Located amid the galleries at Coyote Gulch Art Village, Xetava Gardens Cafe serves creative fare in a chic space, but dining outside in the courtyard makes for a magical evening. The cafe morphs from counter-service coffee shop for breakfast and lunch (think waffles, parfaits, bagels, and ciabatta sandwiches) into an upscale dinner restaurant 4 nights a week, with delicious offerings such as chili-garlic rack of lamb, spicy shrimp, and steaks. There are vegetarian selections for every meal.

815 Coyote Gulch Court, Ivins. www.xetava.com. ⓒ **435/656-0165.** Main courses $7–$12 breakfast, $14 lunch, $16–$20 dinner. Mon–Wed 9am–5pm; Thurs–Sun 9am–9pm. 7 miles west of St. George via Sunset Blvd.

St. George After Dark

The big event of an evening in St. George is actually watching the sun go down. That's about it. With its large non-drinking Mormon population, the city isn't one of the West's hot spots. Locals out on the town attend a performing arts event, and perhaps stop in for a nightcap at one of the local restaurants that serves alcohol. Keep in mind that you'll have to buy food in order to purchase a drink.

Dixie State College's **Avenna Center,** 325 S. 700 East (http://tickets.dixie.edu; ⓒ **435/652-7800),** is St. George's primary performing arts venue. The four-building complex hosts a range of performances, from country and rock concerts to symphony, ballet, and opera performances—and even sports games.

Dixie State College, 225 S. 700 East (www.dixie.edu; ⓒ **435/652-7500),** offers a variety of events throughout the school year. The Celebrity Concert Series, running from October through April, has developed a strong following for its programs of music, ballet, modern dance, and performing arts presented by national and international performers. Tickets are typically around $25.

Not to be outdone, the college's music and drama departments offer numerous performances, including student recitals; band, chamber singer, and jazz ensemble concerts; and theater that runs the gamut from musicals to dramas—and maybe even a Greek tragedy. Admission usually costs between $8 and $12 per person; most performances are presented at Cox Auditorium. Call the box office (http://dixie.edu/ticket-office; © **435/652-7800**) to find out what's scheduled during your visit.

Music lovers will enjoy St. George's own **Southwest Symphonic Chorale** and **Southwest Symphony,** the only full symphony orchestra between Provo and Las Vegas. Its repertoire includes classical, opera, and popular music. Get tickets early for the annual Christmas production of Handel's Messiah—it usually sells out. Concerts are usually scheduled from October to May (www.southwestsymphony.org; © **435/688-8183**).

Broadway musicals and plays are presented September through April by the **St. George Musical Theater,** 735 E. Tabernacle (www.sgmt.org; © **435/628-8755**). Recent productions have included "Annie Get Your Gun" and "Singing in the Rain;" tickets cost $10 to $15.

The **St. George Tabernacle** (p. 194) presents free concerts, including half-hour organ recitals. Call © **435/673-5181** for more information.

Not far from St. George, at 1100 Tuacahn Dr., in Ivins, is the **Tuacahn Amphitheatre and Center for the Arts** (www.tuacahn.org; © **435/652-3300**). Surrounded by towering red-rock cliffs, this 2,000-seat state-of-the-art outdoor theater presents original and Broadway productions from June through September, and at other times is the venue for big-name music acts, such as Kenny Rogers. It also hosts the annual **Christmas Festival of Lights,** when much of Tuacahn is draped with lights. Ticket prices for the musicals vary, but are generally in the range of $20 to $60 for adults and $20 to $40 for children 11 and under. The Amphitheater's **Cafe Hog** is a family-run BBQ/Greek/American cafe serving dinner Monday through Friday from 4 to 9:30pm; on Saturday they offer both lunch and dinner and are open from 11am to 9:30pm.

Those looking for a livelier and mostly younger nightlife have to look hard; remember, this is a mostly Mormon town. But the aptly named **One & Only,** 800 E Saint George Blvd. (© **435/673-9191**), delivers with drinks, a couple of pool tables, a small dance floor, and late hours for Utah, making it a real rarity. It opens at noon daily, closing at 1am Monday through Saturday and at midnight on Sunday. There is a also a national sports bar chain, **Bout Time** (929 W Sunset Blvd.; © **435/673-3607**), and several local hotels have decent bars.

CEDAR BREAKS NATIONAL MONUMENT

Cedar City: 53 miles NE of St. George, 251 miles SW of Salt Lake City; Cedar Breaks National Monument: 21 miles E of Cedar City

So much buzz about the Wasatch and the national parks overshadows this beautiful and uncrowded part of Utah. Cedar Breaks National Monument is like a miniature Bryce Canyon—a stunning multicolored amphitheater of stone, with hiking trails, camping, and a plateau ablaze with wildflowers in summer. But what's special about it is its designation as a "Dark Sky" park.

Rarer than wilderness, dark skies have become a notable feature of the national parks and monuments program. The campground at Cedar Breaks is one the world's few dark sky parks, and the low light pollution makes it a great place for stargazing. Bring a telescope or high-powered binoculars and a star map to find your way around the heavens. You'll find plenty of ranger programs that focus on the rare skies, too.

Brian Head is Utah's southernmost ski resort—where else but southern Utah can you be on the links in the morning and on the slopes by the afternoon? Because Brian Head has the highest base elevation of any of the state's ski areas, it gets about 450 inches of powder each winter. And because Brian Head Resort is off the average skier's beaten track, lift lines are usually nonexistent.

But this area is more than an outdoor play land—with Frontier Homestead State Park Museum and the nationally renowned Utah Shakespearean Festival, Cedar City happens to be a great place to experience a little history as well as some great theater. Even if neither of these attractions appeals to you, you'll probably end up in Cedar City anyway—it's home to most of the area's accommodations and restaurants.

Basing Yourself in Cedar City

The community of Cedar City (elevation 5,800 ft.) is a good base for those exploring this area, especially because Cedar Breaks National Monument has no lodging or dining facilities, though you may camp there. If you're here to ski and you'd like to save money on accommodations, Cedar City also offers an economical alternative to Brian Head's more expensive condos, and it's only 28 miles from Brian Head's slopes (but keep in mind that that can be a mean 28 miles when the weather's bad). In addition to the facilities mentioned below, a good selection of motels, restaurants, campgrounds, gas stations, grocery stores, and other services is strung along I-15 at exits 57, 59, and 62.

ESSENTIALS

GETTING THERE Delta flies into **Cedar City Regional Airport,** possibly the coziest airport in the country—it has a fireplace (www.cedarcity.org; © **435/867-9408**) from Salt Lake City. Car-rental agencies include **Avis**

(© www.avis.com; © **435/867-9898**), **Budget** (www.budget.com; © **435/867-9898**), and **Enterprise** (www.enterprise.com; © **435/865-7636**).

VISITOR INFORMATION   Contact the **Cedar City/Brian Head Tourism Bureau** (www.scenicsouthernutah.com; © **435/586-5124**) for information or visit the office at 581 N. Main St.; it's open daily 9am to 5pm.

FAST FACTS   This area is served by **Cedar City Hospital,** 1303 N. Main St. (© **435/868-5000**). The **post office** is located at 333 N. Main St. (www.usps.com; © **800/275-8777** for hours and other information).

WHERE TO STAY & EAT

Lodging possibilities in Cedar City include the **Abbey Inn,** 940 W. 200 North (www.abbeyinncedar.com; © **435/586-9966**), **Best Western El Rey Inn,** 80 S. Main St. (www.bwelrey.com; © **435/586-6518**), **Best Western Town & Country,** 189 N. Main St. (www.bwtowncountry.com; © **435/586-9900**), **Clarion Inn & Suites,** 1204 S. Main St. (www.daysinn.com; © **435/867-8877**), **Motel 6,** 1620 W. 200 North (www.motel6.com; © **435/586-9200**), **Quality Inn,** 250 N. 1100 West (www.qualityinncedarcity.com; © **435/586-2082**), and **Super 8,** 145 N. 1550 West (www.super8.com; © **435/586-8880**). All of the above charge less than $100 for doubles in winter; rates are higher in summer.

    Cedar City KOA Campground, 1121 N. Main St., Cedar City (© **435/586-9872**) is open year-round and charges $35 to $50 per site.

    The local dining favorite since 1956, **Milt's Stage Stop,** 5 miles east of town on Utah 14 (www.miltsstagestop.com; © **435/586-9344**), still feels a lot like the '50s when you look at the menu: meat and potatoes, seafood (meaning mostly shrimp), even surf and turf at dinner. Entrees range from $15 to $50, and complete liquor service is available. For lighter fare, try the **Pastry Pub,** 86 W. Center St. (www.cedarcitypastrypub.com; © **435/867-1400**), a cafe offering sandwiches, tostadas, egg dishes, baked goods, and even vegan dishes in a Shakespearean-themed space, because, you know, Cedar City is famous for its Shakespeare festival.

    Those planning trips into the nearby mountains—perhaps for a few days at Cedar Breaks National Monument, described below—can pick up supplies in Cedar City at **Smith's Food & Drug Center,** 633 S. Main St. (www.smithsfoodanddrug.com; © **435/586-1203**).

A BRIEF LOOK AT CEDAR CITY'S PIONEER PAST

Frontier Homestead State Park Museum   Charged with scouting new places for Mormons to settle, Parley Pratt's Southern Exploring Company also discovered iron ore here, prompting President Brigham to call for an "Iron Mission" and establish Mormon settlements near what is now Cedar City. Frontier Homestead State Park and museum memorializes that era. Horse-drawn wagons are the main focus here at the site of the original Mormon iron works in Utah. In addition to the usual buckboards, a bullet-scarred Old West stagecoach, and some elaborate, for-the-very-very-rich-only coaches, you'll see an original Studebaker White Top Wagon (predecessor of the present-day station wagon) and several hearses, as well as the only artifact dating back to the original foundry, the town bell.

Also on exhibit are Native American and pioneer artifacts from the region, as well as a diorama depicting the 1850s iron furnace and equipment for which the park is named. Demonstrations of pioneer crafts, such as weaving, spinning, candle making, cooking, and toy making, are held periodically. Changing exhibits feature the work of local artists. Allow about an hour.

The museum also manages Old Iron Town, an 1860s-to-1870s iron foundry west of Cedar City. Ask at the desk for information and directions.

635 N. Main St., downtown Cedar City. www.stateparks.utah.gov. ℂ **435/586-9290.** Admission $4, free for children 5 and under. Open daily 9am–5pm. Closed Thanksgiving, Christmas, and New Year's Day.

Cedar Breaks National Monument ★★

A delightful little park, Cedar Breaks was the second, less poetic name for this natural amphitheater of Technicolor rock. The original name was "Circle of Painted Cliffs," an accurate description, but early settlers mistook the Utah junipers, found at lower elevations, for cedar trees. Badlands, which the pioneers had a lot of experience with, were commonly called breaks, and so the non-descriptive name of Cedar Breaks—less prosaic, and actually incorrect as well—was assigned this gorgeous national monument.

The natural coliseum is reminiscent of Bryce Canyon. It's more than 2,000 feet deep and over 3 miles across and filled with stone spires, arches, and columns shaped by the forces of erosion and painted in ever-changing reds, purples, oranges, and ochers. You can spend part of a day or several days gazing down from the rim into the bowl, hiking the trails, and camping among the spruce, fir, and wildflowers that blanket the plateau in summer.

ESSENTIALS

At more than 10,000 feet elevation, it's always pleasantly cool at Cedar Breaks, but it gets downright cold at night, so bring a jacket or sweater, even if the temperature is scorching just down the road in St. George. The monument opens for its short summer season only after the snow melts, usually in late May, and closes in mid-October—unless you happen to have a snowmobile or a pair of cross-country skis or snowshoes, in which case you can visit year-round.

GETTING THERE Cedar Breaks National Monument is 21 miles east of Cedar City, 56 miles west of Bryce Canyon National Park, and 247 miles south of Salt Lake City.

BY CAR From I-15, drive east of Cedar City on Utah 14 to Utah 148, turn north (left), and follow Utah 148 into the monument. If you're coming from Bryce Canyon or other points east, the park is accessible from the town of Panguitch via Utah 143. From the north, take the Parowan exit off I-15 and head south on Utah 143. It's a steep climb from whichever direction you choose, and vehicles prone to vapor lock or loss of power on hills (such as motor homes) may have some problems.

INFORMATION/VISITOR CENTER A mile from the south entrance gate is the visitor center, open 9am to 6pm daily from late May to mid-October, with exhibits on the geology, flora, and fauna of Cedar Breaks. You can purchase books and maps here, and rangers can help plan your visit.

For advance information, contact the Superintendent of **Cedar Breaks National Monument** (www.nps.gov/cebr; ℂ **435/586-9451,** ext. 4420).

FEES & REGULATIONS Admission is $7 per person for those 16 and older. Regulations are similar to those at most national parks: Leave everything as you find it. Mountain bikes are not allowed on hiking trails. Dogs, which must be leashed at all times, are prohibited on all trails, in the backcountry, and in public buildings.

HEALTH & SAFETY The high elevation—10,350 feet at the visitor center—is likely to cause shortness of breath and tiredness, and those with heart or respiratory conditions should consult their doctors before going. Avoid overlooks and other high, exposed areas during thunderstorms; they're often targets for lightning.

RANGER PROGRAMS During the monument's short summer season, rangers offer campfire talks at the Point Supreme campground several nights a week, daily talks on geology and other subjects, and several guided hikes. There are also special programs on the monument's wildflowers, and, in recent years, stargazing programs have become especially popular. All ranger programs are free. A complete schedule is posted at the visitor center and the campground.

EXPLORING CEDAR BREAKS BY CAR

The 5-mile road through Cedar Breaks National Monument offers easy access to the monument's scenic overlooks and trailheads. Allow 30 to 45 minutes to make the drive. Start at the visitor center and nearby Point Supreme for a panoramic view of the amphitheater. Then drive north, past the campground and picnic ground turnoff, to Sunset View for a closer view of the amphitheater and its colorful canyons. From each of these overlooks, you can see out across Cedar Valley, over the Antelope and Black mountains, into the Escalante Desert.

Continue north to Chessman Ridge Overlook, so named because the hoodoos directly below look like massive stone chess pieces. Watch for swallows and swifts soaring among the rock formations. Then head north to Alpine Pond, a trailhead for a self-guided nature trail (see "Hiking," below) with an abundance of wildflowers. Finally, you'll reach North View, which offers the best look into the amphitheater. The view here is reminiscent of Bryce Canyon's Queen's Garden, with its stately statues frozen in time.

OUTDOOR PURSUITS

HIKING   No trails connect the rim to the bottom of the amphitheater, but the monument does have two high-country trails. The fairly easy 2-mile **Alpine Pond Trail** loop leads through woodlands of bristlecone pines to a picturesque forest glade and pond surrounded by wildflowers, offering panoramic views of the amphitheater along the way. A printed trail guide is available for purchase at the trailhead.

A somewhat more challenging hike, the 4-mile round-trip **Spectra Point/ Ramparts Overlook Trail** follows the rim more closely than the Alpine Pond Trail, offering changing views of the colorful rock formations. It also takes you through fields of wildflowers and by bristlecone pines that are more than 1,600 years old. Be especially careful of your footing along the exposed cliff edges, and allow yourself some time to rest—there are lots of ups and downs along the way.

The 1-mile round-trip **Campground Trail** connects the campground with the visitor center, providing views of the amphitheater along the way. It is the only trail in the monument where pets are permitted.

Late-Summer Bonanza: Cedar Breaks Wildflowers

During its brief summer season, Cedar Breaks makes the most of the warmth and moisture in the air with a spectacular wildflower show. The rim comes alive in a blaze of color—truly a sight to behold. The dazzling display begins practically as soon as the snow melts and reaches its peak in mid-July. The annual 2-week-long **Wildflower Festival,** which celebrates the colorful display, starts the weekend closest to Independence Day. Watch for mountain bluebells, spring beauty, beardtongue, and fleabane early in the season; those beauties then make way for columbine, larkspur, Indian paintbrush, wild roses, and other flowers.

9

There are no trails from the rim to the bottom of the amphitheater completely within the monument, but there are trails just outside the monument that go into the amphitheater. Check with the visitor center for details and directions.

WILDLIFE-WATCHING Because of its relative remoteness, Cedar Breaks is a good place for spotting wildlife. You're likely to see mule deer grazing in the meadows along the road early and late in the day. Marmots make their dens near the rim and are often seen basking on rocks along the Spectra Point Trail. Ground squirrels, red squirrels, and chipmunks are everywhere. Please don't feed them. Pikas, which are related to rabbits, are here, too. It's unlikely you'll see one because they prefer the high, rocky slopes but you may hear their high whistle.

In the campground, birders should have no trouble spotting the Clark's nutcracker, with its gray torso and black-and-white wings and tail. The monument is also home to swallows, swifts, blue grouse, and golden eagles.

WINTER FUN The monument's facilities are shut down from mid-October to late May due to the usually heavy blanket of snow. The snow-blocked roads keep cars out, but they're perfect for snowmobilers, snowshoers, and cross-country skiers, who usually come over from the Brian Head ski area (below) nearby. Snowshoers and cross-country skiers have several different trails to choose from, but snowmobiles are restricted to the main 5-mile road through the monument, which is groomed and marked.

CAMPING

The 28-site campground, Point Supreme, just north of the visitor center, is open from June to mid-September, with sites available on a first-come, first-served basis. It's a beautiful high-mountain setting, among tall spruce and fir. Facilities include restrooms, drinking water, picnic tables, grills, and an amphitheater for the ranger's evening campfire programs. No showers or RV hookups are available. The camping fee is $24 per night. Keep in mind that even in midsummer, temperatures can drop into the 30s (single digits Celsius) at night at this elevation, so bring cool-weather gear.

Brian Head Resort

Like the ski areas in the Ogden and Logan areas, the reasons to visit Brian Head Resort are terrain and snow; the wide range of off-the-snow amenities found in Park City, Deer Valley, and Snowbird just don't exist here. And that's part of its appeal. Brian Head has the distinction of being Utah's southernmost ski resort, just a short drive from the year-round short-sleeve warmth of St. George. Its location makes it particularly popular with skiers from the Las Vegas area and Southern California. But with the highest base elevation of any of the state's ski areas (9,600 ft.), it receives over 400 inches of powdery snow each winter. Another plus is the scenery: The only ski resort in Utah's famed red-rock country, Brian Head Resort offers stunning views.

After the snow melts, bikers and hikers claim the mountain. With elevations of 9,600 to 11,307 feet, Brian Head is stunningly beautiful and always cool and crisp. For those who want to see the mountains without the sweat, chairlift rides are offered in summer Friday to Sunday ($12 adults, $8 children 4–12, free for kids 3 and under). Evenings are busy, too, with live musical entertainment ranging from jazz and country to bluegrass and classical.

Brian Head is fast becoming a major destination for serious and dedicated mountain bikers. This is a wonderful place for mountain biking ★, with endless trails, superb scenery, and about the freshest air you're going to find. What's more, mountain biking here can be oh-so-very easy: A chairlift hauls you and your bike up the mountain ($35 for a full-day pass), or you can take a shuttle to and from several locations)—leaving only the fun parts to pedal. An adult full day bike lift pass plus rental costs $110, less for kids 11 and under, and helmets are $10. Contact the **Brian Head Resort Mountain Bike Park** (© **866/930-1010**, ext. 212), **Brianhead Sports** (www.brian headsports.com; © **435/677-2014**), or **George's Bike Shop** (www.georgsski shop.com; © **435/677-2013**) for details.

Other summer on-mountain activities include the self-guided "Brian Head Family Adventure," earth-science and natural-history-focused activities ranging from orienteering to learning about petroglyphs.

All of these activities are offered on Fridays, Saturdays, and Sundays through Labor Day and then Saturdays and Sundays through September. Hours are 9:30am to 4:30pm (weather conditions permitting) and can be accessed via the Giant Steps chairlift.

On **Giant Steps Mountain,** you'll find challenging intermediate, advanced, and expert-only runs and terrain parks for a family's more advanced skiers and boarders. Giant Steps sits just below 11,307-foot Brian Head Peak, where expert-level skiers and snowboarders enjoy hike-accessed, backcountry bowls. Intermediates will enjoy fine cruising runs a little farther down the mountain, and beginners can ski **Navajo Mountain,** dedicated solely to children and beginning skiers and snowboarders. The terrain is rated 40% beginner, 40% intermediate, and 20% advanced on 65 runs. One double chair and seven triples service 650 skiable acres. The vertical drop is 1,320 feet, 1,548 feet if you hike a little. There are snowmaking capabilities on 170 acres. The ski season generally runs from mid-November to mid-April, with lifts operating daily from 10am to 4:30pm. On weekends and holidays, night skiing and tubing is available until 9pm.

Snowboarders are welcome, with four terrain parks of varying ability levels, plenty of free riding terrain, and a half pipe, conditions permitting. The resort also has a snow tubing park.

In summer, Brian Head is like summer camp for the whole family, with activities that include mountain biking (bike rentals available), mountain biking lessons, disc golf, archery, hiking, and more.

eagle point: **TWO RESORTS IN ONE**

Eagle Point, located 18 miles east of Beaver, via exit 109 or 112 on I-15 (www.skieaglepoint.com; ℂ **855/324-5378** or 435/438 3700) is nestled in the scenic Tushar Mountains. Comprising the former Elk Meadows and Mount Holly ski areas, Eagle Point's current ownership has breathed plenty of new life into the place, which gets a full 450 inches of snow annually on its 625 acres. There are 42 runs here with a 1,500-foot vertical rise served by one quad chair, one triple, two doubles, and a platter. There are plenty of steeps (45% expert) to complement the beginner (20%) and intermediate (35%) terrains, plus a pair of terrain parks, a tubing area, and the "Lookout" warming cabin, with 360° spectacular views of surrounding 12,00-foot peaks. Lift tickets are a bargain at $45 to $60 for adults for a full day, $25 to $45 for kids 7 to 17 and seniors 65 and up. There are condos available on the mountain as well as a restaurant serving three meals daily in winter.

For information, contact **Brian Head Resort,** 329 S. Utah 143 (www.brianhead.com; ℂ **435/677-2035**), or **Brian Head Chamber of Commerce & Visitor Services** (www.brianheadchamber.com; ℂ **435/677-2810**).

From Cedar City, it's 28 miles to Brian Head; take I-15 to exit 75 and head south on the very steep Utah 143 about 12 miles.

LIFT TICKETS A weekday adult all-day lift ticket is $38 regular season and an all-day child's (ages 6–12) or senior's (ages 65 and over) ticket is $27 regular season; half-day tickets are $48 and $35, respectively. Kids 5 and under ski free with a paying adult. Night skiing or snowboarding costs $20.

LESSONS & PROGRAMS The ski school offers private and group lessons, as well as clinics, snowboard classes, and children's ski instruction. Day care is available for children and infants; also available are packages combining day care and ski lessons. Call ℂ **435/677-2049** for current rates.

Cross-Country Skiing: There are numerous cross-country options in Cedar Breaks National Monument. Lessons and rentals are available at **Brianhead Sports** (www.brianheadsports.com; ℂ **435/677-2014**); there's no charge for trail use.

Where to Stay & Eat

The Brian Head area offers a variety of lodging possibilities, with winter rates ranging from about $150 to $300 per night (higher at Christmas; lower in summer). Contact the **Brian Head Chamber of Commerce** (www.brianheadchamber.com; ℂ **888/677-2810**) or Brian Head Reservation Center (www.brianheadtown.com/bhrc; ℂ **435/677-2042**). You can also stay in Cedar City, 28 miles away (see "Basing Yourself in Cedar City," earlier in this chapter).

Cedar Breaks Lodge & Spa ★ 223 Hunter Ridge Rd., Brian Head (www.cedarbreakslodge.com; ℂ **435/677-3000**), near the base of Navajo Mountain, underwent an extensive multimillion-dollar renovation and offers more than

100 studio, one-, and two-bedroom "villas" and "master villas" ranging in price from winter to summer. All rooms have whirlpool tubs, wet bars, refrigerators, microwaves, coffeemakers, and hair dryers; some also have fireplaces. Facilities include a 24-hour front desk, two restaurants, a lounge, an indoor pool, a fireside Jacuzzi, a fitness center, a sauna, and a steam room. Boasting one of Utah's top spas, the lodge has several massage therapists available, offering Swedish full-body massage, deep tissue massage, sports massage, reflexology, aromatherapy baths, hydrating facials, salt glows, and herbal wraps. Rooms start at about $130 for a room and go up to $300 for a 2-bedroom villa. The pet-friendly **Best Western Premier at Brian Head ★**, 314 Hunter Ridge Rd. (www.bwpbrianheadhotel.com; ℂ **435/677-9000**) offers rooms and suites done up in posh Western style with beamed ceilings and flatscreen TVs. Facilities include a restaurant, bar, fitness center, concierge, game room, and spa. Rates are $100 to $200 double.

Quick breakfasts and lunches are served at several places at Brian Head, including the **Navajo Giant Steps Lodge Grill** (329 South Hwy 143; ℂ **435/677-4242**), basically an upscale refueling stop for those who want delicious efficiency, inexpensively. Cedar Breaks Lodge offers several dining options: The **Cedar Breaks Café** serves a breakfast buffet plus a la carte menu daily from 8:30am to noon. **The Cedar Breaks Bar & Grill**, is a local gathering place, with a full bar and the option of ordering from the Cedar Breaks Café menu. **The Grand Steakhouse at the Lodge** serves breakfast and dinner, but does not serve alcohol at this time.

KANAB: CINEMA, SAND DUNES & GRAND CANYON GATEWAY

82 miles E of St. George, 303 miles S of Salt Lake City, 79 miles N of the Grand Canyon

If you get a little deja vu driving into Kanab, it's because you really have seen this all before. Kanab has played a starring role on big and little screens. This is the Wild West you know from old TV shows like "Gunsmoke," "The Lone Ranger," "Death Valley Days," and "F Troop," and from the big screen in "Buffalo Bill," "Sergeants 3," "Bandolero!," and "The Outlaw Josey Wales."

But Kanab (4,925 ft. elevation) lives on more than just memories of the Old West: It's also an old traditional Mormon town and a stopping point for travelers on their way to southern Utah's major sights. Visitors coming from Arizona are likely to pass through on their way to Zion and Bryce Canyon national parks, and the Grand Canyon's north rim directly to the south

Essentials

GETTING THERE   Kanab is 82 miles east of St. George, 80 miles south of Bryce Canyon National Park, 42 miles east of Zion National Park, 68 miles west of Lake Powell and Glen Canyon Recreation Area, 79 miles north of the Grand Canyon, and 303 miles south of Salt Lake City. The town is located on

U.S. 89 at the junction of U.S. 89A, which crosses into Arizona just 7 miles south of town. *Drivers note:* Most gas station are closed on Sundays.

VISITOR INFORMATION For information, check in with the **Kane County Visitors Center,** 78 S. 100 East (U.S. 89), Kanab (www.kaneutah. com; © **435/644-5033**), which is open April through November Monday to Friday 8am to 8pm and Saturdays 9am to 6pm, with shorter hours in the winter.

GETTING AROUND You won't be surprised to hear that Kanab is laid out on a grid, with the heart of town at the intersection of Center and Main streets. U.S. 89 enters from the north on 300 West Street, turns east onto Center Street, south on 100 East Street, and finally east again on 300 South. U.S. 89A follows 100 East Street south to the airport and into Arizona.

FAST FACTS The **Kane County Hospital** is at 355 N. Main St. in Kanab (© **435/644-5811**; www.kanecountyhospital.net). The **post office** is at 39 S. Main St. (www.usps.com; © **800/275-8777** for hours and other information).

Coral Pink Sand Dunes State Park

Off-highway-vehicle users lobbied hard to have this designated a state park, and OHV users can now rev to their hearts' content as long as they follow the rules, which are detailed on the website (https://stateparks.utah.gov/parks/coral-pink). But Coral Pink Sand Dunes is more than a wannabe's racetrack for expensive motorized toys; it's a unique geological phenomenon that deserves exploration and appreciation. Campers, hikers, photographers, and all-around nature lovers come to hunt for wildflowers, glow-in-the-dark scorpions, and lizards, or just wiggle their toes in the smooth, cool shifting sea of red sand. Changed constantly by winds, these mountains and hills of sand can move as much as 50 feet per year. The coral colors are especially rich at sunrise and sunset. Early-morning visitors will find the tracks of yesterday's dune buggies gone, replaced by the tracks of lizards, kangaroo rats, snakes, and the rest of the park's animal kingdom, who venture out in the coolness of night, after the visitors have departed.

ESSENTIALS
GETTING THERE From downtown Kanab, go about 8 miles north on U.S. 89, then southwest (left) on Hancock Road for about 12 miles to the park.

INFORMATION/VISITOR CENTER For copies of the park brochure and off-highway-vehicle regulations, write the park office at P.O. Box 95, Kanab, UT 84741-0095, check the website, or call © **435/648-2800.** At the park entry station, there's a small display area with sand from around the world, local fossils, and live scorpions, lizards, and tadpoles.

FEES & REGULATIONS The day-use fee is $8 per vehicle. The standard state park regulations apply, with the addition of a few extra rules due to the park's popularity for off-roading: Quiet hours are from 10pm to 9am, later in the morning than in most parks. Dunes are open to motor vehicles between

BEST FRIENDS ANIMAL sanctuary

If you're an animal lover, one of the highlights of a trip to this part of Utah is a stop at the **Best Friends Animal Sanctuary** (www.bestfriends.org; ✆ **435/644-2001**), near Kanab. Whether you volunteer, or just stop for a look, you won't soon forget this 5,000-acre spread, home to more than 2,000 cats, dogs, rabbits, horses, birds, and other animals. Founded in the 1980s, the Best Friends Animal Society's mission is simple: to bring the number of pets being euthanized to "essentially zero."

You can see the group's deep commitment to animals at the sanctuary, set amid the red rock of Angel Canyon. The staff works tirelessly to get these often abused or abandoned animals ready for adoption. Their efforts have been chronicled on National Geographic Channel's show "Dog Town."

Free guided tours are available daily; call ahead for a reservation. Many people come and stay for a week or more, and you can rent cottages ($95–$120 double per night), smaller cabins ($60–$75 per night), and RV sites ($45 per night) on the property. You don't need to volunteer in order to stay—some people simply take advantage of the amazing setting, with its network of hiking trails.

Volunteers sign up to help with everything from walking dogs to socializing cats to feeding birds; pick which critters you'd like to work with. Volunteers must be at least 6 years of age, and those 17 and under must be accompanied at all times by an adult. You must make arrangements to volunteer before your visit. Specialized workshops on animal-related topics are also available.

The entrance to Best Friends is about 5 miles north of Kanab on the east side of U.S. 89. The Welcome Center is open daily from 8am to 5pm.

9am and 10pm and to hikers at any time. Vehicles going onto the dunes must have safety flags, available at the entry station; while on the dunes, they must stay at least 10 feet from vegetation and at least 100 feet from hikers. Dogs are permitted on the dunes but must be leashed.

OUTDOOR PURSUITS

FOUR-WHEELING   This giant 3,700-acre sandbox offers plenty of space for off-road-vehicle enthusiasts, who race up and down the dunes. Because the sand here is quite fine, extra-wide flotation tires are needed; lightweight dune buggies are usually the vehicle of choice. Adjacent to the park on Bureau of Land Management property are hundreds of miles of trails and roads for off-highway vehicles.

HIKING   The best time for hiking the dunes is early morning. It's cooler then, the lighting at sunrise and just after produces beautiful shadows and colors, and there are no noisy dune buggies until after 9am. Sunset is also very pretty, but you'll be sharing the dunes with off-road vehicles. Keep in mind that hiking through fine sand can be very tiring, especially for those who go barefoot. A self-guided ½-mile loop nature trail has numbered signs through some of the dunes; allow half an hour.

Other hikes of various lengths are possible within and just outside the park, but because there are few signs—and because landmarks change with the shifting sands—check with park rangers before setting out. Those spending more than a few hours in the dunes will discover that even their own tracks disappear in the wind, leaving few clues to the route back to park headquarters.

CAMPING

The spacious and mostly shady 22-site campground, open year-round, offers hot showers, modern restrooms, and an RV dump station, but no hookups. You can reserve site online but there is an $8 cancellation fee; some sites are first-come first serve. To reserve, call © **800/322-3770** or visit www.stateparks. utah.gov.

More to See & Do in the Kanab Area

Frontier Movie Town Hollywood's vision of the Wild West lives on, with a jail, bunkhouse, bank, ranch house, and numerous other set creations for movies filmed in the Kanab area (once nicknamed "Little Hollywood") over the years. On display are buildings from the sets of Disney's 1973 comedy-drama "One Little Indian"; the 1948 classic western "Black Bart"; and Clint Eastwood's 1976 hit, "The Outlaw Josey Wales," among others.

On the grounds is a large gift/souvenir shop, offering a wide variety of Native American arts and crafts, plus cowboy hats, coonskin caps, and the like. Call to see if a **chuck-wagon dinner** is scheduled during your visit (© **435/689-0706**). Allow about an hour to tour the whole town.

297 W. Center St. www.frontiermovietown.com. © **435/644-5337.** Free admission. Summer daily 8:30am–9pm; shorter hours rest of year.

Heritage House Of the 16 historic houses in the downtown area of Kanab, this is the only one open to the public. Built in 1894, this handsome Victorian was purchased by Thomas H. Chamberlain in 1897, and by the city in 1975. The house has been restored to its original appearance and contains household items from the late 1800s, some belonging to the original owners. Allow about 45 minutes.

At 100 South and Main sts. www.kanabheritage.com © **435/644-3966.** Admission by donation. June–Sept Mon–Fri 1–5pm. One block south of the intersection of Center and Main sts.

Moqui Cave A real roadside attraction in the classic sense, this kitschy but authentic spot is named after American Indians known as the Moqui, believed to have used this cave to store food 800 to 900 years ago. Times have changed since then, and so has the cave—the ancient Moqui would be amazed by what they'd find here today. The Chamberlain family, descendants of Thomas and Mary Chamberlain (see Heritage House, above), bought the cave in 1951, and the following year opened a tavern and dance hall in it. Although you can't order a drink today, the unique bar is still here, along with a huge collection of objects and artifacts that ranges from authentic dinosaur tracks (more than 140 million years old) to a beautiful fluorescent mineral display. A large gift shop specializes in Native American arts and crafts.

1508 S. Kanab Creek Dr., on the east side of U.S. 89, about 5½ miles north of Kanab. www.moquicave.com. © **435/644-8525.** Admission $5 adults, $4.50 seniors 61 and over, $3.50 ages 13–17, $3 children 6–12, free for children 5 and under. Memorial Day to Labor Day Mon–Sat 9am–7pm; winter Mon–Sat 10am–4pm, but check on possible closures.

Where to Stay

In addition to the properties described below, you might consider the moderately priced **Best Western Red Hills,** 125 W. Center St. (www.bestwestern redhills.com; © **435/644-2675**), with rates starting at $149 in summer; the **Holiday Inn Express & Suites,** 217 S. 100 East (www.hiexpress.com; © **435/644-3100**), with rates around $149; or the **Rodeway Inn,** 70 S. 200 West (www.rodewayinn.com; © **877/424-6423** or 435/644-5500), slightly less expensive rates.

Ask about pet policies; many inns in Kanab allow them because of the proximity to Best Friends Animal Sanctuary (p. 213). Note that because Kanab is close to the North Rim of the Grand Canyon, rates are higher in summer.

The Canyons Collection ★ This eclectic group of inns and hotels—from a Victorian B&B to a mid-century-style motor lodge—all have distinctive styles as well as modern amenities like Wi-Fi and bicycles. Extended stay properties and individual cottages are also part of the collection.

www.thecanyonscollection.com. © **844/322-8824.** Rates start at $129 for a double.

Parry Lodge ★ Founded in 1931 and now on the National Register of Historic Places, this is where the stars stayed—Frank Sinatra, Dean Martin, John Wayne, to name just a few—while filming in Kanab. In 1931, Chauncey Parry decided to open a motel for the film people who were regularly coming to town. Two chandeliers from Paris hang in the lobby, while about 200 autographed photos of movie stars are scattered about the public areas of the colonial-feel lodge. Doors to the original guest rooms, which make up about a third of all rooms, are each adorned with the name of an actor who stayed here. The newer units are larger, but lack the charm of the older, smaller rooms. In summer, movies that were filmed in Kanab are screened in the lodge's theater.

89 E. Center St. (U.S. 89), Kanab. www.parrylodge.com. © **800/748-4104** or 435/644-2601. 89 units, including 3 family units. Summer $109 doubles; $129–$138 for movie rooms. Rates include breakfast buffet discount in summer and continental breakfast in winter. Pets accepted ($10 per night). **Amenities:** Restaurant; outdoor heated pool; room service; free Wi-Fi.

CAMPING

Kanab RV Corral Open summer only, this well-kept RV park makes a good base camp for exploring the region. The sites—half back-in and half pull-through—are a bit close together, and you do get some highway noise; however, the bathhouses are exceptionally nice (with extra-large shower stalls), the coin-operated laundry is kept spotless, and the small, kidney-shaped pool is pleasant. Extras include free Wi-Fi access, a dog run, and horseshoe pits.

483 S. 100 East, U.S. 89A. www.kanabrvcorral.com. © **435/644-5330.** 41 sites. $36–$40 a night. Closed Nov to mid-Mar.

Where to Eat

Nedra's Too ★ MEXICAN An outpost of the 1957 Fredonia, Arizona, original, Nedra's is a combination Mexican restaurant/American coffee shop. Choose from tables in the dining room, decorated in Southwestern style, and booths in the adjacent coffee shop. Breakfast is served all day and includes coffee shop favorites like the usual ham and eggs, omelets, and pancakes, as well as an eye-opening chorizo and eggs dish and a delicious huevos rancheros. Lunch and dinner menus offer a variety of charbroiled burgers, such as the Philly (with Swiss cheese, grilled red and green peppers, and Bermuda onions) and several sandwiches. Other options include steaks and seafood, and fried chicken, but Mexican food is the focus. The house-made salsa is famous.

300 S. 100 East. www.nedrascafe.com. © **435/644-2030.** Summer daily 7am–10pm; rest of year daily 8am–9pm.

Rocking V Cafe ★★ NEW AMERICAN After 25 years in the television industry, Vicky and Victor Cooper switched gears, bought the old 1892 mercantile in downtown Kanab, and opened this delightfully artsy eatery. The "slow food" prepared in the Rocking V's kitchen is loaded with fresh ingredients, with an emphasis on great produce—vegan dishes are available. Dinner entrees, such as Thai curry, red trout crusted with cornmeal and pumpkin-seeds, and deep-dish enchiladas topped with chili-tomatillo sauce, give you an idea of the breadth of influences driving the menu. Meat eaters, don't be discouraged—try the buffalo tenderloin. Everything is made in-house, from the breads to the soups to the mouthwatering desserts. (Top pick: key lime pie.) The Coopers' place is a feast for the eyes as well as the taste buds: Original art hangs on the walls and in the second-story Rafters Gallery, showcasing regional talent.

97 W. Center St. www.rockingvcafe.com. © **435/644-8001.** Main courses $15–$38. Thurs–Mon 11:30am–10pm; check the website for possible seasonal changes.

ZION NATIONAL PARK

From Canyon Overlook Trail, Zion looks like the paradise refuge it's named for—the verdant valley is enclosed by towering red cliffs and sculptural rock formations. So it's no wonder Mormon pioneer Isaac Behunin, who settled in the canyon, said, "A man can worship God among these great cathedrals as well as he can in any man-made church; this is Zion." The name endures and the valley does seem like a bit of heaven on earth. The rock formations are open-mouth awe-inspiring—explorer John Wesley Powell named the highest points West and East Temple, and later, Methodist preacher Frederick Fisher drew on the divine when he named Great White Throne, Angels Landing, The Three Patriarchs, and The Watchman. Mormons turned to the Book of Mormon for names like Kolob, Towers of the Virgins, Prodigal Son, and Tabernacle Dome. Visit viewpoints at different times of the day to see the changing light, and let the park and nature work its magic.

Because of its extreme range of elevations (3,666–8,726 ft.) and weather (with temperatures soaring over 100°F/38°C in summer and a landscape carpeted by snow in winter), Zion harbors a vast array of plants and animals. Over 900 native species of plants have been found: cactus, yucca, and mesquite in the hot, dry desert areas; ponderosa pines on the high plateaus; and cottonwoods and box elders along the rivers and streams. Of the 14 varieties of cactus that grow in the park, keep an eye out for the red claret cup, which blooms spectacularly in spring. Wildflowers common to the park include manzanita, with tiny pink blossoms; buttercups; and the bright red hummingbird trumpet. You'll also see the sacred datura—dubbed the "Zion Lily" because of its abundance in the park—with its large funnel-shaped white flowers that open in the cool of night and close by noon.

The different ecosystems in Zion are home to mammals ranging from pocket gophers to mountain lions, hundreds of birds (including golden eagles), lizards of all shapes and sizes, and a dozen species of snakes (only the Great Basin rattlesnake is poisonous).

Zion National Park

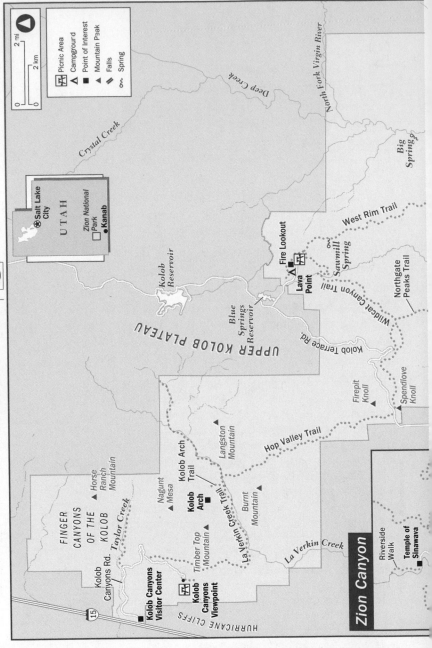

Legend:
- 🏕 Picnic Area
- ⛺ Campground
- ■ Point of Interest
- ▲ Mountain Peak
- ⬧ Falls
- ∿ Spring

2 mi

2 km

Salt Lake City

UTAH

Zion National Park

Kanab

Crystal Creek

Deep Creek

North Fork Virgin River

Big Spring

West Rim Trail

Fire Lookout

Sawmill Spring

Lava Point

Northgate Peaks Trail

Wildcat Canyon Trail

Kolob Reservoir

Blue Springs Reservoir

Kolob Terrace Rd.

UPPER KOLOB PLATEAU

Firepit Knoll

Spendlove Knoll

Langston Mountain

Hop Valley Trail

Horse Ranch Mountain

FINGER CANYONS OF THE KOLOB

Nagunt Mesa

Kolob Arch Trail

Kolob Arch

Burnt Mountain

La Verkin Creek Trail

La Verkin Creek

Riverside Walk

Temple of Sinawava

Taylor Creek

Timber Top Mountain

Kolob Canyons Rd.

Kolob Canyons Visitor Center

Kolob Canyons Viewpoint

HURRICANE CLIFFS

15

Zion Canyon

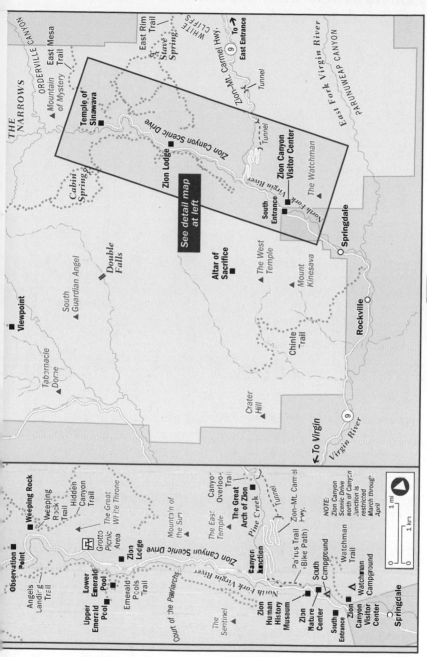

ZION NATIONAL PARK

HOW NATURE painted ZION'S LANDSCAPE

Exploring Zion is a lesson in geology because you can see it happening; for example, witness the "spring lines," areas where water seeps out of rock, create "hanging gardens." Because sandstone is porous, water can percolate down through the rock until it's stopped by a layer of harder rock. Then the water changes direction, moving horizontally to the rock face, where it seeps out, forming the "spring line" that provides nutrients to whatever seeds the wind delivers, which sprout into plants and flowers you can see clinging to the sides of cliffs.

The jaw-dropping wonder of Zion National Park is found simply in its rocks—their formation, uplifting, shifting, breaking, and eroding. Of Zion's nine rock layers, the most important in creating the park's colorful formations is Navajo sandstone—at up to 2,200 feet, the thickest rock layer in the park. This formation was created some 200 million years ago during the Jurassic period, when North America was hot and dry. Movements in the earth's crust caused a shallow sea to rise up and cover sand dunes. Minerals from the water, including lime from the shells of sea creatures, glued sand particles together, eventually forming sandstone. Later crust movements caused the land to lift, draining away the sea but leaving rivers that gradually carved the relatively soft sandstone into the spectacular shapes seen today.

So where do the colors come from? Essentially, from plain old rust. Most of the rocks at Zion are stained by iron or hematite (iron oxide), either contained in the original stone or carried into the rocks by groundwater. Although iron often creates red and pink hues, seen on many of Zion's sandstone faces, it can also result in shades of brown, yellow, black, and even green. Sometimes the iron seeps into the rock, coloring it through, but it can also stain just the surface, often in vertical streaks. Deposits of salt left by evaporating water frequently cause white streaks, and rocks are also colored by bacteria that live on their surfaces. These bacteria ingest dust and expel iron, manganese, and other minerals, which stick to the rock and produce a shiny black, brown, or reddish surface called desert varnish.

Mule deer are common, as well as elk and bighorn sheep, plus foxes, coyotes, ringtail cats, beavers, porcupines, skunks, and plenty of squirrels and bats. Practically every summer visitor sees lizards, often the colorful collared and whiptail varieties, and you often hear the song of the canyon wren and the call of the piñon jay.

ESSENTIALS

Located in southwest Utah, at elevations ranging from 3,666 feet to 8,726 feet, Zion National Park has several sections: **Zion Canyon,** the main part of the park, where everyone goes, and the less-visited **Kolob Terrace** and **Kolob Canyons** areas.

GETTING THERE/ACCESS POINTS   St. George and Cedar City (see chapter 9) are the closest towns with airport service. From either airport, it's easy to rent a car and drive to Zion. Utah 9 connects with Zion National Park, giving the main section of the park two entry gates—south and east. The drive into Zion Canyon (the main part of the park) from I-15 on the park's western side, following Utah 9 or Utah 17, and then Utah 9 to the south entrance at Springdale, is by far the more popular, with two-thirds of park visitors arriving there. Most area lodgings and restaurants are found in Springdale, and the park's two campgrounds and the Zion Canyon Visitor Center are located just inside the south entrance. This approach has the added advantage of avoiding possible delays at the Zion–Mt. Carmel Tunnel. However, this approach is much less scenic than the eastern approach.

From the east, it's a spectacularly scenic 24-mile drive from Mt. Carmel on Utah 9, reached from either the north or south via U.S. 89. However, be aware that this route into the park drops over 2,500 feet in elevation, passes through the mile-long Zion–Mt. Carmel Tunnel, and winds down six steep switch-backs. The tunnel is too small for two-way traffic for any vehicles larger than standard passenger cars and pickup trucks. Buses, large trucks, and most recreational vehicles must be driven down the center of the tunnel, and there-fore, all oncoming traffic must be stopped. This applies to all vehicles over 7 feet 10 inches wide (including mirrors) or 11 feet 4 inches tall (including luggage racks, and so on). Information is available at park entrances or by calling park headquarters (© **435/772-3256**). Such large vehicles must pay a $15 fee before entering the tunnel, good for two trips through the tunnel for that vehicle during a 7-day period. All vehicles over 13 feet 1 inch tall and certain other particularly large vehicles are prohibited from driving anywhere on the park road between the east entrance and Zion Canyon.

Kolob Terrace Road, with additional viewpoints and trailheads, heads north off Utah 9 from the village of Virgin, about 15 miles west of the park's south-ern entrance. This road is closed in the winter.

The Kolob Canyons section, in the park's northwest corner, can be reached via the short Kolob Canyons Road off I-15 exit 40.

Some helpful distances: The park is 83 miles southwest of Bryce Canyon National Park; 120 miles northwest of the north rim of Grand Canyon National Park, in northern Arizona; 309 miles south of Salt Lake City; and 158 miles northeast of Las Vegas, Nevada.

INFORMATION/VISITOR CENTERS   Officials at **Zion National Park,** Springdale, UT 84767 (www.nps.gov/zion; © **435/772-3256**), prefer you write for information (rather than call) at least a month before your planned visit, and they will mail you information; but you will find everything you need and more on the park's website. You can purchase books, posters, maps, DVDs, and CDs related to the park from the nonprofit **Zion Natural History Association** (www.zionpark.org; © **800/635-3959** or 435/772-3265). Some publications are available in foreign languages. Those wanting to help the nonprofit association can join ($45 single or $60 family annually) and get a 15% discount on purchases and most **Zion Canyon Field Institute** classes (https://zionpark.org/zion-canyon-field-institute), and discounts at most other nonprofit bookstores at national parks, monuments, historic sites, and recreation areas.

Don't skip Zion's two visitor centers—they give you a quick overview and allow you to "shop" for the experiences best suited to your timeframe and energy level. The **Zion Canyon Visitor Center,** near the south entrance to the park, has a wide variety of outdoor exhibits. Rangers answer questions and provide backcountry permits; free brochures are available; and books, maps, videos, postcards, and posters are sold. It's open daily from 8am to 6pm; in winter, it closes at 5pm. The **Kolob Canyons Visitor Center,** in the northwest corner of the park, right off I-15, provides information, permits, books, and maps. It is open from 8am to 4pm.

The **Zion Human History Museum,** about 1 mile inside the south entrance, offers museum exhibits, park information, an orientation program, and a bookstore; it's open daily in summer from 9am to 7pm, with shorter hours at other times.

Visitor centers and the museum are closed on Christmas Day.

FEES, BACKCOUNTRY PERMITS & REGULATIONS   Entry into the park (for up to 7 days), which includes unlimited use of the shuttle bus, costs $25 per private car, pickup truck, van, or RV, or $12 per individual 16 or older on motorcycle, bicycle, or foot (maximum charge of $25 per family). America the Beautiful National Parks and Federal Recreational Lands Passes are honored. Oversize vehicles are charged $15 for use of the Zion–Mt. Carmel Tunnel on the east side of the park (see "Getting There/Access Points," above).

Backcountry permits, available at either visitor center, are required for all overnight hikes in the park as well as for any slot canyon hikes. Permits cost $10 for 1 or 2 persons, $15 for 3 to 7, and $20 for 8 to 12 people. Camping costs $16 per night for basic campsites and $18 to $20 per night for sites with electric hookups (located in Watchman Campground).

Bicycles are prohibited in the Zion–Mt. Carmel Tunnel, the backcountry, and on trails, except the Pa'rus Trail. Feeding or disturbing wildlife is forbidden, as are vandalism and disturbing any natural feature of the park. Pets, which must be leashed at all times, are prohibited on all trails (except the Pa'rus Trail, where leashed pets are permitted), in the backcountry, and in public buildings.

SEASONS/AVOIDING THE CROWDS   Zion is one of the most-used national parks in the country. It's open year-round (though visitor centers are closed Christmas Day), 24 hours a day, although weather conditions may limit some activities at certain times. Avoid long hikes in midsummer, when the park bakes under temperatures that can exceed 110°F (43°C), or during and immediately after winter storms, when ice and snow at higher elevations can make trails dangerous.

Try to avoid the peak months of June, July, and August, when Zion receives almost half of its annual visitors. The quietest months are December, January, and February, but, of course, it's cold then; you may have to contend with some snow and ice. Spring and fall are best.

To avoid crowds, simply walk away from them. Choose longer and more strenuous hiking trails or hike into the backcountry. Most visitors don't bother to venture far from the road, and their loss can be your gain. If you're willing to expend a little energy, you can enjoy a wonderful solitary experience. You can also avoid hordes of tourists by spending time in spectacular Kolob Canyons, in the far northwest section of the park; it receives surprisingly little use, at least compared to Zion Canyon.

RANGER & EDUCATIONAL PROGRAMS Rangers present a variety of free programs and activities. Evening programs, which last about 45 minutes, take place most evenings from April through September at the Watchman Campground Amphitheater and Zion Lodge Auditorium. They usually include a slide show, and cover topics such as the animals or plants of the park, geology, the night sky, mankind's role in the park, or some unique aspect of Zion, like slot canyons. Rangers also give short talks on similar subjects during the day at various locations, including the Zion Lodge auditorium and the Zion Human History Museum. Ranger-guided hikes and walks, which may require reservations, might take you to little-visited areas of the park, on a trek to see wildflowers, or on a night hike under a full moon. These range from easy to very difficult. Rangers also lead shuttle tours during summer. The 2-hour "Ride with a Ranger" trip offers an opportunity to see the scenic drive and learn about Zion Canyon from a park ranger's perspective. Activity schedules are posted on boards at the visitor centers, campgrounds, and other locations.

Children up to 12 years old can join the **Junior Rangers/Explorers ★★** and participate in a variety of hands-on activities, earning certificates, pins, and patches. Morning and afternoon sessions, each lasting 1½ to 2½ hours, take place daily from Memorial Day through Labor Day, with children meeting at the Zion Nature Center, near the entrance to South Campground.

The **Zion Canyon Field Institute,** operated by the nonprofit Zion Natural History Association, Zion National Park, Springdale (www.zionpark.org; © **800/635-3959**, 435/772-3265, or 435/772-3264 for the Field Institute), offers a variety of single and multiday outdoor workshops and classes, including the highly recommended photo workshops, which are led by institute director Michael Plyler. Fees for most of the 1-day programs start at $35, and multiday programs cost from $100 to $300.

SEEING THE HIGHLIGHTS

If you have only a day or two at the park, head first to the **Zion Canyon Visitor Center** for the orientation video, and then talk with a ranger about the amount of time you have, your abilities, and interests. Because Zion offers such a variety of landscapes and activities, you can easily create your own itinerary. If your goal is to see as much of the park as possible in 1 day, consider the following:

After a quick stop at the visitor center, hop on the free **shuttle bus,** which runs during the high season and takes you to the major roadside viewpoints. You can get off, look at the formations, take a short walk if you like, and then catch the next shuttle for a ride to the next stop.

You can get off the shuttle at the **Temple of Sinawava** and take the easy 2-mile round-trip **Riverside Walk,** which follows the Virgin River through a narrow canyon past hanging gardens. Then take the shuttle back to Zion Lodge (total time: 2–4 hr.).

Near the lodge is the trailhead for the **Emerald Pools ★.** Especially pleasant on hot days, this easy walk through a forest of oak, maple, fir, and cottonwood trees

---

Wildlife Viewing

The earlier in the day you get out on the Zion Canyon Scenic Drive, the better chance you'll have of seeing wildlife.

---

leads to a waterfall, hanging garden, and the shimmering lower pool. This part of the walk should take about an hour round-trip, but those with a bit more time may want to add another hour and another mile to the loop by taking the moderately strenuous hike on a rocky, steeper trail to the upper pool. Or head back to the south park entrance and stop at **Watchman** (east of Watchman Campground), for the 2-mile, 2-hour round-trip, moderately strenuous hike to a plateau with beautiful views of several rock formations and the town of Springdale. In the evening, try to take in a campground amphitheater program.

EXPLORING ZION BY SHUTTLE OR CAR

If you enter Zion from the east, along the steep **Zion–Mt. Carmel Highway,** you'll travel 13 miles through the park to the **Zion Canyon Visitor Center,** passing **Checkerboard Mesa,** a massive sandstone rock formation covered with horizontal and vertical lines that make it look like a huge fishing net. A fairyland of fantastically shaped rocks of red, orange, tan, and white, as well as the **Great Arch of Zion,** carved high in a stone cliff, will come into view.

A **shuttle-bus** system has been implemented in the main section of the park to reduce traffic congestion and the resultant problems of pollution, noise, and damage to park resources. The shuttle system consists of two loops: one in the town of Springdale and the other along Zion Canyon Scenic Drive, with the loops connecting at the visitor center. From April through October, access to the Zion Canyon Scenic Drive (above Utah 9) is limited to shuttle buses, hikers, and bikers. The only exception: overnight Zion Lodge guests and tour buses connected with the lodge, which have access as far as the lodge. Shuttles run frequently—about every 6 minutes at peak times—and have room for packs, coolers, strollers, and two bicycles. In winter, when the fewest number of visitors are here, you are permitted to drive the full length of Zion Canyon Scenic Drive in your own vehicle.

Those driving into the park at the northwest corner will find a short scenic drive open year-round. The **Kolob Canyons Road** (about 45 min. from Zion Canyon Visitor Center at I-15, exit 40) runs 5 miles among spectacular red and orange rocks, ending at a high vista. Allow about 45 minutes round-trip, and get a copy of the "Kolob Canyons Road Guide" at the Kolob Visitor Center. Here's what you'll pass along the way:

Leaving **Kolob Canyons Visitor Center,** drive along the Hurricane Fault to **Hurricane Cliffs,** a series of tall, gray cliffs composed of limestone, and onward to **Taylor Creek,** where a piñon-juniper forest clings to the rocky hillside, providing a home to the bright blue—and noisy—scrub jay. **Horse Ranch Mountain,** at 8,726 feet, is the national park's highest point. Passing a series of colorful rock layers, where you might be lucky enough to spot a golden eagle, your next stop is **Box Canyon,** along the south fork of Taylor Creek, with sheer rock walls soaring over 1,500 feet high.

Continue until you reach a canyon, which exposes a rock wall that likely began as a sand dune before being covered by an early sea and cemented into stone. Next stop is a side canyon, with large, arched alcoves crowned with delicate curved ceilings. Head on to a view of **Timber Top Mountain,** which has a sagebrush-blanketed desert at

> ## Impressions
>
> Nothing can exceed the wondrous beauty of Zion . . . in the nobility and beauty of the sculptures, there is no comparison.
>
> —Geologist Clarence Dutton, 1880

its base but is covered with stately fir and ponderosa pine at its peak. Watch for mule deer on the brushy hillsides, especially between October and March, when they might be spotted just after sunrise or before sunset.

From here, continue to **Rockfall Overlook;** a large scar on the mountainside marks the spot where a 1,000-foot chunk of stone crashed to the earth in July 1983, the victim of erosion. Yes, geology never stops working. And finally, stop to see the canyon walls themselves, colored orange-red by iron oxide and striped black by mineral-laden water running down the cliff faces.

OUTDOOR PURSUITS

Hiring a guide for activities in the park and surrounding area allows you to safely try things you never dreamed you could: strenuous hiking, canyoneering, rock climbing, and mountain biking. Choose from several reliable local companies, including **Zion Adventure Company,** 36 Lion Blvd., at the corner of Lion Boulevard and Zion Park Boulevard, Springdale (www.zion adventures.com; © **435/772-1001**), which rents gear whatever you're planning to do (such as wetsuits or shoes for hiking the Narrows), and **Zion Rock & Mountain Guides,** 1458 Zion Park Blvd., Springdale (www.zionrock guides.com; © **435/772-3303**). **Zion Cycles,** 868 Zion Park Blvd. in Springdale (www.zioncycles.com; © **435/772-0400**), behind Zion Pizza & Noodle, rents, repairs, and advises about mountain and road bikes. In the park, the free shuttle offers the best way to reach trailheads.

BIKING & MOUNTAIN BIKING Bikes are prohibited on all trails and forbidden to travel cross-country within the national park boundaries, but two developments have helped Zion become one of America's few bike-friendly national parks.

Though it's not the most dramatically scenic path, Pa'rus Trail is paved, open to bicyclists, pedestrians, and those with strollers or wheelchairs, but closed to motor vehicles. It runs 2 miles along the Virgin River from the South Campground entrance to **Zion Canyon Scenic Drive,** near its intersection with the Zion–Mt. Carmel Highway. Along the way, the trail crosses the North Fork of the Virgin River and several creeks, and provides good views of Watchman, West Temple, the Sentinel, and other lower canyon formations.

Bikes are permitted on the park's established roads at any time, except in the Zion–Mt. Carmel tunnel, where they are always prohibited. From April through October, Zion Canyon Scenic Drive north of the Zion–Mt. Carmel Highway is open only to shuttle buses, bicyclists, and hikers, plus tour buses and motorists going to Zion Lodge. The rest of the year, the road is open to private motor vehicles, and the shuttle buses don't run. Bicyclists should stay to the right to allow shuttle buses to pass.

On Bureau of Land Management and state-owned property just outside the park, mountain bikers will find numerous rugged jeep trails that are great for mountain biking, plus more than 70 miles of slickrock cross-country trails and single-track trails. Gooseberry Mesa, above the community of Springdale, is generally considered the best mountain-biking destination in the area, but good trails can be found on nearby Wire and Grafton mesas. Be careful to pay attention to trail markers—this country is easy to get lost in.

Talk with the knowledgeable staff at Zion Cycles (above) about the best trails for your interests and abilities. The full-service bike shop offers maps, bikes, accessories, repairs, and rentals ($38–$55 per day, $28–$45 for a half-day).

For guided mountain or road bike trips, contact Zion Adventure Company (above) or Zion Rock & Mountain Guides (above); both also offer guided mountain bike excursions outside the national park.

HIKING Hiking in Zion can be just what you want it to be: an easy half-hour walk on a paved path or a grueling overnight trek over rocky terrain. Don't worry—there are plenty of options in between the extremes. Hikers with a fear of heights should be careful when choosing trails; many include steep, dizzying drop-offs. Below are a variety of hiking suggestions.

The **Weeping Rock Trail,** among the park's shortest trails, is a .4-mile round-trip walk from the Zion Canyon Scenic Drive to a rock alcove with a spring and hanging gardens of ferns and wildflowers. Although paved, the trail is steep and not suitable for wheelchairs.

Outdoor Pursuits | ZION NATIONAL PARK

Another short hike is the **Lower Emerald Pools Trail ★★**, an easy 1-hour walk. A 0.6-mile paved path from the Emerald Pools parking area through a forest of oak, maple, fir, and cottonwood leads to a waterfall, a hanging garden, and the Lower Emerald Pool, and is suitable for those in wheelchairs, with assistance. If you want to extend your trip to a moderately strenuous 2-hour hike, continue along the loop, a steeper, rocky trail (not appropriate for wheelchairs) continues past cactus, yucca, and juniper another .5 mile to Upper Emerald Pool, with another waterfall. A third pool, just above Lower Emerald Pool, offers impressive reflections of the cliffs. The pools are named for the green color of the water, which is caused by algae.

Hidden Canyon Trail, a 2.4-mile moderately strenuous round-trip hike that takes about 3 hours is worth pushing yourself—it's one of the most scenic trails in Zion. From the Weeping Rock parking area, the trail climbs 850 feet through a narrow, water-carved canyon, with a small natural arch upstream from the mouth of the canyon. Hidden Canyon Trail includes long drop-offs and is not recommended for anyone with a fear of heights.

Another moderately strenuous but relatively short hike is the **Watchman Trail,** which starts near the transit/visitor center. This 2.7-mile round-trip hike gets surprisingly little use, possibly because it can be very hot in midday. Climbing to a plateau near the base of the formation called the Watchman, it offers splendid views of lower Zion Canyon, the Towers of the Virgin, and West Temple formations.

One of the most thrilling hikes in the whole national park system, a strenuous 4-hour, 5.4-mile round trip that's definitely not for anyone with even a mild fear of heights, **Angels Landing Trail** runs through a series of 21 switchbacks built into a cleft in the wall; these are regarded as one of the engineering marvels of the park. The final hair-raising half-mile follows a narrow, knife-edge trail along a steep ridge, where footing can be slippery even under the best of circumstances. Support chains are set along parts of the trail. Plan your hike so you have time to stop at the summit for awhile and savor the spectacular views into Zion Canyon, with the Virgin River gently bending around three sides at the bottom of the canyon, the Great White Throne and Red Arch Mountain to the southeast, and the entrance to the Narrows beyond the Temple of Sinawava to the north. When you look down to see a hawk flying below, you realize you're on top of Zion's world.

Like Angels Landing, hiking **the Narrows ★★** is one of the most iconic Zion experience. It's not really hiking a trail at all—it's river-walking, wading along the bottom of the Virgin River, through a stunning 1,000-foot-deep chasm that, at a mere 20 feet wide, definitely lives up to its name. Passing fancifully sculptured sandstone arches, hanging gardens, and waterfalls, this moderately strenuous 16-mile one-way hike can be completed in less than a day or in several days, depending on how quickly you want to go.

Warning: The Narrows is not an easy hike by any means; it's subject to flash flooding and can be very treacherous. Park service officials remind hikers that they are responsible for their own safety and should always check on current water conditions and weather forecasts before heading out. This hike is not recommended when rain is forecast. Hikers should wear sturdy boots or shoes with good ankle support that they won't mind getting wet, be prepared for cold temperatures with a sweater or jacket, and put everything in water-proof containers. You can rent necessary equipment from Zion Adventure Company (above). Experienced Narrows hikers also recommend that you take a walking stick to help steady yourself against the strong currents. Sticks are sometimes available near the end of the Riverside Walk, but you're better off taking your own—hikers are prohibited from cutting tree branches to make walking sticks. Finally, because of the strong currents, park officials recommend that kids under 4' 8" tall not hike in the river. Permits are required for full-day and overnight hikes (check with rangers for details), but are not needed for easy, short day hikes, which you can access from just beyond the end of the Riverside Walk, a 2.2-mile round-trip trail that starts at the Temple of Sinawava parking area.

HORSEBACK RIDING Guided rides in the park are available March through October from **Canyon Trail Rides** (www.canyonrides.com; **© 435/679-8665**), with ticket sales and information near Zion Lodge. A 1-hour ride along the Virgin River costs $45; a half-day ride on the Sand Bench Trail costs $90. Riders must weigh no more than 220 pounds, and children must be at least 7 years old for the 1-hour ride and 10 years old for the half-day ride. Reservations are advised.

ROCK CLIMBING Despite rangers' warning that much of Zion's rock is loose, or "rotten," and climbing equipment and techniques suitable for granite are often less effective on sandstone, technical rock climbers like the sandstone cliffs in Zion Canyon. Permits ($15 for 1 or 2 persons, $20 for 3 to 7, and $25 for 8 to 12 people) are required for overnight climbs, and because some routes may be closed at times, climbers should check at the Zion Canyon Visitor Center before setting out. Zion Adventure Company and Zion Rock & Mountain Guides (above) offer a variety of guided rock climbing trips, as well as instruction. Typical per-person rates are $139 for a half-day and $169 for a full day for two people, with lower per-person rates for larger groups. Zion Rock & Mountain Guides also offers equipment rentals and sales.

SWIMMING AND WATER SPORTS Technically, hiking in the Narrows is a water sport. Swimming and wading are prohibited in the Emerald Pools. Swimming is permitted south of South Campground amphitheater; check with the visitor center about other areas that would be safe for swimming during your visit. You can also go tubing in the river if the water level allows; check with Zion Adventure Company (above), which rents tubes for $20.

WILDLIFE VIEWING & BIRD-WATCHING Watch out for a chuckwalla, and remember the word to flummox your friends back home. It's the largest of Zion's lizard varieties and can grow to 20 inches. The ringtail cat, a relative of the raccoon, prowls Zion Canyon at night so stow your camping supplies securely. Along the Virgin River, you'll see bank beavers, so named because they live in burrows dug into riverbanks instead of building dams. Of course, mule deer, bighorn sheep, hares, and ground squirrels are everywhere.

The peregrine falcon, among the world's fastest birds, sometimes nests in the Weeping Rock area, where you're also likely to see the dipper, winter wren, and white-throated swift. Also in the park are golden eagles, several species of hummingbirds, ravens, and piñon jays.

Snakes here include the poisonous Great Basin rattler, found below 8,000 feet elevation, as well as nonpoisonous kingsnakes and gopher snakes. Tarantulas are often seen in the late summer and fall. Contrary to popular belief, the tarantula's bite is not deadly, although it can be somewhat painful.

Remember, it's illegal to feed the wildlife.

CAMPING

The best places to camp are at one of the **national park campgrounds ★★★** just inside the park's south entrance. Both of Zion's main campgrounds have paved roads, well-spaced sites, and lots of trees. Facilities include restrooms with flush toilets but no showers, a dump station, a public telephone, and sites for those with disabilities. The fee is $16 per night for basic sites, or $18 to $20 per night for sites with electric hookups. Some campgrounds take **reservations** (www.recreation.gov; call ✆ **877-444-6777**), which is highly recommended during summertime, when campgrounds are usually full by mid-morning.

South Campground has 127 sites (no hookups) and is usually open from early March through October only. Reservations are not accepted and the campground often fills by noon in summer. Some campers stay at nearby commercial campgrounds their first night in the area, then hurry into the park the next morning, circling like vultures until a site becomes available.

Watchman Campground (www.recreation.gov or ✆ **877/444-6777** for reservations) has 164 sites. Of those, 95 have electric hookups and 69 are available only to those camping in tents. Watchman is open year-round (reservations available spring through fall only).

Lava Point, with only six sites, is located on the Koloh Terrace. It has fire grates, tables, and toilets, but no water, and no fee. Vehicles are limited to 19 feet, and it's usually open from June through mid-October.

Outside the Park

Just outside the east and south park entrances are commercial campgrounds with hot showers and RV hookups. Note that the park's visitor center, campgrounds, and most of its attractions are closer to the south entrance.

East Zion Riverside RV Park is located in the Best Western East Zion Thunderbird Lodge complex in Mt. Carmel Junction, about 13 miles east of the east entrance to the national park (at the junction of Utah 9 and U.S. 89; www.zionnational-park.com; ☏ **435/648-2203**). Especially good for self-contained RVs, the park sits along the banks of the Virgin River in the shade of cottonwood trees, and offers campers use of the pool, hot tub, and other amenities at the adjacent Thunderbird Lodge. It has 12 sites, all with hookups, and a dump station. It's open year-round. The fee is $18 per night.

Zion Canyon Campground ★ (www.zioncamp.com; ☏ **435/772-3237**) is at 479 Zion Park Blvd. in Springdale, a half-mile south of the park's south entrance. It's family-owned, open year-round, and offers 200 tent and RV sites, many of which are shaded. Although it gets quite crowded in summer, the campground is clean and well maintained. There are some especially large sites for big RVs, and it has a dump station, a swimming pool, a game room, a playground, and a store. Rates range from $39 for 2 people at a tent site to $49 for an RV; pay extra for additional people and vehicles.

WHERE TO STAY

The only lodging actually in Zion National Park is **Zion Lodge** (below) but there are many options in the village of Springdale, at Zion's south entrance. Be aware that rates change seasonally and deals may be found online. For additional information about lodging, dining, and other services in the area, check in with the Zion Canyon Visitors Bureau, 118 Lion Blvd., Springdale (www.zionpark.com; ☏ **435/772-3434** or 888/518-7070).

In the Park

Zion Lodge ★★★ Built in the heart of the park in 1925 by the Union Pacific Railroad, the lodge was destroyed by fire in 1966, then rebuilt and restored to its historic appearance. It's the only lodging inside the park, and it sits in a valley with spectacular views of the park's rock cliffs. The charming and genuinely historic cabins are first choice here. Each has a private porch, stone (gas-burning) fireplace, two queen-size or double beds, and pine walls. The comfortable modern motel units have two queen-size beds and a private porch or balcony. The plush suites are spacious, with one king-size bed, a separate sitting room with a queen-size hide-a-bed, and a refrigerator. Ranger programs are presented in the lodge auditorium in summer. All units are nonsmoking.

Zion National Park. www.zionlodge.com. ☏ **435/772-7700.** Information and reservations: Xanterra Parks & Resorts (www.xanterra.com; ☏ **888/297-2757** or 303/297-2757). 121 units. Motel rooms $150–$250 double; cabins $140–$237 double; suites $200–$300 double. Discounts (sometimes up to 50% off) and packages available at other times. **Amenities:** 2 restaurants (Red Rock Grill and Castle Dome Cafe, both reviewed below)

Nearby

Best Western East Zion Thunderbird Lodge ★ A well-maintained two-story motel with Southwest decor, the Thunderbird offers quiet, spacious, comfortable rooms, with king- or queen-size beds, wood furnishings, photos or artwork depicting area scenery, and a private balcony or patio. The lodging has a gas station and a convenience store on the premises. All rooms are non-smoking. The complex also includes a campground, the East Zion Riverside RV Park. (See "Camping," above.)

At the junction of Utah 9 and U.S. 89, Mt. Carmel Junction. www.zionnational-park.com. ℂ **800/780-7234** or 435/648-2203. 61 units. May–Oct $169–$199 double; Nov–Apr $120–$180 double. **Amenities:** Restaurant (Thunderbird, see review below); 9-hole golf course; Jacuzzi; large outdoor heated pool (Apr–Oct only); free Wi-Fi.

Best Western Zion Park Inn ★ What you want near Zion is a room with a view, and this a good choice for an upscale, reliable chain motel with a view. Rooms are decorated in a Southwest style; try to book a unit with pitched, high ceilings and windows with views of the colorful rock formations outside.

688 Zion Park Blvd., Springdale. www.bestwestern.com. ℂ **435/429-7650**. $118–$164 double. Rates include breakfast. **Amenities:** Outdoor pool; hot tub; exercise room; coin-op laundry; free Wi-Fi.

Cliffrose Lodge & Gardens ★ With delightful river frontage (they call it "beachside") and 5 acres of lawns, shade trees, and flower gardens, the Cliffrose offers a beautiful setting just outside Zion's entrance. The architecture is Southwestern adobe style, with redwood balconies, and the outdoor rock waterfall whirlpool tub is a delight, especially in the evening. Four luxurious Canyon View Suites sleep up to six guests each. On the lawns, you'll find comfortable seating, a playground, and a lawn swing. All units are nonsmoking.

281 Zion Park Blvd., Springdale. www.cliffroselodge.com. ℂ **800/243-8824** or 435/772-3234. 50 units. Doubles starting at $311; suites and villas begin at $511. Rates lower in off-season. **Amenities:** Jacuzzi; large outdoor heated pool (Apr–Oct only); free Wi-Fi.

Desert Pearl Inn ★ The riverside location makes an especially serene setting for this family-owned inn. Southwest-style rooms arc luxurious and comfortable with great views from private terraces or balconies. Each room has two queen- or one king-size bed, plus a queen-size sofa sleeper. Bathrooms are two rooms: One has a tub/shower combo, toilet, and bidet; the other has a closet, vanity, and sink. There are also luxurious suites. All units are nonsmoking.

707 Zion Park Blvd., Springdale. www.desertpearl.com. ℂ **888/828-0898** or 435/772-8888. 61 units. $280–$417 double; prices may vary with the season. **Amenities:** Jacuzzi; huge outdoor heated pool (Apr–Oct only); free Wi-Fi.

10

ZION NATIONAL PARK | Where to Stay

Driftwood Lodge ★★ Beautiful lawns and gardens enhance this well-kept mid-century modern motel—a quiet, lush complex perfect for sitting back and admiring the spectacular rock formations, particularly the one known as Watchman. The spacious rooms have wood-grain furnishings plus patios or balconies. Most standard rooms have two queen-size beds; others have one king-size. Two family suites each have one king-size and two queen-size beds, and the handsome king suites offer a separate sitting room, king-size bed, and a microwave. The restaurant, King's Landing (reviewed below), has a delightful outdoor patio with splendid views and great food.

1515 Zion Park Blvd., Springdale. www.driftwoodlodge.net. ℂ **888/801-8811** or 435/772-3262. 53 units. Apr–Nov $199–$239 double, rates slightly lower Dec–Mar. Pets accepted at management's discretion, $25 fee. **Amenities:** Restaurant; Jacuzzi; outdoor heated pool (Apr–Oct only); free Wi-Fi.

Flanigan's Inn ★★ This top-of-the-line boutique eco-hotel in Springdale brings the scenic views indoors. Built of natural wood and rock, and set among trees, lawns, and flowers, it's just outside the entrance to Zion National Park. Most units have decks or patios and large windows overlooking a natural courtyard, including a koi pond, heated pool, and hot tub. Suites have microwaves in addition to small refrigerators, and the two furnished villas are beautiful upscale homes, available for rent and separate from the main inn. A nature trail leads to a hilltop labyrinth and spectacular vistas. There is a full-service spa, including a salon and yoga exercise room, and bicycles are available for guests' use. The inn is 50% wind powered and entirely nonsmoking.

450 Zion Park Blvd., Springdale. www.flanigans.com. ℂ **800/765-7787** or 435/772-3244. 36 units. Mid-Mar through Nov $199–$239 double; $349 suite and villa; lower rates at other times. **Amenities:** Restaurant (Spotted Dog Café; see review below); outdoor Jacuzzi; outdoor heated pool (Apr–Oct only); spa; free Wi-Fi.

Harvest House Bed & Breakfast at Zion ★★ People either love or hate B&Bs; it mostly depends on whether you like to eat breakfast with strangers. If you love them, you'll love Harvest House. It's not historic (built in 1989) but the house is Utah territorial-style (similar to Victorian) and the newness means more amenities. Enjoy a garden sitting area with a koi pond and spectacular views of the national park's rock formations. Rooms are charming, comfortable, and quiet, with king- or queen-size beds and private bathrooms. One upstairs room faces west and has grand sunset views, while the other two have private decks facing the impressive formations of Zion. There's a big-screen TV in the living room with access to some 40 movie channels; and the gourmet breakfasts are sumptuous, with fresh-baked breads, fresh-squeezed orange juice, granola, fruit, yogurt, and a hot main course. All units are nonsmoking.

29 Canyon View Dr., Springdale. www.harvesthouse.net. ℂ **800/719-7493** or 435/772-3880. 4 units. $100–$135 double. Rates include full breakfast. No children ages 6 and under. **Amenities:** Outdoor Jacuzzi; no phone; free Wi-Fi.

Majestic View Lodge ★★ This place truly lives up to its name: virtually every room at this sprawling complex offers spectacular glimpses of the surrounding scenery. It's a lovely place to start the day, or to wrap up a long afternoon of hiking, with the added bonus of being very close to the park entrance. The lodge is actually a series of two-story stucco and log buildings, and each unit has its own balcony or patio (perfect for watching the sunset light up the rock formations). The spotless rooms are furnished with rustic aspen decor, including either a king bed or two queen beds, and the deluxe suites have kitchenettes. Spend some time at the restaurant or saloon—both sharing the excellent views—or visit the lodge's sprawling trading post and wildlife museum. There's free shuttle service to the park.

2400 Zion Park Blvd., Springdale. www.majesticviewlodge.com. ℂ **866/772-0665** or 435/772-0665. 69 units. Apr–Oct $159–$169 double; Nov–Mar $89 double. **Amenities:** Restaurant; bar; brewpub; Jacuzzi; heated outdoor pool; free Wi-Fi.

Pioneer Lodge ★ The Pioneer Lodge's exterior is a like a straightforward '60s motel, but standard guest rooms have a homey feel with one king- or two queen-size beds and remote-controlled heating and cooling. There are 40 rooms and three suites, and all units have rustic log furnishings and granite counters. On the premises is a gift shop selling the work of Southern Utah artists, an Internet cafe, and a reasonably priced restaurant where lodge guests receive a 10% discount during their stay. All units are nonsmoking.

838 Zion Park Blvd., Springdale. www.zionpioneerlodge.com. ℂ **888/772-3233** or 435/772-3233. 43 units. Summer $164–$186 double, $208–$329 suite; lower rates in off-season. **Amenities:** Restaurant; Jacuzzi; outdoor heated pool (Apr–Oct only); free Wi-Fi.

Under the Eaves Inn ★★ This romantic 1931 home, located in the heart of Springdale, offers handsomely decorated historic rooms, beautiful gardens and shade trees, and spectacular views from what innkeepers Joe Pitti and Mark Chambers call "the best front porch in Utah." Units range from the basic Hiker's Room to a luxurious suite—covering 1,200 square feet, it has a vaulted ceiling, a wood-burning stove, a kitchenette, and a claw-foot tub plus separate shower. The cute Garden Cottage, built in 1928, was moved here from inside the national park. It contains two small but comfortable rooms on the main floor, and the more rustic, lower level Hiker's Room. Breakfast is off the menu at nearby Oscar's Cafe, served from 7 to 11am. All units are nonsmoking.

980 Zion Park Blvd., Springdale. www.undertheeaves.com. ℂ **866/261-2655** or 435/772-3457. 7 units, including 1 suite. $85–$150 double; $185 suite. Rates include full breakfast. Children allowed at management's discretion. **Amenities:** No phone; free Wi-Fi.

Zion Park Motel ★ You visit Zion for the hiking and the scenery, so you all you really need is a clean, attractive room with a fresh bed to fall into after a day outdoors. This is that place: The slightly small rooms are economical, comfortable, and attractively furnished with one king- or two queen-size beds and bathrooms with showers or tub/shower combos. All rooms are nonsmoking.

865 Zion Park Blvd. (P.O. Box 365), Springdale. www.zionparkmotel.com. ℂ **435/772-3251**. 21 units. $84 double; $104–$149 family unit (sleeps 6) and suite. **Amenities:** Outdoor heated pool (Apr–Oct only); kitchen (in some units); free Wi-Fi.

WHERE TO EAT

With the exception of the Castle Dome Cafe and the Red Rock Grill (below), these restaurants are all located on the main road to the park through Springdale.

In the Park

Castle Dome Cafe ★ SNACK BAR   Located at the north end of Zion Lodge, this simple fast-food restaurant with an outdoor dining patio serves up cinnamon buns, burgers, sandwiches, hot dogs, pizza, ice cream, frozen yogurt, and similar fare. No alcoholic beverages are served.

Zion Lodge, Zion National Park. ℂ **435/772-3213**. Menu items $3.75–$9.95. No credit cards. Summer daily 7am–9pm; shorter hours the rest of the year.

Red Rock Grill ★★ AMERICAN   Try to have at least one meal here during your visit. The restaurant's mountain lodge decor competes for your attention with the spectacular rock formations, visible through the dining room's large windows; for an even better view, dine on the outside patio. The menu changes periodically, but breakfast offer all the usual options, plus a buffet. There's often a buffet at lunch, too, alongside classic a la carte fare like chicken salad, grilled salmon, and burgers. Specialties at dinner might include the excellent Santa Fe flatiron steak (grilled and topped with pico de gallo and fried onions), a bison rib-eye steak with a potato medley, or grilled pork loin with prickly pear sauce. We heartily recommend the lodge's specialty desserts, such as the bourbon pecan pie or turtle Bundt cake. There is full liquor service.

Zion Lodge, Zion National Park. www.zionlodge.com. ℂ **435/772-7760**. Dinner reservations required in summer. Main courses $4–$10 breakfast, $8–$12 lunch, $14–$29 dinner. Daily 6:30–10:30am, 11:30am–3pm, and 5–10pm.

Nearby in Springdale

Bit & Spur Restaurant & Saloon ★★ MEXICAN/SOUTHWESTERN   Rough wood-and-stone walls and an exposed-beam ceiling give this restaurant the look of an Old West saloon. Actually, it's a family dining room with a patio and original art decorating the walls. The menu changes seasonally, but usually includes Mexican standards such as burritos and a traditional green-chili stew with pork and rice. You'll also often find seafood, such as grilled salmon, and our personal favorite, grilled chili-rubbed rib-eye steak with a port wine and blue cheese demiglace. Try the fresh fruit margaritas or choose from an extensive wine list, or a variety of microbrewed beers.

1212 Zion Park Blvd. www.bitandspur.com. ℂ **435/772-3498**. Reservations recommended. Main courses $12–$25. Spring–fall daily 5–10pm; call for winter hours.

King's Landing ★★ MODERN AMERICAN   One of the loveliest places near Zion to dine and drink is on the patio at King's Landing. This inside is refreshingly mid-century modern, but the prize is the patio with its view of the Watchman. The creative menu, created by Chef King and Chef Nguyen, changes seasonally and might feature lamb rage with sweet peas, a pork chop with potato-cauliflower crush, Brussels sprouts petals and grapes, or salmon with saffron couscous. Full bar available.

At the Driftwood Lodge, 1515 Zion Park Blvd. www.driftwoodlodge.net. ✆ **435/772-7422**. Main courses $12–$30. Dinner daily 5–9pm.

Spotted Dog Café ★★ AMERICAN/REGIONAL   This tablecloth restaurant's art-filled interior makes the most of the scenery, with large windows for inside diners plus a Euro-style outdoor patio with spectacular views of Zion Canyon. Selections vary by season and may include Rocky Mountain trout, lamb, free-range poultry, hormone-free beef, environmentally farmed fish, hearty pastas, fresh summer salads, plus local specialties. There is also a healthy children's menu. The express breakfast buffet begins daily at 7am and features country potatoes, bacon, sausage, plus selections of eggs, pastries, yogurt, French toast, and more. The Spotted Dog has an excellent wine cellar, microbrewed draft beers, and complete liquor service.

At Flanigan's Inn, 428 Zion Park Blvd. www.flanigans.com. ✆ **435/772-0700.** Reservations recommended. Main courses $12–$26. Daily 7–11am and 5–9pm; reduced hours in winter.

Whiptail Grill ★★ MEXICAN   This tiny restaurant in a converted gas station (circa 1965) serves some of the best food in Springdale. Eat outside if you can, and the Hathaway's Famous Goat Cheese Chili Relleno is a must: a roasted Anaheim pepper (they tend to be mild) stuffed with goat cheese, coated with crumbs, fried, and served with tomatillo sauce and a cucumber salad. Order it as an app or an entree. Vegetarians will love the spaghetti squash–stuffed enchiladas, and kids like the quesadillas and burgers. Beer and wine available.

445 Zion Park Blvd. www.whiptailgrillzion.com, ✆ **435/772-0283.** Main courses $12–$16. 11:30am–10pm in season; dinner only off-season.

Zion Park Gift & Deli ★ DELI   Want a decent sandwich at an economical price? This is your place. Eat at one of the cafe-style tables inside or on the patio outside, or carry your sandwich off on a hike or to a national park picnic ground. All baked goods, including the sandwich breads and sub rolls, are made in-house. Order your custom sandwich at the counter and wait while it's prepared. This is also a good breakfast stop if you enjoy fresh-baked cinnamon rolls, muffins, banana nut bread, and similar goodies, with a cup of espresso. Locally made candy, including 14 flavors of excellent fudge, and 24 flavors of ice cream and frozen yogurt are offered. No alcohol is served.

866 Zion Park Blvd. http://zionparkgiftanddeli.com. ✆ **435/772-3843.** All items $4.95–$10. Summer Mon–Sat 8:30am–9:30pm; reduced hours in winter.

10

ZION NATIONAL PARK | Where to Eat

WHAT TO SEE & DO IN NEARBY SPRINGDALE

Just outside the south entrance to Zion National Park, in Springdale, are two worthwhile attractions.

The **Tanner Twilight Concert Series** presents a varied performing arts program in the stunning, 2,000-seat outdoor **Tanner Amphitheater,** just off Zion Park Boulevard. Performances range from symphony orchestra concerts and dance performances to rock, jazz, and gospel concerts. Shows begin at 8pm many Saturdays throughout the summer, and cost $10 for adults and $5 for youths (18 and younger). For information, contact **Dixie State College,** in St. George (www.dixie.edu/tanner/index.html; ℭ **435/652-7994**).

The **Zion Canyon Theatre,** 145 Zion Park Blvd. (www.zioncanyontheatre. com; ℭ **888/256-3456** or 435/772-2400), boasts a huge screen—some 60 feet high by 82 feet across. Here you can see the dramatic film "Zion Canyon: Treasure of the Gods," with thrilling scenes of the Zion National Park area, including a hair-raising flash flood through Zion Canyon's Narrows and some dizzying bird's-eye views. The theater also shows a variety of other Hollywood and large-format films. Admission is $8 adults and $6 children under 12. The theater is open daily from 11am in summer; call for winter hours. The theater complex also contains a tourist information center, an ATM, a picnic area, gift and souvenir shops, restaurants, and a grocery store.

BRYCE CANYON NATIONAL PARK

'Hoodoo' means voodoo unless you're in Bryce Canyon—'fairy chimney' or 'earth pyramid' are other names for the otherworldly rock spires rising from the canyon floor. And the names don't lie. There is something bewitching about these geological wonders. **Bryce Canyon ★★★** is a place full of magic, inspiration, and spectacular beauty. These silent rock sentinels invite your imagination to run wild.

Geologically speaking, hoodoos are simply pinnacles of rock, often oddly shaped, left standing after millions of years of water and wind have eroded the surrounding rock. But how much more fun to believe the Paiute legend. These American Indians, who lived in the area for several hundred years before being forced out by Anglo pioneers, told of "Legend People" who once lived here; because of their evil ways, they were turned to stone by the powerful Coyote and even today remain frozen in time.

Whatever the cause, mythical or scientific, Bryce Canyon is certainly unique. Its intricate and often whimsical formations are on a more human scale than the impressive rocks seen at Zion, Capitol Reef, and Canyonlands national parks. Bryce is inviting in its beauty; by gazing over the rim, or spending even just one morning on the trail, you will feel you're on intimate terms with the park.

Besides the attention-grabbing hoodoos, you'll notice deep amphitheaters, with cliffs, windows, and arches, all colored in Utah's signature shades of red. Bryce holds three separate life zones at the various elevations in the park, each with its own unique vegetation, and a kingdom of animals, from the busy chipmunks and ground squirrels to the stately mule deer and its archenemy, the mountain lion.

Human exploration of the Bryce area likely began with the Paiute. It's possible that trappers, prospectors, and early Mormon scouts visited here in the early to mid-1800s before Major John Wesley Powell conducted the first thorough survey of the region in the early 1870s. Shortly after Powell's exploration, Mormon pioneer Ebenezer Bryce and his wife, Mary, moved to the area and tried raising cattle. Although they stayed only a few years before moving on to Arizona, Bryce left behind his name and his oft-quoted description of the canyon as "a helluva place to lose a cow."

ESSENTIALS

Getting There

BY PLANE **Bryce Canyon Airport** (Airport Code BCE; www.brycecanyon airport.com; ℂ 435/834-5239), at 7,586 feet of elevation, is located several miles from the park entrance on Utah 12, and has a 7,400-foot lighted runway. There is no regularly scheduled airline service, but charter service is available from **Bryce Canyon Airlines** (www.rubysinn.com/scenic-flights; ℂ 435/834-8060). The airport offers free shuttle service to local motels and car rentals are available from **Hertz** (www.hertz.com; ℂ 800/654-3131), which is located at the Chevron service station in the Ruby's Inn complex.

You can also fly into St. George (130 miles southwest of the park on I-15) or Cedar City (also on I-15, about 80 miles west of the park), and rent a car (see chapter 9).

From St. George, travel north on I-15 10 miles to exit 16, then head east on Utah 9 for 63 miles to U.S. 89, north 44 miles to Utah 12, and east 13 miles to the park entrance road. The entrance station and visitor center are just 3 miles south of Utah 12. From Cedar City (I-15 exits 57, 59, and 62), take Utah 14 west 41 miles to its intersection with U.S. 89, and follow U.S. 89 north 21 miles to Utah 12, then east 17 miles to the park entrance road.

Situated in the mountains of southern Utah, the park is traversed east to west by Utah 12, with the bulk of the park, including the visitor center, accessible via Utah 63, which branches off from Utah 12 and goes south into the heart of the park. Utah 89 runs north-south west of the park, and Utah 12 heads east to Tropic and Escalante.

From Salt Lake City, it's approximately 240 miles to the park. Take I-15 south about 200 miles to exit 95, head east 13 miles on Utah 20, south on U.S. 89 for 17 miles to Utah 12, and east on Utah 12 for 13 miles to the park entrance road.

From Capitol Reef National Park, take Utah 24 west 10 miles to Torrey, and turn southwest onto Scenic Highway Utah 12 (through Boulder and Escalante) for about 110 miles, until you reach the park entrance road.

Bryce is 83 miles east of Zion National Park and 250 miles northwest of Las Vegas, Nevada.

GETTING AROUND To alleviate congestion along the park's only road, please take the optional **free shuttle.** The $35 car entrance fee (or $20 individual entrance) to Bryce Canyon entitles you to unlimited use of the Bryce Canyon Shuttle buses. Service is in effect from early May to early October, daily from 8am until 6pm Visitors can park their cars at the parking and boarding area at the intersection of the entrance road and Utah 12, 3 miles from the park boundary, and ride the shuttle into the park. Those staying in the park at the Lodge at Bryce Canyon or one of the campgrounds can also use the

239

shuttle. The shuttle has stops at various viewpoints, as well as Ruby's Inn, Ruby's Campground, the visitor center, Sunset Campground, and the Lodge at Bryce Canyon. It runs every 12 to 15 minutes.

INFORMATION/VISITOR CENTER For advance information, contact the park at ℂ 435/834-5322 or visit www.nps.gov/brca. You can find all kinds of information about visiting Bryce on the park's website. You can also get information at www.twitter.com/brycecanyonnps and at www.facebook.com/brycecanyonnps. If you desire even more details to help plan your trip, you can order books, maps, posters, DVDs, and CDs from the nonprofit **Bryce Canyon Natural History Association** (www.brycecanyon.org; ℂ **888/362-2642** or 435/834-4782). Association members (membership costs $35 single or $50 family annually) receive a 15% discount on purchases and also receive discounts at the Bryce Lodge gift shop and other nonprofit bookstores at national parks, monuments, historic sites, and recreation areas.

The **visitor center,** at the north end of the park, has exhibits on the geology and history of the area and a short slide show on the park. Rangers can answer questions and provide backcountry permits. Free brochures are available, and books, maps, videos, and posters can be purchased. The visitor center is open daily year-round except Thanksgiving, Christmas, and New Year's Day. Summer hours are usually from 8am to 8pm, with shorter hours the rest of the year (in the dead of the winter, the visitor center will close at 4:30pm).

FEES, BACKCOUNTRY PERMITS & REGULATIONS Entry into the park (for up to 7 days) costs $35 per private car, pickup truck, van, or RV, which includes unlimited use of the park shuttle (when it's operating). Individuals 16 and older entering the park on bike or foot are charged $20 each for a week; motorcycle fees are $30. Those 15 and under are admitted free. Tent campsites cost $20 per night; RVs are $30.

Backcountry permits are required for all overnight trips into the backcountry, and for up to 7 days cost $5 for 1 or 2 people, $10 for 3 to 6 people, and $15 for 7 to 15 people (group sites only). Backcountry camping is permitted on only two trails (see "Hiking," below).

Backcountry hikers are expected to practice minimum-impact techniques, prohibited from building fires, and required to carry their own water. Bicycles are prohibited in the backcountry and on all trails. Feeding or disturbing wildlife is forbidden, as is vandalizing or upsetting any natural feature of the park. Dogs, which must be leashed at all times, are prohibited on all trails, in the backcountry, and in public buildings.

SEASONS/AVOIDING THE CROWDS Although Bryce Canyon National Park receives only two-thirds the number of annual visitors that pour into Zion, the park can still be crowded, especially during peak season from June through September, when the campgrounds are often full by 2pm. If you visit then, head for some of the lesser-used trails (ask rangers for recommendations), and start your hike as soon after sunrise as possible.

In 2007, the minor planet (most would call it an asteroid) 49272 was named Bryce Canyon by **The International Astronomical Union.** Bryce Canyon (the asteroid) is estimated to be 3 to 5 miles across, and orbits the sun between Mars and Jupiter. It's too dim to be seen with a small telescope. But because Bryce Canyon (the park) is one of the darkest places in the country, visitors can see many other heavenly bodies—sign up for the park's popular twice-weekly summertime **Astronomy Program ★** (telescopes provided; consult the visitor center for details and dates).

A better time to visit, if your schedule allows, is spring or fall; if you don't mind a bit of cold and snow, the park is practically deserted from December through February—and the sight of bright red hoodoos capped with fresh white snow is a rare vision.

SAFETY   While most visitors to Bryce Canyon enjoy an exciting vacation without mishap, accidents can occur, and here—possibly because of the nature of the trails—the most common injuries by far are sprained, twisted, and broken ankles. Park rangers strongly recommend that hikers—even those just out for short day hikes—wear sturdy hiking boots with good traction and ankle support. When hiking, remember that the lower you drop below the rim, the hotter it gets, so carry lots of water and dress in layers that can be removed and easily carried as the temperature rises.

Another concern in the park is bubonic plague, which, contrary to popular belief, is treatable with antibiotics if caught in its early stages. The bacteria that causes bubonic plague has been found on fleas in prairie dog colonies in the park, so you should avoid contact with wild animals, particularly prairie dogs, chipmunks, ground squirrels, and other rodents. Those taking pets into the park should first dust them with flea powder.

RANGER & EDUCATIONAL PROGRAMS   Park rangers present a variety of free programs and activities. One-hour **evening programs,** which may include a slide show, take place at the Lodge at Bryce Canyon, the visitor center, and occasionally at the North Campground amphitheater. Topics vary but may include such subjects as the animals and plants of the park, the park's geology, and the role of humans in the park's early days. Rangers also give half-hour talks several times daily at various locations in the park and lead hikes and walks, including a **moonlight hike ★★** (reservations required, so sign up at the visitor center) and a wheelchair accessible, 1½-hour **canyon rim walk ★★**. Schedules are posted on bulletin boards at the visitor center, General Store, campgrounds, and the Lodge at Bryce Canyon. Especially popular are the park's **Astronomy Programs ★**, which are usually offered 3 evenings a week through the summer. Telescopes are provided.

For an unforgettable view of the canyon, contact **Bryce Canyon Airlines & Helicopters** (www.rubysinn.com/scenic-flights; *©* **435/834-8060**) for scenic flights by helicopter or open cockpit biplane. Tours last from about 35 minutes to several hours, and the longer trips include surrounding attractions. Check the website or call for details.

The **High Plateaus Institute,** which is affiliated with Bryce Canyon Natural History Association, occasionally presents educational programs for the public. For details, check with park offices or the Bryce Canyon Natural History Association (www.brycecanyon.org; *©* **888/362-2642** or 435/834-4782).

During the summer, children 12 and younger can join the **Junior Rangers** for a nominal fee. Junior Rangers participate in a variety of programs, and earn certificates and patches; booklets are available at the visitor center. In addition, park rangers periodically conduct **special kids' activities**—usually lasting about an hour and a half—on subjects such as the park ecology. Reservations are required—contact the visitor center for information.

SEEING THE HIGHLIGHTS

Bryce Canyon is hugely impressive, but its acreage is fairly small, so how much you see depends on how deep you go.

Start at the **visitor center** and watch the short slide show that explains some of the area geology. Then hop on a **shuttle bus** (see "Getting Around," p. 238), which will take you to most of the main viewpoints. If you insist on driving your own vehicle, you'll follow the 18-mile dead end road through the park. Stop at the viewpoints.

Spend time at **Inspiration Point,** which offers a splendid view of **Bryce Amphitheater** and its hundreds of hoodoos. Yes, it actually is inspirational.

Then walk at least partway down the **Queen's Garden Trail.** If you can spare 3 hours, hike down the **Navajo Loop Trail** and return to the rim via the Queen's Garden Trail (p. 245). Those unable to hike into the canyon can enjoy a leisurely walk along the **Rim Trail,** which provides spectacular views into the canyon. The views are especially gorgeous about an hour before sunset.

EXPLORING BRYCE CANYON BY CAR

The park's **18-mile scenic drive** (one-way) follows the rim of Bryce Canyon, offering easy access to a variety of views into the fanciful fairyland of stone sculptures below. Trailers are not permitted on the road, but can be left at several parking lots. All the over-looks are on your left as you begin your drive, so it's best to drive all the way to the end of the road and stop at the overlooks on your return trip. Allow 1 to 2 hours.

From the visitor center, drive 18 miles to **Yovimpa and Rainbow Point overlooks,** which offer expansive views of southern Utah,

---

Top Picnic Spot

On a hot summer day, the best spot in the park for a picnic lunch is **Rainbow Point,** which has picnic tables and restrooms. It's also among the coolest areas because, at 9,115 feet of elevation, it's the highest point in the park.

Arizona, and often even New Mexico. From these pink cliffs, you can look down on a colorful platoon of stone soldiers, standing at eternal attention. A short loop trail from Rainbow Point leads to an **1,800-year-old bristlecone pine,** believed to be the oldest living thing at Bryce Canyon.

From here, drive back north to **Ponderosa Canyon Overlook,** where you can gaze down from a dense forest of spruce and fir at multicolored hoodoos, before continuing to **Agua Canyon Overlook,** which has views of some of the best color contrasts in the park. Looking at the hoodoos is like gazing at clouds—you start to see fantasy characters and buildings. Straight down from Agua, you'll see a hoodoo known as the **Hunter,** wearing a hat of green trees.

Continue to **Natural Bridge,** an arch carved by rain and wind and spanning 85 feet, go on to **Farview Point** for a panoramic view to the distant horizon and the Kaibab Plateau at the Grand Canyon's north rim. Passing through **Swamp Canyon,** turn right off the main road to three viewpoints, the first of which is **Paria View,** with views to the south of the sandstone White Cliffs, carved by the Paria River. To the north of Paria View is **Bryce Point,** a splendid stop for seeing the awesome **Bryce Amphitheater,** the largest natural amphitheater in the park, as well as distant views of the Black Mountains to the northeast and the Navajo Mountain to the south. From here, it's just a short drive to **Inspiration Point,** offering views similar to those at Bryce Point plus the best vantage point for seeing the sleeping "city" cast in stone.

The Best Time to Make the Scenic Drive

The scenic drive is practically deserted in early mornings—any time before 9am. This is the best time to see deer, and the light on the hoodoos is at its richest during this time.

Return to the main road and head north to **Sunset Point,** where you can see practically all of Bryce Amphitheater, including the aptly named **Thor's Hammer** and the 200-foot-tall cliffs of **Wall Street.**

Continue north to a turnoff for your final stop at **Sunrise Point,** which has an inspiring view into Bryce Amphitheater. This is the beginning of the **Queen's Garden Trail ★★★**, one of the best hikes in Utah (p. 245).

11 | OUTDOOR PURSUITS

In addition to the activities in Bryce Canyon National Park, the adjacent national forest has its own share of outdoor activities. For information, stop at the Dixie National Forest's **Red Canyon Visitor Center** (✆ **435/676-2676**), along Utah 12, about 11 miles west of the Bryce Canyon National Park entrance road. It's usually open daily from early May to early October, and offers various interpretative programs on many Saturdays. Or contact the **Dixie National Forest Information Center,** 345 E. Riverside Dr., St. George (www.fs.fed.us/dxnf; ✆ **435/688-3246**).

BIKING & MOUNTAIN BIKING   The park's established scenic drive is open to cyclists, but bikes are prohibited on all trails and forbidden from traveling cross-country within the national park boundaries.

Fortunately, you won't have to go far to find a trail. **Dave's Hollow Trail** ★ starts at the Bryce Canyon National Park boundary sign on Utah 63 (the park entrance road), about a mile south of Ruby's Inn. The double-track trail goes west for about a half-mile before connecting with Forest Road 090, where you turn south and ride for about ¾ of a mile before turning right onto an easy ride through Dave's Hollow to the Dave's Hollow Forest Service Station on Forest Road 087. From here, you can retrace your route for an 8-mile round-trip ride; for a 12-mile trip, turn right on Forest Road 087 to Utah 12 and then right again back to Utah 63 and the starting point. A third option is to turn left on Forest Road 087 and follow it to Tropic Reservoir (see "Fishing," below). This part of the journey does not form a loop, so you would turn around once you've reached the reservoir.

FISHING   The closest fishing hole to the park is **Tropic Reservoir,** a large lake in a ponderosa pine forest. From the intersection of Utah 63 (the park entrance road) and Utah 12, drive west about 3 miles to a gravel road, then about 7 miles south. Facilities include a forest service campground open in summer, a boat ramp, and fishing for rainbow, brook, and cutthroat trout. Locals say the fishing can be better in streams above the lake than in the reservoir itself. For more information, contact the Dixie National Forest (see above).

HIKING   One of Bryce Canyon's greatest assets is that you don't have to be an advanced backpacker to really get to know the park. However, all trails below the rim have at least some steep grades, so wear hiking boots with a traction tread and good ankle support to avoid ankle injuries. During the hot summer months, go hiking either early or late in the day, carry plenty of water, and keep in mind that the deeper you go into the canyon, the hotter it gets.

The **Rim Trail,** which does not drop into the canyon but offers splendid views from above, meanders along the rim for more than 5 miles. Overlooking Bryce Amphitheater, the trail offers excellent views along much of its length. An easy to moderate walk, it includes a half-mile section between two overlooks—Sunrise and Sunset—that is suitable for wheelchairs. This trail is a good choice for an after-dinner stroll, when you can watch the changing evening light on the rosy rocks below.

Your best bet for getting down into the canyon and seeing the most with the least amount of sweat is to combine two popular trails—**Navajo Loop** and **Queen's Garden** ★★★. The total distance is just under 3 miles, with a 521-foot elevation change, and it takes most hikers from 2 to 3 hours to complete the trek. It's best to start at the Navajo Loop Trail head at Sunset Point and leave the canyon on the less-steep Queen's Garden Trail, returning to the rim at Sunrise Point, a half-mile to the north. The Navajo Loop Trail section is considered fairly strenuous; Queen's Garden Trail is rated moderate. Along the Navajo Loop Trail section, you'll pass Thor's Hammer—wondering why it hasn't fallen—and then ponder the towering skyscrapers of Wall Street. Turning onto the Queen's Garden Trail, you'll see some of the park's most fanciful formations—including majestic Queen Victoria herself, for whom the trail was named—plus the Queen's Castle and Gulliver's Castle.

Those up for a challenge might consider the **Hat Shop Trail,** a strenuous 4-mile round-trip with a 1,336-foot elevation change. Leaving from the Bryce Point Overlook, the trail drops quickly to the Hat Shop, so-named for the hard gray "hats" perched on narrow reddish-brown pedestals. Allow 4 hours.

For die-hard hikers who don't mind rough terrain, Bryce has two backcountry trails, usually open in summer only. The **Under-the-Rim Trail** runs for some 23 miles, providing an excellent opportunity to see the park's spectacular scenery on its own terms. **Riggs Spring Loop Trail,** 8½ miles long, offers splendid views of the pink cliffs in the southern part of the park. The truly ambitious can combine the two trails for a weeklong excursion. Permits, available at the visitor center, are required for all overnight trips into the backcountry. They cost $5 for 1 or 2 people, $10 for 3 to 6 people, and $15 for 7 to 15 people (group sites only).

HORSEBACK RIDING Some of the early Utah pioneers were lucky enough to arrive on horseback. **Canyon Trail Rides** (www.canyonrides.com; © **435/679-8665**) offers a close-up view of Bryce's spectacular rock formations from the relative comfort of a saddle. The company has a desk inside Bryce Lodge. A 2-hour ride to the canyon floor and back costs $65 per person, and a half-day trip farther into the canyon costs $9 per person. Rides are offered April through October. Riders must be at least 7 years old for the

---

The Biggest Bird of All

The rarest flying bird in North America, and one of the largest anywhere, by 1987 the **California condor's** population had dwindled to just 22 birds. An aggressive breeding program brought the huge raptors (they have a 10-foot wingspan) back from the edge of extinction and today there are nearly 500 in existence. One of the few spots you might see them is in Bryce Canyon. Ask a park ranger for the likeliest places and times.

Spotting Peregrine Falcons

For a good chance to see peregrine falcons, go to **Paria View** and sit quietly away from the crowds; look out over the amphitheater, where these beautiful birds can often be spotted.

2-hour trip, at least 10 for the half-day ride, and weigh no more than 220 pounds.

Guided horseback rides in Red Canyon are offered by several companies, including **Ruby's Inn Horse Rides** (www.horserides.net; ✆ **435/834-5341**), at Ruby's Inn (p. 248). Rates range from $65 to $135 for a full day, including lunch. Ruby's will also board your horse (call for rates).

WILDLIFE-WATCHING   The park is home to a variety of wildlife, ranging from mule deer to mountain short-horned lizards, which visitors often spot while hiking down into the canyon. Occasionally you might catch a glimpse of a mountain lion, most likely on the prowl in search of a mule-deer dinner; elk and pronghorn may also be seen at higher elevations.

The Utah prairie dog, listed as a threatened species, is actually a rodent. It inhabits park meadows, but should be avoided, as its fleas may carry disease (see "Safety," earlier in this chapter).

There are 175 species of birds in the park; you're bound to hear the triumphant call of the "camp robber" Steller's jay. Watch for swifts and swallows as they perform their exotic acrobatics along cliff faces; binoculars will come in handy.

If you see or hear one, give the Great Basin rattlesnake a wide berth. Sometimes more than 5 feet long, this rattler is the park's only poisonous reptile. However, like most rattlesnakes, it is just as anxious as you are to avoid confrontation.

WINTER FUN

Bryce is beautiful in the winter, when the white snow creates a perfect frosting on the red, pink, orange, and brown stone columns standing strong against the cold winds. Cross-country skiers will find several marked, ungroomed trails (all above the rim), including the **Fairyland Loop Trail ★★**, which leads 1 mile through a pine and juniper forest to the Fairyland Point Overlook. From here, take the 1-mile **Forest Trail** back to the road, or continue north along the rim for another 1¼ miles to the park border.

Snowshoeing is allowed anywhere in the park except on cross-country-ski tracks. There are also connections to ski trails in the adjacent national forest.

Stop at the visitor center for additional trail information, and go to **Best Western Plus Ruby's Inn**

Winter Safety

Although the entire park is open to cross-country skiers, rangers warn that it's extremely dangerous to try to ski on the steep trails leading down into the canyon.

(p. 249), just north of the park entrance (www.rubysinn.com; © **435/834-5341**), for information on cross-country ski trails, snowshoeing, and snowmobiling opportunities outside the park. Ruby's grooms more than 30 miles of ski trails and also rents snowshoes and cross-country ski equipment.

CAMPING

In the Park

Typical of the West's national park campgrounds, the two campgrounds at Bryce offer plenty of trees for a genuine "forest camping" experience, easy access to trails, and limited facilities. **North Campground ★** has 101 sites; **Sunset Campground** has 102 sites. One section in North Campground is open year-round; Sunset Campground is open late spring through early fall only. North Campground is best because it's closer to the Rim Trail—making it easier to rush over to catch those amazing sunrise and sunset colors—but any site in either campground is fine. Neither has RV hookups or showers, but both have modern restrooms with running water. Reservations are available from early May through late September for North Campground and for 20 tent-only sites in Sunset Campground (www.recreation.gov; © **877/444-6777**) for an additional booking fee of $10, regardless of the number of days. If you don't have reservations, get to the campground early to claim a site (usually by 2pm in summer). Cost is $20 per night (tents) and $30 (RVs) at either campground.

Showers ($2), a coin-operated laundry, a snack bar, bundles of firewood, food and camping supplies, and souvenirs are located at the **General Store** (for information, contact the Lodge at Bryce Canyon [p. 251]; © **435/834-5361**), which is usually open daily from mid-April through October. The store is a healthy walk from either campground. The park service operates an RV dump station ($5 fee) in the summer.

Nearby

In addition to the campgrounds listed below, there is camping at Kodachrome Basin State Park (p. 253)

King Creek Campground Located above Tropic Reservoir, this forest service campground, at 7,900 feet elevation, has graded gravel roads and sites nestled among tall ponderosa pines. Facilities include flush toilets, drinking water, and an RV dump station ($5 fee), but no showers or RV hookups. The reservoir has a boat ramp (see "Fishing," above). To get to the campground from the Bryce Canyon National Park entrance, go north 3 miles on Utah 63 to Utah 12, turn west (left), and go 2½ miles to the King's Creek Campground Road; turn south (left) and follow signs to Tropic Reservoir for about 7 miles to the campground. Note: This is a favorite place for ATV enthusiasts; although the vehicles are only allowed to enter and exit the campground, be aware that this very noisy sport will be nearby.

Dixie National Forest Information Center, 345 E. Riverside Dr., St. George. www.fs.fed.
us/dxnf. © **435/688-3246.** 37 sites. No credit cards. Closed Oct to mid-May.

Ruby's Inn RV Park & Campground Ruby's is the closest campground to Bryce Canyon National Park that offers complete RV hookups, and it's also on the park's shuttle-bus route. Many sites are shaded, there's an attractive tent area, and just adjacent to the campground are a lake and horse pasture. Facilities include a swimming pool, coin-op laundry, barbecue grills, and a store with groceries and RV supplies. Also on the grounds are several camping cabins ($56 double) and tepees ($40.95 sleeps 8), which share the campground's bathhouse and other facilities.

300 S. Main St., Bryce Canyon City. www.brycecanyoncampgrounds.com. © **435/834-5301** (Nov–Mar © 435/834-5341). 150 sites. Full hookups $45; electric/water only $42; tent space $32. Closed Oct–Apr.

WHERE TO STAY

Room taxes add about 11% to the cost. Pets are not accepted unless otherwise noted.

In the Park

The Lodge at Bryce Canyon ★★★ This sandstone and ponderosa pine lodge, which opened in 1924, is located extremely close to the Rim and the Rim Trail. The luxurious lodge suites are furnished with charming white wicker furniture, ceiling fans, and separate sitting rooms. Ask for a sunrise or sunset view motel unit, simply pleasant modern motel rooms, with two queen-size beds and either a balcony or a patio for a priceless view. The best choice is one of the historic cabins, restored to their 1920s appearance. They're a bit small, but have two double beds, high ceilings, stone (gas-burning) fireplaces, and log beams. The gift shop has one of the best selections of American Indian jewelry in the area. All units are nonsmoking.

Bryce Canyon National Park, Bryce. www.brycecanyonforever.com. © **435/834-8700.** 114 units, 110 in motel rooms and cabins, 3 suites and 1 studio in lodge. $223 double, double; $231 cabin. Closed Mid-Nov through Mar. **Amenities:** Restaurant (see review, p. 251).

Nearby

Best Western Plus Bryce Canyon Grand Hotel ★★ "Western luxury" sums up the atmosphere at this upscale hotel, just a stone's throw from the entrance to Bryce Canyon National Park. The rooms are well furnished and comfortable, with either one king or two queen beds. The hotel caters to those who want to take care of business while on vacation, with large working desks plus everything else you might want to keep in touch with the office. The spacious deluxe suites, at 770 square feet each, have a king bed, a hide-a-bed couch, and a jetted tub. The hotel is under the same management as the nearby Best Western Plus Ruby's Inn (below). All units are nonsmoking.

31 N. 100 E. (at the entrance to Bryce Canyon), Bryce Canyon City. www.brycecanyon grand.com. ✆ **866/866-6634** or 435/834-5700. 162 units. Summer $196 double, $200–$290 suite; rest of year $75 double, $140–$199 suite. Rates include full breakfast. **Amenities:** Restaurant; fitness center; Jacuzzi; heated outdoor pool (May–Oct only); free Wi-Fi.

Best Western Plus Ruby's Inn ★★

Ruby's is a huge facility, almost a village in itself. The size may be off-putting for some but it is close to the park and you can arrange excursions of all sorts in the lobby, from horseback and all-terrain-vehicle rides to helicopter flights. Spread among nine buildings, the modern motel rooms contain wood furnishings and art that depicts scenes of the area. Deluxe units, located in the main building, have either jetted tubs or two-person jetted spas. Rooms at the back of the complex are a bit quieter. There is also a campground on the property. (See "Camping," above.) All units are nonsmoking.

26 S. Main St. (at the entrance to Bryce Canyon), Bryce Canyon City. www.rubysinn. com. ✆ **866/866-6616** or 435/834-5341. 370 units. June–Sept from $120–$$169 double, $195 suite; Oct–May $70–$140 double, $145 suite. Rates change, so check the website. Pets accepted ($20 per night fee). **Amenities:** 2 restaurants (Canyon Diner and Cowboy's Buffet and Steak Room; see reviews, p. 251 and 252); concierge; 1 indoor and 1 outdoor Jacuzzi; indoor heated pool; free Wi-Fi.

Bryce Canyon Pines

A modern motel with a Western flair, the Bryce Canyon Pines offers well-maintained rooms with wood furnishings and two queen-size beds in most rooms. Some units have fireplaces, some have kitchenettes, and one has its own whirlpool tub. A family suite contains one king-size bed plus two queen-size beds, each in a separate room. There are also some rustic cottages. All units are nonsmoking.

Milepost 10, Utah 12 (3 miles west of intersection with park entry road), Bryce. www. brycecanyonmotel.com. ✆ **800/892-7923** or 435/834-5441. 53 units. Prices range from $150–$171 for a standard room, but may fluctuate with the seasons. **Amenities:** Restaurant; Jacuzzi; covered heated pool (Apr–Oct only); free Wi-Fi.

Bryce Country Cabins ★

There's something special about staying in a genuine log cabin during a national park vacation, but there's also something very appealing about hot showers and warm beds. Bryce Country Cabins offers the best of both worlds, with modern log cabins and a historic pioneer cabin. The grounds are nicely landscaped, with good views, although we wish the units were farther from the highway.

The modern cabins have knotty pine walls and ceilings, exposed beams, and ceiling fans. Each has one or two queen-size beds, a table and chairs, and a porch. Bathrooms have shower/tub combos or showers only. The 1905 pioneer cabin has two spacious rooms with country-style decor. Each has two queen-size beds and a full bathroom, and the rooms can be rented together or individually. There are outdoor barbecues, a fire pit for evening gatherings, and a children's play-fort. All cabins are nonsmoking.

320 N. Utah 12, Tropic. www.brycecountrycabins.com. ℂ **435/679-8643**. 13 units. Summer $160–$189 double; villa with a king or two queens and a twin $326. Lower rates off-season **Amenities:** Free Wi-Fi.

Bryce Valley Inn ★ A member of the America's Best Value Inn & Suites franchise, the Bryce Valley Inn offers simply decorated, basic motel rooms that are a clean, well-maintained, and relatively economical choice for park visitors. Units are furnished with either one king-size bed, one or two queen-size beds, or two double beds. There are also suites with either one queen or one king bed, plus a refrigerator and microwave. All units are nonsmoking. A gift shop on the premises offers a large selection of American Indian arts and crafts, handmade gifts, rocks, and fossils.

199 N. Main St., Tropic. www.brycevalleyinn.com. ℂ **800/442-1890** or 435/679-8811. 65 units. Late spring to early fall $85–$115 double and suite; rates from $50 double the rest of the year. 8 miles east of the park entrance road. Pets accepted ($20 fee). **Amenities:** Restaurant; free Wi-Fi.

Bryce View Lodge ★★ This basic modern American motel offers the best combination of economy and location. It consists of four two-story buildings, set back from the road and grouped around a large parking lot and attractively landscaped area. The simply decorated average-size rooms are comfortable and quiet, with two queen-size beds and artwork depicting the rock formations you'll see in the park, located just down the road. Guests have access to the amenities at Ruby's Inn, across the street. All units are nonsmoking.

105 E. Center St., Bryce Canyon City. www.bryceviewlodge.com. ℂ **888/279-2304** or 435/834-5180. 160 units. Summer double $110 and up, rest of year double $100 and up. Pets accepted ($20 per night fee). **Amenities:** See Best Western Plus Ruby's Inn, p. 249.

Stone Canyon Inn ★★★ This charming inn is the best place to stay outside the park for those who seek upscale accommodations and fantastic views. Each room is unique, with queen- or king-size beds, colorful quilts, handsome wood furnishings, and a classic Western look; most have private hot tubs. In addition to rooms, including a new-in-2018 king room with soaker tub and fridge and one room partly crafted for travelers with disabilities, choose a 2-bedroom, 2-bath cottage that sleeps six, and assortment of guest houses, and a "tree" house. The Stone Hearth Grill serves upscale American food (and plenty of beef); dinner entrees range from $26 to $38. The inn sits well off the main road, on the boundary of the Bryce Canyon National Park, and large windows afford views either into the park or nearby Grand Staircase–Escalante National Monument. Smoking is not permitted.

1220 W. 50 S., Tropic. www.stonecanyoninn.com. ℂ **435/679-8611**. Rates from $235 bungalow to $365 for 2-bedroom cottage; reduced rates in the off-season. Rates include full breakfast. **Amenities:** Restaurant; sauna; free Wi-Fi. From Utah 12 in Tropic, take Bryce Way Rd. west 1 mile to Fairyland Lane, and follow the sign to the inn. Children 4 and under not allowed in the inn; no age restrictions for cottages.

WHERE TO EAT

In addition to the restaurants discussed below, **Ebenezer's Barn & Grill** (https://ebenezersbarnandgrill.com; ℂ **435/834-5341,** ext. 7099) part of the Best Western Plus Ruby's Inn complex, at 26 South Main St., in Bryce Canyon City, offers a Western dinner and slightly hokey show nightly at 8pm during the summer. Diners choose from a set menu then mingle at large tables to eat and enjoy the show, which is a combination of Western-style music and humor. Dinner options include rib-eye steak, baked salmon, baked chicken, and barbecue, with prices from $26 to $32; all meals include beans, potatoes, corn bread, dessert, and a nonalcoholic beverage. Tickets are available at Ruby's Inn.

In the Park

The Lodge at Bryce Canyon ★★ AMERICAN   They call it "parki-techture"—that stone-and-wood design of many national park lodges that evokes a certain era. Here, two handsome stone fireplaces and large windows look out on the park, which is reason enough to dine at the lodge. But the food's good, too, and reasonably priced. Breakfasts offer typical American standards and a good buffet. At lunch, you'll find sandwiches, burgers, salads, and a taco bar. The menu changes periodically, but may include dinner special-ties such as pan-seared Alaskan sockeye salmon topped with sun-dried tomato pesto, and perhaps a rack of lamb. Steaks are also offered, including a bison tenderloin, and other dishes frequently available include chicken with lime and chili. There are also vegetarian items, and the restaurant serves wine and beer.

Bryce Canyon National Park. www.brycecanyonforever.com. ℂ **435/834-8700.** Break-fast a la carte or buffet ($15 adult, $8 12 and under); Lunch entrees $10–$16 or buffet ($16 adult, $8 12 and under). Dinner entrees $18–$35. Daily 7–10am, 11:30am–3pm, and 5–10pm. Closed Mid-Nov through Mar.

Nearby

If you want a break from meat and potatoes, try **The Pizza Place** (http://bryce canyonpizza.com; ℂ **435/679-8888**), open year-round at Bryce Canyon Inn in Tropic, or **Valhalla Pizza** (ℂ **435/834-8709**) and **RoadRunner Pizza** (http://www.roadrunnerpizzafresh.com; ℂ **707/812-2403**), open seasonally in Bryce Canyon City.

Canyon Diner ★ AMERICAN   Part of the Best Western Plus Ruby's Inn complex, this self-serve restaurant offers typical fast-food fare, relatively quick and close to the park. Breakfasts, served until 11am, include bagels and several egg croissants sandwiches; for lunch and dinner, you can get hoagies, burgers, hot dogs, nachos, pretty good stuffed potatoes, pizza, broiled chicken sandwiches, and salads. Specialties include a fish and chips basket. No alcohol is served.

At the Best Western Plus Ruby's Inn, 1000 S. Utah 63, Bryce Canyon City. www.rubysinn. com. ℂ **435/834-8030.** Reservations not accepted. Individual items $4–$7; meals $6–$11. Daily 6:30am–9:30pm. Closed Nov–Mar.

Cowboy's Buffet and Steak Room ★ STEAK/SEAFOOD   The busiest restaurant in the Bryce Canyon area, this main restaurant at the Best Western Plus Ruby's Inn moves 'em through with buffets at every meal, plus a well-rounded a la carte menu and friendly service. The breakfast buffet offers all that you'd expect; the lunch buffet offers country-style ribs, fresh fruit, salads, soups, vegetables, and breads; and the dinner buffet features charbroiled thin-sliced rib-eye steak and other meats, pastas, potatoes, and salads. Regular menu dinner entrees include prime rib, grilled rainbow trout, grilled turkey breast, southern-style catfish, and salads. In addition to the large, Western-style dining room, an outdoor patio is open in good weather. Full liquor service is available.

At the Best Western Plus Ruby's Inn, 26 S. Main St., Bryce Canyon City. www.rubysinn. com. (℃ **435/834-5341.** Reservations not accepted. Breakfast and lunch $3.50–$15, dinner main courses and buffets $12–$30. Summer daily 6:30am–10pm; winter daily 6:30am–9pm.

WHAT TO SEE & DO JUST OUTSIDE BRYCE CANYON

The **Best Western Plus Ruby's Inn** (see "Where to Stay," earlier in this chapter), in Bryce, is practically a one-stop entertainment center for those looking for a bit of kitschy variety in their national park vacation.

Directly across Utah 63 from the inn are **Old Bryce Town Shops** (www. rubysinn.com/old-bryce-town-shops), open daily 8am to 10pm from May through September, where you'll find a rock shop and a variety of other stores offering an opportunity to buy that genuine cowboy hat you've been wanting. There's a trail here especially for kids, where they can search for arrowheads, fossils, and petrified wood; or perhaps they would prefer checking out the jail.

Nearby, **Bryce Canyon Country Rodeo** (℃ **866/782-0002**) showcases bucking broncos, bull riding, calf roping, and all sorts of rodeo fun in a 1-hour program, from Memorial Day weekend through late August, Wednesday through Saturday evenings at 7pm. Admission is $13 for adults, $9 for children 3 to 12, and free for children 2 and under. Adventurous visitors can also ride—bulls for adults and steers and sheep for kids. Call for details.

Red Canyon

About 9 miles west of Bryce Canyon National Park, in the Dixie National Forest, is Red Canyon, named for its vermilion-colored rock formations, which are accented by stands of rich green ponderosa pine. The canyon is a favorite of hikers and mountain bikers in summer and cross-country skiers and snowshoers in winter.

Red Canyon has about a dozen trails; some trails are open to hikers only, others to mountain bikers, horseback riders, and those with all-terrain vehicles. One especially scenic multiuse trail is the 5.5-mile (one-way) **Casto Canyon Trail,** which runs along the bottom of Casto Canyon. It connects with the 8.9-mile (one-way) **Cassidy Trail** (legend has it that outlaw Butch Cassidy used this trail) and 2.9-mile (one-way) **Losee Canyon Trail** to produce a loop of about 17 miles ideal for a multiday backpacking trip. Watch for elk in winter, and pronghorns and raptors year-round. The Casto Canyon and Losee Canyon trails are considered moderate; Cassidy Trail ranges from easy to strenuous.

For maps, directions to trailheads, current trail conditions, and additional information, stop at the **Red Canyon Visitor Center** (✆ **435/676-2676**), along Utah 12, about 11 miles west of the Bryce Canyon National Park entrance road. It's usually open daily from early May to early October, and offers various interpretive programs on many Saturdays. Information can also be obtained from the **Dixie National Forest Information Center,** 345 E. Riverside Dr. in St. George (www.fs.fed.us/dxnf; ✆ **435/688-3246**).

KODACHROME BASIN: A PICTURE-PERFECT STATE PARK

Located about 22 miles from the entrance to Bryce Canyon National Park, Kodachrome Basin lives up to its name—its wonderful scenery practically cries out to be photographed. Named for the classic Kodak color slide film by the National Geographic Society after an expedition there in 1948, the park is chock-full of tall stone chimneys and pink-and-white sandstone cliffs, all set among the contrasting greens of sagebrush and piñon and juniper trees. It also abuts and makes a good base for exploring Grand Staircase–Escalante National Monument, which is discussed below.

Because temperatures get a bit warm here in summer—the park is at 5,800 feet elevation—the best times to visit, especially for hikers, are May, September, and October, when there are also fewer people.

Essentials

GETTING THERE   From Bryce Canyon National Park, go 3 miles north to the junction of Utah 63 and Utah 12, go east (right) on Utah 12 for about 12 miles to Cannonville, turn south onto the park's access road (there's a sign), and go about 7 miles to the park entrance.

INFORMATION, FEES & REGULATIONS   Contact the **park office** (www.stateparks.utah.gov; ✆ **435/679-8562**), for information. Day use costs $8 per vehicle. Dogs are permitted in the park and on trails, but must be kept on leashes no more than 6 feet long. The park office at the pay station at the entrance to the park can give you information.

Outdoor Pursuits

HIKING   Kodachrome Basin offers several hiking possibilities. Starting just south of the campground, the **Panorama Trail** is only moderately difficult, with no steep climbs. At first, it follows an old, relatively flat wagon route, and then climbs to offer views of the park's rock formations before reaching the well-named Panorama Point. Along the way are several possible side trips, including a short walk to the **Hat Shop,** so named because the formations resemble broad-brimmed hats, and **White Buffalo Loop,** where you can try to find a formation that looks like—you guessed it—a white buffalo. The optional **Big Bear Geyser Trail** is a bit more difficult, winding past Big Bear and Mama Bear before returning to Panorama Trail. Allow 2 to 3 hours for the Panorama Trail and an extra hour for Big Bear Geyser Trail.

Fans of arches will want to drive the dirt road to the trailhead for the .5-mile round-trip hike to **Shakespeare Arch.** This trail also provides views of a large chimney-rock formation.

HORSEBACK RIDING   To see Kodachrome Basin from the back of a horse, contact **Red Canyon Trail Rides** (www.redcanyontrailrides.com; ✆ **800/892-7923**). A 1-hour ride costs $40; 2 hours costs $60.

WILDLIFE-WATCHING   Jackrabbits and chukar partridges are probably the most commonly seen wildlife in the park, although you are likely to hear the piñon jay and might see an occasional coyote or rattlesnake.

Where to Stay

Camping   The park's attractive 27-site campground is set among stone chimneys and scattered piñon and juniper trees. It has flush toilets, showers, drinking water, picnic tables, barbecue grills, and an RV dump station. Four sites have full RV hookups. Basic campsites cost $20 to $40 per night, and sites with hookups cost $28 to $40 per night. Call ✆ **800/322-3770** or 801/322-3770, or visit www.reserveamerica.com for reservations ($8 reservation fee).

Lodging & Supplies   Located in the park along the park road (you can't miss it), **Kodachrome General Store** (www.redstonecabins.com; ✆ **435/679-8536**) sells camping supplies, food items, and the like. This is also headquarters for **Redstone Cabins,** where there are six modern cabins for rent. Four have two double beds and two have one king, and all six have bathrooms with showers, refrigerators, microwaves, air-conditioning, private porches with tables and chairs, and outside charcoal barbecue grills. Cost per cabin per night for up to four people is $145 from mid-April to mid-October; rates are cut in half the rest of the year.

GRAND STAIRCASE–ESCALANTE NATIONAL MONUMENT & THE HIGHWAY 12 SCENIC DRIVE

Grand Staircase-Escalante and **Bears Ears National Monument** have become ground zero for the philosophical war over Western wilderness. The vast area of Grand Staircase was set aside by President Clinton in 1996 and many Utahns have been angry about it ever since. President Trump decreased the size of the monument by 50% in 2017, angering those who want to preserve the tone of the continental United States' few remaining wildernesses for future generations. If you're driving between Bryce Canyon and Capitol Reef national parks allow at least 4 hours for the trip, but it's best to allow time to dawdle. Stop in the small community of **Escalante** (see "Basing Yourself in Escalante," later in this chapter), visit its fine state park, and detour through the spectacularly isolated wild area.

Grand Staircase–Escalante National Monument

Known for its stark, rugged beauty, this vast land contains a unique combination of geological, biological, paleontological, archaeological, and historical resources. Originally 1.9 million acres of red-orange canyons, mesas, plateaus, and river valleys, President Trump reduced the size of the monument by a third and, at the time of writing, extraction industries were lining up for permits. Under the jurisdiction of the Bureau of Land Management, the monument is open for grazing and possible oil and gas drilling under existing leases as well as for hunting, fishing, hiking, camping, and other forms of recreation.

Unlike most other national monuments, almost all of this vast area is undeveloped—there are few all-weather roads, only one maintained hiking trail, and two developed campgrounds. But the adventurous will find miles upon miles of dirt roads and practically unlimited opportunities for camping, and hiking, horseback riding, and mountain biking on existing dirt roads.

The national monument can be divided into three distinct sections: the **Grand Staircase** of sandstone cliffs, which includes five life zones from Sonoran Desert to coniferous forests, in the southwest; the **Kaiparowits Plateau,** a vast, wild region of rugged mesas and steep canyons in the center; and the **Escalante River Canyons** section, along the northern edge of the monument, a scenic area containing miles of interconnecting river canyons.

ESSENTIALS

GETTING THERE   The national monument occupies a large section of southern Utah—covering an area almost as big as the states of Delaware and Rhode Island combined—with Bryce Canyon National Park to the west, Capitol Reef National Park on the northeast edge, and Glen Canyon National Recreation Area along the east and part of the south sides.

Access is via Utah 12, one of the most beautiful drives in Utah, along the monument's northern boundary, from Kodachrome Basin State Park and the communities of Escalante and Boulder, and via U.S. 89 to the southwestern section of the monument, east of the town of Kanab, which is about 80 miles south of Bryce Canyon.

INFORMATION/VISITOR CENTERS   The national monument remains a very rugged area, with limited facilities, poor roads, and changeable weather. Before setting out, all visitors are strongly urged to contact one of the monument's visitor centers to get maps and other information, and especially to check on current road and weather conditions. Also see the monument's website, **www.ut.blm.gov/monument**.

Visitor centers include the **Escalante Interagency Visitor Center,** on the west side of Escalante, at 755 W. Main St. (Utah 12), Escalante (© **435/826-5499**), which is open daily from mid-March through September from 7:30am to 5:30pm; from October through Thanksgiving daily from 8am to 4:30pm; and from late November to March Monday through Friday from 8am to 4:30pm. You can also get information at the Bureau of Land Management's

Kanab Visitor Center, 745 E. U.S. 89, Kanab (© **435/644-4680**); it's open from 8am to 4:30pm, daily in summer, and Monday through Friday in winter.

The **Cannonville Visitor Center** is open daily from 8am to 4:30pm, mid-March through mid-November only, at 10 Center St., in Cannonville (© **435/826-5640**), east of Bryce Canyon National Park. The **Big Water Visitor Center** is along U.S. 89, near the southern edge of Glen Canyon National Recreation Area, at 100 Upper Revolution Way, in Big Water (© **435/675-3200**). It is open Thursday to Monday from 8:30am to 4:30pm.

Tip: Each of the visitor centers in Grand Staircase-Escalante is designed around a different aspect of the park—human history, pre-history, geologic history, etc.—the architect echoed the theme in each building and exhibits reflect the focus.

> ### Impressions
>
> On this remarkable site, God's handiwork is everywhere.
> —Former President Bill Clinton

FEES, REGULATIONS & SAFETY There is no charge to enter the monument; those planning overnight trips into the backcountry should obtain free permits at any of the offices listed above. Regulations are similar to those on other public lands; damaging or disturbing archaeological and historic sites in any way is forbidden.

Water is the main safety concern here, whether there's too little or too much. This is generally very dry country, so those going into the monument should carry plenty of drinking water. However, thunderstorms can turn the monument's dirt roads into impassable mud bogs in minutes, stranding motorists, and potentially fatal flash floods through narrow canyons can catch hikers by surprise. Anyone planning trips into the monument should always check first with one of the offices listed above for current and anticipated weather and travel conditions.

OUTDOOR PURSUITS

This rugged national monument offers numerous opportunities for outdoor adventures, including **canyoneering** through narrow slot canyons with the aid of ropes. You can get information on the best areas for canyoneering at the monument's visitor centers, but this is definitely not the place for beginners. To put it bluntly, people die here, and you don't want to be one of them.

Unless you are an expert at this specialized sport, go with an expert. One of the best is Rick Green, owner of **Excursions of Escalante ★★**, 125 E. Main St., Escalante (www.excursionsofescalante.com; © **435/826-4714**). Trips, which are available mid-March through mid-November, usually include four people with one guide, and all equipment is provided. In addition to canyoneering trips, the company offers day hiking and backpacking excursions, specialized tours, and 3-day canyoneering courses ($600). Day trips include lunch. Day hiking trips cost $155 per person, canyoneering costs $175 per person, and a photo safari costs $200 per person. Overnight 4-day, 3-night vehicle trips cost $1,525 per person and includes hot showers and 4-course dinners. Excursions of Escalante also provides a flexible shuttle service; call for a quote.

HIKING, MOUNTAIN BIKING & HORSEBACK RIDING Located about 15 miles northeast of Escalante via Utah 12, the **Calf Creek Recreation Area** has a campground (p. 260), a picnic area with fire grates and tables, trees, drinking water, and flush toilets. The tree-shaded picnic and camping area lies along the creek at the bottom of a high-walled, rather narrow rock canyon. The best part of the recreation area, though, is the moderately strenuous 6-mile round-trip hike to **Lower Calf Creek Falls.** A sandy trail leads along **Calf Creek,** past beaver ponds and wetlands, to a beautiful waterfall that cascades 126 feet down a rock wall into a tree-shaded pool. You can pick up an interpretive brochure at the trailhead. Day use fee is $5 per vehicle.

Although Calf Creek Trail is the monument's only officially marked and maintained trail, numerous unmarked cross-country routes are ideal for hiking, mountain biking (on existing dirt roads only), and horseback riding. Hikers are advised to stop at one of the visitor centers (p. 256) to get recommendations on hiking routes and to purchase topographic maps. Hikers need to remember that this is wild country and can be hazardous. Rangers recommend carrying at least 1 gallon of water per person per day and testing all water from streams before drinking. The potential for flooding is high, and hikers should check with the BLM before attempting to hike through the monument's narrow slot canyons, which offer no escape during flash floods. Other hazards include poisonous snakes and scorpions and, in the wetter areas, poison ivy. Slickrock, as the name suggests, is slippery, so hikers should wear sturdy hiking boots with traction soles.

Among the popular and relatively easy-to-follow hiking routes is the footpath to **Escalante Natural Bridge;** it repeatedly crosses the river, so be prepared to get wet up to your knees. The easy 2-mile (one-way) hike begins at a parking area at the bridge that crosses the Escalante River near Calf Creek Recreation Area, 15 miles northeast of the town of Escalante. From the parking area, hike upstream to Escalante Natural Bridge, on the south side of the river. The bridge is 130 feet high and spans 100 feet.

Also starting at the bridge parking area is a hike downstream to **Phipps Wash.** Mostly moderate, this hike goes about 1.5 miles to the mouth of Phipps Wash, which enters the river from the west. You'll find Maverick Natural Bridge in a north side drainage, and climbing up the drainage on the south side leads to **Phipps Arch.**

Hiking the national monument's **slot canyons** is very popular, but the importance of checking on flood potentials before starting out cannot be stressed enough. A sudden rainstorm miles away can cause a flash flood through one of the monument's narrow canyons, trapping hikers.

One challenging and very strenuous slot-canyon hike is through **Peek-a-boo** and **Spooky canyons,** which are accessible from the Hole-in-the-Rock

Scenic Backway (see "Sightseeing & Four-Wheeling," below). Stop at the Escalante Interagency Office for precise directions.

SIGHTSEEING & FOUR-WHEELING Because this is one of America's least-developed large sections of public land, it offers a wonderful opportunity for exploration by the adventurous. Be aware, though, that the dirt roads inside the monument turn muddy—and impassable—when it rains and that off-highway vehicles (OHVs) have the capacity to damage the landscape you're there to admire.

One particularly popular road is the **Hole-in-the-Rock Scenic Backway,** which is partly in the national monument and partly in the adjacent Glen Canyon National Recreation Area. Like most roads in the monument, this should be attempted in dry weather only. Starting about 5 miles northeast of Escalante off Utah 12, this clearly marked dirt road travels 57 miles (one-way) to the Hole-in-the-Rock. This is where Mormon settlers, in 1880, cut a passage through solid rock to get their wagons down a 1,200-foot cliff to the canyon floor and Colorado River below.

About 12 miles in, the road passes by the sign to **Devil's Rock Garden,** which has classic red-rock formations and arches and a picnic area (about a mile off the main road). The road continues across a plateau of typical desert terrain, ending at a spectacular scenic overlook of Lake Powell. The first 35 miles of the scenic byway are relatively easy (in dry weather); it then gets a bit steeper and sandier, and the last 6 miles of the road require a high-clearance 4×4 vehicle. Allow about 6 hours round-trip, and make sure you have plenty of fuel and water.

Another recommended drive in the national monument is the **Cottonwood Canyon Road,** which runs from Kodachrome Basin State Park south to U.S. 89, along the monument's southern edge, a distance of about 46 miles. The road is sandy and narrow and washboard in places, but it's usually passable for passenger cars in dry weather. It mostly follows Cottonwood Wash, with good views of red-rock formations and distant panoramas from hilltops. About 10 miles east of Kodachrome Basin State Park is a short side road to **Grosvenor Arch.** This magnificent stone arch, with an opening 99 feet wide, was named for the National Geographic Society founder and editor, Gilbert H. Grosvenor, and is well worth the trip.

WILDLIFE VIEWING & BIRDING The isolated and rugged terrain here makes a good habitat for a number of species, including desert bighorn sheep and mountain lions. More than 200 species of birds have been seen, including bald eagles, golden eagles, Swainson's hawks, and peregrine falcons. The best areas for seeing wildlife are along the Escalante and Paria rivers and Johnson Creek. Pack binoculars.

CAMPING

Backcountry camping is permitted in most areas of the monument with a free permit, available at the Interagency Office in Escalante and BLM office in Kanab (p. 262). Sites are first-come, first-served.

The monument also has two designated campgrounds. **Calf Creek Campground,** in the Calf Creek Recreation Area about 15 miles northeast of the town of Escalante via Utah 12, has 13 sites and a picnic area. Open year-round, the tree-shaded campground is situated in a steep, scenic canyon along Calf Creek, surrounded by high rock walls. There is an interpretive hiking trail (p. 258), and facilities include flush toilets and drinking water, but no showers, RV hookups, RV dump stations, or trash removal. In summer, the campground is often full by 10am. From November through March, the water is turned off and only vault toilets are available. Vehicles must ford a shallow creek, and the campground is not recommended for vehicles over 25 feet long. Campsites cost $15 per night; day use is $5 per vehicle.

The national monument's other designated campground is **Deer Creek,** located 6 miles east of the town of Boulder along the scenic Burr Trail Road. There are vault toilets, picnic tables, and grills, but no drinking water or other facilities. Camping at the seven primitive sites costs $10, and the campground is open year-round. RVs and cars can fit onto the sites here.

Escalante Petrified Forest State Park

Large chunks of colorful petrified wood decorate this unique park, which offers hiking, fishing, boating, camping, and panoramic vistas of the surrounding countryside. There's wildlife to watch, trails to hike, and a 30-acre reservoir for boating, fishing, and somewhat chilly swimming. It's open all year, but spring through fall is the best time to visit. Hikers should be prepared for hot summer days and carry plenty of water.

ESSENTIALS
GETTING THERE The park is 44 miles from Bryce Canyon. It's located about 2 miles southwest of Escalante on Utah 12 at Wide Hollow Road.

INFORMATION/VISITOR CENTER The visitor center of the **Escalante Petrified Forest State Park** (www.stateparks.utah.gov; ☎ **435/826-4466**) is located at 710 N. Reservoir Rd., Escalante. It's open daily with displays that include petrified wood, dinosaur bones, and fossils, an exhibit explaining how petrified wood is formed, and an entire 50-ft petrified tree, roots to tip.

FEES & REGULATIONS Entry costs $8 per vehicle, which includes boat launching. As at most parks, regulations are generally based on common sense and courtesy: Don't damage anything, drive slowly on park roads, and observe quiet hours between 10pm and 7am. In addition, you're asked to resist the temptation to carry off samples of petrified wood. Pets are welcome, even on trails, but must be on leashes no more than 6 feet long.

OUTDOOR PURSUITS
FISHING & BOATING **Wide Hollow Reservoir,** located partially inside the park, has a boat ramp and is a popular fishing hole for rainbow trout and bluegill, plus ice-fishing in winter. No rentals.

rock or wood—WHAT IS THIS STUFF?

It looks like a weathered, multicolored tree limb, shining and sparkling in the light—but it's heavy, hard, and solid as a rock. Just what is this stuff? It's petrified wood.

Back in the old days—some 135 to 155 million years ago—southern Utah was not at all like you see it today. It was closer to the equator than it is now, which made it a wet and hot land, with lots of ferns, palm trees, and conifers providing lunch for the neighborhood dinosaurs.

Occasionally, floods would uproot the trees, dumping them in flood plains and along sandbars, and then bury them with mud and silt. If this happened quickly, the layers of mud and silt would cut off the oxygen supply, halting the process of decomposition—and effectively preserving the tree trunks intact.

Later, volcanic ash covered the area, and groundwater rich in silicon dioxide and other chemicals and minerals made its way down to the ancient trees. With the silicon dioxide acting as a glue, the cells of the wood mineralized. Other waterborne minerals produced the colors: Iron painted the tree trunks in reds, browns, and yellows; manganese produced purples and blues.

Sometime afterward, uplift from within the earth, along with various forms of erosion, brought the now-petrified wood to the surface in places like Escalante Petrified Forest State Park and Grand Staircase–Escalante National Monument, breaking it into the shapes of today in the process—one that's taken only a hundred million years or so to complete.

HIKING The 1-mile loop **Petrified Forest Trail** ★ is a moderately strenuous hike among colorful rocks, through a forest of stunted juniper and piñon pine, past a painted desert, to a field of colorful petrified wood. The hike also offers panoramic vistas of the town of Escalante and surrounding stair-step plateaus. A free brochure is available at the visitor center. Allow about 45 minutes. An optional three-quarter-mile loop off the main trail—called **Trail of Sleeping Rainbows**—leads through a large mound of petrified wood, but is considerably steeper than the main trail.

WILDLIFE-WATCHING This is one of the best spots in the region to see wildlife ★. The reservoir is home to ducks, geese, and coots. Chukar partridges wander throughout the park, and you're also likely to see eagles, hawks, lizards, ground squirrels, and both cottontails and jackrabbits. Binoculars are helpful.

CAMPING The 22-unit RV and tent **campground,** within easy walking distance of the park's hiking trails and reservoir, is open year-round. Facilities include hot showers, modern restrooms, and drinking water. There are four sites with water and electric RV hookups. Camping costs $20 per night at Wide Hollow, $28 at Lake View RV. Reservations are available at ✆ **800/322-3770** or 801/322-3770 (www.reserveamerica.com); an $8 nonrefundable fee will be charged.

Basing Yourself in Escalante

Originally called Potato Valley, this community's name was changed in the 19th century to honor Spanish explorer and missionary Father Silvestre Velez de Escalante. But it's believed Escalante never actually visited this particular part of southern Utah on his trek from Santa Fe, New Mexico, to California, a hundred years earlier. Home to nearly 100 historic buildings (a free walking-tour map is available at the information booth and at local businesses), Escalante is your best bet for lodging, food, and supplies as you travel Utah 12. At 5,868 feet elevation, it's also a good base for exploring the nearby mountains and Grand Staircase–Escalante National Monument, or for finally taking a hot shower after a week of backpacking. Be aware, though: Services in this town of 800 are limited in winter.

ESSENTIALS

GETTING THERE Escalante is 50 miles east of Bryce Canyon National Park and 63 miles south of Capitol Reef National Park on the Highway 12 Scenic Byway. Utah 12 becomes Main Street as it goes through town.

VISITOR INFORMATION The National Park Service, Dixie National Forest, and Bureau of Land Management (BLM) operate the **Escalante Interagency Visitor Center** (© 435/826-5499) that provides recreation and other tourist information year-round. It's located on the west side of Escalante, at 755 W. Main St. (Utah 12), and open daily 7:30am to 5:30pm from mid-March through September. Winter hours are 8am to 4:30pm, 7 days a week from October to Thanksgiving; and from late November to mid-March the visitor center is open Monday through Friday from 8am to 4:30pm. The **Escalante Chamber of Commerce,** 280 West Main St. (www.escalanteut. com; © 435/826-4810), can also provide area information. It's open Monday through Friday, 9am to 5pm.

WHAT TO SEE & DO

Several local companies will help you explore this rugged land. **Excursions of Escalante** (p. 257) offers guided day and overnight trips in Grand Staircase–Escalante National Monument and the nearby national forest. **Escalante Outfitters** (see "Where to Stay," below), is one of the few places that offers guided fly-fishing trips in the national monument and on Boulder Mountain (p. 266). Gear is provided. Escalante Outfitters also leads evening natural history hikes and has a well-stocked store where you'll find outdoor clothing, maps, guide books, and other outdoor gear.

But the great outdoors isn't the only reason to visit Escalante. Art lovers should schedule their visits for late September or early October, when Escalante and nearby communities join to sponsor the **Escalante Canyons Arts Festival–Everett Ruess Days,** with demonstrations, workshops, contests, exhibits, talks, music, and more. Subjects range from painting to pottery, plus quilting, ceramics, tie-dying, cowboy poetry—you name it.

Philip and Harriet Priska's **Serenidad Gallery,** 170 S. 100 West, (www.serenidadgallery.com; ☏ **888/826-4577** or 435/826-4720), has seven rooms crammed with beautiful objects that the owners love—fine art, photography, antiques, gift items, jewelry, and even locally handmade soaps and lip balms. Petrified wood and local rocks fill one room. Harriet's huge collection of buttons includes her own hand-painted porcelain creations. The Priskas carry only things they particularly like, so it's fun to talk with them about the selection of items. The gallery/shop is open Monday through Saturday from 8am to 6pm, and Sunday from 1 to 6pm. Note that the shop closes occasionally for meal breaks.

The festival is named for Everett Ruess, a young artist who hiked into the rugged canyon country near here in November 1934—and never came back. His disappearance was a longtime mystery and his fate is still unknown. For additional information on the festival and on Ruess, contact the chamber of commerce (see above), or check out the festival website, **www.everettruessdays.org**.

The scenery here inspires many people to make art, so it's no wonder Escalante has a population of working artists. Pick up a free copy of the brochure "Escalante Arts & Crafts Guide," which includes a map, at the Escalante Interagency Visitor Center (see "Visitor Information," above), or check out the chamber of commerce website, **www.escalante-cc.com**.

WHERE TO STAY

Pets are not accepted unless otherwise noted.

In addition to the lodging choices discussed below, the **Shooting Star RV Resort,** 2020 W. Utah 12, Escalante (www.shootingstar-rvresort.com; ☏ **435/826-4440**), offers a unique opportunity to spend the night in a custom-designed Airstream trailer, decorated as they might have been when movie stars had such accommodations while filming on location. There are eight Airstreams, each with a fully equipped kitchen and full bathroom, and all the amenities you would expect as the Hollywood star you obviously are. There's a drive-in theater—open to lodging guests only—where you sit in a vintage convertible to watch the latest from Cary Grant, Clark Gable, or Marilyn Monroe. Rates range from $129 to $149 for a double and there's also an RV park, where vehicle rates start at $25.

For additional information on lodging, including house rentals, contact the chamber of commerce (see above).

Escalante Outfitters   These cute little log cabins are a favorite of backpackers who want a break from sleeping on the ground. A kind of cross between a motel and a campground; it's most like the auto camps of the 1930s. Each cabin either has one queen-size bed or a pair of bunk beds and two small windows. There's heat in cool weather and fans for warm weather.

That's it. All guests share a simple but adequate and well-maintained bath-house; no private bathrooms are available. On the grounds are barbecue pits, picnic tables, and horseshoe pits. There is also a camping area for about 10 tents ($16 per night). A state liquor store and outdoor gear and clothing store are on the premises.

310 W. Main St. (Utah 12). www.escalanteoutfitters.com. © **435/826-4266.** 7 units. $70 double; cabin $170. Dogs accepted for a $10 per night fee. Closed Nov–Feb. **Amenities:** Restaurant (Esca-Latte Internet Café & Pizza Parlor; see below); no phone, free Wi-Fi.

Escalante's Grand Staircase Bed & Breakfast Inn   This beautiful

B&B has spacious rooms with skylights, full private bathrooms, and beds with pillow-top mattresses. The modern country decor includes some furniture in solid aspen or lodgepole pine, Southwestern drum tables, and pictograph designs on the walls. The full gourmet breakfast consists of a fruit dish, juice, coffee, tea, and hot chocolate, and a main course including breakfast meats or breads. Food allergies can be accommodated with advance notice. The entire property, including the grounds, is nonsmoking.

280 W. Main St. (Utah 12), Escalante. www.escalantebnb.com. © **866/826-4890** or 435/826-4890. 8 units. $135–$150. Children under 16 not accepted; older children accepted with prior approval. **Amenities:** Free Wi-Fi.

WHERE TO EAT

Pizza lovers should stop at the **Esca-Latte Internet Café & Pizza Parlor,** located in Escalante Outfitters, 310 W. Main St. (www.escalanteoutfitters. com; © **435/826-4266**). Build your own 12- or 16-inch pizza by selecting from some 20 toppings, ranging from pepperoni to Utah goat cheese. It also has a salad bar, a variety of hot and cold coffee drinks, and Utah microbrew beer. Most lunch and dinner main courses cost from $10 to $25 (for the most loaded specialty 16-inch pizza); most breakfast items range from $5.50 to $7.50. Ask them to pack a box lunch or dinner to go. The restaurant is open daily from 8am to 9pm, and is usually closed from November through February.

For excellent burgers, including a black bean burger, and slow-smoked locally raised range-fed beef, stop at **Circle D Eatery,** 475 W. Main St., Escalante (www.escalantecircledeatery.com; © **435/826-4125**). House specialties at dinner include brisket, steak, smoked chicken, and pork ribs, or you can choose baked trout filet, a teriyaki veggie stir-fry, sandwiches, or spaghetti with homemade marinara sauce. Lunch is more burgers, sandwiches, and salads, and the breakfast menu includes egg dishes, pancakes, granola, and fruit. Hours are 7:30am to around 9pm from Wednesday through Monday and Tuesday from 5 to 9pm (closed mid-Nov to early Feb). Prices for most main courses are $5 to $11 breakfast and lunch, and $7.50 to $19 dinner. Wine and an excellent selection of beer are served.

One of the most famous restaurants in Utah is on the edge of the monument at **Hell's Backbone Grill** (www.hellsbackbonegrill.com; © **435/335-7464**), about 28 miles northeast of Escalante in the community of Boulder, at 20 N. Hwy. 12. Serving excellent regional cuisine, prepared from organic and natural ingredients, (many of them raised on the restaurant's 6-acre farm), Hell's Backbone is open from mid-March through late November only, 7 to 11:30am and 5 to 9:30pm daily. The menu changes seasonally, but for dinner you're likely to be offered chipotle meatloaf with lemony mashed potatoes and vegetables from the restaurant's own farm or skillet-fried trout with blue corn, pecans, and molasses. Try to leave room for dessert, such as the lemon chiffon cake or a chocolate chili cream pot. Breakfast items include a variety of egg dishes, French toast, homemade granola, and various breakfast meats. Dinner main courses are priced from $17 to $32, while breakfast items cost $6 to $13. Wine and beer are served.

North from Escalante Along Utah 12

Heading toward Capitol Reef National Park from the town of Escalante, the forests of pine and fir make a deep green contrast to the rosy red hues of the region's rock formations.

Picturesque **Posey Lake** (sometimes spelled Posy), under the jurisdiction of the U.S. Forest Service, is open to nonmotorized boats and offers good fishing for rainbow trout. It's at 8,600 feet elevation, some 16 miles northwest of Escalante via Utah 12 and gravel Forest Road 153. Facilities include a picnic area, two floating docks, fish cleaning stations, and a boat ramp. There are several trailheads, and numerous dirt roads are popular with mountain bikers and hikers in summer, cross-country skiers and snowmobilers in winter. The **Posy Lake Campground,** usually open mid-May through early September, has 21 sites (maximum RV length 24 ft.), drinking water, and restrooms, but no showers, RV hookups, or trash pickup. Camping costs $11 per night, and reservations are available for an additional booking fee of $11; call © 877/444-6777 or reserve online at www.recreation.gov. For information on the lake and campground, contact the **Escalante Interagency Visitor Center** (see "Visitor Information," above).

Visitors to **Anasazi State Park Museum,** in the village of Boulder (about 28 miles northeast of Escalante along Utah 12), step back to the 12th century A.D., when the Kayenta Anasazi (also called Ancestral Puebloans) lived here in one of the largest communities west of the Colorado River. The 6-acre park includes the ruins of the village, a full-size six-room replica of a home, a gift shop, picnic area, auditorium, and museum. The museum is open daily from 8am to 6pm from April through October and from 8am to 4pm the rest of the year. It is closed Thanksgiving, Christmas, and New Year's Day. Admission costs $5 per person, $3 for seniors 62 and older, with a $10 maximum per family. There is no campground. For more information, contact **Anasazi State Park Museum,** 460 N. Utah 12, Boulder (www.stateparks.utah.gov; © 435/335-7308).

Boulder Mountain ★★ has some of the most dramatic views along Utah 12. Located northeast of Escalante at an elevation of 9,670 feet, you are practically in the clouds. From viewpoints such as **Point Lookout,** you'll gaze out over the colorful sandstone rock cliffs of Capitol Reef National Park to the imposing Henry Mountains, Navajo Mountain, and sights more than 100 miles away.

Those venturing into the backcountry by foot, four-wheel-drive, mountain bike, or horse will discover rugged, remote beauty; the area is also a trout fisherman's paradise, with dozens of secluded mountain lakes and streams hidden among the tall pines and firs. **Escalante Outfitters** (p. 263) offers guided fly-fishing trips. Don't be surprised to see mule deer, elk, and wild turkey in the open meadows. Contact the **Escalante Interagency Visitor Center** (see "Visitor Information," above) for information.

After Boulder, it's not too much farther to Capitol Reef National Park, but first is the community of Torrey, where Utah 12 intersects with Utah 24. You can turn right here and proceed to the park. See chapter 12 for complete coverage of Capitol Reef.

CAPITOL REEF NATIONAL PARK

Capitol Reef National Park is one of Utah's Mighty Five National Parks but whereas Arches is amazing and Zion is awesome and Bryce is kind of creepy (those hoodoos!), Capitol Reef exudes calm, offering subtle but spectacular southern Utah scenery with lots of fascinating rock formations plus a unique twist and a personality—some might say "vibe"—all its own.

So many of Utah's parks are a colorful swirl of barren but beautiful rocks and red desert. But Capitol Reef is more than that. The Fremont River has helped create a lush oasis in an otherwise unforgiving land, with cottonwoods and willows lining its banks. Nineteenth-century Mormons were sent by Brigham Young to found a settlement (the origin of so many Utah towns); those pioneers found the land so inviting and the soil so fertile that they called the community Fruita and planted orchards that are still there, tended by the Park Service.

Because of differences in geologic strata, elevation, and availability of water in various sections of the park, an assortment of ecosystems and terrains, as well as a variety of activities, coexist. There are hiking trails, mountain-biking trails, and four-wheel-drive touring roads; a lush fruit orchard; desert wildflowers and rich, green forests; an abundance of songbirds; and a surprising amount of wildlife—from lizards and snakes to the bashful ringtail cat (a member of the raccoon family).

Throughout the park, you'll find thousand-year-old petroglyphs, and traces of the more recent Ute and Southern Paiute, Wild West outlaws, and industrious Mormon pioneers (in the one-room Fruita Schoolhouse, their children learned the three Rs and studied the Bible and Book of Mormon).

The name Capitol Reef, which conjures up an image of a tropical shoreline, seems odd for a park comprising cliffs and canyons and situated in landlocked Utah. But many of the pioneers who settled the West were former seafaring men, and they extended the traditional meaning of the word *reef* to include these seemingly impassable rock barriers.

The huge round white domes of sandstone reminded them of the domes of capitol buildings, and so this area became known as Capitol Reef.

A more accurate name for the park might be "the Big Fold." When the earth's crust lifted some 60 million years ago, creating the Rocky Mountains and the Colorado Plateau, most of the lifting was relatively even. But here, through one of those fascinating quirks of nature, the crust wrinkled into a huge fold. Running for 100 miles, almost all within the national park, it's known as the Waterpocket Fold.

ESSENTIALS

GETTING THERE   Capitol Reef National Park is 120 miles northeast of Bryce Canyon National Park, 204 miles northeast of Zion National Park, 224 miles south of Salt Lake City, and 366 miles northeast of Las Vegas, Nevada. The park straddles Utah 24, which connects with I-70 both to the northeast and northwest.

Those coming from Bryce Canyon National Park (see chapter 11) can follow Utah 12 northeast to its intersection with Utah 24, and follow that east into Capitol Reef. If you're approaching the park from Glen Canyon National Recreation Area and the Four Corners region, follow Utah 276 and/or Utah 95 north to the intersection with Utah 24, where you then head west into the park.

The closest major airport is **Grand Junction Regional Airport,** about 200 miles east in Grand Junction, Colorado (www.gjairport.com; © 970/244-9100). It has direct flights or connections from most major cities on **Allegiant, American/American Eagle, Delta,** and **United.** Car rentals are available at the airport from **Alamo** (www.alamo.com; © 970/243-3097), **Avis** (www.avis.com; © 970/244-9170), **Budget** (www.budget.com; © 970/243-3851), **Enterprise** (www.enterprise.com; © 970/254-1700), **Hertz** (www.hertz.com; © 970/243-0747), and **National** (www.nationalcar.com; © **970/243-6626**).

INFORMATION/VISITOR CENTER   For advance information, visit the **Capitol Reef National Park** website at www.nps.gov/care or call © **435/425-3791,** ext. 4111.

The **visitor center** is located on the park access road at its intersection with Utah 24. A path alongside the access road connects the visitor center with the campground, passing the historic Fruita blacksmith shop, the orchards, and a lovely shaded picnic ground. The visitor center, open daily from 8am to 4:30pm, has exhibits on the area's geology and history as well as a 10-minute introductory slide show on the park. You can ask the rangers questions, get backcountry permits, pick up free brochures, and purchase books, maps, videos, postcards, and posters. The **Ripple Rock Nature Center** (© **435/425-2233**) is for the kids. Located in an old artist's studio about ¾ mile south of the visitor center along the Scenic Drive, it offers exhibits and activities created to help kids appreciate the park. Check at the visitor center for its current hours.

Books and maps are available from the nonprofit **Capitol Reef Natural History Association,** Capitol Reef National Park (www.capitolreefnha.org; © **435/425-4106**).

Capitol Reef National Park

butch cassidy: UTAH'S MOST INFAMOUS SON

Robert LeRoy Parker was born into a hardworking Mormon family, in the little Southwestern Utah town of Beaver, on April 13, 1866. The oldest of 13 children, Robert was said to be a great help to his mother, and worked on the small ranch his parents bought near Circleville, about 50 miles north of Bryce Canyon.

It was in Circleville where the problems began. Teenager Robert fell in with some rather unsavory characters, including one Mike Cassidy, the ne'er-do-well role model who reportedly gave the youth his first gun, and presumably from whom young Robert took the alias "Cassidy." The boy made his way to Telluride, Colorado, worked for one of the mines there for a while, and then wandered up to Wyoming. He made his way back to Telluride—and, not coincidentally, the Telluride bank was robbed. Butch Cassidy had officially begun his life of crime.

In the following years, Butch—who gained the nickname after a short stint working in a butcher shop—became an expert at rustling cattle, robbing banks, and, his ultimate glory, robbing trains. Butch wanted to call his gang the Train Robbers Syndicate, but they raised such hell in celebration of their economic successes that saloonkeepers in Vernal and other Utah towns began calling them "that wild bunch," and the name stuck. The Wild Bunch would travel through Utah, hiding out in the desolate badlands that were to become Bryce Canyon, Capitol Reef, and Canyonlands national parks. Capitol Reef's Cassidy

Arch was named after Butch; this area was supposedly one of his favorite hiding places.

If you've seen the 1969 movie "Butch Cassidy and the Sundance Kid," with Paul Newman and Robert Redford, you can't forget the spectacular scene in which Butch and his cohorts blow the door off a railroad car. Then they use way too much dynamite to open the safe, sending bills flying into the air. Apparently, the story is basically true, having taken place on June 2, 1899, near Wilcox, Wyoming. According to reports of the day, they got away with $30,000.

The Union Pacific Railroad took exception to Butch's antics. When the posse started getting a bit too close, Butch, Sundance, and Sundance's lady friend, Etta Place (Katharine Ross in the film), took off for South America, where it's said they continued a life of crime for a half dozen or so years. There are also some stories—unconfirmed—that it was in South America that Butch first killed anyone.

According to some historians (as well as the movie), Butch and Sundance were shot dead in a gun battle with army troops in Bolivia in 1908. But some believe that Butch returned to the United States, visited friends and family in Utah and Wyoming, and eventually settled in Spokane, Washington, where he lived a peaceful life under the name William T. Phillips until he died of cancer in 1937.

FEES, REGULATIONS & BACKCOUNTRY PERMITS Entry to the park is free, although it costs $15 per vehicle (including motorcycles) or $7 per person on foot or bicycle to access the scenic drive beyond the main campground (pass valid for up to 7 days). Free **backcountry permits** (available at the visitor center) are required for all overnight hikes.

Bicycles are prohibited in the backcountry and on all hiking trails. Feeding or otherwise disturbing wildlife is forbidden, as is vandalizing or upsetting any natural, cultural, or historic feature of the park. Because park wildlife refuses to follow park rules regarding wildlife diet, campers should be especially careful of where they store food and should dispose of garbage promptly. Dogs, which must be leashed at all times, are prohibited on all trails, more than 100 feet from any road, and in public buildings.

SEASONS/AVOIDING THE CROWDS   Capitol Reef receives just over a million visitors annually—not many compared to Zion, which is the third most visited. Still, try to avoid the peak summer season. The best time to visit is fall, particularly October and November, when temperatures remain warm enough for comfortable hiking and camping, but are not so hot that they'll send you scurrying for shade. You also don't have to be as cautious about flash floods through the narrow canyons as you do during the July-through-September thunderstorm season.

SAFETY   Hikers should carry plenty of water, especially in summer, and watch out for rattlesnakes, which have been seen in the rocks of the Grand Wash and around Fruita. Afternoon thunderstorms in July, August, and September can bring flash floods, which fill narrow canyons without warning. Steep-walled Grand Wash can be particularly hazardous—avoid it whenever storms are threatening.

RANGER PROGRAMS   Rangers present a variety of free programs and activities from spring through fall. Campfire programs take place most evenings at the outdoor amphitheater next to Fruita Campground. Topics vary, but could include animals and plants, geology, and human history in and of the area. Rangers also lead hikes and walks and give short talks on history at the pioneer Fruita Schoolhouse. Schedules are posted on bulletin boards at the visitor center and campground.

Kids can become Junior Rangers or Junior Geologists—they'll learn to map ancient earthquakes, inspect water bugs, and so on. Get details at the visitor center.

SEEING THE HIGHLIGHTS BY CAR

As with most national parks, it would be easy to spend a week or more here, hiking the trails, admiring the views, and enjoying the parts of the park unseen by most visitors. However, many of us have a limited amount of time, or prefer or require a car. Fortunately, Capitol Reef is relatively easy to explore through a car window.

Start at the **visitor center** and watch a short slide show explaining the park's geology and early history. From the center, the paved 25-mile round-trip **Scenic Drive** leads south into the park, offering good views of dramatic canyons and rock formations. Pick up a copy of the Scenic Drive brochure the visitor center and set out, stopping at viewpoints to admire the colorful cliffs, monoliths, and commanding rock formations.

If the weather's dry, drive down the gravel **Capitol Gorge Road** (5 miles round-trip) at the end of the paved Scenic Drive for a look at what many consider the best backcountry scenery in the park. If you're up for a short walk, the relatively flat 2-mile (round-trip) **Capitol Gorge Trail,** which starts at the end of Capitol Gorge Road, takes you to the historic **Pioneer Register,** a rock wall where traveling pioneers "signed in" (p. 274).

Another dry-weather driving option is the **Grand Wash Road,** a maintained dirt road that's subject to flash floods, but in good weather offers an easy route into spectacular backcountry. Along the 2-mile round-trip, you reach **Cassidy Arch,** where famed outlaw Butch Cassidy is said to have hidden out nearby.

Utah 24, which crosses Capitol Reef from east to west, also has several viewpoints offering good looks at the park's features, such as monumental **Capitol Dome,** which resembles the dome of a capitol building; the aptly named **Castle** formation; the historic **Fruita Schoolhouse;** and some roadside **petroglyphs** left by the prehistoric Fremont people (below).

Burr Trail Road

The Burr Trail road, originally a cattle trail blazed by stockman John Atlantic Burr, extends from Notom-Bullfrog Road to the town of Boulder on Utah Hwy 12. Much of the road lies outside the boundary of Capitol Reef and traverses the Circle Cliffs, Long Canyon, and The Gulch. The 8½-mile stretch of road inside Capitol Reef includes a breathtaking set of switchbacks rising some 800 feet in only half a mile. These switchbacks are not considered suitable for RVs or vehicles towing trailers. Visitors should inquire about road and weather conditions before traveling.

PETROGLYPHS TO PIONEERS: CAPITOL REEF'S HISTORIC SITES

The **Fremont** people lived along the Fremont river as early as A.D. 700, staying until about A.D. 1300. Evidence of that ancient past is evident throughout Capitol Reef. Primarily hunters and gatherers, the Fremont also grew corn, beans, and squash to supplement their diet; when they abandoned the area, they left little behind. They lived in pit houses, so called because they were dug into the ground—the remains of one can be seen from the **Hickman Bridge Trail.** Many of the Fremont people's petroglyphs (images carved into rock) and some pictographs (images painted on rock) are still visible on the canyon walls. If you could read them, they might even say why these early Americans left the area—a puzzle that continues to baffle historians and archaeologists.

Fast-forwarding to the 19th century, prospectors and other travelers passed through the **Capitol Gorge** section of the park in the late 1800s, leaving their names on a wall of rock that came to be known as the **Pioneer Register.** You can reach it via a 2-mile loop; see p. 274.

Mormon pioneers established the appropriately named community of **Fruita** when it was discovered that this was a good locale for growing fruit. The tiny 1896 **Fruita Schoolhouse** served as a church, social hall, and community-meeting hall, in addition to functioning as a one-room schoolhouse. The school closed in 1941, but it was carefully restored by the National Park Service in 1984 and is authentically furnished with old wood and wrought-iron desks, a woodstove, a chalkboard, and textbooks. The hand bell used to call students to class still rests on the corner of the teacher's desk. Nearby, the **orchards** planted by the Mormon settlers continue to flourish, tended by park workers who invite you to sample the "fruits" of their labors. In season, visitors may also pick fruit.

The historic **Gifford Farmhouse,** built in 1908, is a typical early-20th-century Utah farmhouse. Located about a mile south of the visitor center, the authentically renovated and furnished farmhouse is open daily from mid-April through September. In addition to displays of period objects, there are often demonstrations of early homemaking skills and crafts, such as quilting and rug making. Park across the road at the picnic area; a short path leads to the farmhouse.

OUTDOOR PURSUITS

Among the last areas in the continental United States to be explored, many parts of Capitol Reef National Park are still practically unknown, perfect for those who want to see real wilderness. Several local companies offer **guide services,** both in the national park and nearby. **Hondoo Rivers and Trails,** 90 E. Main St., Torrey (www.hondoo.com; *©* **435/425-3519**), offers multiday horseback trail rides plus half- and full-day hiking and four-wheel-drive tours, including special tours for photographers and expeditions to rock art sites, plus shuttle services for hikers and mountain bikers. **Backcountry Outfitters,** 677 E. Utah 12, Torrey (www.ridethereef.com; *©* **435/425-2010**), offers a variety of guided trips, including hiking, canyoneering, biking, fishing, horseback riding, and four-wheel-drive excursions.

Four-Wheel Touring & Mountain Biking

As in most national parks, bikes and four-wheel-drive vehicles are restricted to established roads, but Capitol Reef has several so-called roads—actually little more than dirt trails—that provide exciting opportunities for those using 4×4s or pedal power. Use of ATVs is not permitted in the park.

The only route appropriate for road bikes is the 25-mile round-trip Scenic Drive, described above. However, both the Grand Wash and Capitol Gorge roads (see p. 272 for descriptions of these roads), plus three much longer dirt roads, are open to mountain bikes as well as four-wheel-drive vehicles. Rain can make the roads impassable, so check on current conditions with park rangers before setting out.

The **Cathedral Valley Loop** is recommended for mountain bikers and four-wheel-drivers. This road covers 60 miles on a variety of surfaces, including dirt, sand, and rock, and requires the fording of the Fremont River, where water is usually 1 to 1½ feet deep. You are rewarded with beautiful, unspoiled scenery, including bizarre sandstone monoliths and majestic cliffs, in one of the park's most remote areas. There is a small, primitive campground in Cathedral Valley. Access to the loop is from Utah 24, just outside the park, 12 miles east of the visitor center at the river ford; or 19 miles east of the visitor center on the Caineville Wash Road. It's best to begin at the river ford to be sure you can make the crossing.

Hondoo Rivers and Trails and **Backcountry Outfitters** (see above) offer full-day four-wheel-drive tours, including lunch, at rates from $120 to $175 per person. Early-morning starting times are available for photographers who want to catch the light at sunrise, and specialized tours, including trips to rock art sites, are also available. Backcountry Outfitters, whose motto is "Get Out and Stay Out!," also rents mountain bikes starting at $40. You can rent a 4WD vehicle for $95 to $125 per day, including 150 miles, at **Thousand Lakes RV Park & Campground** (see "Camping" below).

Hiking

Trails through the national park offer sweeping panoramas of colorful cliffs and soaring spires, eerie journeys through desolate steep-walled canyons, and cool oases along the tree-shaded Fremont River. Watch carefully for petroglyphs and other reminders of this area's first inhabitants. Little has changed from the way cowboys, bank robbers, settlers, and gold miners found it in the late 1800s. In fact, one of the best things about hiking here is experiencing the unique combination of scenic beauty, American Indian art, and Western history.

Park rangers can help you choose trails best suited to the time of year, weather conditions, and your personal physical condition; those planning serious backpacking treks will want to buy topographic maps, available at the visitor center. The summer sun is wicked, so hats and sunscreen are mandatory, and a gallon of water per person per day is recommended.

Among the best short hikes at Capitol Reef is the 2½-mile round-trip **Capitol Gorge Trail.** It's easy, mostly level walking along the bottom of a narrow canyon. Starting at the end of the dirt Capitol Gorge Road, the hiking trail leads past the **Pioneer Register,** where prospectors and other early travelers carved their names. The earliest legible signatures were made in 1871 by J. A. Call and "Wal" Bateman.

An easy hike that's best at sunset is the aptly named **Sunset Point Trail.** The hike is less than a half-mile but affords panoramic views of cliffs and domes at their most dramatic, at sunset. The trailhead is at Panorama Point turnoff, on Utah 24, 3 miles west of the visitor center, then 1 mile on a gravel access road.

Another short hike, but quite a bit more strenuous, is the 3.5-mile round-trip **Cassidy Arch Trail.** This route offers spectacular views as it climbs steeply from the floor of Grand Wash to high cliffs overlooking the park. The trail provides several perspectives of Cassidy Arch, a natural stone arch named for outlaw Butch Cassidy. The

trail, which has an elevation change of 1,150 feet, is off the Grand Wash dirt road, which branches off the east side of the highway about halfway down the park's Scenic Drive.

Capitol Reef offers a variety of backpacking opportunities, including the 15-mile round-trip **Upper Muley Twist Canyon** route, which follows a canyon through the Waterpocket Fold and offers views of arches and narrows, as well as panoramic vistas from the top of the fold; and the 22-mile round-trip **Halls Creek Narrows,** which follows Halls Creek through a beautiful slot canyon (where you may have to wade or swim). Free backcountry permits (available at the visitor center, p. 268) are required for all overnight hikes. Discuss any plans with park rangers first, as these routes are prone to flash floods.

Guided hikes in the park and in other nearby locations are available from **Hondoo Rivers and Trails** and **Backcountry Outfitters** (see above). Prices vary, but as an example, half-day guided hiking trips cost about $90 per person, and full-day guided hikes, including lunch, cost about $125.

Horseback Riding

Horses are welcome in some areas of the park but prohibited in others; check at the visitor center for details. Multiday guided trail rides that include the national park or other areas are offered by **Hondoo Rivers and Trails** (see above), at rates of about $1,600 to $2,400 per person for a 6-day trip, including all food and equipment; Hondoo also leads custom trips. **Backcountry Outfitters** (see above) also provides multiday trail rides, and, in addition, offers kids' pony rides (5 and younger) for $20, plus half-day rides for $120, and full-day rides, with lunch, for $180.

Wildlife-Watching

Although summer temperatures are hot and there's always the threat of a thunderstorm, this is a good season for wildlife viewing. Many species of lizards reside in the park; you might spy one warming itself on a rock. The western whiptail, eastern fence, and side-blotched lizards are the most common, but the loveliest is the collared lizard, dark in color but with light speckles that allow it to blend easily with lava rocks and become almost invisible to its foes. Watch for deer throughout the park, especially along the path between the visitor center and Fruita Campground. This area is also where you're likely to see chipmunks and antelope ground squirrels. Don't feed them!

If you keep your eyes to the sky, you may spot a golden eagle, Cooper's hawk, raven, and some of the songbirds that pass through each year. Although they're somewhat shy and only emerge from their dens at night, the ringtail cat, a member of the raccoon family, also makes the park his home, as do the seldom-seen bobcat, cougar, fox, marmot, and coyote.

A Tasty Excursion

Mesa Farm Market (http://mesafarmmarket.com; ℭ **435/456-9146**) is a local treasure known mostly to the best chefs in Utah. It's located on the east side of Caineville Utah, 13 miles west of Hanksville at mile marker 102 on Highway 24, 24 miles east of the visitor center at Capitol Reef National Park; it's the little purple store on Highway 24. The tiny roadside stand and 50-acre farm and goat dairy serves fresh fruits and vegetables picked daily from their own gardens and orchards, artisan breads from the wood-fired oven, pastured meats from the chickens and goats, and, most notably, several cheeses made with milk from their goat dairy. Proprietor, goatherd, cheesemaker, gardener, baker, pizza-maker Randy Ramsley is zealous about sustainability—ask him how it works at Mesa Farm.

CAMPING

In the Park

The 71-site **Fruita Campground** ★★ offers a delightful forest camping experience—a welcome break from the desert sun—with large, well-spaced sites. Open year-round, it offers modern restrooms, drinking water, picnic tables, fire grills, and an RV dump station (in summer only), but no showers or RV hookups. It's located along the main park road, 1 mile south of the visitor center. Camping costs $20; reservations are not accepted.

The park also has two primitive campgrounds, free and open year-round on a first-come, first-served basis. Both have tables, fire grills, and pit toilets, but no water. Check road conditions before going; unpaved roads may be impassable in wet weather. **Cedar Mesa Campground,** with six sites, is located in the southern part of the park, about 23 miles down Notom-Bullfrog Road (paved for only the first 10 miles), which heads south off Utah 24 just outside the eastern entrance to the park. **Cathedral Valley Campground,** with six sites, is located in the northern part of the park. From the visitor center, head east on Utah 24 about 12 miles to the Fremont River ford, cross the river, and turn north on unpaved Hartnet Road for about 25 miles. A high-clearance or four-wheel-drive vehicle is necessary.

Backcountry camping is permitted in much of the park with a free permit, available at the visitor center. Fires are forbidden in the backcountry.

Nearby

Sandcreek RV Park The open, grassy area in this pleasant park affords great views in all directions, and there are numerous trees. Facilities include a large, clean bathhouse; horseshoe pits; a gift shop with handmade stone and antler jewelry; a dump station; and pay laundry. There are 24 sites plus two attractive cabins that share the campground bathhouse ($30 double). And, coolest of all, you can rent a 1954 vintage trailer on site for $36 a night (call to reserve trailer; it's not available through the online reservation system).

540 Utah 24, 5 miles west of the park entrance, Torrey. www.sandcreekrv.com. *©* **435/425-3577.** 24 sites, including 12 tent and 12 RV sites, plus 2 cabins. $15 tent site; $33–$37 RV site; $30 cabin with shared bath; extra charge for additional people. Closed mid-Oct to Mar.

Single Tree Campground ★ Located in a forest of tall pines at an elevation of 8,200 feet, this campground features nicely spaced paved sites, with sites that can accommodate large RVs. Most popular are sites offering distant panoramic views of the national park. Facilities include a picnic table, grill, and fire ring at each site; restrooms with flush toilets but no sinks or showers; water hydrants scattered about; an RV dump station; and a horseshoe pit and volleyball court. There are no RV hookups. *Note:* The campground is part of the Dixie National Forest but is managed by the Fishlake National Forest.

Utah 12, about 16 miles south of Torrey. Fremont Ranger District, Fishlake National Forest, 138 S. Main St., Loa. www.fs.fed.us/r4. *©* **435/836-2800.** Reservations must be made at least 4 days in advance by calling *©* **877/444-6777** or visiting www.recreation.gov. 26 sites. $12. No credit cards on-site. Wi-Fi $5 a day. Closed Nov to mid-May.

Thousand Lakes RV Park & Campground Good views of surrounding rock formations are one of the perks of staying at this well-maintained campground, which also has some shade trees. RV sites are gravel; tent sites are grass. Facilities include the usual bathhouse, plus a gift-and-convenience store, a coin-op laundry, a dump station, a heated outdoor swimming pool, horseshoes, barbecues, and Wi-Fi. And a hair salon! Rentals of 4×4s are available at $160 per day. Eight cabins range from basic with a shared bathhouse to complete with shower and toilet, plus several upscale units. The onsite Torrey Grill & BBQ serves dinner from 5 to 9pm Monday through Saturday ($18–$23 adults, $8 children 12 and younger).

Utah 24, 6 miles west of Capitol Reef National Park, Torrey. www.thousandlakesrvpark.com. *©* **435/425-3500** for reservations. $20 tent site; $40 RV site; cabins $39–$109. Closed late Oct to late Mar.

Wonderland RV Park ★★ The closest full-service RV park and campground to the national park, Wonderland offers great views, immaculately maintained grounds and bathhouses, plus shade trees, grass, big rig sites, and croquet, horseshoes, volleyball, and basketball. Wi-Fi, cable TV, and use of gas barbecue grills are included in the rates. There are fire pits and a dump station. Also on the grounds and sharing the bathhouse are two basic camping cabins and two "mountain cabins," with two queen beds, color TVs, microwave, and fridge. There's also a cute sheep wagon ($48 double).

Junction of Utah 12 and 24, Torrey. www.capitolreefrvpark.com. ℭ **435/425-3665.** 43 sites, include 10 tent sites and 33 RV sites. $24 tent site; $40–$64 RV site; $60 cabins. Closed Nov–Mar.

WHERE TO STAY

The park itself has no lodging or dining facilities, but the charming town of Torrey, just west of the park entrance, can take care of most needs. In addition to the properties discussed below, Torrey has a **Days Inn,** 825 E. Utah 24 (www.daysinn.com; ℭ **435/425-3111**). Rustic cabins are available at several area campgrounds; check out **Sandcreek RV Park, Thousand Lakes RV Park & Campground,** and **Wonderland RV Park** under "Camping," above.

For additional information on area lodging, dining, and activities, contact the **Wayne County Travel Council Information Center** (www.capitolreef. travel; ℭ **435/425-3365**), which operates a **visitor center** at the junction of Utah highways 12 and 24, from April through October, daily 9am to 5pm.

Austin's Chuck Wagon Motel ★ Family-owned-and-operated, this well-maintained property includes modern motel rooms, which have Southwestern decor, phones, and two queen-size beds, and a family suite with a large living room, fully equipped kitchen, and three bedrooms that sleep six. The best choice here, however, is one of the cozy (but still Western-style) cabins. Each cabin has two bedrooms (each with a queen-size bed), a living room with a queen-size sofa bed, a complete kitchen, a full bathroom, a covered porch, and a small yard with a barbecue grill and a picnic table surrounded by a lawn and large trees; also on the property is a grocery store/bakery with a well-stocked deli. JacuAll rooms are nonsmoking.

12 W. Main St., Torrey. www.austinschuckwagonmotel.com. ℭ **435/425-3335.** 24 units. Motel rooms $67–$119; cabins $183 for up to 4; family suite $150 for up to 4. **Amenities:** Grocery store; bakery; outdoor heated pool; Jacuzzi; free Wi-Fi. Closed Dec–Feb.

Best Western Capitol Reef Resort ★★ Located a mile west of the national park entrance, this is one of the best Best Westerns. It's close to the park, and the rooms on the back side of the motel building have great views of red rock formations, and guest accommodations go beyond basic motel rooms (you can opt for cottage, a covered wagon, or a teepee). Standard units have either one king-size or two queen-size beds; minisuites have a king-size bed and a queen-size sofa sleeper, plus a refrigerator, microwave, and wet bar; full suites add a separate sitting room for the sofa sleeper, a second TV and telephone, a jetted tub, and patio. The sun deck and pool are situated out back, away from road noise, with glass wind barriers and spectacular views.

2600 E. Utah 24, Torrey. ℭ **435/425-3761.** 97 units. June–Sept $169 double, $140–$150 minisuite and suite, $259 teepee, $239 wagon, $279 cabin. Lower rates from Oct–May. Children 12 and under stay free in parent's room. Pets accepted in designated pet rooms. **Amenities:** Restaurant; Jacuzzi; outdoor heated pool; tennis court; free Wi-Fi.

Capitol Reef Inn & Café ★ This older, Western-style motel—small and slightly eccentric—offers guest rooms that are homey and comfortable, with furnishings handmade of solid wood but it's the surroundings that are most charming, including the desert garden with petrified stone walls and paths, and a stone kiva. Adjacent, under the same ownership, is a good restaurant as well as a gift shop that sells American Indian crafts, guidebooks, and maps.

360 W. Main St. (Utah 24), Torrey. www.capitolreefinn.com. ✆ **435/425-3271.** 10 units. $59–$84 double. Children 2 and under stay free in parent's room. Closed late Oct to mid Mar. **Amenities:** Restaurant (reviewed below); large Jacuzzi.

Torrey Schoolhouse Bed and Breakfast ★★ The three-story red sandstone building served as Torrey's school from 1917 until 1954; during its early days, it also hosted plays, boxing matches, and dances. Beautifully restored, it now houses a charming B&B that maintains the schoolhouse theme on the first and second floors, with furnishings such as an antique writing desk and musical instruments. The large third-floor rooms have a pioneer theme along with high ceilings that them feel even bigger. The inn offers a good mix of historical ambience and modern conveniences, including top-of-the-line beds and massage recliners. The organic breakfasts, often from locally grown ingredients, might include a breakfast quiche, Belgian waffles with fruit topping, or a breakfast burrito. All units are nonsmoking.

150 N. Center St. Torrey. www.torreyschoolhouse.com. ✆ **435/633-4643.** 10 units. $130–$160 double. Rates include full breakfast. No children 11 or under. **Amenities:** Free Wi-Fi. Closed Nov–Mar.

WHERE TO EAT

In addition to the restaurants discussed below, you'll find a good deli and bakery at **Austin's Chuck Wagon Motel,** 12 W. Main St., Torrey (www.austins chuckwagonmotel.com; ✆ **435/425-3335**), open daily with varying hours from mid-March through October (closed the rest of the year). It offers hot and cold sandwiches, wraps, and burritos and enchiladas, at prices from $3 to $7. The deli is primarily for takeout, but there are several small tables. A grocery store shares the building.

Cafe Diablo ★★★ SOUTHWESTERN Looks are deceiving. What appears to be a simple, Western cafe strives to be more with innovative beef, pork, chicken, seafood, and vegetarian selections, many with a Southwestern flair. The rack of glazed pork ribs, slow-roasted in chipotle, molasses, and rum glaze, is spectacular. Other noteworthy dishes include pumpkin seed–crusted red trout served with cilantro-lime sauce and wild rice pancakes, and Mayan tamales—eggplant, poblano peppers, roasted tomatoes, *masa,* and Casera cheese steamed in a banana leaf. The pastries—at least eight different ones are prepared daily—and homemade ice creams are wonderful. In addition to the dining room there is a heated patio. Beer, wine, and cocktails are served.

599 W. Main St., Torrey. www.cafediablo.net. ✆ **435/425-3070.** Main courses $20–$36. Daily 3–10pm. Closed late Oct through Mar.

Capitol Reef Inn & Café ★ AMERICAN   Known for its locally raised trout (available at every meal), the cafe is equally famous for its 10-vegetable salad. Vegetables are grown locally, and vegetarian dishes include spaghetti and mushroom lasagna. There are several steaks, including an excellent tenderloin, plus chicken. The atmosphere is casual, with comfortable seating, American Indian crafts, and large windows. The restaurant offers beer and wine.

At the Capitol Reef Inn & Cafe, 360 W. Main St. www.capitolreefinn.com. ℭ **435/425-3271.** Main courses $6–$11 breakfast and lunch, $10–$20 dinner. Daily 7am–9pm. Closed late Oct to mid-Mar.

Rim Rock Restaurant ★★ AMERICAN   Fine dining Utah-style is casual by New York standards but this is a local favorite for special occasions. The menu is beef-heavy—try the grilled tenderloin with cranberry demi-sauce or the blackened top sirloin with caramelized onions and button mushrooms—but the smoked pork barbecue ribs, the smoked trout appetizer, and the pasta of the day, lighten things up slightly. There are a few vegetarian items, and homemade pies. The casual dining room has a Western look, with lots of windows providing stupendous views and a raised outdoor dining area. Full liquor service is available.

2523 E. Utah 24. www.therimrock.net. ℭ **435/425-3388.** Main courses $15–$30. Daily 5–9:30pm. Closed Nov to late Mar.

Slacker's Burger Joint ★ BURGERS/SANDWICHES   This fast-food restaurant serves good burgers—about a dozen varieties including Utah's signature Pastrami burger—plus sandwiches, fries, fish and chips; for those who insist on eating healthy, several salads and a garden burger are offered. A small dining room pays homage to the '50s and a lawn is set with picnic and patio tables. A wide variety of ice-cream cones and thick milkshakes are also available; no alcohol is served.

165 E. Main St., Torrey. ℭ **435/425-3710.** All items $2–$9. Daily 9am–8pm. Closed Oct–Mar.

LAKE POWELL & GLEN CANYON NATIONAL RECREATION AREA

This huge canyon is a spectacular wonderland of stark contrasts—parched desert, deep blue water, startlingly red rocks, rich green hanging gardens. A (controversial) joint effort by man and nature, Lake Powell's water is essential to the survival of much of the West. Lake Powell and Glen Canyon National Recreation Area is a huge water park, with more shoreline than the West Coast of the continental United States. It's also a place of almost unbelievable beauty, where millions of visitors each year take to the water to explore, fish, water ski, swim, or simply lounge in the sun.

Named for Major John Wesley Powell, a one-armed Civil War veteran who led a group of nine explorers on a scientific expedition down the Green and Colorado rivers in 1869, the lake is 186 miles long and has almost 100 major side canyons that give it 1,960 miles of shoreline. And with more than 160,000 surface acres of water when full—which has been seldom in the 21st century), it has the second-largest capacity of any man-made lake in the United States after Lake Mead. Both reservoirs have been at historically low levels in recent years.

Glen Canyon National Recreation Area, with Lake Powell at its heart, is three parks in one: a major destination for boaters and fishermen, a treasury of scenic wonders, and an important historic site. Lake Powell is best enjoyed by boat—you can glide through the numerous side canyons among sandstone formations that are intricate, sensuous, and sometimes bizarre, the millions of years of erosion resulting in marvelous formations like Rainbow Bridge National Monument, a huge natural stone bridge sacred to the Navajo and other area tribes. You can also explore the 1870s stone fort and trading post at Lees Ferry, the Ancestral Puebloan (also called Anasazi) ruins of Defiance House, and the dam, which supplies water and electric power to much of the West.

ESSENTIALS

ACCESS POINTS: THE MARINAS Located in southern Utah and northern Arizona, Lake Powell and Glen Canyon National Recreation Area has four major access points: Wahweap Marina and Lake Powell Resort (www.lakepowell.com and www.lakepowellmarinas.com; ℭ **888/896-3829** or 928/645-2433), on the lake's south end, is the most developed area of the recreation area, with the largest number of facilities, and the closest to additional lodging, dining, and services in nearby Page, Arizona; **Bullfrog Marina** (ℭ **435/684-3000**) and **Halls Crossing Marina** (ℭ **435/684-7000**) are midlake, and are also fairly well developed. **Hite Marina** (ℭ **435/684-2278**), which has been closed quite a bit in recent years because of low water, is normally the lake's northernmost access point. It is the smallest and least developed marina, with limited services off-season.

These four marinas, operated by Lake Powell Resorts & Marinas, are accessible by car, operate year-round, and provide boat rentals, docks, fuel, fishing and other supplies, and accommodations. A fifth marina, **Dangling Rope,** is accessible by boat only (it's 40 lake miles north of the dam and 55 lake miles south of Halls Crossing and Bullfrog marinas) and is mainly a fuel stop, though it does offer minor repairs, limited supplies, a free dump/pump-out station, emergency medical services, and some of the best soft-serve ice cream around. A sixth marina, **Antelope Point** (www.antelopepointlakepowell.com; ℭ **928/645-5900**), has a launch ramp onto the original channel of the river, small courtesy docks, a large graveled parking area, restrooms, a beach access road, a covered fuel dock, and boat rentals. This ramp may close during low-water levels. **Lees Ferry** is a popular river crossing, but does not offer direct access to Lake Powell.

GETTING THERE Wahweap Marina and Glen Canyon Dam are just off U.S. 89, 6 miles north of Page, Arizona. Wahweap is 150 miles southeast of Bryce Canyon National Park; 130 miles northeast of the north rim of Grand Canyon National Park; 65 miles east of Kanab; 267 miles east of Las Vegas, Nevada; and 381 miles south of Salt Lake City. By road, Halls Crossing is 220 miles northeast of Wahweap, and Bullfrog is 283 miles northeast (both are about 100 miles from Wahweap by boat); both are reachable via Utah 276. Hite, 40 miles uplake from Halls Crossing and Bullfrog, is off Utah 95.

Motorists can reach the dam and **Wahweap Marina** via U.S. 89 from Kanab or Grand Canyon National Park, and via Ariz. 98 from the east. To get to the **Lees Ferry** section, south of Wahweap, drive south on U.S. 89 and then north on U.S. 89A to Marble Canyon, where you can pick up the Lees Ferry access road.

Bullfrog and **Halls Crossing** marinas, which are connected by a toll ferry mid-lake, are accessible via Utah 276, which loops southwest from Utah 95. The 3-mile crossing takes about 30 minutes; it does not run in winter. For the current schedule and rates, contact either Bullfrog or Halls Crossing marinas (see "Access Points: The Marinas," above).

Glen Canyon National Recreation Area

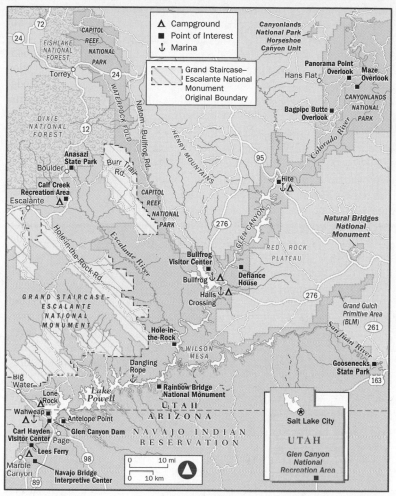

Flights between Page and Southwestern cities including Phoenix and Denver are available from **Great Lakes Airlines** (www.greatlakesav.com; ✆ **800/554-5111**).

INFORMATION/VISITOR CENTERS   For advance information, contact the **Glen Canyon National Recreation Area** in Page (www.nps.gov/glca; ✆ **928/608-6200**), or call the **Carl Hayden Visitor Center** (✆ **928/608-6072**). Books, maps, and other materials are available from the nonprofit **Glen Canyon Natural History Association,** Page (www.glencanyonnha.org; ✆ **928/608-6358**).

For lodging, tour, and boat-rental information, contact the licensed park concessionaire, **Lake Powell Resorts & Marinas,** 100 Lakeshore Dr., Page (www.lakepowell.com; ☎ **888/896-3829** or 928/645-2433).

Information about lodging, dining, and other services is available in **Carl Hayden Visitor Center,** at Glen Canyon Dam, 2 miles north of Page via U.S. 89 (☎ **928/608-6404**). The center also presents exhibitions on the construction of the dam, dinosaurs, and other related subjects. Audiovisual programs, free brochures, and books, maps, and videos are also available. The visitor center is open daily 8am to 6pm from Memorial Day through Labor Day, the rest of the year daily 8:30am to 4:30pm.

The **Bullfrog Visitor Center,** at mid-lake off Utah 276 (☎ **435/684-7423**), has a variety of exhibits and information. It's open intermittently May through October and closed at other times. An **interpretative center** at Navajo Bridge, along U.S. 89A near Lees Ferry (☎ **928/355-2319**), is open from 9am to 5pm. The **Halls Crossing Boater Contact Station,** a self-serve visitor information center, is usually open daily from 8am to 6pm during the summer.

FEES & REGULATIONS   Entry into the park costs $25 per vehicle or $12 per person for up to 7 days. Boating fees are $16 for the first vessel and $8 for each thereafter, for up to 7 days. Backcountry permits (free) are required for overnight trips into the Escalante River section of the national recreation area.

The standard National Park Service regulations, such as not damaging anything and driving only on established roadways, apply here; additional regulations are aimed at protecting the water quality of the lake by prohibiting any dumping of garbage into the water, plus requiring the containment and proper disposal of human wastes within a quarter-mile of the lake. Safe-boating requirements include mandatory use of life jackets by children 12 and under. Remember, boating regulations are slightly different in Utah and Arizona; brochures of regulations are available at the marinas. Pets must be leashed at all times, except on houseboats, and are prohibited in public buildings.

SEASONS/AVOIDING THE CROWDS   The park is open year-round and is busiest in summer—when it's also the hottest, with temperatures often topping 100°F (38°C). Spring is pleasant, but can be a bit windy. October is great, when the water's still warm enough for swimming but most of the

---

A Bird's-Eye View of Lake Powell

The quickest way to see the sights of Lake Powell is by air. **Westwind Air Service** (www.westwindairservice.com; ☎ **480/991-5557** or 928/645-2494) provides half-hour flights over the dam, Rainbow Bridge, and other scenic attractions. Longer flights take in the Grand Canyon, Canyonlands, Monument Valley, and even Bryce Canyon. Tours start at $148 per person for a 45-minute trip to Rainbow Bridge or Horseshoe Bend (two-person minimum) and go up to about $275 per person for expeditions to the Grand Canyon (three-person minimum).

crowds have gone home. Winter can also be beautiful, with snow only rarely dusting the rocks and daytime temperatures usually in the 40s and 50s (single digits and teens Celsius). Another advantage to visiting in the off-season: discounts on lodging and tours November through March and on boat rentals from October to May.

RANGER PROGRAMS **Amphitheater programs** at Wahweap Campground take place several evenings each week in summer. Topics vary, but may include such subjects as the animals or plants of the park, geology, or the canyon's human history. Schedules are posted on bulletin boards at the campground and at the visitor center.

Kids 12 and under can become **Junior Rangers** and receive badges by completing projects in an activity book available at the Carl Hayden and Bullfrog visitor centers.

EXPLORING LAKE POWELL BY BOAT

The best way to see Lake Powell and Glen Canyon National Recreation Area is by boat, either your own or a rental, or on a boat tour. Exploring by **rented houseboat** ★★ for a week and wandering among the numerous side canyons is the best—and most popular—way to get to know the lake.

If your time is limited, try to spend a few hours touring the dam and seeing the exhibits in the Carl Hayden Visitor Center, particularly the excellent relief map that helps you see the big picture. Then take one of the boat tours, such as the half-day trip to **Rainbow Bridge.** Adventurous types might want to buy some good maps, rent a boat for the day, and explore the canyons on their own. But whatever you do, try to get to Rainbow Bridge.

BRINGING YOUR OWN BOAT The best Lake Powell sightseeing is from your own boat, whether it's a one-person kayak or family-size cabin cruiser. Boat-launching ramps are located at Wahweap, Lees Ferry, Bullfrog, Halls Crossing, and Hite (the locations of these marinas are described earlier in the chapter). Fuel, supplies, sewage pump-out stations, drinking water, and boat repairs are available at all of the above except Lees Ferry. Services and supplies are also available at Dangling Rope Marina, about 40 miles uplake from Wahweap Marina and accessible only by boat. As part of the Lake Powell Pure campaign, facilities have been added for the disposal of human waste. You can get directions to them at the marinas or visitor center.

BOAT RENTALS **Lake Powell Resorts & Marinas** (p. 283) and **Antelope Point Marina** (www.lakepowellhouseboating.com; ✆ **800/255-5561**) rent powerboats of all sizes, from two-passenger personal watercraft to luxurious 75-foot houseboats.

Late spring through early fall is the best time to be on the water, and consequently the most expensive: Rates for houseboats that sleep up to 20 people range from $2,200 to $9,000 for 4 days, or $3,700 to $15,000 for 7 days. Rates are considerably lower—sometimes by as much as 30%—in winter. Rates for small fishing boats, ski boats, and personal watercraft range from about $300 to $700 per day. Ask about packages that include boat rentals plus lodging, houseboats with smaller powerboats, and powerboats with water-skiing equipment. Nonmotorized water toys are also available for rent. Most types of boats, although not necessarily all sizes, are available at Wahweap, Bullfrog, Halls Crossing, and Antelope Point marinas. Making reservations well in advance is strongly recommended (see p. 283 for the marina telephone numbers).

You can sometimes get lower rates away from the marinas. About 12 miles northwest of Page, Arizona, in Big Water, Utah, is **Skylite Boat Rentals,** at U.S. 89 Mile Marker 6 (www.skylite.net; © **800/355-3795** or 435/675-3795), offering water toys—there are some great tubes that kids will love—and a range of powerboats.

Generally, anybody who can drive a car can pilot a boat, though Skylite Boat Rentals requires renters have some experience. The only tricks are learning to compensate for wind and currents. Be sure to spend a few minutes practicing turning and stopping; boats don't have brakes! No lessons or licenses are required; the marinas supply all the equipment needed and offer some training as well.

BOAT TOURS Year-round boat tours will take you to those hidden areas of the lake that you may never find on your own. Options range from 1½-hour trips ($32 adults, $18 children 11 and under) to all-day tours to Rainbow Bridge ($100 per adult, $72 per child). Ask about dinner cruises, float trips, and numerous packages that combine activities with lodging and/or RV spaces. For information and reservations, contact **Lake Powell Resorts & Marinas** (p. 283).

WHAT TO SEE & DO

The lake as a whole is a spectacular experience but some particular places deserve special mention. Sites are arranged geographically below, from the south end of the lake to the north.

LEES FERRY Downriver from Glen Canyon Dam, Lees Ferry is a historic river crossing and the site of a stone fort built by Mormon pioneers in 1874 for protection from the Navajo. It was later used as a trading post. You can see the remains of the fort and a 1913 post office. Nearby at Lonely Dell, you'll find 19th- and early-20th-century ranch buildings, an orchard, and a blacksmith shop. Upriver, during low water, you can spot the remains of a steamboat, the *Charles H. Spencer,* a 92-foot-long paddle wheeler that was used briefly in the early 1900s to haul coal for a gold-dredging operation.

Lees Ferry is also the starting point for white-water river trips through the Grand Canyon, and is known for its trophy trout fishing.

GLEN CANYON DAM Contested by environmentalists and others who saw the lake as destructive to the landscape and Anasazi petroglyphs, nevertheless, construction began on this U.S. Bureau of Reclamation project in October 1956. By the time the $155-million dam was completed in September 1963, almost 10 million tons of concrete had been poured, creating a wall 710 feet high and 1,500 feet long. It took until 1980 for the lake to reach its "full pool," covering much of the area that had been explored over 100 years earlier by Major John Wesley Powell. Today, the dam provides water storage, mostly for agriculture and hydroelectric power. Its eight generators, which cost an additional $70 million, produce more than 1 million kilowatts of electrical energy per day.

RAINBOW BRIDGE NATIONAL MONUMENT ★★ This awe-inspiring natural bridge is held sacred by Native Americans. The Navajo call it a "rainbow turned to stone," and in the summer of 1995, they briefly blocked the route to the bridge to conduct a blessing ceremony and protest what they considered to be the bridge's commercialization. Located about 50 miles by boat from Wahweap, Bullfrog, and Halls Crossing marinas, the bridge is so spectacular that it was named a national monument in 1910, long before the lake was created. Believed to be the largest natural bridge in the world, Rainbow Bridge is almost perfectly symmetrical and parabolic in shape, measuring 278 feet wide and standing 290 feet above the streambed. The top is 42 feet thick and 33 feet across.

DEFIANCE HOUSE This archaeological site 3 miles up the middle fork of Forgotten Canyon, uplake from Halls Crossing, is believed to have been occupied by a small clan of Ancestral Puebloans between A.D. 1250 and 1275. The cliff-side site includes ruins of several impressive stone rooms, food storage areas, and a kiva for religious ceremonies. The rock art panel, high along a cliff wall, includes a pictograph for which the ruin is named—an image of three warriors carrying clubs and shields. The panel also contains paintings of sheep and men.

OUTDOOR PURSUITS

FISHING   Although March through November is the most popular season, the fishing is good year-round, especially for huge rainbow trout, which are often caught in the Colorado River between the dam and Lees Ferry. Lake fishermen also catch largemouth, smallmouth, and striped bass; catfish; crappie; and walleye. Because Glen Canyon National Recreation Area lies within two states, Utah and/or Arizona fishing licenses are required, depending on where you want to fish. The marinas sell licenses as well as fishing supplies.

HIKING, MOUNTAIN BIKING & FOUR-WHEELING

Although boating and watersports are the main activities, Lake Powell makes up only 13% of the area—most of this recreation area is solid rock so aquaphobes can have fun here too. Hikers need to be alert: There are few marked trails, and changing water levels create a constantly shifting shoreline.

HIKING   Several short hikes lead to panoramic vistas of Lake Powell. For a view of the lake, Wahweap Bay, the Colorado River channel, and the sandstone cliffs of Antelope Island, drive half a mile east from the Carl Hayden Visitor Center, cross a bridge, and turn left onto an unmarked gravel road; follow it for about a mile to its end and a parking lot in an area locally known as the **Chains** (day-use area only). Heading north from the parking lot, follow the unmarked but obvious trail across sand, up slickrock, and across a level gravel section to an overlook that provides a magnificent view of the lake. This is usually a 10-minute walk (one-way). To extend the hike, you can find a way down to the water's edge, but beware: The steep sandstone can be slick.

Several hikes originate in the Lees Ferry area, including a moderate 2.5-mile round-trip hike through narrow **Cathedral Wash** to the Colorado River. The trailhead is at the second turnout from U.S. 89A along Lees Ferry Road. This hike isn't along a marked trail, but rather down a wash, so there's really only one path to follow—on either side are high rock formations. In wet weather, be alert for flash floods and deep pools. Allow 1 to 1½ hours for the round-trip hike.

Another relatively easy hike, the **River Trail,** starts just upriver from the Lees Ferry fort and follows an old wagon road to a ferry-crossing site, passing the historic submerged steamboat, the *Charles H. Spencer.* Allow about an hour for the 2-mile round-trip walk. A self-guiding booklet is available at Lees Ferry.

A heavy-duty 45-mile hike through the **Paria Canyon Primitive Area,** which departs from Lonely Dell Ranch at Lees Ferry, takes you through beautiful but narrow canyons. *Warning:* Flash flooding can be hazardous. This hike requires a permit from the Bureau of Land Management office in Kanab (www.blm.gov/ut; ✆ **435/644-4680**).

Although most visitors take an easy half- or full-day boat trip to see iconic Rainbow Bridge National Monument, you can hike to it, although the 14-mile one-way trail is difficult and not maintained. It crosses the Navajo Reservation and requires a permit. Contact the **Navajo Nation Parks and Recreation Department** (www.navajonationparks.org; ✆ **928/871-6647**)

If you saw the movie "127 Hours" then you know how important it is for backcountry hikers to obtain current maps of the area and discuss their plans with rangers before setting out. Hikers should carry at least 1 gallon of water per person, per day.

FOUR-WHEELING Mountain bikers and 4WD enthusiasts must stay on established roadways within the recreation area itself, but you can find challenging dirt roads in the recreation area and on adjacent federal land. Get information from the Glen Canyon National Recreation Area office (p. 283).

MOUNTAIN BIKING In the Hite area, the **Orange Cliffs** are particularly popular among mountain bikers. The 53-mile one-way **Flint Trail** connects Hite with Hans Flat in the far-northern section of the recreation area. It's rocky, with some sandy stretches and steep grades.

For a shorter ride, the **Panorama Point/Cleopatra's Chair Trail** is 10 miles (one-way) from Hans Flat to Cleopatra's Chair, providing a spectacular view into Canyonlands National Park. Camping in the Orange Cliffs area requires a permit, and strict regulations apply; contact the **Canyonlands National Park** office (www.nps.gov/cany; ✆ **435/719-2313**).

The Escalante River canyons of the national recreation area are accessible by four-wheel-drive vehicle via the 56-mile one-way **Hole-in-the-Rock Road,** which leaves Utah 12 5 miles east of Escalante, traversing part of the Grand Staircase–Escalante National Monument (chapter 11). Managed by the Bureau of Land Management (ww.blm.gov/ut; ✆ **435/644-1300**), the dirt and sometimes rocky road passes through **Devil's Rock Garden,** an area of unique rock formations, and offers a spectacular overlook of Lake Powell. Although four-wheel-drive is not always needed, the last 6 miles of the road require a high-clearance vehicle. Regardless of what you're driving, avoid the road in wet weather. Allow at least 6 hours round-trip.

CAMPING National recreation area concessionaire **Lake Powell Resorts & Marinas** (p. 284) operates year-round full-service RV parks at Wahweap, Bullfrog, and Halls Crossing, with complete RV hookups, modern restrooms, RV dump stations, drinking water, groceries, and LP gas. Wahweap and Halls Crossing have showers and coin-op laundries as well. Rates for two people range from around $40 to $50; reservations are accepted through the concessionaire. Package deals that include RV sites and boat tours are offered.

The National Park Service operates a campground year-round at Lees Ferry, with 54 sites, flush toilets, and drinking water, but no showers or RV hookups. Reservations are not accepted; rates are $20 per site. The only camping at Hite is a primitive campground with no amenities. The cost is $12 per vehicle, and it's open year-round. Several other primitive campgrounds charge similar rates per night.

Free dispersed camping is permitted throughout the recreation area, except within 1 mile of marinas and Lees Ferry, and at Rainbow Bridge National Monument. Those camping within a quarter-mile of Lake Powell are required to have and use self-contained or portable toilets.

MORE WATER SPORTS

Houseboats and powerboats are the most popular way to get on the water on Lake Powell, but the water is good for other types of craft —kayaks and paddleboards—that get you closer to the water and let you experience the thrill of exploring solo.

Lake Powell Paddleboards on Vista Avenue in Page ((C) **928/645-4017**) rents and sells kayaks and paddleboards and everything needed for a day on the lake, as well as advice and instruction for the inexperienced. Single kayaks cost $30 per day, double kayaks cost $45 per day; and paddleboards go for $40 per day. It's open daily in season, March through September from 8am to 6pm and October through April from 9am to 5pm. Winter weekends are by appointment.

WHERE TO STAY & EAT

Lake Powell Resorts & Marinas (p. 284) operates all of the recreation area's lodging facilities, as well as houseboat rentals; call to make reservations or to get additional information.

Although plenty of hotels, motels, and condominium-type units are available, the best choice for lodging is that wonderful floating vacation home, the **houseboat.** Powered by two outboard motors and complete with a full kitchen, bathrooms with hot showers, and sleeping areas for up to 22 people, houseboats serve not only as your home away from home, but also as your means of exploring the fascinating red-rock canyons that make Lake Powell the unique paradise it is. You can accommodate your vegan, omnivore, or paleo diet easily—there's a fridge, a kitchen stove with an oven, and a gas barbecue grill. For prices and additional information, see "Exploring Lake Powell by Boat," above.

In addition to the facilities described below, a variety of motels are located in Page, Arizona. For information, contact the **Page–Lake Powell Tourism Bureau** (p. 283).

AT WAHWEAP

The **Lake Powell Resort** (formerly the Wahweap Lodge; (www.lakepowell. com; (C) **888/896-3829** or 928/645-2433) has the largest hotel in the area, with 350 units. Located right at the Wahweap Marina, it offers good access for boat tours and rentals; has two pools, a hot tub, and sauna; and provides shuttle service into Page. Many of the rooms have spectacular views of Lake Powell. Rates for two ranges from $240 to $354, depending on the type of room and the season.

Restaurants at Lake Powell Resort include the **Rainbow Room** (© **928/645-1162**), serving American and Southwestern dishes alongside a panoramic view of Lake Powell. All three meals are served daily (closed in winter); dinner main courses cost $19 to $35. Other dining options include a lounge, a coffee shop, and a casual grill.

NEAR WAHWEAP

Amangiri ★★★ If money is no object, consider a stay at Amangiri, the second of Singapore-based Amanresorts' North American properties. A secluded, minimalist desert compound, Amangiri offers design, comfort, service, and opulence that are nothing short of superlative, in line with the $1,000-plus price tag. Rooms are ultra-chic, with two outdoor sitting areas each (the suite even has a private pool), and transcendent desert views. Four-digit nightly rates aside, it serves as a great base for desert recreation of all kinds. The resort itself is surrounded by trails into the surrounding desert wilderness, and the in-house Adventure Center offers everything from kayaking trips on Lake Powell to helicopter tours to Grand Canyon. Amangiri is also home to one of the best pools in the West, featuring a late Jurassic rock formation snaking down the cliffs into its crystal-clear depths.

1 Kayenta Rd., Canyon Point. www.amanresorts.com. © **800/477-9180** or 877/695-3999. 34 suites. $1,000–$1,600 double; $3,600 pool suite. **Amenities:** Restaurant; lounge; outdoor heated pool; spa; free Wi-Fi.

AT BULLFROG & THE OTHER MARINAS

The **Defiance House Lodge** (www.lakepowell.com; © **888/896-3829**), at Bullfrog Marina, has a restaurant and 48 rooms with beautiful views of the lake; prices for two are around $176—the lodge closes in winter.

Three-bedroom mobile home **family units** (lakepowell.com/lodging/family-units) are available at Bullfrog, Halls Crossing, and Hite marinas. Prices for up to six people are about $269 spring to fall—and considerably lower in winter.

MOAB, ARCHES & CANYONLANDS NATIONAL PARKS

They call it Canyonlands country—a seemingly infinite high desert of rock, with spectacular formations and rugged gorges that have been carved over the centuries by the forces of the Colorado and Green rivers. Massive sandstone spires and gravity-defying arches colored by iron and other minerals in shades of orange, red, and brown, define the national parks of southeastern Utah. This is a land that begs to be explored—if you've come to Utah for mountain biking, hiking, four-wheeling, or rafting, then this is the place. And the region holds a few surprises, too, from Ancestral Puebloan (also called Anasazi) dwellings and rock art to dinosaur bones.

14

MOAB: GATEWAY TO THE NATIONAL PARKS

238 miles SE of Salt Lake City

Make no mistake—it's the biggest town in Southeast Utah, but Moab is not a destination in itself. The main drag is lined with gear shops and pizza joints—not a lot of charm here. The attraction of Moab (named for a biblical kingdom at the edge of Zion, the promised land) is the landscape around it. Moab is the base camp for mountain bikers, four-wheel-drive enthusiasts, hikers, kayakers, and rafters eager to explore the red-rock canyon country. Not far from the Colorado River, the dramatic red sandstone cliffs have lured Hollywood filmmakers for hits such as John Wayne's "The Comancheros," the biblical epic "The Greatest Story Ever Told," "Indiana Jones and the Last Crusade," "Thelma & Louise," and "City Slickers II."

Like most Utah towns, Moab was established by Mormon pioneers sent by church leader Brigham Young. But Moab was actually founded twice. The first time, in 1855, missionaries set up Elk Mountain Mission to see to the spiritual needs of the local Ute.

Salt Lake City

UTAH

To Price
↑ 191
Green River
Green River State Park
24
To Goblin Valley State Park

Crescent Junction
70
191
128

ARCHES NATIONAL PARK
See detailed map "Arches National Park" later in this chapter
Visitor Center
279
Moab
141

Green River
HORSESHOE CANYON

Canyonlands National Park
Visitor Center
313
Dead Horse Point State Park
MANTI-LA SAL NATIONAL FOREST

GLEN CANYON NATIONAL RECREATION AREA
ORANGE CLIFFS
CANYONLANDS NATIONAL PARK
Colorado River
Visitor Center
46
191

CATARACT CANYON
211
Newspaper Rock

C O L O R A D O
U T A H

See detailed map "Canyonlands National Park" later in this chapter

Monticello
491

Lake Powell
MANTI-LA SAL NATIONAL FOREST

Natural Bridges National Monument
96
275
Edge of the Cedars State Park Museum
Blanding
95
191

Glen Canyon National Recreation Area
276
261
steep, narrow switchbacks
Bluff
262
262
Hovenweep National Monument

163
San Juan River
262
Aneth

Goosenecks State Park
163
Mexican Hat
191
NAVAJO INDIAN RESERVATION

To Mesa Verde National Park ↗

Four Corners Monument

0 — 10 mi
0 — 10 km

MONUMENT VALLEY NAVAJO TRIBAL PARK
U T A H
A R I Z O N A
160
NEW MEXICO

Apparently unimpressed with the notion of abandoning their own religion for the LDS Church, the Ute killed several missionaries, sending the rest back to Salt Lake City in a hurry. Twenty years later the persevering Mormons tried again; this time, they established a small farming and ranching community.

Moab (elevation 4,000 ft.) is still a small town, with just under 5,000 permanent residents. Right next to Arches National Park, Moab is also close to Canyonlands National Park and is surrounded by the Manti-La Sal National Forest and vast spaces under the jurisdiction of the Bureau of Land Management (BLM).

Essentials

GETTING THERE Situated on U.S. 191, Moab is 30 miles south of I-70 (take exit 182 at Crescent Junction) and 53 miles north of Monticello. Moab is 399 miles northeast of the north rim of Grand Canyon National Park and 238 miles southeast of Salt Lake City. From Salt Lake City, follow I-15 south to Spanish Fork, take U.S. 6 southeast to I-70, and follow that east to Crescent Junction, where you'll pick up U.S. 191 south to Moab.

Sixteen miles north of downtown Moab, **Canyonlands Field** (www.moab airport.com; ✆ **435/259-4849**) has daily scheduled flights between Moab and Denver and Moab and Las Vegas on **Sky West** (✆ **435/259-0408** and car rentals from **Enterprise** (www.enterprise.com; ✆ **435/259-8505**). Shuttle service into Moab is also available from several companies, including **Roadrunner Shuttle** (www.roadrunnershuttle.com; ✆ **435/259-9402**).

The closest major airport is **Grand Junction Regional Airport,** about 112 miles east in Grand Junction, Colorado (www.gjairport.com; ✆ 970/244-9100). It has direct flights or connections from most major cities on **Allegiant, American/American Eagle, Continental, Delta, United,** and **US Airways.** Car rentals are available at the airport from **Alamo** (www.alamo.com; ✆ 970/243-3097), **Avis** (www.avis.com; ✆ 970/244-9170), **Budget** (www.budget.com; ✆ 970/243-3841), **Enterprise** (www.enterprise.com; ✆ 970/254-1700), **Hertz** (www.hertz.com; ✆ 970/243-0747), and **National** (www.nationalcar.com; ✆ 970/243-6626).

Another option for air travelers is to fly into **Salt Lake City International Airport** (www.slcairport.com; ✆ **800/595-2442** or 801/575-2400), about 240 miles from Moab, which has service from most major airlines and rental-car companies. You can rent a car at the airport and drive to Moab, or check with **Roadrunner Shuttle** (www.roadrunnershuttle.com; ✆ **435/259-9402**) or **Moab Luxury Coach** (www.moabluxurycoach.com; ✆ **435/940-4212**) about current shuttle rates and schedules.

Amtrak's (www.amtrak.com; ✆ **800/872-7245**) California Zephyr stops in Green River, about 52 miles north of Moab, and provides service to Salt Lake City and Grand Junction, Colorado. If you plan to go from Green River to Moab, make reservations with **Roadrunner Shuttle** or **Moab Luxury Coach** (see above).

VISITOR INFORMATION For area information, contact the **Moab Area Travel Council,** 84 N. 100 East (www.discovermoab.com; ✆ **435/259-8875**). When you arrive, stop by the **Moab Information Center,** 25 E. Center St., open Monday through Saturday 8am to 7pm and Sunday from 9am to 6pm from mid-March through October, with shorter hours the rest of the year. This multiagency visitor center has information from the Park Service, Bureau of Land Management, U.S. Forest Service, Grand County Travel Council, and Canyonlands Natural History Association. You can get advice, watch a number of videos on Southwest attractions, pick up brochures on local businesses and outfitters, and purchase books, videos, and other materials. A board displays current weather conditions and campsite availability.

GETTING AROUND Rentals (standard passenger cars, vans, and 4WD vehicles) are available from **Enterprise** (www.enterprise.com; ✆ **435/259-8505**). Rugged 4WD vehicles are available from **Farabee's Jeep Rentals** (www.farabeejeeprentals.com; ✆ **435/259-7494**); **Canyonlands Jeep Adventures** (www.canyonlandsjeep.com; ✆ **435/259-4413**), which also rents regular passenger cars; and **Cliffhanger Jeep Rental** (www. cliffhangerjeeprental.com; ✆ **435/259-0889**), which also rents camping trailers. Want a cab? Call **Moab Taxi** (✆ **435/210-4297**). Uber and Lyft are also available.

FAST FACTS The full-service **Moab Regional Hospital,** 450 Williams Way (www.amhmoab.org; ✆ **435/719-3500**), offers 24-hour emergency care. The **post office** is at 50 E. 100 North (www.usps.com; ✆ **800/275-8777**).

The best grocery store in town is **City Market,** 425 S. Main St. (www. citymarket.com; ✆ **435/259-5181**), open daily from 6am to midnight. Pick up sandwiches from the deli, mix it up at the excellent salad bar, or choose fresh-baked items from the bakery before hitting the trail. The store also sells fishing licenses, money orders, and stamps; offers photo finishing; and has a pharmacy.

Outdoor Pursuits

Moab area is the heart of Utah's main outdoor playgrounds, an ideal base for hiking, boating, camping, or just plain horsing around (with or without the horse). In addition to the nearby national parks, Arches and Canyonlands, which are covered in full later in this chapter, there's plenty of room to roam on land administered by the **Bureau of Land Management**'s Moab office, 82 E. Dogwood Ave. (www.blm.gov/utah/moab; ✆ **435/259-2100**), and the **Manti-La Sal National Forest's Moab Ranger District,** 62 E. 100 North (www.fs.fed.us/r4; ✆ **435/259-7155**). The best source for information is the **Moab Information Center** (above).

Because of the extreme desert heat in summer, the best time for most outdoor activities is spring or fall—even the relatively mild winters are inviting. If you end up vacationing in the middle of summer, do your serious hiking and mountain biking early in the day, enjoy a siesta along the river or beside a

MOAB, ARCHES & CANYONLAND | Moab: Gateway to the National Parks

Bring your binoculars and a bird book, and take a break at **Scott M. Matheson Wetlands Preserve** ★, 934 W. Kane Creek Blvd. (www.nature.org/wherewework; © **435/259-4629**). Owned by the Nature Conservancy, this unexpectedly lush oasis attracts more than 200 species of birds and other wildlife, such as river otters, beavers, and muskrats. The preserve has a wheelchair-accessible 1-mile loop trail, with boardwalks over the wet areas, and a two-story viewing blind. Guided bird walks are given (call for the current schedule), and bird and wildlife lists and self-guided tour brochures are available.

In late spring and summer, visitors are advised to bring mosquito repellent. The preserve is open daily year-round from dawn to dusk, and admission is free. From downtown Moab, go south on Main Street to Kane Creek Boulevard (btw. McDonald's and Burger King), and go west about ¾ mile, passing the Moab Public Works Department, to a Y in the road. Take the left fork, and continue for about another half-mile to the preserve entrance. From the parking area, a footpath and bridge lead over Mill Creek to an information kiosk and into the preserve.

swimming pool during the heat of the afternoon, and take a short hike in the evening, just before sundown.

OUTFITTERS

Lots of folks are perfectly prepared and experienced so that they can take off on outdoor adventures on their own. But inexperience and lack of proper equipment shouldn't stop anyone from exploring Utah's outdoors. More than 60 local outfitters offer guided excursions from lazy canoe rides to hair-raising jet-boat and four-wheel-drive adventures. The chart below lists some of the major companies that can help you fully enjoy this beautiful country, and you can get additional recommendations at the **Moab Information Center** (p. 295). All are located in Moab. Advance reservations are often required. It's best to check with several outfitters before deciding on one; in addition to asking about what you'll see and do and what it costs, it doesn't hurt to make sure the company is insured and has the proper permits with the various federal agencies. Also ask about its cancellation policy, just in case.

FOUR-WHEELING

The Moab area has thousands of miles of four-wheel-drive roads, most left over from mining days. These roads offer a popular way to explore this scenic country without exerting too much energy.

A number of local companies (see "Outfitters," above) provide guided trips, starting at about $70 per adult and $60 per child under 16 or 17 for a half-day. You can also rent a 4×4 and take off on your own (see "Getting Around," above).

When hitting the trail on your own, either in a rental or personal 4×4, you will encounter everything from fairly easy dirt roads to "You-don't-really-expect-me-to-take-this-$50,000-SUV-up-*there*-do-you?" piles of rocks.

Outfitter	4WD	Bike	Boat	Horse	Rent
Adrift Adventures 378 N. Main St. ☎ 800/874-4483, 435/259-8594 www.adrift.net	•		•	•	
Canyon Voyages Adventure Co. 211 N. Main St. ☎ 435/259-6007 www.canyonvoyages.com	•	•	•	•	
Dan Mick's Guided Jeep Tours 600 Mill Creek Dr. ☎ 435/259-4567 www.danmick.com	•				
Escape Adventures[1] Moab Cyclery, 391 S. Main St. ☎ 800/451-1133, 435/259-5774 www.escapeadventures.com		•			
Magpie Cycling 497 N. Main St. ☎ 435/259-4464 www.magpieadventures.com		•			
Moab Adventure Center 225 S. Main St. ☎ 435/259-7019 www.moabadventurecenter.com	•	•	•	•	•
Moab Rafting and Canoe Co. 805 N. Main St. ☎ 435/259-7722 www.moab-rafting.com			•		•
Navtec Expeditions 321 N. Main St. ☎ 435/259-7983 www.navtec.com	•		•		•
Sheri Griffith River Expeditions 2231 S. U.S. 191 ☎ 800/332-2439 www.griffithexp.com			•		
Western Spirit Cycling 478 Mill Creek Dr. ☎ 435/259-8732 www.westernspirit.com		•			•

1 Las Vegas–based Escape Adventures runs several guide and cycling services in Moab, offered through Moab Cyclery.

Several four-wheel-drive trips are described in the Canyonlands section, later in this chapter, and a free brochure, available at the Moab Information Center (p. 295), covers several others.

Poison Spider Mesa Trail ★★★, which covers 16 miles of 4×4 road, providing stupendous views down to the Colorado River and Moab Valley, is a favorite of four-wheelers. It's considered difficult; a short-wheelbase high-clearance vehicle is best. Allow at least 4 hours. To reach the trail from the Moab Information Center, drive north on U.S. 191 for about 6 miles and turn west (left) onto Utah 279. Continue another 6 miles to the dinosaur tracks sign, where the trail leaves the pavement to the right, passing over a cattle guard. From here, simply follow the main trail (which is usually obvious) up switchbacks, through a sandy canyon, and over some steep, rocky stretches. From a slickrock parking area on top, you can take a short walk to Little Arch, which isn't really so little.

One easy 4×4 road is the **Gemini Bridges Trail,** which four-wheelers share with mountain bikers (see below). Those with 4×4s often drive the route in the opposite direction of the mountain bikers, starting at a dirt road departing from the west side of U.S. 191, about 10 miles north of the Moab Information Center. This involves more uphill driving, which is safer for motor vehicles— mountain bikers usually prefer going downhill.

The self-guided **Mill Canyon Dinosaur Trail** provides a close-up view of dinosaur bones and fossils from the Jurassic period, including a sauropod leg bone, vertebrae, ribs, toe bones, and the fossil remains of a large tree trunk. To reach the trailhead, drive about 15 miles north of Moab on U.S. 191, then turn left at an intersection just north of highway mile marker 141. Cross the railroad tracks and follow a dirt road for about 2 miles to the trailhead. Allow about 1 hour. On the south side of the canyon are the remnants of an old copper mill that operated in the late 1800s. Also nearby are the ruins of the Halfway Stage Station, a lunch stop in the late 1800s for stagecoach travelers making the 35-mile trip between Moab and Thompson, the nearest train station at that time. From the dinosaur trail head, go north as though you're returning to U.S. 191, but at the first intersection, turn right and drive to a dry wash, where you turn right again onto a jeep road that takes you a short distance to the stage station. The trail is managed by the **BLM**'s Moab office (p. 295).

GOLFING

Some of us don't get why you would spend the day on a man-made golf course in the middle of all this natural scenery, but golfers do. The 18-hole, par-72 **Moab Golf Club** course, 2705 East Bench Rd. (http://moabgolfcourse. com; ✆ **435/259-6488**) is located 5 miles south of downtown Moab in Spanish Valley (take Spanish Trail Rd. off U.S. 191). It's a challenging course nestled among red sandstone cliffs, with spectacular views in every direction. Open daily year-round (weather permitting), the course has a driving range, a pro shop and lessons, and a snack bar open for breakfast and lunch.

HIKING

The Moab area offers hundreds of hiking possibilities, many of them just a few miles from town. Get information at the Moab Information Center (p. 295) and pick up the free brochure that describes seven local trails. Hikes in nearby Arches and Canyonlands national parks are described later in this chapter.

Heads up: Particularly in the summer, carry at least a gallon of water per person per day and wear a broad-brimmed hat.

A local favorite is the **Negro Bill Canyon Trail,** named for William Granstaff, who lived in the area in the late 1800s. Allow about 4 hours for this 4-mile-plus round-trip hike, which is considered easy to moderate. You may get your feet wet, depending on the level of the stream you follow up the canyon. To get to the trailhead, go north from Moab on U.S. 191 to Utah 128, turn east (right), and go about 3 miles to a dirt parking area. A little over 2 miles up the trail, in a side canyon to the right, is the Morning Glory Bridge, a natural rock span of 243 feet. Watch out for the poison ivy that grows by a pool under the bridge. (In case you don't remember from your scouting manual, poison ivy has shiny leaves with serrated edges, and leaves grow in clusters of three.)

The **Hidden Valley Trail** is a bit more challenging, taking you up a series of steep switchbacks to views of rock formations and a panorama of the Moab Valley. Allow at least 3 hours for the 4-mile round-trip. To get to the trailhead, drive about 3 miles south of the Moab Information Center on U.S. 191, turn west (right) onto Angel Rock Road, and go 2 blocks to Rimrock Road. Turn north (right) and follow Rimrock Road to the parking area. The trail is named for a broad shelf, located about halfway up the Moab Rim. Many hikers turn around and head back down after reaching a low pass with great views of huge sandstone fins (the 2-mile point), but you can extend the hike by continuing all the way to the Colorado River on a four-wheel-drive road.

The highly recommended **Corona Arch Trail** offers views of three impressive arches, a colorful slickrock canyon, and the Colorado River. Allow 2 hours for this 3-mile round-trip hike, which involves a lot of fairly easy walking plus some rather steep spots with handrails and a short ladder. From Moab, go north on U.S. 191 to Utah 279, turn west (left), and go about 10 miles to a parking area on the north side of the road. A registration box and trailhead are near the railroad; after crossing the tracks, follow an old roadbed onto the trail, which is marked with cairns (piles of stones).

HORSEBACK RIDING

For those who want to see the canyons from horseback, several companies lead guided rides; the Moab Information Center (p. 295) will have info on current availability. **Adrift Adventures** (see "Outfitters," above) offers combination rafting/horseback riding excursions.

MOUNTAIN BIKING

With hundreds and hundreds of miles of trails, a wide variety of terrains, and spectacular scenery, Moab is easily the mountain-bike capital of Utah, and possibly of the United States. In addition to the mountain-biking possibilities on four-wheel-drive roads in the national parks (see sections on Arches and Canyonlands national parks, later in this chapter), there are abundant trails on BLM and national forest lands that are much less trafficked than national park routes.

When you get into town, stop by the Moab Information Center (p. 295) for a free copy of the "Moab Area Mountain Bike Trails" pamphlet. The very knowledgeable employees here can help you find the trails most suitable for your interests, ability, and equipment—just ask. You can also get information, as well as rent or repair bikes, at **Poison Spider Bicycles,** 497 N. Main St. (www.poisonspiderbicycles.com; ℗ **800/635-1792** or 435/259-7882), which recommends shuttle services from **Porcupine Shuttle** (℗ **435/260-0896**). Bike rentals and repairs, plus shuttle services, will be found at **Chile Pepper Bike Shop,** 702 S. Main St. (www.chilebikes.com; ℗ **888/677-4688** or 435/259-4688). Bike rentals range from $60 to $75 per day, with multiday discounts. Bike shuttle services are also available from several other companies, including **Coyote Shuttle** (www.coyoteshuttle.com; ℗ **435/260-2097**) and **Roadrunner Shuttle** (www.roadrunnershuttle.com; ℗ **435/259-9402**).

Several local companies (see "Outfitters," above) also offer guided mountain-bike tours, with rates starting at about $95 for a half-day and about $145 for a full day. Multiday biking/camping trips are also available.

The area's most famous trail is undoubtedly the **Slickrock Bike Trail ★★★,** a scenic but challenging 11-mile loop that crosses a mesa of heavily eroded pale orange Navajo sandstone just a few minutes from downtown Moab. Along the way, the trail offers views that take in the towering La Sal Mountains, the red-rock formations of Arches National Park, a panorama of Canyonlands National Park, and the Colorado River. The trail, open to both mountain bikes and motorcycles, is physically demanding and technically difficult and not recommended for children, novices, or anyone who is out of shape or has medical problems. Allow 4 to 5 hours, and expect to walk your bike in some areas. If you're not sure you're ready for the trail, get started on the 2¼-mile practice loop. To access the trailhead from the visitor information center, take Center Street east to 400 East. Turn south (right) and follow 400 East to Mill Creek Drive. Turn east (left) and follow Mill Creek Drive to Sand Flats Road, which you take 2⅓ miles east to the BLM's Sand Flats Recreation Area and the trailhead.

Those looking for a somewhat less challenging experience might try the **Gemini Bridges Trail,** a 14-mile one-way trip that shows off the area's colorful rock formations, including the trail's namesake: two natural rock bridges. Considered relatively easy, this trail follows a dirt road mostly downhill, ending at U.S. 191 just under 10 miles from the center of Moab, so it's best to arrange a shuttle (see above). To get to the trailhead from the Moab Information Center, drive north along U.S. 191 to Utah 313, turn west (left), and go about 13 miles. Allow a full day, including getting to and from the trail, and be sure to watch for the magnificent view of Arches National Park from a hilltop as you approach U.S. 191 near the end of the ride.

Although dozens of fabulous trails are waiting for you to explore in the immediate area, mountain bikers who really want to go somewhere—perhaps all the way to Colorado—will want to check out Kokopelli's Trail and the San Juan Hut System. Winding for 142 miles across sandstone and shale canyons, deserts, and mountains, **Kokopelli's Trail** connects Moab and Grand Junction, Colorado. It combines all types of mountain biking, from demanding single track to well-maintained dirt roads, and passes primitive campsites along the way. The elevation change is about 4,200 feet. The west end of the trail is near Sand Flats Road in Moab; the east end is at the Loma Boat Launch, 15 miles west of

Grand Junction. For more information contact the **Colorado Plateau Mountain Bike Trail Association** (www.copmoba.org; © 970/244-8877).

The **San Juan Hut Systems** (www.sanjuanhuts.com; © 970/626-3033) links Moab with Telluride and Durango, both in Colorado, via two 215-mile mountain-bike trail systems. Approximately every 35 miles there is a primitive cabin with eight bunks, a woodstove, a propane cooking stove, cooking gear, and groceries. The route is appropriate for intermediate-level mountain-bikers in good physical condition; more experienced cyclists will find advanced technical single tracks near the huts. The mountain-biking season generally runs from June through September. The cost for riders who plan to make either complete trip is $850 per person, which includes use of the six huts, food, sleeping bags at each hut, and maps and trail descriptions. Shorter trips and shuttles are also available.

ROCK CLIMBING

Those with proper skills and rock-climbing equipment will find plenty of places to scramble in the Moab area; check with the BLM (p. 295). Several companies offer instruction and guided climbs, with rates for full-day climbs generally from $150 to $315 per adult for two climbers. Contact **Desert Highlights,** 50 E. Center St., Moab (www.deserthighlights.com; © **800/747-1342** or 435/259-4433), **Moab Desert Adventures,** 39 E. Center St., Moab (www.moabdesertadventures.com; © **804/814-3872** or 435/260-2404), or **Moab Cliffs & Canyons,** 253 N. Main St., Moab (www.cliffsandcanyons.com; © **877/641-5271** or 435/259-3317). For climbing equipment, you'll find one of the best selections anywhere, at reasonable prices, at **Gearheads,** 471 S. Main St. (© **435/259-4327**), which also offers free filtered water (bring your own jugs).

WATERSPORTS: BOATING, CANOEING, RAFTING & MORE

Canyonlands is more than hot sun and red sandstone rock formations. The Moab area is the only town in Utah that sits along the West's most famous river, the **Colorado ★★**.

You can travel down the river, all the way down to Canyonlands National Park, in a canoe, kayak, large or small rubber raft (with or without motor), or a speedy, solid jet boat. Do-it-yourselfers can rent kayaks or canoes for $40 to $65 for a full day, or rafts starting at $100 for a full day. Half-day guided river trips start at about $55 per person; full-day trips are usually $100 to $190 per person. Multiday rafting expeditions, which include meals and camping equipment, start at about $300 per person for 2 days. **Moab Jett,** 50 W. 400 North (www.moabjett.com), offers 1-hour jet-boat tours for about $77 per person, and from $99 for 3 hours. Children's rates are usually 10% to 20% lower. Some companies also offer sunset or dinner trips. See "Outfitters," p. 296. Be aware that low-water levels may cause cancellations.

Public boat-launching ramps are opposite Lion's Park, near the intersection of U.S. 191 and Utah 128; at Take-Out Beach, along Utah 128 about 10 miles east of its intersection with U.S. 191; and at Hittle Bottom, also along Utah 128, about 24 miles east of its intersection with U.S. 191. For recorded information on river flows and reservoir conditions statewide, contact the **Colorado Basin River Forecast Center** (www.cbrfc.noaa.gov; © **801/524-5130**).

What to See & Do

Film Museum at Red Cliffs Lodge   Moab, and much of this part of Utah, has been a popular location for moviemaking since it was "discovered" by famed director John Ford. Ford filmed much of "Stagecoach," starring a young John Wayne, in Monument Valley in the 1930s; in the 1940s, Ford found Moab. The Red Cliffs Ranch provided the spectacular scenery for many of Ford's movies, including "Wagon Master" and "Rio Grande." In recent years, feature films shot in the Moab area have included "City Slickers II" and "Thelma & Louise." The museum has exhibits from the earliest films to the most recent, including props, posters, and photos—and the scenery's still spectacular. Allow 1 hour.

Red Cliffs Lodge, 14 miles east of Moab on Utah 128 (milepost 14). www.redcliffslodge. com/museum. © **866/812-2002** or 435/259-2002. Free admission. Daily 8am–10pm.

Museum of Moab   This growing museum, which is also known as the Dan O'Laurie Museum of Moab, has numerous displays depicting the history of Moab from prehistoric times to the present. It starts with dinosaur skeletons and bones and also has exhibits on the geology of the area and the resultant uranium and radium mining. A hands-on testing area allows for identification of minerals. The archaeology section includes a large basket unearthed near Moab plus Ancestral Puebloan and early Fremont pottery. You can try your hand (actually your feet) at the restored player piano. Early home-medical remedies are on display, as is the first incubator, which used only a 25-watt bulb and was invented by a local doctor. There is a large hand-carved relief map of the Moab area, as well as the expected ranching and farming exhibits. Another display discusses the National Park Service, Bureau of Land

Management, and U.S. Forest Service, describing their role in the area—a large one—and how they work together. Allow about an hour.

118 E. Center St. (2 blocks east of Main St.). www.moabmuseum.org. © **435/259-7985.** Admission $5 for those 17 and older, free for youths 16 and under, $10 family. Apr–Oct Mon–Sat 10am–5pm; Nov–Feb Mon–Sat noon–5pm. Closed Thanksgiving, Christmas, and New Year's Day.

Where to Stay

Room rates are generally highest from March through October—with the highest rates often in September—and sometimes drop by up to half in winter. High season rates are listed here; call or check websites for off-season rates. Pets are not accepted unless otherwise noted.

Most visitors are here for the outdoors and don't plan to spend much time in their rooms; as a result, many book into one of the fully adequate chain and franchise motels, most of which are located on Main Street. Franchises here include **La Quinta Inn,** 815 S. Main St. (www.lq.com; © 435/259-8700), which is pet friendly and charges from $169 double. Other more-than-adequate franchises, with rates in the same general area, include **Super 8,** at 889 N. Main St. (www.super8.com; © 435/259-8868), **Best Western Plus Canyonlands Inn,** 16 S. Main St. (www.bestwesternutah.com; © 435/259-2300), **Best Western Plus Greenwell Inn,** 105 S. Main St. (www.bestwesternutah.com; © 435/259-6151), and **Comfort Suites,** 800 S. Main St. (www.choicehotels.com; © 435/259-5252). You'll generally find lower rates at **Days Inn,** 426 N. Main St. (www.daysinn.com; © 435/259-4468), **Motel 6,** 1089 N. Main St. (www.motel6.com; © 435/259-6686), and **Sleep Inn,** 1051 S. Main St. (http://moabsleepinn.com; © 435/259-4655). But all are a little pricier than they look. Alternatives include the cabins at **Arch View Resort RV Camp Park, Canyonlands Campground & RV Park,** and **Moab Valley RV Resort** (see "Camping," below).

Big Horn Lodge ★★ Typically Western log furniture and knotty pine walls give the Big Horn its lodge-like feel. All of the well-maintained units (all nonsmoking) have two queen-size beds. Bikes are permitted in the rooms.

550 S. Main St., Moab. www.moabbighorn.com. © **800/325-6171** or 435/259-6171. 58 units. $117–$175 double. Pets permitted with $5 per-night fee. **Amenities:** Restaurant; Jacuzzi; outdoor heated pool; free Wi-Fi.

Bowen Motel ★ This older family-owned-and-operated motel has clean, basic rooms with attractive wallpaper and a king-size or one or two queen-size beds. Family units sleep up to six persons each, and there is an 1,800-square-foot guest house with three bedrooms, two full bathrooms, and a complete kitchen (about $425 per night). All units are nonsmoking.

169 N. Main St., Moab. www.bowenmotel.com. © **800/874-5439** or 435/259-7132. 40 units. $142–$172 double; $425 family unit. Rates include continental breakfast. Pets accepted with $10 per-night fee. **Amenities:** Heated outdoor pool, free Wi-Fi.

Cali Cochitta Bed & Breakfast ★★ The most charming places to stay are outside of Moab proper, and this is a prime example. The Cali Cochitta (Aztec for "House of Dreams") is a handsomely restored late-1800s Victorian home, with great views of the surrounding mountains and red rock formations. The guest rooms have queen-size beds with down comforters, wood furnishings (including many antiques and many that look like antiques), and cotton robes, but no phones. Our favorite is the romantic Cane, with a high queen-size mahogany sleigh bed and French glass doors. The cottages have refrigerators, and the suite can be rented as one or two rooms. Breakfasts include a hot entree (often prepared with herbs from the inn's garden), plus fresh muffins or other baked goods, fruit, and beverages. Wine and snacks are served in the afternoon. Bike storage is available. All units are smoke-free.

110 S. 200 E., Moab. www.moabdreaminn.com. ℭ **888/429-8112** or 435/259-4961. 6 units. Mar–Oct around $175 double; lower rates in winter. Rates include full breakfast. **Amenities:** Heated outdoor pool; free Wi-Fi.

Lazy Lizard International Hostel ★ This hostel offers clean, comfortable lodging at bargain rates on the south side of town. The main house, which is air-conditioned, has basic dorm rooms plus two private rooms. A separate building contains four private rooms, which look much like older motel units. The best facilities are the cabins, constructed of real logs, with beds for up to six. There's also a camping area (no hookups). Everyone shares the bathhouses and there's a phone in the main house, but none in the guest rooms. Guests also have use of a fully equipped kitchen; living room with TV and movies; gas barbecue grill; and picnic tables. Groups should inquire about the nearby houses, which can be rented by the night ($120–$260 for 12–30 people).

1213 S. U.S. 191, Moab. www.lazylizardhostel.com. ℭ **435/259-6057.** 25 dorm beds, 10 private rooms, 8 cabins; total capacity 65 persons. $32 dorm bed; $37 private room double occupancy; $37–$58 cabin double occupancy; $7 per person camping space; inquire about houses. Showers $3 for nonguests. Hostel membership not necessary. No phone.

Redstone Inn ★ This centrally located motel offers quite a bit for the price. The cabin-like structure has log furniture and colorful posters and maps of area attractions on the knotty pine walls. Rooms are smallish side, but spotless. Three rooms accessible to travelers with disabilities have combination tub/showers. There is a mountain bike work stand and bike wash, and bikes are permitted in the rooms. On-site is a covered picnic area with tables and gas barbecue grills, and guests have free access to the heated outdoor pool at a sister motel across the street.

535 S. Main St., Moab. www.moabredstone.com. ℭ **800/772-1972** or 435/259-3500. 52 units. $ 113–$179 double. Pets accepted ($5 fee). **Amenities:** Indoor Jacuzzi; access to heated outdoor pool across the street; free Wi-Fi.

Sunflower Hill Luxury Inn ★★★ This upscale country-style retreat, 3 blocks off Main Street, is a relaxing haven after a day on the trail/river/rocks.

Each of the elegant rooms has its own vibe—for instance, the Summer House Suite boasts a colorful garden-themed mural—with handmade quilts on the queen-size beds, and bathrobes and Molton Brown toiletries. Deluxe rooms have jetted tubs and private balconies. The popular French Bedroom includes a hand-carved antique bedroom set, stained-glass window, vaulted ceiling, white lace curtains, and large whirlpool tub and separate tiled shower. The lush grounds are grassy and shady, with fruit trees and flowers and a swimming pool. There is locked bike storage, a swing, a picnic table, and a barbecue. The substantial breakfast buffet includes fresh-baked breads and pastries, honey-almond granola, fresh fruit, and a hot entree such as a vegetable frittata, Belgian waffles, or potato omelet. All units are nonsmoking.

185 N. 300 East, Moab. www.sunflowerhill.com. ℂ **800/662-2786** or 435/259-2974. 12 units. Rates are seasonal but average $125–$235 double and include full breakfast and evening refreshments. Children 9 and under are generally not allowed. **Amenities:** Jacuzzi; outdoor heated pool; free Wi-Fi.

CAMPING

In addition to the commercial campgrounds discussed here, you can also camp at Canyonlands and Arches national parks, at Dead Horse Point State Park, and at Newspaper Rock, which are discussed elsewhere in this chapter. Pets are permitted in campgrounds unless otherwise noted. Those camping on public lands where there are no showers can get a list of businesses offering public showers from the **Moab Area Travel Council**'s website (www.discovermoab.com; "Area Info & Services" section) or at the **Moab Information Center** (p. 295). The cost runs from $2.25 to $8.

Arch View Resort RV Camp Park This well-maintained campground offers all the usual RV hookups, showers, and amenities you'd expect in a first-class commercial RV park, plus great views into Arches National Park, especially at sunset. Located about 6 miles from the park entrance, Arch View has trees throughout the park, a grassy tent area, a convenience store, a pool, a playground, a coin-op laundry, Wi-Fi, and propane, gasoline, and diesel sales. Basic log cabins and more upscale, fully equipped cottages are available for $79 and up for two people.

U.S. 191, at the junction with U.S. 313, 9 miles north of town, Moab. highwaywestvacations.com. ℂ **800/813-6622** or 435/259-7854. 83 sites. For 2 people, $36 tent, $45–$53 RV. Inquire about glamping options. Closed mid-Nov to mid-Mar.

Canyonlands Campground ★ This campground is surprisingly shady and quiet, given its convenient downtown location, which makes it our top choice for a commercial campground here. Open year-round, it has tent sites as well as partial and full (including cable TV) RV hookups. Facilities include a dump station, self-service laundry, convenience store, playground, and outdoor heated pool. It also offers Wi-Fi. There are also six cabins ($58 double). A City Market grocery store is within walking distance (p. 295).

555 S. Main St., Moab. www.canyonlandsrv.com. ℂ **800/522-6848** or 435/259-6848. 122 sites. For 2 people, $25–$29 tent, cabins $90–$115. Dogs not permitted in cabins.

Moab Valley RV Resort Situated on the north side of Moab, near the intersection of U.S. 191 and Utah 128, this campground is just 2 miles from Arches National Park. Practically any size RV can be accommodated in the extra-large pull-through sites, and some tent sites are covered. All sites have great views of the surrounding rock formations. There are trees and patches of grass, and full RV hookups include cable TV connections. Facilities include an RV dump station, coin-op laundry, convenience store, bike wash, outdoor pool and whirlpool tub, a playground, and Wi-Fi. Eighteen cabins and cottages are available starting at $89 for two people.

1773 N. U.S. 191, Moab. www.moabvalleyrv.com. ℂ **435/259-4469.** 115 sites. Tent sites available. Closed Nov–Feb. Dogs permitted in RV sites, but not in tent sites or cabins.

Where to Eat

Because you might get desperate late at night, Moab has a 24-hour **Denny's** at 191 N. U.S. 191 (www.dennys.com; ℂ **435/259-8839**). Also, see the **Bar-M Chuckwagon** and **Canyonlands by Night & Day,** under "Moab After Dark," below. To view the menus of practically every restaurant in town, see **www. moabhappenings.com.**

Eddie McStiff's ★ AMERICAN This bustling, noisy brewpub is half family restaurant and half bar, with a climate-controlled garden patio bar as well. The dining room has a Southwest decor, and the bar has the look of an Old West saloon—long bar, low light, and lots of wood. Fresh-ground burgers are the deal here—beef, buffalo, salmon, turkey, and veggie—but the menu also includes a variety of grill items, pasta, and pizzas. Prime rib is available after 4:30pm. About a dozen fresh-brewed beers are on tap, and full liquor service is available.

In McStiff's Plaza, 57 S. Main St. (just south of the information center). www. eddiemcstiffs.com. ℂ **435/259-2337.** Main courses $9–$21. Daily 11:30am–midnight.

Moab Brewery ★ ECLECTIC Fresh ales brewed on-site are the main attraction, and the menu is largely beer-friendly: steaks, sandwiches, salads, soups, vegetarian dishes, and assorted specialties. The open microbrewery and restaurant is popular with families, who gobble down basic American fare such as half-pound burgers; fresh fish, including good salmon tacos; and, our top choice here, the St. Louis smoked pork ribs. Finish with house-made gelato. The dining room decor includes light woods, outdoor sports equipment—including a hang glider on the ceiling—and local artwork. Patio dining is available. You can sample the brews—from wheat ale to oatmeal stout—at the separate bar. You can also purchase growlers—beer-to-go in half-gallon jugs. In the restaurant, diners can purchase beer, wine, or mixed drinks. In the package store, you can buy local vodka and beer.

686 S. Main St. www.themoabbrewery.com. ℂ **435/259-6333.** Main courses $8–$22. Sun–Thurs 11:30am–10:30pm; Fri–Sat 11:30am–11:30pm.

Moab: Gateway to the National Parks

MOAB, ARCHES & CANYONLAND

Moab Diner & Ice Cream Shoppe ★ AMERICAN/SOUTHWESTERN
Late risers can get breakfast—could be the best in town—all day here, featuring the usual egg dishes, biscuits and gravy, and a spicy breakfast burrito. Hamburgers, sandwiches, and salads are the offerings at lunch. For dinner, it's steak, shrimp, and chicken, plus liver and onions. The green chili is famous. In addition to ice cream, you can get malts and shakes, plus sundaes with seven different toppings. The decor is old-time diner, with comfy red vinyl booths, a bit of neon, photos of classic cars, and old Coca-Cola ads. No alcoholic beverages are served.

189 S. Main St. www.moabdiner.com. ℂ **435/259-4006.** Main courses $5.75–$11 breakfast and lunch, $7.25–$15 dinner. Mon–Thurs 6am–9pm Fri–Sat 6am–10pm. Closed New Year's, Thanksgiving, and Christmas.

Sunset Grill ★★ AMERICAN   Perched on a hill at the north edge of Moab, this fine restaurant offers the best sunset views in town. Once the home of uranium miner Charles Steen, the Sunset Grill contains four traditional dining rooms and three patios. A special occasion destination for locals, the restaurant serves hand-cut steaks and upscale dishes like roasted half duck with a raspberry sauce, and a grilled salmon filet with an Asian glaze served in a light soy-sherry cream sauce. Texas-style prime rib sells out often, so get here early if it's your first choice. The menu also includes chicken dishes and several pasta selections. Full liquor service is available.

900 N. U.S. 191. www.sunsetgrillmoab.com. ℂ **435/259-7146.** Main courses $14–$26. Mon–Sat 5–10pm.

Moab After Dark

For a small town in conservative, nondrinking Utah, this is a pretty wild place. After a day on the river or in the back of a jeep, don't be surprised to see your outfitter letting his or her hair down at **Eddie McStiff's** (p. 306), a microbrewery that's part family restaurant and part bar, with several TVs and a game room with pool tables, foosball, shuffleboard, and, if you must, Wi-Fi. Another good option for beer lovers is the **Moab Brewery** (p. 306). The **Rio Sports Bar & Grill,** 2 S. 100 West, a block west of Main Street on Center Street (ℂ **435/259-6666**), is a longtime locals' favorite watering hole known for its large selection of alcoholic beverages. For a relaxing, somewhat sophisticated and more upscale bar, stop at **Vista Lounge,** located inside Buck's Grill House.

Those looking for a foot-stompin' good time and a Western-style dinner will want to make their way to the **Bar-M Chuckwagon Live Western Show and Cowboy Supper,** 7 miles north of Moab on U.S. 191 (www.barmchuckwagon.com; ℂ **800/214-2085** or 435/259-2276). Diners go through a supper line to pick up sliced roast beef or barbecued chicken, baked potatoes, baked pinto beans, cinnamon applesauce, buttermilk biscuits, cake, and nonalcoholic beverages. Vegetarian meals can be prepared with advance notice, and beer and wine coolers are available. After dinner, a stage show entertains with Western-style music, jokes, and down-home silliness from the

MOAB, ARCHES & CANYONLAND

Moab: Gateway to the National Parks

Bar-M Wranglers. The grounds, which include a small Western village and gift shop, open at 6:30pm, with gunfights starting at 7pm, dinner at 7:30pm, and the show following supper. The Bar-M is usually open from April through mid-October, but is closed several evenings each week; call for the current schedule. Supper and the show cost $32 for adults, $16 for children 4 to 12, and free for kids 3 and younger. Reservations are strongly recommended.

Canyonlands by Night & Day (www.canyonlandsbynight.com; *(C)* 435/259-5261) offers a variety of excursions in the area, including an evening river trip, operating spring through fall, that combines a 1½-hour sunset jet-boat ride with a Dutch-oven dinner. Cost for the boat trip and dinner is $89 for adults and $70 for children 4 to 12 (minimum age 4), with a family rate of $278 for two adults and two children. A 4-hour daytime jet-boat ride costs $99 for adults and $89 for children 4 to 12 (minimum age 4), with a family rate for two adults and two kids of $312. Reservations are recommended. The office and dock are just north of Moab at the Colorado River Bridge.

ARCHES NATIONAL PARK ★★

233 miles SE of Salt Lake City

Look at the Utah license plate—natural stone arches and fantastic rock formations are the defining features of this park. And of the state, and they exist in remarkable numbers and variety. Just as soon as you've seen the most beautiful, most colorful, most gigantic stone arch you can imagine, walk around the next bend and there's another—bigger, better, and more brilliant than the last. It would take forever to see them all, with more than 2,000 officially listed and more being discovered or "born" every day.

Some people think of arches as bridges, but to geologists there's a big difference between the two. Bridges are formed when a river slowly bores through solid rock. But the often bizarre and beautiful contours of arches result from the erosive force of rain and snow, which freezes and thaws, dissolving the "glue" that holds the sand grains together and chipping away at the stone until gravity finally pulls a chunk off.

Although arches usually grow slowly—*very* slowly—something dramatic happens every once in a while: like that quiet day in 1940 when a sudden crash instantly doubled the size of the opening of Skyline Arch, leaving a huge boulder lying in its shadow. Luckily, no one (that we know of) was standing underneath it at the time. The same thing happened to the magnificently delicate Landscape Arch in 1991, when a slab of rock about 60 feet long, 11 feet wide, and 4½ feet thick fell from the underside of the arch. Now there's such a thin ribbon of stone that it's hard to believe it can continue standing at all.

Spend a day or a week here, exploring the terrain, watching the rainbow of colors deepen and explode with the long rays of the setting (or rising) sun, and gazing at the moonlight glistening on the tall sandstone cliffs. Watch for mule deer, cottontail rabbits, and bright green collared lizards as they go about the

Arches National Park

Salt Lake City

UTAH

Arches ■
National Park

🏕	Picnic area
■	Point of Interest
▲	Campground
⛰	Unpaved road
⛰	Four-wheel-drive road
⟋	Hiking trail

EAGLE PARK

KLONDIKE BLUFFS
■ Tower Arch

Marching Men

DEVILS GARDEN
Dark Angel ■
Double O Arch ■
Landscape Arch ■
Devils Garden Trailhead ■
Devils Garden Campground ▲
Skyline Arch ■
Broken Arch ■
Sand Dune Arch ■

SALT VALLEY

FIERY FURNACE
■ Fiery Furnace Viewpoint
■ Salt Valley Overlook
Wolfe Ranch ■
Delicate Arch ■
Delicate Arch Viewpoint ■

HERDINA PARK
■ Eye of the Whale Arch
■ Panorama Point

WILLOW FLATS
ROCK PINNACLES
Balanced Rock ■
Cove of Caves ■
Double Arch ■
Parade of Elephants ■
Turret Arch ■

THE GREAT WALL

THE WINDOWS

SEVEN MILE CANYON
313
To Canyonlands National Park
191

Petrified Dunes Viewpoint ■
PETRIFIED DUNES

Tower of Babel ■
Courthouse Towers Viewpoint ■
COURTHOUSE TOWERS
The Organ ■
Visitor Center ■
Park Avenue ■
La Sal Mountains Viewpoint ■

Colorado River
128

279

MOAB VALLEY
191

279

MOAB

difficult task of desert living. And let your own imagination run wild among the Three Gossips, the Spectacles, the Eye of the Whale, the Penguins, the Tower of Babel, and the thousands of other statues, towers, arches, and bridges that await your discovery in this magical playground.

Essentials

See the Moab section of this chapter for camping options outside the park, plus lodging, restaurants, and other nearby services.

GETTING THERE   From Moab, drive 5 miles north on U.S. 191. Arches is located 27 miles east of Canyonlands National Park's Island in the Sky Visitor Center, 233 miles southeast of Salt Lake City, 404 miles northeast of the north rim of Grand Canyon National Park in Arizona, and 371 miles west of Denver, Colorado.

INFORMATION/VISITOR CENTERS   For advance information, contact **Arches National Park** (www.nps.gov/arch; ℓ **435/719-2299**).

Books, maps, and videos on Arches as well as Canyonlands National Park and other southern Utah attractions can be purchased from the nonprofit **Canyonlands Natural History Association,** 3015 S. U.S. 191 (www.cnha.org; ℓ **800/840-8978** or 435/259-6003). Some publications are available in foreign languages.

The attractive **Arches National Park Visitor Center** is just inside the entrance gate. It offers maps, brochures, and other information, and a museum explains arch formation and other features of the park. Be sure to take time to watch the orientation film, "Secrets of Red Rock," shown in the auditorium. The visitor center is open daily from 7:30am to 5pm. On Christmas Day, the park is open but the visitor center is closed.

FEES, REGULATIONS & BACKCOUNTRY PERMITS   Entry for up to 7 days costs $30 per private vehicle or $15 per person on foot, $25 motorcycle, or bike. A $25 annual pass is also available; it's good for Arches and Canyonlands national parks as well as Natural Bridges and Hovenweep national monuments. Campsites cost $25 per night, and guided ranger walks into Fiery Furnace cost $16 for adults and $3 for children 5 to 12 (p. 312). Required permits for overnight trips into the backcountry, available at the visitor center, are free.

Backcountry hikers should practice minimum-impact techniques, packing out all trash. Feeding or otherwise disturbing wildlife is prohibited, as is vandalizing or disturbing any natural, cultural, or historic feature of the park. Wood fires are not permitted. Dogs, which must be leashed at all times, are prohibited in public buildings, on all trails, and in the backcountry.

SEASONS/AVOIDING THE CROWDS   Summer days here are hot, often exceeding 100°F (38°C), and winters can be cool or cold, dropping below freezing at night, with snow possible. The best time to visit, especially for hikers, is in spring or fall, when daytime temperatures are usually between 60° and 80°F (16°–27°C) and nights are cool.

Visitation to Arches is highest from March through October, with August the peak month. Parking lots are crowded and the campground is often full by late morning. As with most popular parks, avoid visiting during school vacations if possible.

RANGER PROGRAMS From spring through fall, rangers lead guided hikes on the Fiery Furnace Trail (see "Outdoor Pursuits," below), as well as daily nature walks at various park locations. Evening campfire programs, also from spring through fall, are held on topics such as rock art, geological processes, and wildlife. A schedule of events is posted at the visitor center.

Kids between the ages of 6 and 12 can pick up a **Junior Ranger** booklet at the visitor center. After completing activities and participating in several programs, kids pick up their badge and certificate at the visitor center.

Seeing the Park's Highlights by Car

Arches is the easiest of Utah's national parks to see in a day, if that's all you can spare. An 18-mile (one-way) **scenic drive** offers splendid views of countless natural rock arches and other formations, and several easy hikes reveal additional scenery. Allow 1½ hours for the round-trip drive, adding time for optional hikes.

You can see many of the park's most famous rock formations without even getting out of your car—although venturing out and exploring on foot is always the best way to see them. You have the option of walking short distances to a number of viewpoints, or stretching your legs on a variety of longer hikes along the way (see "Outdoor Pursuits," below). The main road is easy to navigate, even for RVs, but parking at some viewpoints is limited. Please be considerate and leave trailers at the visitor center parking lot or in a Moab campground.

Start out by viewing the short slide show at the **visitor center** to get a feel for what lies ahead. Then drive north past the Moab Fault to the overlook parking for **Park Avenue,** a solid rock "fin" that reminded early visitors of the New York skyline.

From here, your next stop is **La Sal Mountain Viewpoint,** where you look southeast to the La Sal Mountains, named by early Spanish explorers who thought the snow-covered mountains looked like huge piles of salt. In the overlook area is a "desert scrub" ecosystem, composed of sagebrush, saltbush, blackbrush, yucca, and prickly pear cactus. Animals that inhabit the area include the kangaroo rat, black-tailed jackrabbit, rock squirrel, several species of lizards, and the coyote.

Please: *Don't Bust the Crust!* It doesn't look like much—just a lumpy black lichen-like covering on the ground and rocks. But do not disturb it. This is cryptobiotic soil or crust and it's essential to every growing thing in the desert. These tiny communities—they're alive—are the beginnings of soil, which will allow plants to grow. They fix nitrogen and hold the soil together. Cryptobiotic crusts are fragile; once destroyed, they can take years to grow back.

Continuing the scenic drive, you'll see the major sights: At **Courthouse Towers,** large monoliths, such as Sheep Rock, the Organ, and the Three Gossips, dominate the landscape. Leaving Courthouse Towers, watch for the **Tower of Babel** on the east (right) side of the road, then proceed past the petrified sand dunes to **Balanced Rock,** a huge boulder weighing about 3,600 tons, perched on a slowly eroding pedestal. You can take an easy .3-mile round-trip walk around the base of the pedestal from the Balanced Rock parking area. Continuing, take a side road to the east (right) to the **Windows.** Created when erosion penetrated a sandstone fin, they can be seen after a short walk from the parking area. Also in this area are **Turret Arch** and the **Cove of Caves.** Erosion is continuing to wear away at the back of the largest cave, which means it will probably become an arch one day. The North and South Windows are also off this trail. Once you reach them, take the loop around back and see for yourself why they are sometimes called Spectacles. A short walk from the parking lot takes you to **Double Arch,** which looks exactly like what its name implies. It is possible to climb right up underneath the arch; just take care not to disturb the delicate desert vegetation. To the right of Double Arch are several alcoves that may one day become arches. If you're visiting in the spring, look for the sego lily, Utah's state flower. It has three lovely cream-colored petals with a reddish-purple spot fading to yellow at the base. From the end of this trail, you can also see the whimsical **Parade of Elephants.**

Return to the main park road, turn north (right) and drive to **Panorama Point,** which offers an expansive view of Salt Valley and the Fiery Furnace, which can really live up to its name at sunset.

Next, turn east (right) off the main road onto the Wolfe Ranch Road and drive to the **Wolfe Ranch** parking area. A very short walk leads to what's left of this ranch. John Wesley Wolfe and his son Fred moved here from Ohio in 1898; in 1907, they were joined by John's daughter Flora, her husband, and their children. The cabin seen here was built for Flora's family (John's cabin was destroyed by a flash flood). In 1910, the family decided this was not the greatest location for a ranch, and they packed up and returned to Ohio. If you follow the trail a bit farther, you'll see some Ute petroglyphs.

More ambitious hikers can continue for a moderately difficult 3-mile round-trip excursion to **Delicate Arch,** with a spectacular view at trail's end of the "license plate arch." If you don't want to do the hike, you can still see this lovely arch, albeit from a distance, by getting back in your car, continuing down the road for 1 mile, and walking a short trail (about a 5-min. walk) to the **Delicate Arch Viewpoint.**

Returning to the park's main road, turn north (right) and go to the next stop, the **Salt Valley Overlook.** The various shades of color in this collapsed salt dome are caused by differing amounts of iron in the rock, among other factors.

Continue to the vantage point for **Fiery Furnace,** which offers a dramatic view of colorful sandstone fins. This is where 3-hour ranger-guided hikes begin.

From here, drive to a pullout for **Sand Dune Arch,** located down a short path from the road, where you'll find shade and sand along with the arch. This is a good place for kids to play. The trail leads across a meadow to Broken Arch (which isn't broken at all—it just looks that way from a distance).

Back on the road, continue to **Skyline Arch,** whose opening doubled in size in 1940 when a huge boulder tumbled out of it. The next and final stop is the often-crowded parking area for the **Devils Garden Trailhead.** From here, you can hike to **Landscape Arch,** which is among the longest natural rock spans in the world. It's a pretty easy 1.6-mile round-trip hike.

From the trailhead parking lot, it's 18 miles back to the visitor center.

Outdoor Pursuits

BIKING   Bikes are prohibited on all trails and are not allowed to travel cross-country within national park boundaries. The park's established scenic drive is open to cyclists, although you need to be aware that the 18-mile dead-end road is narrow and winding in spots and can be a bit crowded with motor vehicles in summer.

Mountain bikers also have the option of tackling one of several 4WD roads (see below). For guided mountain-bike trips outside the park, as well as rentals, repairs, and supplies, see the Moab section earlier in this chapter.

FOUR-WHEELING   Arches doesn't have many four-wheel-drive opportunities , but it has a few, including the **Salt Valley Road** and the **Willow Flats Road,** both of which can be extremely slick after a rain and are open to four-wheel-drive vehicles and mountain bikes. Check at the visitor center for directions and current conditions.

HIKING   Most trails here are short and relatively easy, although because of the hot summer sun and lack of shade, it's wise to wear a brimmed hat and carry a good amount of water on any jaunt of more than 1 hour.

One easy walk is to **Sand Dune Arch,** a good place to take kids who want to play in the sand. It's only .3 miles (round-trip), but you can add an extra 1.2 miles by continuing on to Broken Arch. Sand Dune Arch is hidden among and shaded by rock walls, with a naturally created giant sandbox below the arch. Resist the temptation to climb onto the arch and jump down into the sand: Not only is it dangerous, but it can also damage the arch. Those who continue to Broken Arch should watch for mule deer and kit foxes, which inhabit the grassland you'll be crossing. Allow about 30 minutes to Sand Dune Arch and back and 1 hour to Broken Arch.

From the **Devils Garden Trail,** you can see about 15 to 20 arches on a strenuous and difficult hike of 7.2 miles round-trip, or view some exciting scenery by following only part of the route. Take at least the easy-to-moderate 1.6-mile round-trip hike to **Landscape Arch ★,** a long, thin ribbon of stone that's one of the most beautiful arches in the park. Watch for mule deer along the way, and allow about an hour. Past Landscape Arch, the trail becomes more challenging but offers numerous additional views, including panoramas of the curious **Double O Arch** and a large, dark tower known as Dark Angel. From the section of the trail where Dark Angel is visible, you are 2.5 miles from the trailhead. If you turn back at this point, the round-trip will take about 3 hours; if you keep going, you'll have the primitive loop almost to yourself as most people turn back at Double O Arch.

The park's best and most scenic hike, the 3-mile round-trip **Delicate Arch Trail ★★**, is a moderate-to-difficult hike, with slippery slickrock, no shade, and some steep drop-offs along a narrow cliff. Hikers are rewarded with a dramatic and spectacular view of Delicate Arch, as well as a visit to the John Wesley Wolfe ranch, and an opportunity to take a side trip to a Ute petroglyph panel that includes what may represent a bighorn sheep hunt. When you get back on the main trail, watch for collared lizards—up to a foot long—which are usually bright green with stripes of yellow or rust, with a black collar. Collared lizards feed in the daytime, mostly on insects and other lizards, and can stand and run on their large hind feet in pursuit of prey. (Very reminiscent of "Jurassic Park.")

Continuing along the trail, watch for **Frame Arch,** off to the right. Its main claim to fame is that numerous photographers have used it to "frame" a photo of Delicate Arch in the distance. Just past it, the trail gets a little weird— narrow and twisting—having been blasted out from the cliff. Allow 2 to 3 hours.

The **Fiery Furnace Guided Hike ★** is a strenuous 2-mile round-trip naturalist-led hike to some of the most colorful formations in the park. Guided hikes are given into this restricted area twice daily from March through October, by reservation. Cost is $10 per adult, $5 per child from 5 to 12. Children ages 5 to 13 must be accompanied by an adult, and children under 5 are not permitted. Reservations must be made at least 4 days in advance (no more than 6 months in advance) online at www.recreation.gov. As you hike along, a ranger describes the desert plants, points out hard-to-find arches, and discusses the geology and natural history of the Fiery Furnace. Rangers recommend against it, but you can hike in the Fiery Furnace on your own. You must first obtain a permit and watch a short video (get details at the visitor center). Other restrictions apply, and there are no marked trails, so it's best to join a guided hike.

Another strenuous hike is to **Tower Arch.** This 3.4-mile round-trip hike on a primitive trail starts with a steep incline to the top of the bluff and proceeds up and down, with great views of the Klondike Bluffs to the right. Beware of the slickrock that makes up part of the trail, and watch carefully for the cairns leading the way—there are many piles of rocks along the way; make sure the ones you're following are manmade. The hardest part is near the end, where you struggle uphill through loose sand. Your reward is a grand sight: the immense Tower Arch standing among a maze of sandstone spires. Climb up under it for a soul-soothing view while you take a much-deserved break. In the spring, the majestic, snowcapped La Sal Mountains can be seen to the east through the arch opening.

The backcountry has no trails or campsites, and very little of the park is open to overnight camping, but backcountry hiking is permitted. Ask park rangers to suggest routes. No fires are allowed, and hikers must carry their own water and practice low-impact hiking and camping techniques. Those planning to be out overnight need free backcountry permits, available at the visitor center (p. 310).

CAMPING **Devils Garden Campground** ★, at the north end of the park's scenic drive, is Arches' only developed camping area, offering a perfect location for exploring the park. The 50 well-spaced sites are nestled among rocks, with plenty of piñon and juniper trees, and some sites can accommodate RVs up to 30 feet long. From March through October, the campground accepts reservations (www.recreation.gov; © **877/444-6777**), with a $10 additional booking fee. In summer, the campground fills very early, with people arriving early trying to garner any unreserved sites, so reservations are strongly recommended. Sites costs $25 per night. You'll find drinking water and flush toilets, but no showers or RV hookups. See the Moab section earlier in this chapter for information on public showers and nearby commercial campgrounds.

CANYONLANDS NATIONAL PARK ★★

34 miles W of Moab, 304 miles SE of Salt Lake City

Utah's largest national park is not for the sightseer out for a Sunday afternoon drive. This is not a landscape inspiring oohs and ahs—its beauty is more subtle than that. Instead, it rewards those willing to spend time and energy— *lots* of energy—exploring the rugged backcountry. Sliced into districts by the Colorado and Green rivers, which are the park's primary architects, this is a land of extremes: vast panoramas, dizzyingly deep canyons, dramatically steep cliffs, broad mesas, and towering red spires.

The most accessible part of Canyonlands is the **Island in the Sky District,** in the northern section of the park, where a paved road leads to sites such as Grand View Point, which overlooks some 10,000 square miles of rugged wilderness. Island in the Sky has several easy-to-moderate trails offering sweeping vistas. A short walk provides views of Upheaval Dome, which resembles a large volcanic crater but may actually have been created by the crash of a meteorite. For the more adventurous, the 100-mile White Rim Road takes experienced mountain bikers and those with high-clearance four-wheel-drive vehicles on a winding loop tour through a vast array of scenery.

The **Needles District,** in the southeast corner, offers only a few viewpoints along the paved road, but boasts numerous possibilities for serious hikers and backpackers, and those with high-clearance 4×4s or mountain bikes. Named for its tall, red-and-white-striped rock pinnacles, this diverse district is home to impressive arches, including the 150-foot-tall **Angel Arch,** as well as grassy meadows and the confluence of the Green and Colorado rivers. Backcountry visitors will also find ruins and rock art left by the Ancestral Puebloans (also known as Anasazi) some 800 years ago.

Most park visitors don't get a close-up view of the **Maze District,** but instead see it off in the distance from **Grand View Point** at Island in the Sky or Confluence Overlook in the Needles District. That's because it's inhospitable and practically inaccessible. A lot of endurance and at least several days are necessary to see even a few of its sights, such as the appropriately named **Lizard Rock** and **Beehive Arch.** Hardy hikers can visit **Horseshoe Canyon** in 1 day, where they can see the **Great Gallery,** an 80-foot-long rock art panel. The Maze is a bucket-list destination, spectacular but hard to access and hard to navigate. One recent year's estimates suggest that about 40,000 people visited the Island in the Sky, about 20,000 visited the Needles, but only 546 ventured into the Maze.

The park is also accessible by boat, which is how explorer Major John Wesley Powell first saw the canyons in 1869, when he made his first trip down the Green to its confluence with the Colorado, and then even farther downstream, eventually reaching the Grand Canyon. River access is from the towns of Moab and Green River; several local companies offer boat trips (see the Moab section earlier in this chapter or the Green River section later in this chapter).

Essentials

No lodging facilities, restaurants, or stores are located inside the national park. Most visitors use Moab as a base camp.

GETTING THERE/ACCESS POINTS To reach the Island in the Sky Visitor Center, 34 miles west of Moab, take U.S. 191 north to Utah 313, which you follow south into the park. To reach the Needles Visitor Center, 75 miles southwest of Moab, take U.S. 191 south to Utah 211, which you follow west into the park. Getting to the Maze District is a bit trickier: From I-70 west of Green River, take Utah 24 south. Watch for signs and follow two- and four-wheel-drive dirt roads east into the park.

INFORMATION/VISITOR CENTERS Contact **Canyonlands National Park** (© 435/719-2313) or visit www.nps.gov/cany for information. Books, maps, and DVDs can be purchased from the nonprofit **Canyonlands Natural History Association,** 3015 S. U.S. 191, Moab (www.cnha.org; © 435/719-2313). Some publications are available in foreign languages.

Canyonlands National Park operates two visitor centers—**Island in the Sky Visitor Center,** in the northern part of the park, and **Needles Visitor Center,** in the southern section—where you can get maps, free brochures on hiking trails, and, most important, advice from rangers. The terrain at Canyonlands can be extremely brutal, and it's important to know not only your own limitations, but also the limitations of your vehicle and other equipment. The Island in the Sky Visitor Center is open daily 8am to 6pm from early March through

Canyonlands National Park

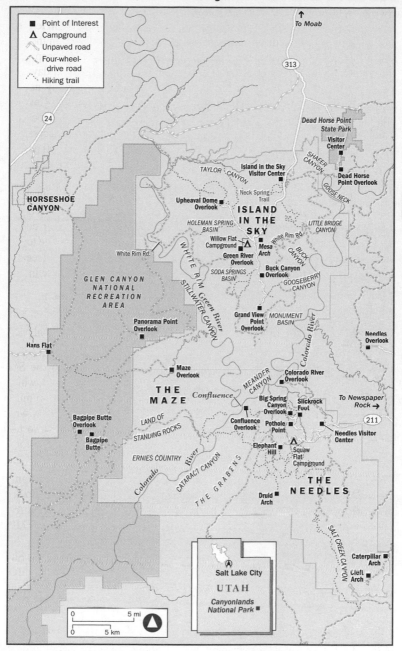

Legend:
- ■ Point of Interest
- △ Campground
- Unpaved road
- Four-wheel-drive road
- Hiking trail

↑ To Moab

313

Dead Horse Point State Park
Visitor Center

SHAFER CANYON

Dead Horse Point Overlook

GOOSE NECK

24

TAYLOR CANYON

Island in the Sky Visitor Center

Neck Spring Trail

HORSESHOE CANYON

Upheaval Dome Overlook

ISLAND IN THE SKY

LITTLE BRIDGE CANYON

HOLEMAN SPRING BASIN

Willow Flat Campground △

Mesa Arch

White Rim Rd.

BUCK CANYON

White Rim Rd.

Green River Overlook

Buck Canyon Overlook

SODA SPRINGS BASIN

GOOSEBERRY CANYON

GLEN CANYON NATIONAL RECREATION AREA

WHITE RIM

Green River

STILLWATER CANYON

Grand View Point Overlook

MONUMENT BASIN

Panorama Point Overlook

Colorado River

Needles Overlook

Hans Flat

Maze Overlook

MEANDER CANYON

Colorado River Overlook

THE MAZE

Confluence

Big Spring Canyon Overlook

Slickrock Foot

To Newspaper Rock →

211

LAND OF STANDING ROCKS

Confluence Overlook

Pothole Point

Needles Visitor Center

Bagpipe Butte Overlook

Bagpipe Butte

Colorado River

Elephant Hill

Squaw Flat Campground △

ERNIES COUNTRY

CATARACT CANYON

THE GRABENS

THE NEEDLES

Druid Arch

SALT CREEK CANYON

Caterpillar Arch

Cleft Arch

Salt Lake City

UTAH

Canyonlands National Park ■

0   5 mi
0   5 km

December; from January through early March it's open Friday through Tuesday with reduced hours. The Needles Visitor Center is open daily 8am to 5pm early March through late November, and closed the rest of the year. Those going into the Maze District can get information at the Hans Flat Ranger Station, usually open daily from 8am to 4:30pm.

FEES, REGULATIONS & BACKCOUNTRY PERMITS   Entry into the park (for up to 7 days) costs $10 per private vehicle or $5 per person on foot, bike, or motorcycle. A $25 annual pass is also available; it's good for Canyonlands and Arches national parks as well as Natural Bridges and Hovenweep national monuments. The camping fee at Squaw Flat Campground in the Needles District is $15; camping at Willow Flat Campground in the Island in the Sky District costs $10.

Backcountry permits, available at either visitor center, are required for all overnight stays in the park, except at the two established campgrounds. **Permit reservations** can be made in advance (www.nps.gov/cany; ✆ 435/259-4351). Permits for overnight four-wheel-drive, overnight backpacking trips, and mountain-bike trips are $30. The permit for white-water boating through Cataract Canyon is $30 per group plus $20 per person.

There is a $5 day-use fee for those taking four-wheel-drive vehicles into the Needles District.

Backcountry hikers should practice minimum-impact techniques, packing out all trash. Feeding or disturbing wildlife is prohibited, as is vandalizing or upsetting any natural, cultural, or historic feature of the park. Wood fires are also prohibited.

Dogs, which must be leashed at all times, are prohibited in public buildings, on all trails, and in the backcountry (even in vehicles on 4WD roads).

SEASONS/AVOIDING THE CROWDS   Summers here are hot, with temperatures often exceeding 100°F (38°C). Winters can be cool or cold, dropping well below freezing at night, with light snow possible. The best time to visit, especially for hikers, is in spring or fall, when daytime temperatures are usually from 60° to 80°F (16°–27°C) and nights are cool. Late-summer and early-fall visitors should be prepared for afternoon thunderstorms.

Although Canyonlands does not get nearly as crowded as most other national parks in Utah, summer is still the busiest time, and reservations for backcountry permits are recommended from spring through fall. As with most parks, if you want to escape humanity, pick the longest and most difficult trail you can handle.

SAFETY   Due to the extreme variety and ruggedness of the terrain, the main safety problem at Canyonlands is that people underestimate the hazards. Rangers warn hikers to carry at least 1 gallon of water per person per day, be especially careful near cliff edges, avoid overexposure to the intense sun, and carry maps when going into the backcountry. During lightning storms, avoid lone trees, high ridges, and cliff edges. Four-wheel-drive-vehicle operators should be aware of their vehicle's limitations and carry extra food and emergency equipment. Anyone heading out into the backcountry should let someone know where they are going and when they plan to return. Traveling alone in Canyonlands is not a good idea.

RANGER PROGRAMS A variety of ranger programs are presented from March through October. Several programs are offered daily in the **Island in the Sky District,** including geology presentations at Grand View Point and talks at the visitor center. In the **Needles District,** there are 1-hour evening programs at Squaw Flat Campground most nights of the week. In the **Maze District,** guided hikes in Horseshoe Canyon are offered most weekends in spring and fall.

Seeing the Highlights

Canyonlands is not an easy place to see in a short period of time. In fact, if your schedule permits only a day or less, you might want to simply skip the Needles and Maze districts entirely and drive directly to the **Island in the Sky Visitor Center.** After looking at the exhibits, drive to several of the overlooks, stopping along the way for a short hike or two. Make sure you stop at the **Grand View Point Overlook,** at the south end of the paved road. Hiking the **Grand View Point Trail,** which is especially scenic in the late afternoon, literally gives you the "grand view" of the park. Allow about 1 hour for this easy 2-mile walk. The 1-mile **Upheaval Dome Overlook Trail** is another interesting walk; it takes about 30 minutes and leads you to a mile-wide crater of mysterious origins,.

EXPLORING CANYONLANDS BY CAR

No driving tour has yet been designed to show off Canyonlands. The Island in the Sky District has about 20 miles of paved highway, some gravel roads accessible to two-wheel-drive vehicles, and several viewpoints. The Needles District has only 8 miles of paved roads and fewer viewpoints. Many (but not all) of Needles' viewpoints and trailheads are accessible only by high-clearance four-wheel-drive vehicles, mountain bikes, or plain old foot power. The Maze District has no paved roads. Essentially, both of the park's main roads lead to trailheads, and unless you plan to leave your car and hike for at least a half-hour or so, it would be better to skip Canyonlands and spend your time at nearby Arches National Park, which is much more accessible by car.

Of course, if your "car" happens to be a serious 4×4, and you're equally serious about doing some hard-core four-wheeling, this is the park for you (see "Outdoor Pursuits," below). Due to the constantly changing conditions of the dirt roads, however, it is strongly recommended that you discuss your plans with rangers before setting out.

Outdoor Pursuits
BIKING & MOUNTAIN BIKING

Bikes of any kind are prohibited on hiking trails or in the backcountry, except on designated two- and four-wheel-drive roads. Road bikes are of little use,

MOAB, ARCHES & CANYONLAND

Canyonlands National Park

except for getting to and from trailheads, viewpoints, visitor centers, and campgrounds in the Island in the Sky and Needles districts.

Mountain bikers will find themselves sharing four-wheel-drive roads with motor vehicles of every size, plus occasional hikers and horseback riders. Because some of the four-wheel-drive roads have deep sand in spots—which can turn into quicksand when wet—mountain biking may not be as much fun here as you'd expect, although it certainly is a challenge. It's wise to ask rangers about current conditions on specific roads before setting out. Roads that are popular with mountain bikers include the **Elephant Hill** and **Colorado River Overlook** jeep roads, both in the Needles District. The 100-mile **White Rim Road,** in the Island in the Sky District, also makes a great mountain-bike trip, especially for bikers who can arrange for an accompanying 4×4 vehicle to carry water, food, and camping gear (see "Four-Wheeling," below).

FOUR-WHEELING

Unlike most national parks, where all motor vehicles and mountain bikes must stay on paved roads, Canyonlands has miles of rough 4WD roads where mechanized transport is king, and jacked-up jeeps with oversize tires rule the day. Four-wheelers must stay on designated 4×4 roads, but keep in mind that the term "road" can mean anything from a graded, well-marked, two-lane gravel byway to a pile of loose rocks with a sign that says "that-a-way." Many of the park's jeep roads are impassable during heavy rains and for a day or two after. Rangers warn that many of the park's 4×4 roads are suitable only for high-clearance 4WD vehicles. ATVs and non-street-legal dirt bikes are not permitted.

The best four-wheel-drive adventure in the Island in the Sky District is the **White Rim Road ★★**, which winds some 100 miles through the district and affords spectacular views, from broad panoramas of rock and canyon to close-ups of red and orange towers and buttes. A high-clearance 4×4 is necessary. Expect the journey to be slow, taking 2 to 3 days, although with the appropriate vehicle, it isn't really difficult. There are primitive campgrounds along the way, but reservations and backcountry permits are needed (see "Essentials," above). Mountain bikers also enjoy this trail, especially when accompanying a four-wheel-drive vehicle that can carry supplies and equipment.

Four-wheeling in the Needles District can be an end in itself, with a variety of exciting routes, or simply a means to get to some of the more interesting and remote hiking trails and camping spots. Four-wheel-drive fans will find an ultimate challenge on the **Elephant Hill** road, which begins at a well-marked turnoff near Squaw Flat Campground. Although most of the 10-mile trail is only moderately difficult, the stretch over Elephant Hill itself (near the beginning of the drive) can be a nightmare, with steep, rough slickrock, drifting sand, loose rock, and treacherous ledges. Coming down the hill, one switchback requires you to back to the edge of a steep cliff. This road is also a favorite of mountain bikers, although bikes will have to be walked on some stretches because of the abundance of sand and rocks. The route offers views of numerous rock formations, from striped needles to balanced rocks, plus panoramas of steep cliffs and rock "stairs"; side trips can add another 30 miles. Allow from 8 hours to 3 days. Backcountry permits are needed for overnight trips.

For a spectacular view of the Colorado River, the **Colorado Overlook** ★ road can't be beat. This 14-mile round-trip is popular with four-wheelers, backpackers, and mountain bikers. Considered among the park's easiest 4×4 roads, the first part is very easy indeed, accessible by high-clearance two-wheel-drives, but the second half has rough and rocky sections that require four-wheel-drive. Starting at the Needles Visitor Center parking lot, the road takes you past numerous panoramic vistas to a spectacular 360-degree view of the park and the Colorado River, some 1,000 feet below.

HIKING

With little shade, no reliable water sources, and temperatures soaring to 100°F (38°C) and higher in summer, it can get hot in Canyonlands. Hikers should carry at least a gallon of water per person per day, along with sunscreen, a hat, and all the usual hiking and emergency equipment. If you expect to do some serious hiking, try to plan your trip for the spring or fall, when conditions are much more hospitable, and never hike alone. Because some of the trails may be confusing, hikers attempting the longer ones should carry good topographic maps, available at park visitor centers and at stores in Moab. Although the park offers dozens of hiking possibilities, the few below are highlighted for their variety of ability requirements, and are listed by district.

HORSESHOE CANYON This detached section of the park was added to Canyonlands in 1971 mainly because of its **Great Gallery** ★★★, an 80-foot-long rock art panel with larger-than-life human figures, believed to be at least several thousand years old. Only one road leads into the Horseshoe Canyon Unit, and you'll have to drive some 120 miles (one-way) from Moab and then hike 6½ miles (round-trip) to see the rock art, which includes pictographs and petroglyphs. To get to the area by two-wheel-drive vehicle, take I-70 west from Green River about 11 miles to U.S. 24, go south about 24 miles to the Horseshoe Canyon turnoff (near the WATCH FOR SAND DRIFTS sign), turn left, and follow this maintained dirt road for about 30 miles to the canyon's west rim, where you can park. From here, it's a 1½-mile hike down an 800-foot slope to the canyon floor, where you turn right and go 1.75 miles to the Great Gallery. There's no camping in Horseshoe Canyon, but primitive camping is available on BLM property on the rim just outside the park boundary.

ISLAND IN THE SKY The **Mesa Arch Trail** provides the casual visitor with an easy ½-mile (round-trip) self-guided nature walk through an area forested with piñon and juniper trees, mountain mahogany, cactus, and a plant called Mormon tea, from which Mormon pioneers made a tealike beverage. The loop trail's main scenic attraction is an arch made of Navajo sandstone that hangs precariously on the edge of a cliff, framing a spectacular view of nearby mountains. Especially scenic at sunrise, allow about a half-hour.

Another half-hour round-trip hike, although a bit steeper and moderately strenuous, leads to the **Upheaval Dome Overlook.** Upheaval Dome doesn't fit with the rest of the Canyonlands terrain—it's obviously not the result of gradual erosion like the rest of the park, but rather a dramatic deformity in which rocks have been pushed into a domelike structure. At one time, it was believed that the dome was formed by a hidden volcano, but a more recent theory suggests that a meteorite may have struck the earth here some 60 million years ago. This hike is about 1 mile round-trip; a second overlook adds about 1 mile round-trip and at least 15 minutes.

An easy 2-mile hike, especially scenic at sunset, is the **Grand View Point Trail ★**, which follows the canyon rim from Grand View Point and shows off numerous canyons and rock formations, the Colorado River, and distant mountains. Allow about 1 hour.

Those looking for a real challenge can explore the **Lathrop Canyon Trail,** which meanders some 5 miles down into the canyon to the White Rim Road, affording beautiful views as you descend. Allow 5 to 7 hours for this strenuous hike over steep terrain and loose rock, remembering that it's another 5 miles back. It's possible to continue down to the Colorado River from here, which makes your round-trip close to 22 miles, but check with rangers about the feasibility of this overnight trip before attempting it.

THE MAZE Getting to the trailheads in the Maze District involves rugged four-wheel-drive roads; rangers can help you with directions.

The 3-mile **Maze Overlook Trail** is not for beginning hikers or anyone with a fear of heights. It is quite steep in places, requiring the use of your hands for safety. At the trailhead, you get a fine view of the many narrow canyons that inspired this district's name; the trail then descends 600 feet to the canyon bottom. The 9-mile **Pictograph Fork to Harvest Scene Loop** is a 7- to 10-hour hike (or an overnight) that leads over slickrock and along canyon washes—watch for the cairns to be sure you don't wander off the trail—to a magnificent example of rock art.

NEEDLES Trails here are generally not too tough, but keep in mind that slickrock can live up to its name, and that this area has little shade. One relatively easy hike is the **Roadside Ruin Trail,** a short (.3-mile), self-guided nature walk that takes about 20 minutes round-trip and leads to a prehistoric granary, probably used by the Ancestral Puebloans some 700 to 1,000 years ago to store corn, nuts, and other foods. Although easy, this trail can be muddy when wet.

For a bit more of a challenge, try the **Slickrock Trail,** a 2.4-mile loop that leads to several viewpoints and takes 2 or 3 hours. Slickrock—a general term for any bare rock surface—can be slippery, especially when wet. Viewpoints show off the stair-step topography of the area, from its colorful canyons and cliffs to its flat mesas and striped needles. Also, watch for bighorn sheep.

From **Elephant Hill Trailhead,** you can follow several interconnecting trails into the backcountry. The road to the trailhead is gravel, but is graded and drivable in most two-wheel-drive passenger cars; those in large vehicles such as motor homes, however, will want to avoid it. The 11-mile round-trip **Elephant Canyon–Druid Arch hike** can be accomplished in 4 to 6 hours and is moderately difficult, with some steep drop-offs and quite a bit of slickrock. But the views are well worth it, as you hike through narrow rock canyons, past colorful spires and pinnacles, and on to the huge Druid Arch, its dark rock somewhat resembling the stone structures at Stonehenge.

The **Confluence Overlook Trail,** a 10-mile round-trip day or overnight hike, leads to a spectacular bird's-eye view of the confluence of the Green and Colorado rivers and the 1,000-foot-deep gorges they've carved. The hike is moderately difficult, with steep drop-offs and little shade, but it splendidly reveals the many colors of the Needles District, as well as views into the Maze District of the park. Allow 4 to 6 hours.

For those staying at Squaw Flat Campground, the **Big Spring to Squaw Canyon Trail** is a convenient, moderately difficult 7.5-mile loop that includes some sections not good for those with a fear of heights. This trail can be hiked in 3 to 4 hours. It winds through woodlands of piñon and juniper, but has some steep grades that can be dangerous when wet, and offers views of nearby cliffs and mesas as well as distant mountains. Watch for wildflowers from late spring through summer.

CAMPING

The park has two campgrounds, both open year-round. In the Island in the Sky District, **Willow Flat Campground** (elevation 6,200 ft.) has 12 sites, picnic tables, fire grates, and vault toilets, but no water. Maximum RV length is 28 feet; camping is $10. In the Needles District, **Squaw Flat Campground** (elevation 5,100 ft.) has 26 sites, fire grates, picnic tables, flush toilets, and year-round drinking water. Maximum RV length is 28 feet; the fee is $15 per night. Neither campground accepts reservations and both typically fill from late March through June and early September to mid-October. Primitive campsites are also available throughout the park for four-wheelers and back-packers (permits required; see "Essentials," earlier in this chapter).

Near Island in the Sky, the campground at **Dead Horse Point State Park** has electric hookups (see "More to See & Do Nearby," below). Additional camping facilities are available on nearby public lands administered by the

Bureau of Land Management and U.S. Forest Service; commercial camp-grounds and public showers are located in Moab (see the Moab section, earlier in this chapter).

More to See & Do Nearby

DEAD HORSE POINT STATE PARK ★

One of Utah's most scenic state parks, Dead Horse might be considered a mini-Canyonlands. The Dead Horse Point Overlook offers a splendid view across the river to the nearby national park, as well as down some 2,000 feet past seven distinctive and colorful layers of rock to the Colorado River. A strip of land only 30 yards wide connects the point with the rest of the mesa, and in the late 1800s, this natural corral was used by cowboys who herded wild horses in, roped all they wanted, and left the rest to find their way out.

From Canyonlands' Island in the Sky Visitor Center, drive north out of the park for 3½ miles to the intersection with Utah 313, and turn right. The state park's visitor center is about 7½ miles down the road. From Moab, head northwest on U.S. 191 for 9 miles, and turn south on Utah 313 for about 23 miles to the park (passing the access road for Canyonlands National Park).

For information, contact **Dead Horse Point State Park** (www.stateparks. utah.gov; ℂ **435/259-2614**).

The **visitor center/museum** is near the entrance to the park, with exhibits on the park's geology, history, plants, and animals. Rangers are on hand to assign campsites and answer questions; books, posters, maps, and souvenirs are available for purchase. A video presentation on the human and geologic history of the area is shown by request; in summer, nightly campfire programs and short guided walks are scheduled. Also, from late spring through early fall, the **Pony Expresso Coffee Shop,** open 8am to 5pm daily, sells snacks, sandwiches, soft drinks, and, of course, coffee.

The day-use fee is $10 per vehicle. In addition to the usual regulations requiring vehicles and bikes to stay on roads and pets to be leashed, visitors are asked to conserve water (which has to be trucked in) and to avoid stepping on cyanobacterial crusts—the fragile, bumpy, black mats composed of bacteria, algae, lichen, moss, and fungi found along trails and roads.

EXPLORING THE PARK Dead Horse Point Overlook is about 2 miles from the visitor center via a paved road. A short, wheelchair-accessible paved walkway leads from the parking area to a platform overlook that provides a magnificent panoramic view of the deep red canyons, the Colorado River, and distant mountains. The light is best either early or late in the day, but this is a worthwhile stop at any time.

Although you can easily drive to Dead Horse Point Overlook, it's a fun hike if you have the time. The main trail starts at the visitor center, follows the east rim of the mesa to the overlook, and returns on the west side. The fairly easy loop is 4 miles; you can add another 3 miles in side trips out to overlook points. Along the way, you pass a variety of rock formations while scrambling over the slickrock.

Another 3½-mile loop leads from the visitor center to a series of potholes (holes in the rock that catch rainwater and may contain tadpole shrimp and other aquatic life) and a canyon overlook.

CAMPING   The park's attractive campground has 21 sites, all with electric hookups and covered picnic tables, plus flush toilets and an RV dump station. However, because water must be trucked in, there are no showers, and campers are asked to conserve the small amount of water available. Electric outlets are hidden on the underside of picnic tables, which may be 50 or 60 feet from the site parking area, so those with recreational vehicles will likely need long extension cords. Camping costs $20; reservations are accepted (and encouraged Mar–Oct) with an $8 processing fee (www.reserveamerica.com; ✆ 800/322-3770).

NEWSPAPER ROCK

This site is famous for a large sandstone panel covered with petroglyphs that date from A.D. 1500 to modern times, created by a long line of humans, from the Ancestral Puebloans to the Utes. The panel also includes initials and names left by early European-American settlers, including one J. P. Gonzales of Monticello, who herded sheep in the canyon in the early 1900s. Administered by the Bureau of Land Management's **Monticello Field Office,** 365 N. Main St., Monticello (www.blm.gov/ut/st/en/fo/monticello.html; ✆ 435/587-1500), the site is located in Indian Creek Corridor, along the road to Canyonlands' Needles District, Utah 211.

North & West of the Parks

GREEN RIVER

Travelers heading north to Salt Lake City or west toward Nevada will undoubtedly pass through the village of Green River, which sits at an elevation of 4,100 feet, on I-70 along the banks of the Green River, about 54 miles northwest of Moab.

The **John Wesley Powell River History Museum,** 1765 E. Main St. (www.jwprhm.com; ✆ 435/564-3427), details the phenomenal river expedition of explorer John Wesley Powell, a one-armed Civil War veteran who explored the Green and Colorado rivers in the late 1800s. Museum exhibits also discuss the geology of the region and the history of river running, from a replica of Powell's heavy wooden boat, the *Emma Dean,* to examples of boats and rafts used on the river since then. A 25-minute film, shown throughout the day, brings Powell's adventures to life. Admission is $6 per person 13 and older, $2 for children 5 to 12, free for those 4 and under, and a family rate of $15. From mid-May through mid-September, the museum is open Monday through Saturday 9am to 7pm and Sunday noon to 5pm; the rest of the year it is usually open Tuesday through Saturday 9am to 5pm. You can also get information on other Green River area attractions, activities, and lodging at the museum.

Tip: Since 1943, **Ray's Tavern**, 25 S. Broadway (© **435/564-3511**), has been the first stop for those just off the river or trail. The appeal is simple: Ray's famous burger and cold beer.

Green River State Park, on Green River Road (www.stateparks.utah.gov; © **435/564-3633**), is a lush green oasis with big, old Russian olive and cottonwood trees. There's a **boat ramp** for launching your raft or canoe, but be aware that once you start heading downstream, you'll need a motor or mighty powerful arms to fight the current back to the park. The park also has a 9-hole championship **golf course** (© **435/564-8882**). Situated right along the river, it's open year-round (weather permitting) and has a pro shop, snacks, and carts. Day-use park entry costs $5 per vehicle, which includes use of the boat ramp. The shady and spacious 40-site **campground,** open year-round, has modern bathhouses with toilets and hot showers (closed Dec–Feb), and a dump station, but no RV hookups. Camping costs $35; reservations are accepted from March through October with an $8 nonrefundable fee (www. reserveamerica.com; © **800/322-3770**).

Several river-running companies offer day and overnight trips on the Green.

A MAGICAL STATE PARK

Goblin Valley State Park ★★ (www.stateparks.utah.gov; © **435/275-4584**) is filled with fantasyland rock formations; hence its name. The landscape is so strange, in fact, that it starred in the 1999 sci-fi movie "Galaxy Quest." But have no fear. Although in the light of the full moon the little munchkins almost come alive, with shadows giving them facelike features, these goblins are friendly. Bikes and motor vehicles are restricted to paved areas, but visitors are welcome to hike among the goblins. Park residents include kit foxes, rabbits, and lizards.

The 24-site **campground** is laid out in a semicircle among tall, multicolored rocks of varying heights. Facilities include showers and a dump station, but no RV hookups. The day-use fee is $7 per vehicle; camping is $16. There are also several yurts (similar to camping cabins, with heat and electricity but no bathroom) that cost $60 per night. Reservations are accepted from March through November with an $8 nonrefundable fee (www.reserveamerica.com; © **800/322-3770**).

To get here from Green River, head west on I-70 for about 10 miles to exit 149, and turn south on Utah 24 for about 25 miles to Temple Mountain Junction, where you turn west and follow signs for about 12 miles to the park.

The San Rafael Swell, a vast 2,000 square miles of public land, is known for deep canyons, natural sandstone sculptures, and wide panoramas. It's Utah's fastest-growing tourist destination, largely because it's still relatively unknown and uncrowded so you can get a sense of its vastness. The San Rafael Reef, once identifiable by horizontal layers of earth, is now lifted by an anticline—a giant underground dome—creating a maze of canyons. Much of the Swell is in the San Rafael Reef Wilderness Study Area. (Contact the Price BLM office © **801/636-3600**). Besides the stupendous geology, the

Swell is full of Archaic, Fremont, and Ute rock art and wild horses and burros roam the area. This is a wilderness area—the one-day use stop has toilets and picnic tables. Take plenty of food and water.

The **Wedge Overlook,** also known as Utah's Little Grand Canyon, offers unequalled views of the San Rafael River's deep gorge in the Northern Swell. There are picnic tables, restrooms, and camping areas available at this facility, but no water.

For more information call the **BLM-Price Field Office (*©* 435/636-3600)** or visit www.blm.gov/ut/st/en/fo/price/recreation/SanRafaelDesert.html.

TO THE DINOSAURS OF PRICE & BEYOND

The town of Price, founded in 1879, began as a railroad and coal-mining center. A popular midway stopover for those traveling between southern Utah's national parks and the Salt Lake City area, Price is gaining in reputation as a destination, especially for those interested in dinosaurs.

Price (elevation 5,600 ft.) is 119 miles from Moab and 63 miles from the town of Green River. From I-70 exit 157, follow U.S. 191/6 northwest 57 miles. Take the business loop through the center of town and follow signs to the information center, located in the CEU Prehistoric Museum (see below), to pick up maps and brochures on the area, including a walking-tour brochure to the town's seven buildings listed on the National Register of Historic Places.

For advance information, contact **Castle Country Travel Region** (*©* **435/636-3701**) or visit www.castlecountry.com.

One of the area's top attractions is the excellent **Prehistoric Museum ★★,** 155 E. Main St. (http://usueastern.edu/museum/visit/index; *©* **435/613-5060**), operated by the College of Eastern Utah and USU. Among the exhibits are the huge skeletons of an allosaurus, a Utah raptor, and a strange-looking duck-billed dinosaur known as the prosaurolophus. Watch for the large Colombian mammoth, with its long tusks, which resembles a modern elephant and roamed this area over 10,000 years ago. You'll also see exhibits on the early Native Americans of Utah—describing how they lived and adapted to changing environments—and displays of rare 1,000-year-old clay figures created by the mysterious Fremont people. A variety of interactive exhibits was designed just for kids, including a sandbox where they can do their own paleontological dig. The museum is open Monday through Saturday from 9am to 5pm. It's closed major holidays. Admission costs $6 for adults, $4 for seniors 65 and older, $3 for children 2 to 12, and free for infants 1 and under.

To see more dinosaurs, you need to drive about 32 miles out of town. Designated a National Natural Landmark, the **Cleveland-Lloyd Dinosaur Quarry** contains the densest concentration of Jurassic Age dinosaur bones ever found, as well as the largest known collection of the bones of meat-eating dinosaurs. The visitor center has a complete allosaurus skeletal reconstruction and a stegosaurus wall mount on display. At the quarry itself—enclosed in two metal buildings—from several viewing areas, you can see bones in place where they were found, and sometimes watch scientists at work. Three easy-to-moderate trails, totaling just under 5 miles, are nearby and include a 1.4-mile loop interpretative trail, with a descriptive brochure available at the trailhead, a 1.25-mile round-trip scenic trail to a viewpoint, and a one-way trail of over a mile that branches off the scenic trail and leads to another viewpoint. Leashed pets are permitted, and drinking water, restrooms, and picnic tables are available.

From late March through May, the quarry is open 10am to 5pm Monday to Saturday and noon to 5pm Sunday. From August through October, it's open 10am to 5pm Monday, Thursday, Friday, and Saturday, and noon to 5pm Sunday. It is closed the rest of the year. Admission costs $5 for all those 16 and older, and free for youths 15 and under. For details, contact the BLM office in Price at 125 S. 600 West (www.blm.gov/ut/st/en/fo/price/recreation/quarry.html; ℘ 435/636-3600). To get here from Price, take Utah 10 south-west about 15 miles to Utah 155 south, following dinosaur signs to the quarry. The last 12 miles are on a gravel road; allow about 1 hour from Price.

For a look at the somewhat more recent history of the area, go north of Price 11 miles on U.S. 191/6 to the town of Helper, and follow signs to the **Western Mining and Railroad Museum,** 296 S. Main St. (www.wmrrm.org; ℘ **435/472-3009**). Crammed into the four stories of the old Helper Hotel, built in 1913, are thousands of objects and exhibits illustrating the area's mining and railroad days of the late 1800s and early 1900s. Highlights include a complete jail cell, a simulated coal mine, mine models, wine- and whiskey-making equipment from Prohibition days, pictures of mine disasters, railroad equipment and photos, relics from outlaw Butch Cassidy's exploits in the area, and operating model trains. You can watch a video on the area's history, wander past the early mining equipment, caboose, and railroad snowplow in the outdoor displays, and browse the gift shop. The museum is open Monday through Saturday, 10am to 5pm, from mid-May through mid-September; Tuesday through Saturday, 11am to 4pm, the rest of the year. Admission is free, although donations are welcome.

THE FOUR CORNERS AREA

D espite the thousands of family photos that have been taken at Four Corners—where the borders of Colorado, New Mexico, Arizona, and Utah allegedly meet—this is one of the least interesting features of this area, not to mention that it was discovered in 2009 that the monument marking the spot is off by about 1,800 feet. More importantly, what makes this area fascinating is that it's a major U.S. archaeological center (see the map of Southeast Utah, p. 293). A vast complex of ancient villages dominated this region a thousand years ago. Among the red-brown rocks, abandoned canyons, and flat mesas lies another world, once ruled by the Ancestral Puebloans (also known as the Anasazi) and today largely the domain of the Navajo.

15

Wander among the scenic splendors of Monument Valley, where Navajo people tend sheep and weave rugs, and trace the history of a civilization that vanished more than 7 centuries ago, leaving behind more questions than answers. Those particularly interested in the ancient and modern Native American tribes of the region will want to continue their travels into Arizona, New Mexico, and Colorado. "Frommer's Arizona" and "Frommer's EasyGuide to Colorado" guidebooks can provide additional information.

The southeast corner of Utah is sparsely populated—desolate and deserted, some might say—and you're not going to find your favorite chain motel, fast-food restaurant, or brand of gasoline right around every corner. That's assuming you can even *find* a corner. So, many travelers discover a place they like, rent a room or campsite for a few days, and take day trips. This chapter is laid out using the village of **Bluff** as a base—a series of excursions rings the tiny town. First, you are right in the center of the much-disputed **Bears Ears National Monument** (see p. 333).

After you are settle in, you can head southwest **to Monument Valley** and then northwest to **Natural Bridges National Monument.** Then head east, to **Hovenweep National Monument** and the misplaced **Four Corners Monument.** Finally, this chapter takes you into Colorado, to visit **Mesa Verde National Park,** site of the most impressive cliff dwellings in the United States.

A BASE CAMP IN BLUFF

100 miles S of Moab, 338 miles SE of Salt Lake City

The tiny and very friendly village of Bluff sits near the intersection of U.S. 191 and U.S. 163, with roads leading off toward all the attractions of the Four Corners. Situated on the Trail of the Ancients Scenic Byway, Bluff (elevation 4,320 ft.) is basic. Founded by Mormon pioneers in 1880, the town had already been the site of both Ancestral Puebloan and Navajo occupations. Local businesses distribute a free walking- and biking-tour guide that shows where ancient rock art and archaeological sites are located, and points out the locations of some of Bluff's handsome stone homes and other historic sites from the late 19th century.

For more information on Bluff, check out the website of the **Business Owners of Bluff** (www.bluffutah.org). You can also get information on Bluff and the other southeast Utah communities of Monticello, Mexican Hat, and Monument Valley from **Utah's Canyon Country,** 117 S. Main St. Monticello (www.utahscanyoncountry.com; ✆ **435/587-3235,** ext. 5006). There is no visitor center in Bluff.

White-Water Rafting & Other Organized Tours

Situated along the San Juan River, Bluff is a center for river rafting. **Wild Rivers Expeditions,** 2621 S. Hwy. 191 (www.riversandruins.com; ✆ **435/672-2244),** offers river trips on the San Juan led by archaeology and geology professionals. The expeditions take boaters past dozens of Native American sites, such as the spectacular Butler Wash Petroglyph Panel—a 250-yard-long wall of petroglyphs—plus fascinating rock formations. Trips, offered from March through October, range from a full day to more than a week, with rates starting with a full-day excursion for $199 per adult and $139 per child 15 or younger, including lunch.

Guided tours to scenic areas and archaeological sites such as Cedar Mesa and Comb Ridge are offered by **Far Out Expeditions,** 7th East Street and Mulberry Avenue (www.faroutexpeditions.com; ✆ **435/672-2294**), which also creates custom guided backpacking trips. Day trips run $200 per person for groups of two people; backpacking trips are $295 per person per day for groups of two or three people. Far Out Expeditions also offers lodging (p. 332).

Note that both of the above companies also collect per-person user fees charged by the Bureau of Land Management (BLM).

More to See & Do

In town, check out the remains of **Historic Fort Bluff** and the **Chacoan Ruin** sites, both worthy of a quick stop or detour.

About 2¼ miles west of town is **Sand Island Recreation Site,** operated by the BLM. Located along the San Juan River among cottonwoods, Russian olives, and salt cedar, this area offers boating and fishing. Boaters must obtain river permits in advance, and because there are usually more people wanting permits than there are permits available, a lottery is held in January to determine who gets the permits. Fees are charged, based on the time of year, section of river, and number of people in your party. As early as possible, preferably in December for the following summer, contact the Bureau of Land Management (www.blm.gov/ut; ✆ **435/587-1500** or 435/587-1544 8am–noon Mon–Fri for permits and applications). Nestled between the river and a high rock bluff are picnic tables, vault toilets, and graveled campsites; camping is $10 per night and drinking water is available. Head west from the boat launch to see a number of petroglyphs, some of which can be seen easily on foot; others require a boat to see. Unfortunately, you must have your own boat with you, as there are no nearby places to rent boats.

    Goosenecks State Park (www.stateparks.utah.gov; ✆ **435/678-2238**), set on a rim high above the San Juan, offers spectacular views out over the twisting, turning river some 1,000 feet below. It's named for the sharp turns in the river, which meanders more than 5 miles to progress just 1 linear mile and provides a look straight down through 300 million years of geologic history. (The park also has some Hollywood history: It served as the location for the climactic scene in "Thelma & Louise.") A gravelly open area at the end of the paved road has picnic tables, trashcans, vault toilets, and an observation shelter, but no drinking water. The park is open around the clock and admission is free; primitive camping is permitted at no charge. The park is about 24 miles from Bluff, just off the route to Monument Valley Navajo Tribal Park. Head west on U.S. 163 for about 20 miles, turn north (right) on Utah 261 for about a mile, and then west (left) on Utah 316 for 2½ miles.

    Another worthwhile area attraction is **Valley of the Gods,** a 16-mile driving loop south of Bluff proper, featuring a stunning landscape of isolated red mesas on a flat valley floor below sheer cliffs. It is located 8 miles northwest of Mexican Hat off U.S. 163; there are several hiking trails.

Where to Stay

In addition to the choices below, about 25 miles southwest of Bluff near Mexican Hat, the **San Juan Inn,** U.S. 163 (www.sanjuaninn.net; ✆ **800/447-2022**), is a fairly nondescript roadside motel in a location that's anything but: perched above the San Juan River. Rooms range from a simple yurt ($105) to the three-bedroom Trading Post suite ($375); a double queen is $124. The complex includes a trading post and restaurant.

    Campgrounds include **Cadillac Ranch RV Park,** 640 E. U.S. 191, Bluff (✆ **435/672-2262**), a down-home sort of place on the east side of town with sites around a small pond. It has 14 RV sites—all large pull-throughs—and 10 tent sites plus free Wi-Fi and restrooms with showers. The campground is open year-round, but water is turned off in winter. The cost per site is $23 for tents and $33 for RVs. Showers are $5.

Desert Rose Inn ★★   Built in 1999, this imposing lodge-style building offers a mix of accommodation, including simple doubles, suites with king beds and separate living rooms (some with wraparound porches), and slightly more rustic cabins, each with a large walk-in shower (no tubs), one king bed and a sofa sleeper, fridge and microwave, knotty pine walls and ceilings, a porch, and cathedral ceiling with exposed beams. Smoking is not permitted.

701 W. U.S. 191 (Main. St.), Bluff. www.desertroseinn.com. (C) **435/672-2303.** 35 units. Free Wi-Fi. $169–$199 double, $119–$149 cabin. Call for seasonal rates. **Amenities:** Restaurant; heated indoor pool; fitness center; free Wi-Fi.

Far Out Guest House ★ This restored historic home has two bedrooms, decorated in Southwestern style, with artwork and photos depicting scenes of the area. Each room has six bunk beds and a private bathroom. Both share a comfortable living room, screened porch, and fully equipped kitchen. Smoking is not permitted. The house is operated by Far Out Expeditions (p. 330), which offers day tours and backcountry trips led by local owner and renowned guide Vaughn Hadenfeldt.

7th East St. and Mulberry Ave., Bluff. www.faroutexpeditions.com. (C) **435/672-2294.** 2 units. $90 for 1–2 people; $100 for 3–4 people; $110 for 5–6 people; $200 for the entire house.

Recapture Lodge ★ Western decor and a nature trail that follows the San Juan River along the back of the property set this motel apart. Located on the main street near the center of town the double rooms have no air-conditioning but do contain evaporative cooling; several budget units, each with one double bed, are also available.

220 E. U.S. 191, Bluff. www.recapturelodge.com. (C) **435/672-2281.** 26 units. $98 double. Rates include continental breakfast. **Amenities:** Heated outdoor pool (May–Oct); hot tub; firepit; BBQ grills.

Where to Eat

Cottonwood Steakhouse ★★ This Old West–style restaurant—think lots of wood and a handsome stone fireplace—knows what to do with beef and buffalo (not to mention homemade pie). Grilled chicken or ribs, shrimp, and catfish are accompanied by salads, grilled potatoes, and beans. In warm weather, diners can sit at picnic tables outside under cottonwood trees. Beer is available.

U.S. 191 on the west side of town (Main and 4th St. E). www.cottonwoodsteakhouse. com. (C) **435/672-2282.** Main courses $13–$28. Apr–Oct daily 5:30–9:30pm. Closed in winter.

Twin Rocks Café ★ In the shadow of the prominent Twin Rocks formation, the cafe has an open, airy dining room with large windows offering views of the surrounding red-rock walls. The selections range from half-pound burgers to vegetarian specialties. You can also choose from a variety of sandwiches, steak, and chicken dishes. But best to try the regional dishes—the sheepherder's sandwich, Navajo taco, and beef stew with Navajo fry bread, a thick, deep-fried bread. You can also mix your cultures with a Navajo pizza— a variety of toppings served on Navajo fry bread. Besides the standards the breakfast menu offers a spicy breakfast burrito. Microbrews and other beers are available with meals. While you're there, be sure to check out the museum-quality American Indian arts and crafts at Twin Rocks Trading Post, under the same management, next door.

913 E. Navajo Twins Dr. (off U.S. 191, on the east end of town). www.twinrockscafe.com. © **435/672-2341.** Lunch and dinner entrees $9–$22. Summer daily 7am–9pm; slightly reduced hours in winter.

BEARS EARS NATIONAL MONUMENT

At the end of 2016, President Barack Obama established this national monument, setting aside the 1,351,849 acres of land that had long been held as sacred or significant by a number of the region's Native American tribes. One year later, President Donald Trump reduced the scale of the monument by 85% to 201,876 acres, a move that quickly led to bitter disputes at the federal, state, and local level, ongoing at the time of writing.

A pair of buttes, nearly 9,000 high, inspired the local tribes to call the area Bears Ears, each in their own language. Still largely undeveloped, Bears Ears is managed by a coalition of BLM and United States Forest Service and five local Native American tribes: the Navajo Nation, Hopi, Ute Mountain Ute, Ute Indian Tribe of the Uintah and Ouray Reservation, and the Pueblo of Zuni. The hundreds of archaeological sites in the monument had been looted of their Ancestral Puebloan artifacts for many years and unregulated off-road vehicle use has damaged the natural landscape and archaeological sites.

GETTING THERE Located west of the towns of Blanding, Monticello, and Bluff and north of Mexican Hat in San Juan County, Bears Ears is 5 hours from Salt Lake City International Airport, 3 hours from the regional airport in Grand Junction, Colorado, and 30 minutes north of Monument Valley Navajo Tribal Park.

There is no official visitors center, so your best bet for information is at the **Kane Gulch BLM Ranger Station** on Utah Highway 261 (© **435/587-1500**), 36 miles west of Blanding and about 4 miles south of Hwy. 95. The office is open from March 1 to June 15 and September 1 to October 31, daily from 8am to noon.

WHEN TO GO Like most of southern Utah, spring and fall are the best times to visit, with the caveat that spring rains can make hiking hazardous and turn the mostly dirt roads in the monument to undrivable mud. July and August heat can exceed 100°F (38°C) in some areas, and there are also monsoons, which can bring flash floods. Much of this area is high desert country, often exceeding 6,000 feet about sea level. Bring plenty of water.

WHAT TO SEE Mule Canyon requires a hiking permit, which is available at the trailhead. Advance reservations for overnight trips in the Bears Ears area may be obtained on recreation.gov or at the Kane Gulch Ranger Station.

Valley of the Gods

Technically outside the new boundaries of the Bears Ears, Valley of the Gods features tall, isolated mesas, buttes, and cliffs reminiscent of a scattered red sandstone Stonehenge. Hiking trails are undeveloped and you can see a lot from your car, though if it's wet, you may need a 4x4. Begin your drive at either the west entrance (Highway 261) or the east (Highway 163)—the direction of travel doesn't matter. Feel free to get out of the car and explore at any location you choose (park at pull-offs). No off-road travel is allowed.

House on Fire, one of the most popular cliff dwellings in the area, is within the boundaries of Bears Ears National Monument—on Highway 95 between Blanding and Natural Bridges in the South Fork of Mule Canyon. It's a quarter- mile drive on well-maintained native-surface road, then a short hike, 3 miles round trip. It's called House on Fire because in the morning the sunlight makes the ruin look like it's glowing with flames.

MONUMENT VALLEY NAVAJO TRIBAL PARK ★★

50 miles SW of Bluff; 150 miles S of Moab; 395 miles S of Salt Lake City; 160 miles W of Cortez, Colorado

For most of us, Monument Valley *is* the Old West. You've seen it dozens of times in movie theaters, on television, and in magazine and billboard advertisements. In 1938, Harry Goulding, who had been operating a trading post for local Navajo for about 15 years, convinced Hollywood director John Ford that Ford's current project, "Stagecoach," should be shot in Monument Valley. Released the following year, "Stagecoach" not only put Monument Valley on the map, but it also launched the career of a little-known actor by the name of John Wayne.

Ford and other Hollywood directors were attracted to Monument Valley by the same elements that draw visitors today. This is the genuine, untamed American West, with a simple, unspoiled beauty of carved stone, blowing sand, and rich colors—no special effects necessary. The same erosive forces of wind and water carved the surrounding scenic wonders of the Grand Canyon, Glen Canyon, and the rest of the spectacular red-rock country of southern Utah and northern Arizona. But here the result is different: Colors seem deeper, natural rock bridges are almost perfect circles, and the vast emptiness of the land around them gives the towering stone monoliths an unequaled sense of drama and wildness.

Essentials

Operated as a tribal park by the Navajo Nation (the country's largest tribe), Monument Valley (elevation 5,200 ft.) straddles the border of southeast Utah and northeast Arizona. U.S. 163 goes through the valley from north to south, and a tribal park access road runs east to west.

GETTING THERE   From Moab, Monticello, and most points in eastern Utah, take U.S. 191 south to Bluff, turn west (right), and follow U.S. 163 to Monument Valley. An alternative is to turn off Utah 95 south onto Utah 261 just east of Natural Bridges National Monument, follow Utah 261 to U.S. 163, turn southwest, and follow U.S. 163 to Monument Valley. This latter route is quite scenic, but because of switchbacks and steep grades it is not recommended for motor homes or vehicles with trailers. Those coming from Arizona can take east-west U.S. 160 to U.S. 163, turn north, and follow it into Monument Valley.

INFORMATION/VISITOR CENTER   The **visitor center/museum** is located about 4 miles east of U.S. 163 on the Monument Valley access road. It contains a viewing deck, exhibits on the geology and human history of the valley, restrooms, drinking water, a gift shop, and a restaurant that serves Navajo and American dishes for all three meals daily.

For additional information, try **Monument Valley Navajo Tribal Park** (utah.com/monument-valley; ✆ **435/727-5874** or 727-5870) and the **Navajo Nation Parks and Recreation Department** (www.navajonationparks.org; ✆ **928/871-6647**).

HOURS, FEES & REGULATIONS   The tribal park is open daily; fro April through September it's open from 6am to 8pm and October through March it's open from 8am to 5 pm. The tribal park is closed Christmas, New Year's Day, and Thanksgiving).

Admission is $20 per vehicle, $10 per walk-in, bicycle, or motorcycle; free for children 9 and under. *Note:* The park is operated by the Navajo Nation and not the U.S. government, so federal interagency passes are not accepted.

Because the park is part of the Navajo Nation, laws here differ somewhat from those in Utah, in Arizona, or on public lands. All alcoholic beverages are prohibited within the boundaries of the Navajo reservation. Visitors must stay on the self-guided Valley Drive unless accompanied by an approved guide, and rock climbing and cross-country hiking are prohibited. Although photography for personal use is permitted, permission is required to photograph Navajo residents and their property, and you will usually need to pay them.

Both Utah and Arizona are on Mountain Time, and although the state of Arizona does not recognize daylight saving time, the Navajo Nation does.

Exploring Monument Valley by Car

Driving the **17-mile self-guided loop** lets you see most of the major scenic attractions of Monument Valley Navajo Tribal Park at your own pace, and at the lowest cost. The dirt road is a bit rough—not recommended for low-slung sports cars or vehicles longer than 24 feet, although it is passable for smaller motor homes. The road's first half-mile is the worst, and you have to drive it both at the beginning and end of the loop. There are no restrooms, drinking water, or other facilities along the route, and motorists should watch for livestock. Allow about 2 hours.

A brochure (free) and a more detailed booklet (fee) provide rough maps and information on 11 numbered sites, such as the **Mittens**—rock formations that resemble (you guessed it) a pair of mittens—and the aptly named **Elephant** and **Camel** buttes, **Totem Pole,** and the **Thumb.** You'll also see **Yei Bi Chei,** a rock formation that resembles a Navajo holy man, and **John Ford Point,** one of famed Hollywood director John Ford's favorite filming locations, where he shot scenes from "Stagecoach," "The Searchers," and "Cheyenne Autumn." It's still popular with producers—watch for crews working on feature films, TV shows, or commercials.

Guided tours are the best way to see Monument Valley—without a guide, visitors are restricted to the 17-mile scenic drive, but **Navajo guides** ★ can take you into lesser-visited areas of the tribal park, give you their personal perspectives, and often arrange weaving demonstrations and other activities. Inquire at the visitor center for the types of tours (including the possibility of a sunset tour) currently available.

Tours are also available from **Goulding's** (see below), with differing rates for basic tours, sunrise or sunset tours, all-day tours, and full moon tours. Discounts apply for children 8 and under. Their prices include the park admission fee.

You can also see Monument Valley by horseback with Navajo-owned-and-operated **Roy Black's Monument Valley Tours** (www.royblacksmonument valleytours.com; ✆ **928/429-0637** or 505/701-9609). Prices are about $80 per person for a 90-minute trail ride and $200 per person for a 6-hour ride; riders also have to pay the monument entrance fee.

More to See & Do

There is one hike you can take without a guide, the 3.2-mile **Wildcat Trail** around West Mitten Butte. Bring water and expect the hike to take about 2 hours.

Goulding's Trading Post Museum, at Goulding's Lodge (see "Where to Stay & Eat," below), is the original Monument Valley trading post opened by Harry and Leona (Mike) Goulding in 1924; it served as their home as well as a trading post for many years. Furnished much as it was in the 1920s and 1930s, the museum contains exhibits of Goulding family memorabilia, old photos of the area, Navajo and Ancestral Puebloan artifacts and crafts, and posters and other items from movies that were filmed at the trading post and in Monument Valley. It's open year-round (call the lodge for hours); a $2 donation is requested, and goes toward scholarships for local children. Allow a half-hour. Nearby, a more modern trading post sells souvenirs, books, videos, and top-quality American Indian arts and crafts.

The **Earth Spirit Theater,** next to Goulding's Lodge (p. 337), shows a rotation of films including a 20-minute show on the valley's history and geology, utilizing magnificent photos of the area and classic movies that used Monument Valley as a setting—yes, that means lots of John Wayne. Showings are $2 per person, and free for those who also take a Monument Valley tour with Goulding's.

Camping

Primitive **camping** in the park (meaning no running water, only portable restrooms) is operated by the tribal park administration (p. 335).

Goulding's Monument Valley Campground (www.gouldings.com; _©_ 435/727-3231), on the Monument Valley access road about 3 miles west of its intersection with U.S. 163, offers splendid views, plus full RV hookups including cable TV, an indoor heated swimming pool, modern restrooms with showers, a playground, a self-serve laundry, and a large convenience store. The campground is open year-round, but with limited services from November to mid-March. Tent sites cost $30, RV sites start at $57, and cabins are $139, with discounts in winter.

Where to Stay & Eat

View Hotel (www.monumentvalleyview.com; _©_ 435/727-5555), the Navajo-owned hotel located within the Navajo Nation and the Navajo Tribal park at Monument Valley, offers a contemporary take on local heritage. It's perched on the bluff next to the park's visitor center and the architecture blends into the red-rock country. Every room has a private balcony with a drop-dead view of the Mittens and other valley landmarks. Rooms are modern, with flatscreen TVs, fridges, and other amenities. The property features an upscale restaurant that serves three meals a day, in-house guide service, and a trading post stocked with Navajo blankets and jewelry. Rooms range from $178 to $411, depending on the season, plus the room's type and location.

Goulding's Lodge (www.gouldings.com; _©_ 800/874-0902 or 435/727-3231), on the Monument Valley access road about 2 miles west of its intersection with U.S. 163, has 63 modern motel rooms, each with Southwestern decor and flatscreen TVs; suites and houses add bedrooms, living space, and kitchens. The Lodge has a small indoor heated pool and a restaurant serving three meals daily—American cuisine plus traditional Navajo dishes, with dinner prices in the $10-to $30 range. Room rates for two are $217 to $260 with reduced rates the rest of the year.

NATURAL BRIDGES NATIONAL MONUMENT

60 miles NW of Bluff, 360 miles S of Salt Lake City

Utah's first National Park Service area, Natural Bridges was designated primarily to show off and protect its three outstanding natural rock bridges, carved by streams and other forms of erosion beginning some 10,000 to 15,000 years ago. You can see the bridges from roadside viewpoints, take individual hikes to each one, or hike a loop trail that connects all three.

Giant **Sipapu Bridge** is considered a "mature" bridge. It's 220 feet high, with a span of 268 feet, and is believed to be the second-largest natural bridge in the world, after Rainbow Bridge in nearby Glen Canyon National

Recreation Area. **Owachomo Bridge,** which appears to be on the brink of collapse (then again, it could stand for centuries more), is the smallest of the three at 106 feet high, with a span of 180 feet. **Kachina Bridge,** 210 feet high with a span of 204 feet, is the thickest of the monument's bridges at 93 feet.

All three bridges were given Hopi names: Sipapu means "gateway to the spirit world" in Hopi legend; Owachomo is Hopi for "rock mound," so called for a rounded sandstone formation atop one side of the bridge; and Kachina was named as such because rock art on the bridge resembles decorations found on traditional Hopi kachina dolls.

Essentials

Natural Bridges National Monument is about 40 miles west of Blanding, 60 miles northwest of Bluff, 43 miles north of Mexican Hat, and about 50 miles east of Glen Canyon National Recreation Area's Hite or Halls Crossing marinas.

GETTING THERE   Natural Bridges is located in southeast Utah, off scenic Utah 95 via Utah 275. From Monument Valley, follow U.S. 163 north to Utah 261 (just past Mexican Hat); at Utah 95, go west to Utah 275 and the Monument. Beware, though: Utah 261, although a pretty drive, has 10% grades and numerous steep switchbacks. It's not recommended for motor homes, those towing trailers, or anyone who's afraid of heights. The less adventurous and RV-bound should stick to the approach from the east, via Utah 95.

Make sure you have enough fuel for the trip to Natural Bridges; the closest gas stations are at least 40 miles away in Mexican Hat or Blanding. In fact, no services of any kind can be found within 40 miles of the monument.

INFORMATION/VISITOR CENTER   For a park brochure and other information, write or call **Natural Bridges National Monument,** HC 60 Box 1, Lake Powell, UT 84533-0101 (www.nps.gov/nabr; ✆ **435/692-1234,** ext. 16).

A **visitor center** at the park entrance is open daily spring through fall from 9am to 5pm (closed on Tues–Wed in winter) and features exhibits and a video program on bridge formation, the human history of the area, and the monument's plants and wildlife. Rangers are available to advise you about hiking trails and scheduled activities. The visitor center is the only place in the monument where you can get drinking water.

FEES & REGULATIONS   Entry to the monument is $15 per vehicle, $7 on foot or bicycle, $10 for motorcycle. Regulations are similar to those in most areas administered by the National Park Service, with an emphasis on protecting the natural resources. Be especially careful not to damage any of the fragile archaeological sites in the monument; climbing on the natural bridges is prohibited. Overnight backpacking is not permitted within the monument, and vehicles may not be left unattended overnight. Because parking at the overlooks and trail heads is limited, anyone towing trailers or extra vehicles is asked to leave them at the visitor center parking lot. Pets must be leashed and are not allowed on trails or in buildings.

SEASONS/AVOIDING THE CROWDS Although the monument is open year-round, winters can be a bit harsh at this 6,500-foot elevation; the weather is best between late April and October. Because trailhead parking is limited and most people visit in June, July, and August, the best months to see the park, if your schedule permits, are May, September, and October.

RANGER PROGRAMS Guided hikes and walks, evening campground programs, and talks at the visitor center patio are presented from spring through fall. Schedules are posted at the visitor center.

Seeing the Highlights

Natural Bridges National Monument probably won't be your major vacation destination, but you can easily spend a half- or full day, or even 2 days, here. For those who want to take a quick look, stop at the visitor center for a brief introduction, and then take the 9-mile loop drive to the various natural bridge overlooks. Those with the time and the inclination might also take an easy hike down to Owachomo Bridge; it's just a half-hour walk.

Outdoor Pursuits

Hiking is the number-one activity here. From the trailheads, you can hike separately to each of the bridges, or start at one and do a loop hike to all three. Be prepared for summer afternoon thunderstorms that can cause flash flooding. Although the possibility of encountering a rattlesnake is very small, you should still watch carefully. During the hot summers, all hikers should wear hats and other protective clothing, use sunscreen, and carry a gallon of water per person for all but the shortest walks.

The easiest hike—more of a walk—leads to **Owachomo Bridge** (½ mile round-trip), with an elevation gain of 180 feet. Look toward the eastern horizon to see the twin buttes named Bear's Ears. Allow a half-hour.

The Sipapu and Kachina Bridge trails are both considered moderately strenuous—allocate about 1 hour for each. The trek to **Sipapu Bridge** has a 500-foot elevation change, climbing two flights of stairs with three ladders and handrails on a 1.2-mile round-trip trail. This is the steepest trail in the park, and it ends with a splendid view of the bridge about halfway down. The hike takes about 1 hour.

The 1.5-mile round-trip hike to massive **Kachina Bridge** has a 400-foot elevation change, descending steep slickrock with handrails. Under the bridge is a pile of rocks that fell in June 1992, slightly enlarging the bridge opening. Allow about 1 hour.

Those planning to hike the **loop to all three bridges** can start at any of the trailheads, although rangers recommend starting at Owachomo. The round-trip, including your walk back across the mesa, is about 9 miles. Although the trails from the rim to the canyon bottom can be steep, the walk along the bottom is easy.

Camping

A primitive 13-site campground has pit toilets, tables, tent pads, and fire grates, but no drinking water, showers, or other facilities. It's limited to vehicles no more than 26 feet long, and only one vehicle is allowed per site. Cost is $15; sites are allotted on a first-come, first-served basis.

HOVENWEEP NATIONAL MONUMENT ★★

35 miles NE of Bluff; 122 miles S of Moab; 366 miles SE of Salt Lake City; 42 miles W of Cortez, Colorado

Hovenweep is the Ute/Paiute word for "deserted valley," appropriate because Hovenweep's 1,250 inhabitants apparently left around A.D. 1300. Located along the Colorado-Utah border, Hovenweep contains six separate sites with some of the most striking (and most isolated) **archaeological sites ★★** in the Four Corners area. These include castle-like towers, cliff dwellings, a kiva (a circular underground ceremonial chamber), stone rooms, walls, and petroglyphs.

Essentials

No lodging, food, gasoline, supplies, or even public phones are available in the national monument; but there are bathrooms with running water. The closest motels and restaurants are in Bluff (p. 330) and Blanding, Utah, or Cortez, Colorado.

GETTING THERE   You can get to Hovenweep's Square Tower Site, where the visitor center is located, via paved roads from either Colorado or Utah. From Utah, follow U.S. 191, southeastern Utah's major north-south route, to Utah 262, between the towns of Blanding and Bluff. Head east on Utah 262 to Hatch Trading Post; then, watching for signs, follow paved roads to the monument. One option is to take Utah 163 east from Bluff toward the village of Aneth, turn north (left) onto an unnamed paved road, and follow signs to the monument.

From Cortez, Colorado, follow U.S. 491 (formerly U.S. 666) north to the community of Pleasant View and turn west (left) onto newly paved road, following signs to the monument.

VISITOR INFORMATION   For more information or questions about current road conditions call **Hovenweep National Monument** at ℭ **970/562-4282** or visit www.nps.gov/hove.

FEES, HOURS, REGULATIONS & SAFETY   Entry to the national monument is $6 per vehicle or $3 per person. The monument is open 24 hours a day, but trails are open from sunrise to sunset only. The visitor center, with exhibits, restrooms, and drinking water, is open daily from 9am to 5pm (closed Tues–Wed in winter).

Regulations are much the same here as at most National Park Service properties, with an emphasis on taking care not to damage archaeological sites. Summer temperatures can reach 100°F (38°C) and water supplies are limited; bring your own and carry a canteen, even on short walks. In late spring, gnats can be a real nuisance, so bring insect repellent. Leashed dogs are permitted on trails.

Exploring the Monument

Hovenweep is noted for its mysterious and impressive 20-foot-tall sandstone towers, some of them square, others oval, circular, or D-shaped. Built by the Ancestral Puebloans (also known as Anasazi), the solid towers have small windows up and down the masonry sides. Archaeologists have suggested myriad possible uses for these structures—their guesses range from guard towers to celestial observatories, ceremonial structures to water towers or granaries. In addition to the towers, the monument contains the remains of cliff dwellings and a kiva, petroglyphs, stone rooms, walls, and a reconstructed dam.

Your walk among the 700-year-old buildings will take you through yucca, cactus, saltbush, juniper, and even some cottonwood trees. Watch for lizards, snakes, rabbits, hawks, ravens, and an occasional deer or fox.

The **Square Tower Site,** where the visitor center is located, should be your first stop. The other five sites are difficult to find, and you'll need to get detailed driving directions and check on current road conditions before setting out. Be aware that GPS units may lead you astray. Use maps. (Ask about the Cajon site, a great place to snap sunset photos.)

At the Square Tower Site, the 2-mile **Square Tower self-guided trail** is a loop, the first part of which is paved and suitable for wheelchairs with assistance. The trail winds past the remains of ancient Puebloan buildings, including the impressive **Hovenweep Castle,** probably built around A.D. 1200. Once home to several families, this site contains two D-shaped towers plus additional rooms. A trail guide, based at the visitor center, discusses the ruins and identifies desert plants used for food, clothing, and medicine. Allow about 2 hours.

Camping

The 31-site Hovenweep Campground, at the Square Tower Site, is open year-round. It has restrooms, drinking water, picnic tables, and fire grills, but no showers or RV hookups. Most sites will accommodate short trailers and motor homes under 36 feet in length. Cost is $15 per night; reservations are not accepted, but the campground rarely fills, even during the peak summer season.

FOUR CORNERS MONUMENT

Operated as a Navajo Tribal Park (with the Colorado section owned by the Ute Mountain Tribe), a flat monument marks the spot where Utah, Colorado, New Mexico, and Arizona meet—or were thought to have met, until a 2009 survey found the marker to be up to 2½ miles away from the true intersection of the four states—on which visitors can pose for photos. Official seals of the four states are displayed, along with the motto FOUR STATES HERE MEET IN FREE-DOM UNDER GOD. Surrounding the monument are the flags of the four states, the Navajo Nation and Ute tribes, and the United States. Despite its inaccurate location, which it owes to an 1868 survey, it's still legally recognized as the intersection of the four states (so says the Supreme Court), and makes for a good photo opportunity.

There are often crafts demonstrations here, and jewelry, pottery, sand paintings, and other crafts are for sale, along with T-shirts and other souvenirs. In addition, traditional Navajo food, such as fry bread, is available, and a small visitor center offers information on visiting the Navajo Nation.

A half-mile northwest of U.S. 160, the monument is open daily from 7am to 8pm from May through September and 8am to 5pm the rest of the year. It's closed on Thanksgiving, Christmas, and New Year's Day. Entry costs $5 per person. For information, contact the **Navajo Nation Parks and Recreation Department** (www.navajonationparks.org; ℭ **928/871-6647**). Allow a half-hour.

EAST TO COLORADO & AN ARCHAEOLOGICAL PRESERVE

The Four Corners region was once a bustling metropolis, the home of the Ancestral Puebloan people (also called Anasazi). The single best place to explore this ancient culture is Mesa Verde National Park.

Mesa Verde National Park ★★★

Mesa Verde National Park (www.nps.gov/meve; ℭ **970/529-4465**) is the only U.S. national park devoted entirely to the works of humans. And it's the largest **archaeological preserve** in the United States. More than 5,000 known sites dating from A.D. 600 to 1300 can be found here, including the most impressive cliff dwellings in the Southwest.

The earliest-known inhabitants of Mesa Verde (Spanish for "green table") built subterranean pit houses on the mesa tops. During the 13th century, they moved into shallow alcoves and constructed complex cliff dwellings. These homes were obviously a massive construction project, yet the residents occupied them for only about a century, leaving in about 1300 for reasons as yet undetermined.

The area was little known until ranchers Charlie Mason and Richard Wetherill chanced upon it in 1888. Looting of artifacts followed their discovery until a Denver newspaper reporter's stories aroused national interest in protecting the site. The 52,000-acre site was declared a national park in 1906.

A series of lightning-sparked fires has blackened over 50% of the park since 2000, closing it for several weeks one summer. Officials said that although the park's piñon-juniper forests were severely burned, none of the major archaeological sites were damaged. In fact, the fires uncovered some sites that officials were not aware existed.

ESSENTIALS

The park entrance is about 10 miles east of Cortez, Colorado; 56 miles east of Hovenweep National Monument; 125 miles east of Bluff; and 390 miles southeast of Salt Lake City. Admission to the park for up to 1 week for private vehicles is $20 from May through October, and $15 the rest of the year; motorcyclists and bicyclists pay $10 and $16 for the same periods; and individuals pay $7 year-round.

The LEED-certified (Leadership in Energy and Environmental Design) **Mesa Verde Visitor and Research Center,** located at the park entrance about 15 miles off U.S. 160, is the park's primary facility for orienting visitors to opportunities within the park and surrounding area. It also houses a state-of-the-art research and storage facility for more than 3 million artifacts. It's open daily, from early January to early April, from 8:30am to 4:30pm; from early April to late May 8am to 5pm; early September to early November from 8:30am to 5pm; and from early November to early December from 8:30am to 4:30pm. **Chapin Mesa,** site of the park headquarters, a museum, and a post office, is 21 miles south of the park entrance on U.S. 160. The **Chapin Mesa Museum,** open daily year-round January to early March, 9am to 4:30 pm; early March to early April, 9 am to 5pm; early April to mid October, 8am to 6:30pm; mid October to early November, 8 am to 5pm; early November to late December, 9am to 5pm), also houses artifacts and specimens related to the history of the area.

The cliff dwellings can be viewed daily, and, in summer, rangers give evening programs at Morefield Campground. In winter, many facilities are closed; check the website for updates. Food, gas, and lodging are generally available in the park from mid-April to mid-October only.

SEEING THE HIGHLIGHTS

Balcony House, Cliff Palace, and Long House can be seen up close only on ranger-led tours, which are offered only during the warmer months; tickets ($5) are available at the park visitor center and the Colorado Welcome Center at Cortez (see below). You must purchase tickets in person and in advance. The **Cliff Palace,** the park's largest and best-known site, is a four-story apartment complex with stepped-back roofs forming porches for the dwellings above. Its towers, walls, and kivas are all set back beneath the rim of a cliff. Rangers lead a twilight tour for $20 per person. Climbing a 32-foot ladder permits exploration of **Balcony House,** while **Long House,** on Wetherill Mesa, is the second-largest cliff dwelling at Mesa Verde.

From late spring through early fall, rangers lead **bus tours** that include a few short hikes to archeological sites along Mesa Top Loop Road and a hiking tour of Cliff Palace. The 4-hour **700 Years Tour** (Apr 13–Oct 23) a morning trip that costs $55 for adults, $33 for children under 12. The **Classic Pueblo Tour** is a 3½-hour afternoon tour that costs $35 for adults and $18 for children under 12. Tour tickets are available at Far View Lodge, Far View Terrace, Morefield Campground Store, and online at **www.visitmesaverde.com.**

Spruce Tree House, another of the major cliff-dwelling complexes, has been closed indefinitely for safety reasons.

Although the draw here is ancient cliff dwellings rather than outdoor recreation, you will have to hike and climb to reach the sites. None of the trails are strenuous, but the 7,000-foot elevation can make the treks tiring for visitors who aren't accustomed to the altitude. To avoid hiking and climbing, the **Mesa Top Loop Road** is a 6-mile loop that offers access to 12 different pit houses and cliff-side overlooks. If you'd really like to stretch your legs and get away from the crowds, however, take one of the longer **hikes** into scenic Spruce Canyon, but you must register at the ranger's office before setting out.

WHERE TO STAY & EAT

Only one lodging facility, Far View Lodge (see below), is actually in the park and it features two restaurants and a bar. The company that runs the lodge also operates two other restaurants in the park—one near the campground and another near Chapin Mesa Museum. Numerous lodging and dining possibilities are in nearby Cortez. Stop at the **Colorado Welcome Center at Cortez,** Cortez City Park, 928 E. Main St. (ⓒ **970/565-3414**) for info; it's open Thursday through Tuesday from 8am to 5pm in summer, with shorter hours the rest of the year and closed Thanksgiving, Christmas, New Year's Day, and Easter. **Mesa Verde Country Visitor Information Bureau** (www. mesaverdecountry.com; ⓒ **970/565-8227**) and the **Cortez Area Chamber of Commerce** (www.cortezchamber.org; ⓒ **970/565-3414**) can also help. See "Frommer's EasyGuide to Colorado" for lodging and dining choices in the Cortez area.

Far View Lodge ★★   Right in the heart of Mesa Verde National Park, Far View offers not only the most convenient location for visiting the park, but also the best views of any accommodations in the area. The facility lodges guests in 17 separate buildings spread across a hilltop. Rooms aren't fancy, and some are a bit on the small side, but all have Southwestern decor and great views. The upscale Kiva rooms boast handcrafted furniture, CD players, and other amenities. There are no TVs, but each unit has a private balcony and the views are magnificent in all directions. All rooms are nonsmoking.

Mesa Verde National Park. www.visitmesaverde.com. ⓒ **800/449-2288.** 150 units. $141–double; $448 Kiva room. Open seasonally (roughly mid-Apr through Oct). **Amenities:** 2 restaurants; free Wi-Fi.

CAMPING

Morefield Village, an area of Mesa Verde's **Morefield Campground** (www. visitmesaverde.com; ⓒ **800/449-2288**), has 365 sites, including 15 with full RV hookups. It's about 4 miles south of the park entrance station on the main park road (Colo. 10). It's open roughly from mid-April through mid-October, but call or check the website to confirm dates.

The campground is set in rolling hills in a grassy area with scrub oak and brush. The attractive sites are fairly well spaced and mostly separated by trees and other foliage. Facilities include picnic tables and grills, modern restrooms, coin-operated showers and laundry (not within easy walking distance of most campsites), a convenience store, and an RV dump station. Tent sites cost $30 per night, and full hookup sites cost $40 per night. Reservations are accepted.

PLANNING YOUR TRIP TO UTAH

A t one time Utah was known for its polygamous past and its alcohol-free present—when people saw pictures of Rainbow Bridge or powdered slopes, they thought they were looking at Arizona or Colorado. But Utah has come into its own. The economic and demographic boom that started with the 2002 Winter Olympics has continued. But this wide-open state is unlike any place else on earth. Take the time, and drive the extra mile.

Utah is an easy state to visit—roads are good and generally uncrowded, and you can often expect to pay less for food and lodging than you would in other parts of the country. But once you leave the Wasatch Front—the area around Salt Lake City, Ogden, and Provo—distances between towns are long, with few services along the way. Plan your trip carefully and make reservations far in advance for popular areas such as the national parks, and for popular times, such as ski season.

The presence and influence of the Mormon Church—officially known as the Church of Jesus Christ of Latter-day Saints (LDS)—makes visiting Utah a unique experience, from ordering an alcoholic beverage to visiting a historic home with two identical bedrooms—one for each wife. To learn more about modern Mormonism, as well as Utah's history in general, see chapter 2, "Utah in Depth."

GETTING THERE

BY PLANE Utah's only major airport is Salt Lake City International Airport (www.slcairport.com; ✆ **800/595-2442** or 801/575-2400), located just north of I-80 at exit 115, on the west side of the city. Its airport code is SLC. And it's in the middle of an expansion, so watch out for the orange traffic cones.

Airlines serving Salt Lake City include **American Airlines** (www.aa.com), **Delta Air Lines** (www.delta.com), **Frontier Airlines** (www.frontierairlines.com), **JetBlue Airways** (www.

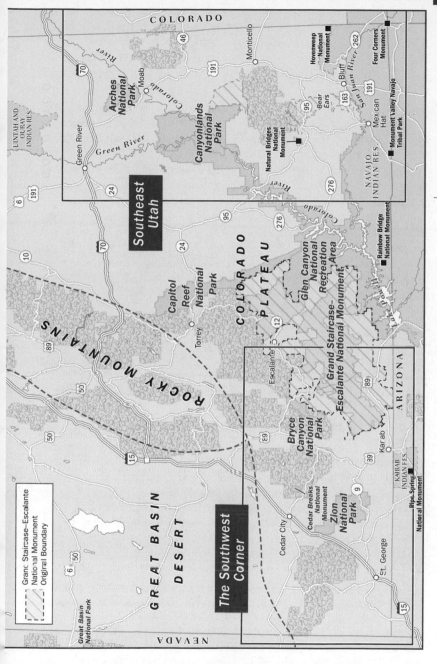

347

jetblue.com), **Southwest Airlines** (www.southwest.com), and **United Airlines** (www.united.com).

An alternative for visitors planning to go to southern Utah is to fly into **McCarran International Airport** in Las Vegas, Nevada (www.mccarran.com; ☏ **702/261-5211**), which is only 120 miles southwest of St. George. Budget-conscious travelers should check airline and vehicle-rental prices at both airports to see which will provide the better deal for their particular circumstances.

BY CAR About 80% of Utah's visitors arrive by car, in part because it's so easy: The state is accessed by **I-80** from the west or east, **I-70** from the east, **I-15** and **I-84** from the north, and **I-15** from the southwest. Salt Lake City is 600 miles from Albuquerque, 500 miles from Denver, 430 miles from Las Vegas, and 650 miles from Phoenix. Keep in mind that there will be long distances between services —especially on Sundays—when traveling in and around Utah.

International visitors should note that insurance and taxes are almost never included in quoted rental car rates in the U.S. Be sure to ask your rental agency about any additional fees. They can add a significant cost to your car rental. While the minimum age for driving in Utah is 16, many car-rental agencies will not rent a vehicle to anyone under 25 years of age; others have a minimum age of 21.

BY TRAIN There are four Amtrak stations in Utah along the **California Zephyr** line, which runs from Chicago to Emeryville, California: Salt Lake City, Provo, Helper, and Green River. Call ☏ **800/872-7245** or visit www.amtrak.com for details. In state, **Trax** runs in metro Salt Lake City, and the **FrontRunner** train connects Salt Lake City, Provo, the airport and Ogden. Call ☏ **888/743-3882,** or visit www.rideuta.com for additional information.

GETTING AROUND

BY PLANE Attention visitors to the U.S. from abroad: Some major airlines offer transatlantic or transpacific passengers special discount tickets under the name Visit USA, which allows mostly one-way travel from one U.S. destination to another at very low prices. Unavailable in the U.S., these discount tickets must be purchased abroad in conjunction with your international fare. This system is the easiest, fastest, cheapest way to see the country. Inquire with your air carrier.

BY CAR The best way to see Utah is by car—you simply can't get to many of its iconic sites any other way.

Before you set out on a road trip, you might want to join the **American Automobile Association** (**AAA;** www.csaa.com for Northern California, Nevada, and Utah information; ☏ **800/222-4357**), which has hundreds of offices nationwide. The Salt Lake City office is located at 560 E. 500 South (☏ **800/541-9902** or 801/364-5615), and is open Monday through Friday from 8:30am to 5:30pm. AAA also has offices in Ogden (☏ **801/476-1666**), Orem

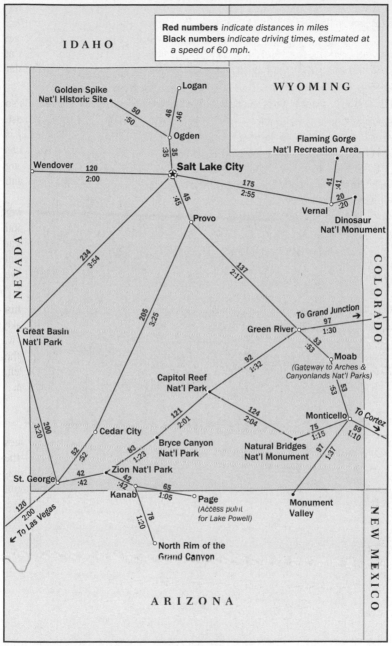

Red numbers indicate distances in miles
Black numbers indicate driving times, estimated at a speed of 60 mph.

IDAHO

WYOMING

Logan

Golden Spike Nat'l Historic Site

50
:50

49
:49

35
:35

Ogden

Flaming Gorge Nat'l Recreation Area

Wendover

120
2:00

Salt Lake City

175
2:55

41
:41

20
:20

Vernal

Dinosaur Nat'l Monument

45
:45

Provo

234
3:54

137
2:17

NEVADA

205
3:25

To Grand Junction →

Green River

97
1:30

53
:53

Great Basin Nat'l Park

Moab
(Gateway to Arches & Canyonlands Nat'l Parks)

92
1:32

Capitol Reef Nat'l Park

124
2:04

53
:53

COLORADO

Monticello

To Cortez

200
3:20

121
2:01

75
1:15

59
1:10

Cedar City

Bryce Canyon Nat'l Park

Natural Bridges Nat'l Monument

52
:52

63
1:23

97
1:37

St. George

42
:42

Zion Nat'l Park

42
:42

65
1:05

Kanab

Page
(Access point for Lake Powell)

120
2:00

To Las Vegas ←

78
1:20

Monument Valley

NEW MEXICO

North Rim of the Grand Canyon

ARIZONA

(© **801/225-4801**), St. George (© **435/656-3990**), and several other locations. Members receive excellent road maps and emergency road service, and AAA will even help you plan an exact itinerary.

Gasoline taxes are already included in the printed price. At press time, the average price for a gallon of gas was around $3. One U.S. gallon equals 3.8 liters or .85 imperial gallons.

If you're visiting from abroad and plan to rent a car in the United States, keep in mind that foreign driver's licenses are usually recognized in the U.S., but you may want to consider obtaining an international driver's license.

BY TRAIN   International visitors can buy a **USA Rail Pass,** good for 15, 30, or 45 days of unlimited travel on **Amtrak** (www.amtrak.com; © **800/USA-RAIL** in the U.S. or Canada; © **001/215-856-7953** outside the U.S.). The pass is available online or through many overseas travel agents. See Amtrak's website for the cost of travel within the western, eastern, or northwestern United States. Reservations are generally required and should be made as early as possible. Regional rail passes are also available.

BY BUS   Greyhound (www.greyhound.com; © **800/231-2222** in the U.S.; © **001/214-849-8100** outside the U.S. with toll-free access) is the sole nationwide bus line. International visitors can obtain information about the Greyhound North American Discovery Pass. The pass, which offers unlimited travel and stopovers in the U.S. and Canada, can be obtained outside the United States from travel agents or through www.discoverypass.com.

TIPS FOR PEDESTRIANS   Downtown SLC is compact and instead of constantly moving your car, take a walk. Take note of the orange flags at crosswalks—grab one when you cross the street so motorists see you. Listen for the chirping sounds indicating when it's safe to cross. And if you don't want to walk, pick up a Green Bike.

TIPS ON ACCOMMODATIONS

Utah offers a variety of lodging options, from typical American chain motels to luxury hotels—primarily in Salt Lake City, Park City, and Deer Valley, but also tucked away in scenic wilderness—plus bed-and-breakfasts, rustic cabins, and pleasant and inexpensive mom-and-pop independent motels.

The chains here are the same ones you see everywhere else in America: Best Western, Comfort Inn, Days Inn, Embassy Suites, Hampton Inn, Hilton, Holiday Inn, Motel 6, Quality Inn, Sheraton, Super 8, and so on. You already know what these places look like. In most cases, their rooms are little more than boring boxes of various sizes, with the usual amenities. But face it: Enjoying the magnificent *in*doors is probably not the reason you've come to Utah, so these chains might be all that you require.

On the other hand, if you are exploring Temple Square and enjoying the numerous cultural offerings in downtown Salt Lake City, the best choice for lodging would be the Monaco or one of the offerings at Airbnb or VRBO. At

Bryce Canyon National Park, go for one of the delightful Bryce Lodge cabins. And if you really want to be pampered after a hard day on the slopes, you can't beat the upscale properties at Park City and Deer Valley.

Another option is a B&B. Numerous bed-and-breakfasts are discussed throughout the book, and when you take into consideration the delicious breakfasts prepared at most of them, the rates are fairly reasonable. Why spend $90 for a boring motel room and then another $10 to $15 for breakfast when, for just a bit more, you can instead sleep in a handsome home, often uniquely decorated, and be served a delightful home-cooked breakfast?

Other lodging choices in Utah include cabins and a handful of small independent motels. Both are usually fairly inexpensive, although they often lack the facilities, such as pools, spas, exercise equipment, and so on, that you'll find in most chains. The cabins and independents are still preferable because they're often a very good value, and the rooms usually have at least some personality (can anybody actually describe the decor of the last Super 8 or Days Inn he or she stayed at?)—and cabins, although sometimes a bit primitive, are often in beautiful settings.

In some areas, like the national parks, your options will be fairly limited: You can either camp, stay in one of the few in-park lodgings, or choose from one of the lodgings in a gateway town. You can save some money at Utah's numerous ski resorts by staying in a nearby town and taking a bus (often a free shuttle to the slopes). The accommodations in Salt Lake City are very reasonable, even in peak ski season, when the room rates at Snowbird and Park City go through the roof. The rates drop precipitously in the winter in southern Utah, and there are many nice days to be had in the national parks when the crowds are sparser and the weather mild.

For camping throughout Utah, you can make reservations through either **Utah State Parks** (http://stateparks.utah.gov or www.stateparks.utah.gov; ✆ **800/322-3770**) or the **National Parks Reservation Service** (www.recreation.gov; ✆ **877/444-6777**), depending on the park or recreation area. Some campsites operate only on a first-come, first-served basis.

To learn more about camping and bringing your RV through Utah, see chapter 4.

SAVING ON YOUR HOTEL ROOM

The **rack rate** is the maximum rate that a hotel charges for a room. Hardly anybody pays this price, however, except in high season or during holidays. To lower the cost of your room:

○ **Ask about special rates or other discounts.** You may qualify for corporate, student, military, senior, frequent flier, trade union, or other discounts.

○ **Dial direct.** When booking a room in a chain hotel, you'll often get a better deal by calling the individual hotel's reservation desk rather than the chain's main number.

o **Book online.** Many hotels offer Internet-only discounts, or supply rooms to Priceline, Hotwire, Orbitz, Travelocity.com, Hotels.com, or Expedia at rates much lower than the ones you can get through the hotel itself. Comparison shop on hotel websites for great deals on hotel rooms and multiday packages.

o **Remember the law of supply and demand.** Resort hotels are most crowded and, therefore, most expensive on weekends, so discounts are usually available for midweek stays. Business hotels in cities are often busiest during the week, so expect big discounts over the weekend. Avoid holidays and school vacations, typically busy times for families and school groups.

o **Look for family-friendly pricing.** Many resorts and chain hotels entice families with big breaks on kids' costs, from letting kids under 12 stay free in a parent's room or promoting a "kids-eat-free" policy. Ski resorts often offer "kids-stay-free" or "kids-ski-free" incentives.

o **Look into group or long-stay discounts.** If you come as part of a large group, you should be able to negotiate a bargain rate. Likewise, if you're planning a long stay (at least 5 days), you might qualify for a discount. As a general rule, expect 1 night free after a 7-night stay.

o **Sidestep excess surcharges and hidden costs.** Many hotels have the unpleasant practice of nickel-and-diming their guests with opaque surcharges. When you book a room, ask what is included in the room rate, and what is extra. Avoid dialing direct from hotel phones, which can have exorbitant rates. And don't be tempted by the room's minibar offerings. Ask about local taxes and service charges, which can add 15% or more.

o **Book an efficiency.** A condo or a room with a kitchenette allows you to shop for groceries and cook your own meals. This is a big money saver, especially for families on long stays.

o **Consider enrolling in hotel "frequent-stay" programs,** which are upping the ante to win the loyalty of repeat customers. Frequent guests can now accumulate points or credits to earn free hotel nights, airline miles, in-room amenities, merchandise, tickets to concerts and events, and discounts on sporting events. Perks are awarded not only by many chain hotels and motels, but also by individual inns and B&Bs. Many chain hotels partner with other hotel chains, car-rental firms, airlines, and credit card companies to give consumers additional incentive to do repeat business.

[FastFACTS] UTAH

Area Codes The area codes are 385 and **801** in the Wasatch Valley, which includes Salt Lake City, Provo, and Ogden. Most of the rest of the state is in the **435** area code.

Business Hours Banks are usually open Monday through Friday from 9am to 5pm, often until 6pm on Friday; some have hours on Saturday. Small stores are usually open Monday through Saturday, with some also open on Sunday afternoon. Most department stores, discount stores, and supermarkets are open daily until 9pm. Some supermarkets are open 24 hours a day.

Cellphones See "Mobile Phones," later in this section.

Crime See "Safety," later in this section.

Customs The Customs agency is **U.S. Customs & Border Protection** (CBP), 1300 Pennsylvania Ave. NW, Washington, DC 20229 (www.cbp.gov; Ⓒ **877/287-8667**).

Disabled Travelers

Disabled travelers can expect accessible lodgings and attractions throughout the state; some trails in the state and national parks are accessible and several ski resorts have programs for disabled guests.

Doctors Ask your hotel for references to local doctors. Also see "Hospitals," later in this section.

Drinking Laws

Although private clubs are a thing of the past, liquor laws are still complicated, and in some cases, apparently arbitrary. You can buy 3.2% beer in supermarkets and convenience stores 7 days a week; stronger beer, wine, and hard liquor are available only at state-owned liquor stores and package agencies, which are closed Sundays and state holidays. You can buy beer directly from many breweries. Some establishments are licensed as taverns and can sell 3.2% beer only. The legal age for purchase and consumption of alcoholic beverages is 21;

proof of age is required at bars, nightclubs, and restaurants, so bring ID whenever you go out. Do not carry open containers of alcohol in your car or any public area that isn't zoned for alcohol consumption. The police can fine you on the spot. Don't even think about driving while intoxicated. Call Uber or Lyft.

Electricity Like Canada, the United States uses 110 to 120 volts AC (60 cycles), compared to 220 to 240 volts AC (50 cycles) in most of Europe, Australia, and New Zealand. Downward converters that change 220 to 240 volts to 110 to 120 volts are difficult to find in the United States, so bring one with you.

Embassies & Consulates All embassies are in the nation's capital, Washington, D.C. Some consulates are in major U.S. cities, and most nations have a mission to the United Nations in New York City. If your country isn't listed below, call for directory information in Washington, D.C. (Ⓒ **202/555-1212**), or check **www.embassy.org/embassies**.

The embassy of **Australia** is at 1601 Massachusetts Ave. NW, Washington, DC 20036 (Ⓒ **202/797-3000**; www.usa-embassy.gov.au). Consulates are in New York, Honolulu, Houston, Los Angeles, and San Francisco.

The embassy of **Canada** is at 501 Pennsylvania Ave. NW, Washington, DC 20001 (Ⓒ **202/682-1740**; www.

canadainternational.gc.ca/washington). Other Canadian consulates are in Buffalo (New York), Detroit, Los Angeles, New York, and Seattle.

The embassy of **Ireland** is at 2234 Massachusetts Ave. NW, Washington, DC 20008 (Ⓒ **202/462-3939**; www.embassyofireland.org). Irish consulates are in Boston, Chicago, New York, San Francisco, and other cities. See the website for a complete listing.

The embassy of **New Zealand** is at 37 Observatory Circle NW, Washington, DC 20008 (Ⓒ **202/328-4800**; www.nzembassy.com). New Zealand consulates are in Los Angeles, Salt Lake City, San Francisco, and Seattle.

The embassy of the **United Kingdom** is at 3100 Massachusetts Ave. NW, Washington, DC 20008 (Ⓒ **202/588-6500**; http://ukinusa.fco.gov.uk). Other British consulates are in Atlanta, Boston, Chicago, Cleveland, Houston, Los Angeles, New York, San Francisco, and Seattle.

Emergencies Call Ⓒ **911.**

Family Travel Utah is a terrific family destination, from the museums to the ski resorts. To locate accommodations, restaurants, and attractions that are particularly kid-friendly, look for the "Kids" icon throughout this guide.

Gasoline Please see the section "By Car," under "Getting Around," earlier in this chapter.

Health Utah's extremes—from burning desert to snow-covered mountains—can cause health problems for the ill-prepared. If you haven't been to the desert before, the heat, dryness, and intensity of the sun can be difficult to imagine. Bring a hat, strong sun block, sunglasses with ultraviolet protection, and moisturizing lotion for dry skin. Hikers and others planning to be outdoors should carry water—at least a gallon per person, per day.

Another potential problem for short-term visitors is elevation. There's less oxygen and lower humidity in Utah's mountains, which rise to over 13,500 feet. If you have heart or respiratory problems, consult your doctor before planning a trip to the mountains. Even if you're in generally good health, you may want to ease into high elevations by changing altitude gradually. Don't fly in from sea level in the morning and plan to hike 10,000-foot Cedar Breaks National Monument that afternoon. Spend a day or two at 4,000- or 5,000-feet elevation to let your body adjust. Also, get lots of rest, avoid large meals, and drink plenty of nonalcoholic fluids, especially water.

State health officials warn outdoor enthusiasts to take precautions against the hantavirus, a rare but often fatal respiratory disease first recognized in 1993. About half of the country's 200-plus confirmed cases have been reported in the Four Corners states of Colorado, New Mexico, Arizona, and Utah, and about 45% of the cases have been fatal. The disease is usually spread by the urine, feces, and saliva of deer mice and other rodents, so health officials recommend that campers avoid areas with signs of rodent droppings. Symptoms of hantavirus are similar to flu, and lead to breathing difficulties and shock.

Most cities in Utah have hospitals with 24-hour emergency rooms, but the smaller towns and less populated regions often have little in the way of health care. It is best to find out where the nearest medical facilities are to your specific destination.

Bugs, Bites & Other Wildlife Concerns Rattlesnakes, hobo spiders, and wood ticks are native to Utah, and each can inflict a nasty bite, the former two being venomous and the latter carrying a number of diseases. If you experience pain or swelling after a hike or camping, it could be a bug bite. Anti-itch cream will help diminish the itch, but time is the best medication—unless of course, the symptoms are dramatic, in which case you should seek medical attention or call 🕻 **911** immediately. While hiking or camping, insect repellent is always a good idea.

Respiratory Illnesses Air quality can be an issue on the Wasatch Front, where numerous cities have struggled to meet federal standards for various pollutants. For the daily air quality report, visit www.airquality.utah.go

High-Altitude Hazards For many people who live at or near sea level, the most common health issue is discomfort caused by Utah's high elevations. Altitude sickness is a process that can take a day or more to dissipate. Symptoms include headache, fatigue, nausea, loss of appetite, muscle pain, and lightheadedness. Doctors recommend that, until acclimated, travelers should avoid heavy exertion, consume light meals, and drink lots of liquids, avoiding those with caffeine or alcohol.

Sun/Elements/Extreme Weather Exposure In the desert area, extreme heat is common; wintertime in the

THE VALUE OF THE US$ VS. OTHER POPULAR CURRENCIES

US$	A$	C$	€	NZ$	£
1	1.35	1.30	0.86	1.47	0.76

WHAT THINGS COST IN UTAH	US$
Taxi from the airport to downtown Salt Lake City	20.00
Double room, moderate	100.00
Double room, inexpensive	50.00
Three-course dinner for one without wine, moderate	30.00–40.00
Bottle of beer	5.00
Cup of coffee	1.00–2.00
1 gallon/1 liter of premium gas	3.45/0.91
Admission to most museums	2.00–10.00

Rockies can bring freezing temperatures and powerful blizzards. Depending on the time of year and your destination, it is best to be prepared with plenty of water and a wide range of layers for clothing. Symptoms of sunstroke include dizziness, clouded vision, and fainting. The best cure is shade, rest, and plenty of water. Seek medical attention if symptoms are dramatic.

Waterborne Illnesses Two waterborne hazards are *Giardia* and *Campylobacter,* with symptoms that wreak havoc on the human digestive system. If you pick up these pesky bugs, they might accompany you on your trip home. Untreated water from lakes and streams should be boiled for at least 5 minutes before consumption or pumped through a fine-mesh water filter specifically designed to remove bacteria.

Hospitals Salt Lake City has the state's most comprehensive medical facilities, including **LDS Hospital,** 8th Avenue and C Street (www.ldshospital. com; *©* **801/408-1100**), and **Salt Lake Regional Medical Center,** 1050 E. South Temple (www. saltlakeregional.com; *©* **801/350-4111**); both have 24-hour emergency rooms. Many of the national parks have clinics. For emergencies, dial *©* **911.**

Insurance For information on traveler's insurance, trip cancellation insurance, and medical insurance while traveling, please visit www.frommers. com/planning.

Internet & Wi-Fi In Salt Lake City, Provo, Ogden, and Utah's major resorts, Wi-Fi is commonplace. It's generally not difficult to access the Internet in any urban area, but may be a little harder to find in some of the state's less populated areas.

Legal Aid While driving, if you are pulled over for a minor infraction (such as speeding), never attempt to pay the fine directly to a police officer; this could be construed as attempted bribery, a much more

serious crime. Pay fines by mail, or directly into the hands of the clerk of the court. If accused of a more serious offense, say and do nothing before consulting a lawyer. In the U.S., the burden is on the state to prove a person's guilt beyond a reasonable doubt, and everyone has the right to remain silent, whether he or she is suspected of a crime or actually arrested. Once arrested, a person can make one telephone call to a party of his or her choice. The international visitor should call his or her embassy or consulate.

LGBTQ Travelers Although most Utahns are tolerant people, the Mormon Church has been criticized in the past for homophobia. Nevertheless, Salt Lake City has a large and thriving LGBTQ population.

Mail At press time, domestic postage rates were 35¢ for a postcard and 50¢ for letters. For more information go to **www. usps.com.**

If you aren't sure what your address will be in the United States, mail can be sent to you, in your name, c/o General Delivery at the main post office of the city or region where you expect to be. (Call ✆ 800/275-8777 for information on the nearest post office.) The addressee must pick up mail in person and must produce proof of identity (driver's license, passport, and the like). Most post offices will hold mail for up to 1 month, and are open Monday to Friday from 8am to 6pm, and Saturday from 9am to 3pm.

Always include zip codes when mailing items in the U.S. If you don't know your zip code, visit www.usps.com/zip4.

Medical Requirements

Unless you're arriving from an area known to be suffering from an epidemic (particularly cholera or yellow fever), inoculations or vaccinations are not required for entry into the United States.

Mobile Phones

Just because your cellphone works at home doesn't mean it'll work everywhere in the U.S. (thanks to our nation's fragmented cellphone system). It's a good bet that your phone will work in major cities, but take a look at your wireless company's coverage map on its website before heading out. If you're not from the U.S., you'll be appalled at the poor reach of our **GSM (Global System for Mobile**

Communications) wireless network, which is used by much of the rest of the world. Your phone will probably work in most major U.S. cities; it definitely won't work in many rural areas. And you may or may not be able to send SMS (text messaging) home from some of Utah's most secluded corners, either.

Money & Costs

Frommer's lists prices in the local currency. The currency conversions provided were correct at press time. However, rates fluctuate, so before departing consult a currency exchange website such as **www.oanda.com/currency/converter** to check up-to-the-minute rates. See "Money & Costs" box.

Costs in Utah are moderate for the United States. Lodging is lower than many comparable destinations, and there are more deals at ski resorts than neighboring Colorado, although Park City is now owned by Vail so lift ticket prices are equalizing. Many hotels and motels have low off-season rates. Conversions provided were correct at press time. However, rates fluctuate, so consult a currency-exchange website such as **www.xe.com** to check up-to-the-minute rates before departing.

Multicultural Travelers

Most Utahns are tolerant people, but the Mormon Church has been criticized in the past for racism and homophobia, although

recent church initiatives have demonstrated more progressive attitudes. However, the state remains one of the least diverse in the United States, and strains of intolerance remain.

Newspapers & Magazines

The state's two largest dailies, both published in Salt Lake City, are the "Salt Lake City Tribune" (www.sltrib.com) and the "Deseret Morning News" (www.desnews.com). The "Salt Lake City Weekly" (www.slweekly.com) is the alternative weekly. Several other communities have daily newspapers, and many smaller towns publish weeklies. There are a few local magazines, the foremost being "Salt Lake Magazine" (www.saltlakemagazine.com).

Packing

Weather changes frequently and abruptly in Utah; bring layers and be prepared to see winter and summer in one day. For more helpful information on packing for your trip, download our convenient Travel Tools app for your mobile device. Go to www.frommers.com/go/mobile, and click on the Travel Tools icon.

Senior Travel

Seniors can expect discounts at many attractions, including museums, restaurants, and ski resorts. The U.S. National Park Service offers an **America the Beautiful—National Park and Federal Recreational Lands Pass—Senior Pass** (formerly the

Golden Age Passport), which gives seniors 62 years or older lifetime entrance to all properties administered by the National Park Service—national parks, monuments, historic sites, recreation areas, and national wildlife refuges—for a one-time processing fee of $80. The pass must be purchased in person at any NPS facility that charges an entrance fee. Besides free entry, the America the Beautiful Senior Pass also offers a 50% discount on some federal-use fees charged for such facilities as camping, swimming, parking, boat launching, and tours. For more information, go to www.nps.gov/fees_passes.htm.

Smoking The Utah Indoor Clean Air Act prohibits smoking in any public building or office and in all enclosed places of public access. This includes restaurants but not private clubs, lounges, or taverns.

Taxes A combination of state and local sales taxes, from 6% to 8.5%, is added to your bill in all areas of Utah except Indian reservations. Local lodging taxes usually add an additional 3% to 6%. The United States has no value-added tax (VAT) or other indirect tax at the national level. Every state, county, and city may levy its own local tax on all purchases, including hotel and restaurant checks and airline tickets. These taxes will not appear on price tags.

Time Utah is in the **Mountain Standard Time Zone.** The continental United States is divided into **four time zones:** Eastern Standard Time (EST), Central Standard Time (CST), Mountain Standard Time (MST), and Pacific Standard Time (PST). Alaska and Hawaii have their own zones. For example, when it's 9am in Los Angeles (PST), it's 7am in Honolulu (HST),10am in Denver (MST), 11am in Chicago (CST), noon in New York City (EST), 5pm in London (GMT), and 2am the next day in Sydney.

Daylight saving time (summer time) is in effect from 1am on the second Sunday in March to 1am on the first Sunday in November, except in Arizona, Hawaii, the U.S. Virgin Islands, and Puerto Rico. Daylight saving time moves the clock 1 hour ahead of standard time.

For help with time translations, and more, download our convenient Travel Tools app for your mobile device. Go to www.frommers.com/go/mobile, and click on the Travel Tools icon.

Tipping In hotels, tip **bellhops** at least $1 per bag ($2–$3 if you have a lot of luggage) and tip the **chamber staff** $1 to $2 per day (more if you've left a big mess for him or her to clean up). Tip the **doorman** or **concierge** only if he or she has provided you with some specific service (for example, calling a cab for you or obtaining

difficult-to-get theater tickets). Tip the **valet-parking attendant** $2 every time you get your car.

In restaurants, bars, and nightclubs, tip **service staff** and **bartenders** 20% of the check, tip **checkroom attendants** $1 per garment, and tip **valet-parking attendants** $1 per vehicle.

As for other service personnel, tip **cab drivers** 15% of the fare, tip **skycaps** at airports at least $1 per bag ($2–$3 if you have a lot of luggage), and tip **hairdressers** and **barbers** 15% to 20%.

For help with tip calculations, currency conversions, and more, download our convenient Travel Tools app for your mobile device. Go to www.frommers.com/go/mobile, and click on the Travel Tools icon.

Toilets You won't find public toilets or "restrooms" on the streets in most U.S. cities but they can be found in hotel lobbies, bars, restaurants, museums, department stores, railway and bus stations, and service stations. Large hotels and fastfood restaurants are often the best bet for clean facilities. Restaurants and bars in resorts or heavily visited areas may reserve their restrooms for patrons.

Visitor Information
For information on the state as a whole, as well as an official state map, contact the **Utah Office of Tourism** (www.utah.com; ⓒ **800/200-1160** or 801/538-1030). For information on Utah's national

forests, contact the **U.S. Forest Service Intermountain Region,** 324 25th St., Ogden (www.fs.fed.us/r4; *ⓒ* **801/625-5306**). The Utah State Office of the **U.S. Bureau of Land Management (BLM)** is at 440 W. 200 South, Ste. 500, Salt Lake City (www.blm.gov/ut; *ⓒ* **801/539-4001**). For information on Utah's state parks, contact **Utah State Parks,** 1594 W. North Temple, Salt Lake City 84114 (www.stateparks.utah.gov; *ⓒ* **800/322-3770,** or 801/538-7220 for campground reservations). You can find additional resources for planning your outdoor adventures in chapter 4.

Wi-Fi See "Internet & Wi-Fi," earlier in this section.

Index

Accommodations

Restaurants

Map List

Photo Credits

Frommer's Utah 2019, 11th Edition

Published by
FROMMER MEDIA LLC

Copyright © 2019 FrommerMedia LLC, New York, NY. All rights reserved. No part of this publication may be reproduced, stored in a retrieval system or transmitted in any form or by any means, electronic, mechanical, photocopying, recording, scanning or otherwise, except as permitted under Sections 107 or 108 of the 1976 United States Copyright Act, without the prior written permission of the Publisher. Requests to the Publisher for permission should be addressed to Support@Frommer Media.com.

Frommer's is a registered trademark of Arthur Frommer. Frommer Media LLC is not associated with any product or vendor mentioned in this book.

ISBN 978-1-62887-404-4 (paper), 978 1 62887 405 1 (e-book)

Editorial Director: Pauline Frommer
Editor: Lorraine Festa
Production Editor: Kelly Dobbs Henthorne
Cartographer: Roberta Stockwell
Photo Editor: Meghan Lamb
Cover Design: Dave Riedy

For information on our other products or services, see www.frommers.com.

Frommer Media LLC also publishes its books in a variety of electronic formats. Some content that appears in print may not be available in electronic formats.

Manufactured in the United States of America

5 4 3 2 1

ABOUT THE AUTHOR

A degree in Latin and a teenage summer in Greece and Turkey gave **Mary Brown Malouf** a love of language and a taste for culinary travel—she's been to India, Nepal, Britain, Botswana, Mexico, and all over the United States. Currently Executive Editor of *Salt Lake* magazine, she is excited to be writing about the culture and incredible scenery of Utah.

DEDICATION

Dedicated to the memory of Glen Warchol, who showed me everything.

ABOUT THE FROMMER TRAVEL GUIDES

For most of the past 50 years, Frommer's has been the leading series of travel guides in North America, accounting for as many as 24% of all guidebooks sold. I think I know why.

Though we hope our books are entertaining, we nevertheless deal with travel in a serious fashion. Our guidebooks have never looked on such journeys as a mere recreation, but as a far more important human function, a time of learning and introspection, an essential part of a civilized life. We stress the culture, lifestyle, history, and beliefs of the destinations we cover, and urge our readers to seek out people and new ideas as the chief rewards of travel.

We have never shied from controversy. We have, from the beginning, encouraged our authors to be intensely judgmental, critical—both pro and con—in their comments, and wholly independent. Our only clients are our readers, and we have triggered the ire of countless prominent sorts, from a tourist newspaper we called "practically worthless" (it unsuccessfully sued us) to the many rip-offs we've condemned.

And because we believe that travel should be available to everyone regardless of their incomes, we have always been cost-conscious at every level of expenditure. Though we have broadened our recommendations beyond the budget category, we insist that every lodging we include be sensibly priced. We use every form of media to assist our readers, and are particularly proud of our feisty daily website, the award-winning Frommers.com.

I have high hopes for the future of Frommer's. May these guidebooks, in all the years ahead, continue to reflect the joy of travel and the freedom that travel represents. May they always pursue a cost-conscious path, so that people of all incomes can enjoy the rewards of travel. And may they create, for both the traveler and the persons among whom we travel, a community of friends, where all human beings live in harmony and peace.

Arthur Frommer